The Silence

Ruth Wajnryb is an applied linguist, researcher and writer with twin interests in language and teacher education. She has published widely in the language teaching field prior to *The Silence*. She has a son and a daughter and lives in Sydney.

The Silence

How tragedy shapes talk

Ruth Wajnryb

ALLEN&UNWIN

First published in 2001

Allen & Unwin
83 Alexander Street
Crows Nest NSW 2065
Australia
Phone: (61 2) 8425 0100
Fax: (61 2) 9906 2218
Email: info@allenandunwin.com
Web: www.allenandunwin.com

National Library of Australia
Cataloguing-in-Publication entry:

Wajnryb, Ruth.
    The silence: how tragedy shapes talk.

    Includes index.

    ISBN 1 86508 512 X.

    1. Silence—Psychological aspects. 2. Psycholinguistics. 3. Nonverbal
    communication. 4. Interpersonal communication. 5. Psychic trauma.
    6. Children of holocaust survivors—Australia. 7. Wajnryb, Ruth, 1948–.
    8. Wajnryb family. I. Title.

401.9

Set in 11 pt Jansen Text by Midland Typesetters, Maryborough
Printed by and bound by Australian Print Group, Maryborough

10 9 8 7 6 5 4 3 2 1

Contents

To Laura and Sasha, and now, Sheila

Acknowledgements

Book-writing is a slow process. When Theo Richmond was in Sydney giving public talks about *Konin: A Quest*, I found out that he had spent some seven years in the research and writing. He'd learned to read and translate Yiddish, he'd travelled widely and he'd interviewed many people across the globe. I remember thinking, as I heard him speak, what a tremendously brave undertaking this was.

When I began the research for *The Silence*, I did not imagine that it too would last seven years. It involved less travel and, regrettably, no further contact with Yiddish, yet every step of the way felt like a quest. From the outset it was an emotional tug-of-war. The project was a jealous lover, uncompromisingly demanding an all-or-nothing relationship. For months at a time, the material would sit on a shelf—sometimes it seemed to be glaring at me!—while I attended to more urgent deadlines. Many were the times that I regretted ever having started. Over time what developed was a love–hate relationship of the first order. Yet as I look back now, from the comfortable perspective of a finished work, I believe that it was love that fuelled the project and sustained my will.

I bow deeply to the many people who in various ways engaged with the project on its long road to completion. To begin with, there are the people who told me their stories. One way of describing the genre of *The Silence* is as a polyphonic ethnography. The polyphony in this case consists of the voices of the 37 people interviewed—27 children of Holocaust survivors and ten others who had parallel experiences of trauma and silence. It is to these people (whom I cannot name, as anonymity has been promised) that I express my first debt of thanks—for their time and their trust.

For help in turning a project into a book, again I have many to thank. Morris Kaplan read about the research in the media and, urging me to publish for a readership wider than academia, brought David Holland to my home. Within a very brief period, David became both my literary agent and friend. David's connections brought me to Sophie Cunningham, of Allen & Unwin, and this too has been a close and rewarding connection. Sophie has a very special gift based in part on being an excellent listener. She creates an encouraging space in which a writer can work autonomously yet feel the gentle constancy of a wider support. Sophie brought in as editor Sarah Brennan, whose skill and intelligence turned my raw-edged manuscript into a finished work. Then Emma Cotter took over and again I felt confident in the expertise and good will with which my book was being managed. And alongside this chain of people has been a small team of readers, led by the intrepid Alan Gold who praised and exhorted me in turn, and imposed only one condition on his unwavering support—that the work be titled *The Silence*.

At the level of ideas, many people gave generously. Ruth Nathan's insight and breadth of knowledge inspired the project in its early stages. Jonathan Crichton's contribution at the conceptual level was indispensable; I am also grateful for the line he solemnly repeated whenever I thanked him: 'I'm very proud to be part of this'. Narrative poet Ursula Duba read the entire manuscript, weaving comment and wisdom into her emailed edits. Long discussions about cultural sever-ance with Erika Apfelbaum and Janine Altounian, both of Paris, focused and enriched my thinking. Karen Arnold subjected the entire manuscript to exacting scrutiny, challenging me at every turn of page to rethink and reshape my assumptions. The book is the richer for these contributions; any deficiencies, of course, remain my own.

For contributions of the personal kind, I am indebted to many. Ann Mulheron, a bereavement therapist to whom I turned in the wake of my father's death, enabled me ultimately to turn crippling grief into creative energy. Claire McWilliams was the first person to have contact with the manuscript as it rolled off the printer: chapter by chapter, she read, commented, edited, suggested and encouraged. Louise McCoke was an untiring research assistant. Ben Taaffe has been a Rock of Gibraltar through all the times I gave up. There are others who nour-ished the project, each in her own individual way: Lili Bellamy, Libi Burman, Marietta Elliott, Jenny Hannan, Cecily Moreton, Ruth Rosen and Ecaterina Varga. And because nothing happens these days without computers, I am grateful to Rick Williams.

Lastly, I thank Sasha and Laura for sharing their mother with something they probably only partly understand as yet. And because cultural lineage is what memory ennobles and silence threatens, it is to my children, and to the memory of my parents and my grand-parents that I dedicate this book.

Ruth Wajnryb
Sydney, January 2001

None of us coming to the Holocaust afterwards can know these events outside the ways they are passed down.
J.E. Young (1988)

The one who is silent means something just the same
Yiddish proverb

Preface

I was born in 1948 in Australia, a galaxy away from the Europe that my refugee parents had fled. I never knew my grandparents, on either side. They died in the German occupation of Poland.

It has taken me some 50 years to piece together the stark details of my family's deaths. Yet the facts are quite simple. My father's mother, father and sister were gassed, I think, at Treblinka. My mother's mother died on the day of the liquidation of the Vilna ghetto, her head beaten in by Nazis, while my mother stood there, helpless, with two untouched cyanide suicide pills in her pocket. My mother's father was sent, along with my father, to a German concentration camp in Estonia. He died there, in that bleak and icy landscape, in my father's arms. These people were literally silenced by the Holocaust. They died before I was born.

Nor did I know *about* them. What I now know of their deaths—these stark, bald facts—is more than I know or ever knew about their lives. This fact, like the facts of their deaths, is the stuff of tragedy. And this fact—that their lives were unspoken—is the stuff of this book.

My mother and father survived the war and rebuilt their lives in Australia. From them, I might have gained a vicarious knowledge of things past. I might have learned about the world they had left and lost, about the families they had, the heritage they cherished, the languages they spoke. I might have learned something of my grandparents' lives, or those of the aunts, uncles and cousins—I imagine there were many. But I didn't.

My parents survived the war but were silenced—metaphorically. Their deaths, my mother's in 1987 and, six years later, my father's, put a literal end to a story that was in fact never told.

Tragedy so devastating sweeps away everything in its path—and more, even the capacity to represent it. The home I grew up in was bathed in a silence wrought by trauma. Yet because silence transmits its own messages, it is impossible not to communicate. Meanings are constructed. Snippets of text and fragments of allusion are calibrated against context and sense is haltingly induced. I grew up apprenticed in the skills of inference and versed in the language of the oblique. I became literate in the grammar of silence.

One outcome of these personal circumstances is this book. It has grown in me for some 40 years, a struggle of competing interests. The yearning to understand has vied uncomfortably with the urge not to know. A love–hate relationship with memory and truth, this book has been started, put aside, returned to, abandoned many times. Ultimately, what has won is the imperative to understand.

I dedicate it to the memory of family lost, and many millions of others besides. It is written for them, about them, because of them and through them. It is also written for others of my generation, and those who are raised in the aftermath of trauma, steered by the silence they inherit. It is a tribute to our struggle to know about the forces that shaped us.

1

A Personal Journey

This work began as a feeling, an abiding and uncomfortable feeling, a pervasive, never-articulated constant in my life. I carried it through infancy and childhood, then into adolescence and young adulthood without ever getting closer to giving it a name. I was 45, with children of my own, and fully immersed in my own intellectual pursuits, before I was able to wrap words around sentiments I had carried with me for half a lifetime.

The process of naming this phenomenon had to wait until I was able to stand some distance away from events that had embraced me at birth. This distance in time was needed in the same way distance in space is needed to see a pattern in a picture. You don't see it when the picture is right in front of you. Discovering the pattern was the first step in naming and understanding. Before this could occur, however, I had to bury both my parents. It is the abiding, irremediable sadness of my life—an uninterrupted dull ache of sorrow—that my understanding, as will become clear, was predicated on their passing.

What began, then, as an unarticulated feeling developed into a question urgently seeking an answer. A nagging question of this sort could have compelled another person into therapy or some avenue of artistic creativity. My nagging question instead took its particular shape as research: beginning with a question, reviewing the field and background, selecting an instrument for the collection of data, analysing the data, seeing patterns in the chaos, naming these, drawing conclusions and suggesting explanations. Despite its intensely personal nature, the research was lent an eerie calm by the procedures and objectivity of a formal investigation. I doubt that this was an accident. Rather, I suspect that the intellectual framework of research gave me the scaffolding I needed to manage the emotions that were exposed, both mine and those of the people I interviewed.

Research, of course, is different things to different people. For some it is people in white lab coats, elbows resting on pristine surfaces, peering down microscopes, inching their way towards a medical breakthrough. For others, the scene conjured up is a library archive with dusty papers and manuscripts untidily strewn about, as the historian or journalist searches out the vital fugitive detail of an investigation. Research like this project of mine is of the order of an odyssey, a means of making sense of something so close to me that I could not perceive it unaided, something wholly personal, something I needed to understand.

I would like to believe that understanding is achievable. I have a naive, unexamined conviction that understanding will bring with it some comfort or composure. I would like to think that there will come a time when I will cease being overwhelmed, reeling back with disbelief each time I am confronted with the savagery of Holocaust events, as if each time were the first time. Once I asked a friend, rhetorically: 'When will this horror cease to horrify?' and he replied, sagely and sadly, 'That's when we should begin to worry'. Perhaps it is inherent in the nature of the material that it should shock, and inherent in the nature of being human that we be shocked.

Perhaps the extreme and visceral response I describe here is bound up with what it means to be a descendant. I find it impossible to confront the horror without interposing my parents. In any Holocaust picture, whether it be of Nazi thugs taunting an elderly rabbi in a Berlin street in 1934, or of sealed cattle cars transporting Jews, or of the icy backdrop of a Ukrainian winter with a killing scene in the foreground, what I see is always a stage set and the protagonists are always my parents.

Actual memorabilia make it worse, of course. When I was cleaning out my mother's things after she died, I found a faded, torn ID pass in the name of 'Helena Smarska'. It was issued on 7 December 1944 in the Polish city of Lublin. The photo is of my mother in Polish military uniform, and the signature is in her handwriting, though it is not her name. The signature and photo have an official stamp in which the only word I can make out is Lublin. I assume these are the false papers which she carried in the last year of the war to prove she wasn't a Jew. I stare at the photo, knowing the immensity of narrative that lies within it, and knowing I'll never know.

Similar feelings were evoked when I walked through a cattle car that is in the Holocaust Museum in Washington DC, having been brought from Europe for this purpose. It serves as a form of egress from one section of the museum to another and you have to go through it to proceed to the next part of the permanent exhibition. How can I not think of my father in such a place? Like other fragments of stories that we heard, it elicits memories of events never personally experienced but many times imagined.

So it was that, through my research, I picked and probed at the scar tissue in my life and others' lives, quite quickly coming to realise that the phenomenon under my microscope was larger than me, larger than my home, my family. What I was confronting was something that had afflicted a generation.

The question that drove me and the conclusions I drew eventually became this book. This chapter will personalise and contextualise what is recounted in later chapters. The first part, 'Echoes', recalls two moments of interaction between my daughter and me, one where language defies the pressure of silence; and one where silence reigns. These two incidents capture echoes from a generation earlier. The second part, 'Memory', incorporates my recollections of childhood and the role that remembering assumed in my immediate family. The third part, 'Awakening', recounts the events of adult life that catapulted me into the roles of researcher, historian and linguist, in the quest to resolve the inner discordance that had long haunted me.

Echoes

It's strange how being with your own children, listening to them and to yourself, can trigger flashes of insight into your own childhood. Experiences long since buried and apparently forgotten, emerge anew and as you encounter them, there's an uncanny familiarity.

'Who's that?' asked Laura, my three-year-old daughter, pointing to a small picture of my mother who had died two-and-a-half years earlier.

'That's my mother', I replied. My words sounded dully in my own ears.

'That your mother? *Your* mother, Mum?' The idea of my having a mother was novel, and interesting, and she wanted to explore it.

'Yes.'

Long pause. Child is thinking.

'Who's that?' Same question. Maybe she thought she'd get a

different answer this time, something that she could run with, something that was familiar. Certainly she had heard little about mothers having mothers. Quite probably, that was a weird concept.

I responded as I had the first time: 'That's my mother'. I remember keeping my voice low, even dull, every part of me wanting to discourage this line of talk.

This time she followed up with a different question:

'Where's she?' This came out as though she meant 'Where are you keeping her?' or 'Why haven't I seen her around the house?'

I said, 'She's dead now'. Once again the words felt dull and heavy in my mouth, even alien, as if they weren't my words. It was a struggle to speak, like trying to retrieve a phrase of a foreign language long lost from schooldays. I knew I wanted this conversation over. I resolved to be calm but minimal, hoping to deflect further interest.

But Laura wasn't finished. 'Dead? She dead?'

OK, I thought, crouching down to the eye height of a three-year-old. Do this gently. 'Yes, darling. She died when you were just a little tiny baby.'

Again a long pause. I figured she was struggling with the very abstract notion of death.

Then she said, with the monumental egocentricity of the child, 'She love me?'

Here I was torn. To answer simply, in the present tense—'yes she loves you'—would be to suggest a vision of eternal life. Instead, I turned the present tense into a gentle past conditional: 'Yes, she would have loved you very much'.

Amazingly, Laura picked up on the conditional, inferring correctly that I was repeating perhaps obliquely, what I'd said before—that my mother was dead. Defiantly, she responded, 'She not dead. She mum's mum'.

Still crouching down and maintaining eye contact, I said, very gently, 'Yes, she is dead, darling'.

Her reply was, 'Look—she's sitting up'.

I had thought that Laura was failing to accept the grim truth of her grandmother's death. But in fact she was merely being as concrete a thinker as a three-year-old can be. Simple. Look, in the picture the woman is sitting up, wide awake; not at all dead.

For the remainder of the day, we went on with our lives and it seemed the conversation had blended in with a thousand others that collectively are the stuff of childhood. I hoped that was the end of it. I was disconcerted by how uncomfortable I had felt, but also disinclined to dwell on it too much.

Later in the same day, as I passed the shelf where the picture frame stood, I moved it up to adult height, thinking Laura wouldn't notice, and that would be the end of the matter. A cowardly evasive act, I concede, and one that backfired. The next time Laura passed by the shelf, she noticed the photo had been moved to a higher shelf. With a slick, imperative tone in her voice, she said, 'Bring it down here!'

Compliantly, silently, I did as I was bid and she added, 'And now, leave it there!' She ran off, tossing over her shoulder as if it were an afterthought or a Greek chorus, 'That my mum's mum. She not dead'.

There were no pictures of older-looking people on the shelves of my childhood. I didn't have any grandparents. No aunts, uncles. No cousins. No kin, by blood or marriage.

I didn't know why I didn't have grandparents like all the kids at school. Sometimes they'd talk about 'visiting Gran' on the weekends. I had no idea what they meant and I didn't ask. On occasion, when I went over to someone's place, there might have been a 'Pop' on the sofa, watching TV or a 'Nanna' in the kitchen helping get dinner. While I recognised the phenomenon as something we didn't have in our house, I didn't feel I was missing out. To miss assumes that you recognise what is absent, or even, that there *is* an absence.

The only old person I had ever spoken to was a Mrs Nott, who sometimes babysat for us, when my parents were out. I had never ever seen anyone as old as Mrs Nott and she was amazing for that very reason. For many years, she was my mental yardstick for how long a human being can live. Thinking back now, she probably wasn't anywhere near as ancient as she seemed. I just didn't have much to measure age against. There weren't even any people whom my parents had known for very long: no school friends from their childhood, no one they finished school with, no pals from their university days. There was no one to tangibly connect them with another time.

There were a few exceptions to this rather gross generalisation. One was a group of Polish-Jewish doctors. They lived in the city and we'd visit them on occasion, but I didn't understand then that their accent signalled the world they had come from. Because they were all doctors like my parents, I thought an accent was something doctors have. There was a different group of people with whom they spoke Yiddish. Perhaps because we lived a long way away from these people, and lacked daily contact with them, I failed to interpret these relationships coherently. Certainly I made no connections then between these contacts and my parents' past.

It was as if we'd arrived from another planet, with no records or recollections, no memory. We lived *in* the present and *for* the future. We were busy. We had plans. We had ambitions. We had this space in time that was now. And we were working hard towards what we could imagine ahead of us. But there was no past. The past was cordoned off, sealed out. There was a complete severance with what went before. But of course I didn't know it was a severance, because to know that it was severed is to know what came before, and I didn't. I wasn't told. And I didn't ask. I must sometimes have strayed into forbidden terrain, because I'll always remember my mother's line, 'Let's not talk about that', and the tone and expression that accompanied the words, the combination of which efficiently put an end to any foray, deliberate or accidental, into the past.

There were some topics to which questions simply did not attach— at least, not voiced questions. I figured out quite young that I shouldn't ask questions about what I discovered other people had but we didn't— relatives, especially grandparents. They just weren't there—defined by their absence in a blanket of silence. And after a while, questions that hovered around unspoken in my head didn't seem at all real. Unless they come out and are asked, and get answers of a sort, they lose their currency, and become defunct. That's when I'd start to wonder whether I ever had a question in my head at all. Maybe I just imagined I did. All in all, it was much less complicated to wonder less and to live in the present while looking forward, always forward, toward the future.

So when Laura picked up the photo of my mother, her dead grandmother, whom she never knew, and turned her little face to mine, her eyes squarely on mine, and asked 'Who's that?', there was, to my mind, an amazing freedom in action here: a freedom to talk about dead grandparents. It was a circumstance that would never have yielded a conversation when I was a child. I had had no way of asking about people who were not spoken of, whose faces were not in pictured frames on the mantelpiece. In my recall, there was no such conversation, ever. So in responding to Laura, I truly was in a foreign country, where the customs and rituals and language were all unfamiliar. I was lost for a code that would work.

A few days later she passed the same shelf where the photo was, as ordered, at her eye level. She was smugly pleased about this. She picked up the frame again, possessively. As if aware of her mysterious power to 'work' this conversation to her own ends, she caught my eye and said, 'She your mum, look. She not dead, Mum'. I fought the impulse to remain silent. I looked about for an answer that would work in the circumstance, some sort of compromise between her three-year-old reality and mine. 'Yes, Laura, that's my mum. She's not dead. Not in the photo.'[1]

Fast-forward ten years. Laura is now thirteen years old and we're in Paris. I'm aware how precious these years are. My son has already passed through them and beyond, and I know how they slip through the fingers. I am anxious to create some shared moments with Laura that might later serve as landscapes in her memory. I'd love her to look back one day and say, 'The year 2000? That's the year I went to Paris with my mum'.

We took the school holidays and went to Paris. We stayed on the Left Bank and did all the right things: the Eiffel Tower, the Champs Elysées, Notre Dame, Sacre Coeur. And we did one other little trip. After some investigating I had finally uncovered the address of the attic apartment where my parents had decamped on their journey from Holocaustal Europe to Australia. For them, Paris had been a temporary refuge en route to something more permanent. There they lived and worked and shared what little they had with co-refugees, other remnants of the world they'd known. It was a hiatus of freedom-from-slavery, and though they had nothing in the way of worldly goods, they ever more referred back to their year or so in Paris as if they had lived a 5-star lifestyle. I didn't understand back then that this is what being alive and being free must have felt like for them.

Before we set out to track down this apartment, in the Mont-martre area, I tried to contextualise the event for Laura. I always find this difficult to do, lacking a language to talk about the Holocaust with my children, but I tried. I was only dimly aware that from the time she had looked at the photo of her 'mum's mum', when she was three, until this time in Paris, she had not learned much more about her grandparents or their world.

We found the apartment and with what I thought was a wisdom and prudence beyond her years, Laura let me be alone with my thoughts of my parents, waiting patiently for me to come back into the present.

A few weeks later, she was back at school, hard at work for the new term. Her English teacher set a poem as homework. The girls had to write a poem located in a particular time or place that is personally meaningful to them. Laura said, resolutely, 'I'm going to write about that place in Paris where your parents lived'. And she did, naming the poem after its address, *10 rue Duhesme*.

I stand on the pavement
Of this narrow incline of a street
Facing 10 rue Duhesme.
Elegant and austere
Restored with ornate detail
French doors, white shutters,
Pretend wrought-iron balconies.

I know my mum needs space
And time
To capture this moment.
I let her go and watch
As the postman allows her past
With a 'bonjour madame'.
She disappears from view.

It's my moment too.
They were my grandparents.
They lived here
In this building
In the tiny attic room
Vivid in my mind
My neck straining to glimpse
My imagination
Is accustomed
To working overtime.

1945.
The war is over.
Survivors, but only just.
Paris becomes the refuge.
Now I'm here.
More than half a century later.
Paris is my holiday.

French.
A new language. New culture.

How did they cope?
I struggle.
Strange words in my mouth.
Ordering a meal
Buying a Metro ticket
Asking directions.
Did they struggle too?

I know 10 rue Duhesme.
Not much more than that.
No stories
No tales of childhoods
Of family myths and legends.
No one speaks of the past.
Silence severs links
And disconnects.

Suddenly my mum is at the door.
I take a last photo
Of her, there.
I know now's not a time
For speaking.
We walk
Up to Sacre Coeur.
Back to the present.

In reading the poem, I see now that Laura has been filling in blanks just as I did throughout my childhood. Aware of silences but needing answers, she wants to know about her grandparents, just as I did about mine. She wants a connection, just as I did. She wants me to tell her little stories about 'when I was a child' so that she can picture that place from which she is herself derived. But I am largely lost for words to describe a world that was not told to me in words. And I have not developed a talent for using words about the past, because I was brought up without one.

Memory

I grew up in Campbelltown, then a small lazy town located some two hours' drive southwest of Sydney. At that time—from the early 1950s to the mid-1960s—Campbelltown was country-town Australia in every sense of the term. There was one of everything, or nearly everything: one post office, one small police station, one newsagent, one lawyer. There was one dress shop for special occasions. There were two pharmacies, one next door to where we lived and one a minute's walk away. There was one town drunk, called Danny, who slept in the park. (The word 'homeless' wasn't used then.) On Sundays, when my dad celebrated the weekend by not shaving till the afternoon, we'd call him 'Danny' because of the bristles on his chin. There was one cinema, where it seemed everyone-and-his-dog converged with great singularity of purpose on Saturday afternoons. One shilling and sixpence purchased a cartoon, a serial, a short feature film, the main advertised film, a packet of Smith's crisps and a Coke. We always went home with sticky fingers, high spirits and no money. It never occurred to me at the time, but the parents probably treasured those lazy Saturday afternoons *sans enfants*.

I rode a bike to high school. So did most of us, I think. They were old worn things, handed down the sibling ladder of mostly large families. We left our bikes at a spot not far from the teachers' car park, and though there weren't any locks, they were always there when we came out at 3.30. We never thought they wouldn't be. Sometimes, I'd get a lift to and from school if one of my parents was doing house-calls (both were doctors). On occasion, I'd come out at 3.30 p.m. and see my mum parked in the green and white Zephyr on the far side of the road, outside the 'home for crippled children', as it was called before we had 'disabled'. She waited there for my father. When he went inside, everyone greeted him with a smile and he too would smile a lot, perhaps because there was reason to try harder. Every Christmas, the staff and children there bought him a hardback book, usually the best-seller of the moment, typically a Leon Uris if there was a new one out. He would read it and then my mum would, and they'd talk about it together. My mother didn't see any patients in the crippled children's home. That was an unspoken thing. I knew even without knowing that I knew, that it was because it hurt too much to hold tears in.

We lived around the corner from the RSL Club where the 'Lest We Forget' motto was displayed outside. I remember not knowing what 'lest' meant but being aware that we were being admonished not to forget something without being quite sure what that thing was, and somehow thinking there was some connection with beer. Saturday nights were the noisiest. From our place, we could hear the shouting across the back fence.

Dad was called out on house calls almost every night and some-times I went along for the ride. We'd always go past the RSL Club and on Saturday nights young kids in pyjamas often loitered on the steps outside, waiting with varying degrees of patience for their parents to have had enough. I never went inside the Club and I'm not sure what was on offer there beyond drinks and the pokies. On Sunday mornings, it was not unusual for Dad to have a battered wife arrive at the surgery, which was at our house. Eyes cast down, she'd say she'd run into a door, again, and refuse to allow my father to ring the police. He'd learned not to insist. 'Domestic violence' may not have been known as such; nameless, it just happened. But I knew that there was a link between a battered wife at the surgery on a Sunday morning and the importance of getting an education. I gathered it was a question of having options. Getting an education meant that one didn't have to 'tolerate the intolerable'. I knew that phrase but for a long time I didn't know what it meant.

The only take-away food outlet was a fish-and-chip shop near the base of a hill at the top of which was the Town Hall. Ballet classes were held in the Town Hall and I used to go on Thursday afternoons. I was a reluctant and unpromising student of ballet, but for a while, it fulfilled a little romantic illusion of my mother's. What made it toler-able were the hot chips that I'd buy at the bottom of the hill and munch walking up the hill. Wrapped in newspaper (the best chips are), sprinkled with more salt than I ever saw at any other time, there was something crudely, greasily real about those chips, juxtaposed as they were with the taut preciousness of French ballet class. I remember the need to lick your fingers well before going through the side door, usually to be ticked off by Madame, both literally and metaphorically. She had a sharp tongue and a keen eye and she didn't miss much.

Somewhere around that part of town was the shoe-repair man. I don't know if he really was chronically grouchy; maybe it was the impression lent by his foreign accent. But he was the only other person in town, apart from my parents, who was foreign and, in-comprehensibly, I sensed some affinity there. In a town like Campbelltown in the 1950s, people were suspicious of accents. At school, I once heard it said that people who talked foreign must be Nazis. I wasn't very sure what this meant. And I only vaguely connected it with us.

There were four doctors in the town, including my parents. One was an older surgeon who probably served my parents as a kind of mentor. Dad would often come back from an operation with some of the gems of human wisdom that this old man had passed on. He retired not long after we came to Campbelltown. The fourth was a tall and very quiet man, a Doctor Parnell, who seemed to want no part of getting to know us. Perhaps he thought of us disdainfully as 'the new arrivals'. His practice was just a few streets away but there was no contact except of the most formal kind. There were kids at school who went out of their way to make sure I knew that their families would never consider going to any doctor other than Parnell. I remember being puzzled about why they felt they needed to tell me, and tell me so many times. People had trouble with our surname, of course. But a loyal following seemed to grow up pretty quickly, and to them, it was Dr Abe and Dr Nellie.

Queen Street was the only main street, and we lived on it. The house, at Number 200, was up the end of a battle-axe drive that bloomed annually with magnificent lilac wisteria. (Recently I planted a wisteria against the front wall of my property, a case of nostalgia flying in the face of good horticultural advice.) On one side of the front path, was the barber, and he and his wife lived behind the shop. His name was Clissold. I remember that because it rhymed with 'rissoles'—then a favourite family meal. It wasn't long before we came to call Mum's little meat patties by the endearing name of 'Clissoles', a kind of in-family joke. On the other side of the path, the Commonwealth Bank stood proudly. The bank manager, Mr Gibson, had a large mole on the side of his nose. He was the very soul of respectability and my parents were proud to know him. Those were the days when you were off to a good start if you left school with a character reference from the bank manager.

Everyone knew everyone. I think sociologists call this a 'multiplex' community—people have multiple different points of contact with each other. You went to school with the same kids that you played tennis or footy with on weekends, and you saw them during the week at Cubs or Brownies, at ballet, at Sunday School, at band practice, or at the movies on Saturday afternoon.

Above all else, I remember a slow pace where the cycles of life were lived out, mostly harmoniously. People were allowed their three-score years and ten, and most lived them peacefully and predictably. As a town doctor, my father would often leap out of bed at night to race to neighbouring Camden Hospital to deliver a baby, and then later in the same day be called on by the coroner for a death certificate for an elderly patient who had died in his or her sleep. In between times, he dealt with the plethora of concerns, only some of them strictly medical, that in those days country people brought to their doctor. I remember the struggles he had with the Catholic women who wanted no more children but who denied themselves contraception. I remember the joy with which he accepted the invitation to the wedding of a young man he'd delivered, some twenty years earlier. I remember the sadness with which he stopped off at what today would be called a hospice, where Julie, a 34-year-old patient of his, was shortly to die of breast cancer. I stayed in the car and when he came back and sat down with a sigh in the driver's seat, I asked what he had come there for. He said, 'To say goodbye to a brave woman'.

Despite the tranquillity of this childhood setting and the apparently untroubled surface of the calm sea of my life, what I am has always been bound up with war. For my parents, life in the idyllic landscape of a country town must have been as far removed from war-ravaged Europe as one could hope to be. The temptation to seal off the past so as not to allow its horrors to intrude into the present must have been overwhelming. I don't know if they made a pact not to talk about where they came from, what they'd seen and experienced, what they'd lost. But it was as if they had. I am aware now of the enormous energy invested daily, yearly and across the decades, in keeping the past in the past, preventing it from engulfing us. Back then, however, I had no words to describe what was not said and what lay outside of our visual field. How can you know what is not there, when what you know is shaped largely by the world you know, the here and now?

Children live the life into which they are born, accepting as given the world that surrounds and shapes them. It takes many years for some experiences to assume form and clarity, and make a larger sense. I remember that against the backdrop of 1950s Campbelltown, there were discordances. Much didn't make sense, and answers to follow-up questions made even less sense. For example, I recall asking 'Why did we come to Australia?' I was told 'Because it's the farthest place from Europe'. The child wonders: *What's Europe? Why go far from Europe? What happened in Europe that would make you go so far away?* I'd hear, 'Don't give your mother a hard time. She has suffered enough'. *When did she suffer? I didn't notice she was suffering. Did I do something to make her suffer?* 'Why don't you want to go and visit Poland?' 'Because Poland is a cemetery.' *How can a whole country be a cemetery? What does this mean?* 'I'm hungry.' 'You're hungry! You think you know what "hungry" means?' *Yeah, sure, this feeling I have now, this is 'being hungry', isn't it?* 'Eat up. It's good to have an extra layer.' *Layer of what? For what? Why is it good? What will happen if I don't have the extra layer?*

Strange things happened, rituals like the calico box evenings. My mother would gather together a whole lot of useful things—from old clothes to blankets to tinned food and soap, and place everything compactly into a large cardboard box. Then she would wrap it in white calico and sew the seams up so that the box was covered. Then my father would write an address on the top of it in black texta colour and tie the whole box up tightly with string. Sometimes he would get me to hold the string down, to enable him to tie a neat knot. I can see them now, working wordlessly, heads bowed, fingers nimbly attending to their tasks, my father whistling quietly and tunelessly as he concentrated on what he was doing. The names and places he wrote were foreign. I noticed 'Polonia', and wondered why it wasn't 'Poland'. *Are they the same place? Who is there that they still contact? Do they receive things from there or only send them?* I'd ask, 'Why are you putting all those things in the box?' 'To send to someone.' 'Who?' 'An old woman. Not someone you know.' 'But who is she? And where does she live and why do you send her things?' 'She's very poor and these things help her live. She did some good things once a long time ago.' *What good things? For whom? Why? Who is she? Is she part of our family?*

I think children can smell narrative the way airport police dogs can smell drugs. And they are drawn to it in the same way. I knew there was a story to do with the calico boxes but I never found out any more details. One day I must have stopped asking questions and put it together somehow. In my head, unconfirmed and now unverifiable, I have the story that an old Polish peasant woman had saved my mother's life. (I deduced that she was a peasant from an attitude of my mother's towards well-off, educated folk: she let slip a few times that money and education did not make you human, that humanity could be found anywhere up and down the social ladder.) Many years later, when I was interviewing children of survivors for this book, a person referred to the boxes in white calico that her parents sent to Poland from time to time, as a gesture of gratitude for what was done for them during the war. I was transfixed by this revelation, never having considered the possibility that the calico box routine was not unique to my home. Of course, while I was growing up, my awareness of the calico boxes, as with other cues to the past, happened largely at a subliminal level. It must have been many years after the last box was sent that I realised that the ritual had stopped.

There were other things that threw me into confusion. An inner momentary panic would overtake me when I heard the word 'Christian'. It was used to mean 'a good person'. At school assembly, the deputy would give out awards for the 'good Christians' of the week. I tried to make sense of it. I knew we weren't Christians but I didn't know what that meant and I didn't think we were bad people. So, was it possible that non-Christians could be 'good'? And could Christians ever be 'bad'? I remember keeping my eyes down and my body very still and willing myself into invisibility when this kind of talk came up.

One venue where the quandary would often reappear was in Scripture class. The teachers didn't know what to do with me for the compulsory weekly Scripture period, when the different denominations would congregate together in prescribed rooms. The Church of England class was overflowing, as was the Roman Catholic, and both these were in the largest rooms. There was plenty of room in the Methodist room, so I was sent there.

One day the Methodist Scripture teacher cleaned the blackboard and put a line down the middle, dividing the left side from the right side. At the top of the left side, she wrote 'those whom God loves'. And on the top of the right side, she wrote, 'Those whom God does not love'. At the top of a list of Christian denominations on the left side, she wrote 'Methodist'. Once all the Christian denominations were written up (I imagine the rank order was not without significance), she moved to the right side (I remember dreading this move) and wrote in big letters 'the Jews' as the only category of people whom God didn't love. I willed myself into the smallest, stillest person I could imagine, praying to the God who didn't love me to keep my pariah status a secret from my peers. I never knew what they knew. I didn't actually know what there was to know.

On another occasion, this same Scripture teacher started the class with the question: 'Is there anyone in this class who is not a Christian?' To this day, I remember where my seat was that morning: close to the middle aisle, three desks from the front. I froze. I had no idea what to do. All I knew was that I had to do what everyone else didn't do. If they all stood, I had to remain seated. If they all remained seated, I had to stand. Keeping absolutely still, I waited for the sound of chairs scraping as people stood. (As I was near the front, I was aware that I would hear before I saw their response). Silence. Then the unthinkable happened. I realised that I had to do what I most dreaded—stand up alone to identify myself as un-Christian.

I didn't go home from school and talk about these incidents and others like them. I kept them close to my chest, hoping they would somehow resolve themselves or disappear. As I think back to such events, I see them now as discordant moments on the landscape of a childhood. One of the most discordant was what I have come to think of as 'the fish incident'. It happened during the summer vacation when we used to rent a house in the coastal town of Austinmer. It was on a hill up from the beach. I was playing on the rocks near the beach, aware rather shyly of some local boys playing close by. They had some fish that they'd caught and were doing things in the tradition of little boys and cruelty to animals—boys who pick off the wings of butter-flies or attach a firecracker to a cat's leg. These boys were picking up the fish, many still flicking about as fish out of water do, and bashing them against the wall till they went limp and came apart. There was much accompanying shrieking and laughter. I was a witness to this event, rendered mute by the strange detached cruelty, something I had never encountered before. Suddenly my mother appeared; she had been calling me for lunch. She saw what the boys were doing and she quite simply went berserk. They fled from her, leaving the bloodied mass of fish littering the rocks. Embarrassed by the hysteria, I asked her why. She replied through clenched teeth and with face turned away, but I made out the words 'babies', 'walls', 'heads cracked open'. Nothing on this subject was ever said again. When I was older, I read reports that resonated with the details I recalled. What I remember of that day was a tremendous fury, unleashed momentarily, then locked away again.

Every family has its own mythology—*leitmotifs* that become the stuff of a culture. In ours, one such was my brother's birth. In 1947, this was the first new life in the family. Given all the death they had seen, it must have been a momentous event. Yet all references to his birth, I recall throughout our childhood, were always clouded with bitterness. His birth had been very difficult: born premature, he remained small and sickly, and lacked appetite. There was an expecta-tion that he would not make it—perhaps they were steeling themselves so as to be able better to take it if and when it happened. My father used to recount that he created a chart on which he tracked the food the baby ate and the food he needed to survive, and from this, the baby's expected time of death. One day, the baby stopped eating altogether; he was hospitalised and fed forcibly. It must have seemed that this child was mocking them, refusing food in a land of plenty, parodying the brutality of induced starvation. But I am only guessing. It was another year before I was born. What I remember is the family *leitmotifs* of his birth—'hunger strike' and near-demise— and how angry they were that he did this to them.

Food and death were connected, this I knew. We were not allowed not to eat. I became pretty expert at smuggling food off my plate into my lap, and off my lap into my room, and from my room out of the house. I'm told this is typical eating disorder behaviour. But as a child all I knew was that I would gag if I ate more—yet I had to eat what was on my plate. So the solution seemed simple: remove what was on the plate. At the same time, I felt guilty about being so thin—I knew my protruding ribs infuriated them—and I knew that what they wanted was for me to be round and plump and 'healthy'. But even if I had had layers and layers of fat on me, I don't think it would have been enough. Food was an issue. There was plenty of it but it was an issue. I could never understand why it was treated with such reverence and why the reverence was bound up with so much panic and pain.

Discordance and contradiction. While my parents sought to keep their past cordoned off from our lives, I was aware that it had a hold on them. I remember being told by my father at a very early age that 'seven died for him'. It took me some years to make sense of this: it meant, I later discovered, that for every person who survived, seven perished. The one surviving, in my father's mind, was then duty-bound to make the lives of the other seven meaningful through his own, by remembering and by telling; by living; by doing good; by not forgetting. I can distinctly remember the feeling that I was competing with something 'behind' my father, something in his past, for his attention, his love, his loyalty. It was if, Janus-like, he were facing two ways at the same time—backwards, to his past and his losses and his debt of memory; and forwards, to the future, his recovery, his new life, his children. With the egotism of the child that I then was, I wanted all his love and loyalty and the space in his heart for me! I was jealous of the hold that the past had on him. Some kids have sibling rivalry. I had this rivalry for what had happened to my father before my birth. And I knew that it was an unwinnable battle. Not only could I not win, but the battle had no end. He was never going to be satisfied that he had told his story fully or properly. His debt to the unnamed seven remained unpaid and unpayable. As I sat with him on his deathbed, not long after his eighty-first birthday, he spoke again about 'his seven', still with the same restless disquiet. His entire postwar life, I realised, was inexorably tied to the death of others.

As for my mother, her memories remained unspoken, locked up in some hermetically sealed chamber. l learned about them from my father's writings only after she died. All I knew, or half-knew, was that she was partially closed off to me. It was a kind of unavailability. When I was at school as a young child, we had to ask our mothers to make a hair ribbon to match our sports shirt so we could cheer for our house on sports days. Awkwardly I asked a friend to persuade her mother to make two, one for her and one for me. That meant I didn't have to ask my mother to deal with the matter of the ribbon. I knew coloured ribbons and sports carnivals didn't feature very prominently on her list of serious priorities. I found it easier to avoid the matter in this circuitous way. It was not the last time, by any means, that I felt that my ordinary, childish, growing-up concerns were petty and frivolous when set against the weightiness of the larger issues at home.

I believe that my parents lived on the cusp between the imperative to remember and tell and the imperative to forget and move on. A story will illustrate the dilemma. From an early age I knew that through my middle names (Marie Eugene) I was named for dead relations, as is the Jewish way. In my case it was for a maternal and paternal grandmother. Yet I knew so little about each grandmother that to this day I am never entirely sure which name was whose.

One day, I asked where 'the Ruth came from'. My parents said I was named after the daughter of the family that sponsored my parents after the war and took care of them in the years after their arrival in Australia. This other little Ruth—a few years older than me—symbolised everything about the new country: youth, health, innocence, the future. But I sensed even then that in being named for the future, I was being *not* named for the past. I knew, too, that something was not being said, something that was best left unspoken. I knew that there was more to the story than I was being told but I dared not ask.

Many years later, when I found the courage to ask again where 'the Ruth' came from, my mother let slip the fact that in the Vilna ghetto she had made a promise to a dying woman whom she had been caring for. The promise was to name any daughter she might one day have, if she were to survive, after this woman's little daughter, Karen, who had just died. Against all odds, my mother survived and she did have a daughter. When the time came to honour the promise, she was torn between a name that took her back to a time of enormous sadness, and an alternative that had the lightness of no baggage. Indeed, the choice was not so much of 'Ruth' as 'not Karen'. Though she must have blamed herself for a promise broken, it's hard not to forgive her.

It is not unusual to want to tell about the past, about where you come from, especially if you are dislocated from that place. It must be a core feature of the human condition. Peoples have done it through time, allowing the caress of continuity to weave its way through the past, into the present and the future: threads of narrative woven and rewoven by one set of hands, then another and another. Perhaps it is humankind's response to mortality. In my parents' case, the urge to tell was a conventional urge caught up in an abnormal circumstance. It is this circumstance that gave rise to this book: it is bound up with the complexity of how to tell the story when the story is wracked by trauma. From the parents' perspective, the dilemma was how to tell what they could not bear their children to have to hear. From the child's perspective, it was how to hear what they could not bear their parents to have to tell.

Between these falls my story.

Awakening

Biography shapes and constructs the events of our life. I suspect that many whose adult profession embraces research, particularly in the social sciences, make good use of the formal instruments of their profession to untie and smooth out knots in their own lives. One such is the Oliners' *The Altruistic Personality*, which reports on a large-scale research project into the kind of person who risked their lives to help Jews during the Holocaust.[2] The anecdote with which the book begins—about a twelve-year-old boy who survives a ghetto liquidation and is saved and cared for by a Polish peasant—is in fact autobiographical. That twelve-year-old boy is one of the authors. I am no different in having my own biography play a part in the drama I am to recount. Specifically, two events in middle life touched on the emotions that I have hinted at earlier and catapulted me into an intensive search for satisfactory answers.

The first event had to do with my intellectual self. It was preceded by a period of several years when I immersed myself fully in study leading towards a PhD. I had already worked in the area of applied linguistics for a number of years, and when it came to choosing a topic for my doctoral studies I was torn between a number of options. Most of these topics would have meant a relatively unproblematic, if passion-free course of study. Caution suggested that I choose among them.

I didn't. Rather, though I had no background in it, I found myself intuitively attracted to the field of Pragmatics. Pragmatics is the study of language as shaped and determined by the context in which it occurs. It is best understood by being differentiated from Semantics, which deals with the dictionary definition of what words mean. If you look up 'hungry' in the dictionary, you'll read something like 'needing to eat'. But if we consider what 'hungry' means as spoken by a homeless man, palm upturned, in the street as we pass by, compared to what our child means when he or she says 'I'm hungry' at 9 p.m. in yet another move designed to delay bedtime, then we begin to approach the essence of Pragmatics. In the view of a pragmaticist, words do not carry their meanings around with them.[3] Rather, meanings are born of a context or situation: what is said by whom, to whom, in what place and for what purpose. In the determination of pragmatic meaning, context reigns supreme.

I vacillated aimlessly for some time between a safe, familiar area to investigate and something in the field of Pragmatics. What decided me to go with my intuitions was the realisation that a shelf in my study housed most of the books I needed. This is a shelf in a much-cluttered room where I put all my impulse purchases—the books I buy when I can't stop myself, on topics that I'd love to read about but rarely have the time for. Suddenly, I realised that nearly all of them were Pragmatics-oriented. All that was required was a good dusting. I took this as a sign.

My doctorate ended up being in an area of Pragmatics called 'uncomfortable speech events'. It involved looking at what happens in the language when two people are involved in an exchange which involves a degree of discomfort for one or both of them. In the strange journey that is a doctorate, you take a tiny area of human experience and probe it so deeply and thoroughly that by the end of the study there are probably not many people in the world who know more about the topic than you. Certainly, I found that fairly soon my supervisor Harry, a charming man and excellent teacher, had begun to say 'Well, Ruth, you *sound* as if you know what you're talking about'.

When it was over and successfully behind me, I began ruminating one day on the questionable value of academic specialisation. I thought back on my own career of study—how I'd narrowed from a broad interest in the liberal arts, embracing language, literature, history, anthropology, to work in one domain within one sub-branch of one discipline associated with language study. I had become something of an expert in face-to-face spoken discomfort. In considering the peculiarity of such specialisation, I was suddenly looking at my life from afar, the fly-on-the-wall perspective, if you like. All at once I saw that this was not the result of conscious, well-deliberated decisions made at critical junctures; nor was it any accident of academic circuitry that had made me end up thus. Rather, I realised in a flash of insight, that the place I had arrived at was in fact wholly pre-determined, wholly steered by events outside my adult self.

My early life had been a training ground. In a household of two survivors, I had mastered a particular type of communication. Like many of my generation, I had grown up in—around, beside, under, within—an intensely uncomfortable speech event: namely, being a first-hand receiver of Holocaust narrative from the lips of Holocaust survivors. In fact I had arrived, some 40-odd years later, where I had started and, as T.S. Eliot puts it, I had come to 'know the place for the first time'.[4]

This then accounted for my intuitive pull towards Pragmatics. I realised that my doctorate, just completed, was no more than a prelude, a kind of apprenticeship in the skills of research that would bring me to my real topic, my *magnum opus:* the unpacking of the complexity of communication in the household of Holocaust survivors.

This may become more apparent if I detail the kinds of skills involved in a Pragmatics-based inquiry. You learn to probe at the gap that separates what is said and what is meant. You learn to weave together text and context so that the composite message is integrated and meaningful. You learn to read minimalist text, to know what is hinted at, alluded to. You learn to interpret messages in fragments of text. You learn to disentangle verbal and non-verbal messages, reading the cues of face and gesture, especially when they are in conflict with language. You learn to read irony, indirection, incongruities of all kinds. You learn to pick up on dissonance—for example, mismatches between sound and text. You learn to recognise the allowable, the disallowable, the taboo. You learn to recognise and read avoidance strategies. Finally, cumulatively and perhaps most importantly, you learn to identify and evaluate what is absent. You learn to read the silence.

As will become clear through this book, a childhood lived in a survivor household was indeed an apprenticeship in Pragmatics. Later, when I started interviewing people as part of my research, I was to discover that a whole generation of us learned how to put the jigsaw together, how to take the fragments we were given and from them construct larger meanings in the attempt to make sense of our world.

I have said that this book's genesis lies in two events. The first event, in my intellectual life, has been outlined above. The second involves incidents in my personal life that tipped me in this direction. Chief among these was the death of my father.

When he died, it was as if a whole era had ended. Something was over, something larger than him. It was my first experience of over-whelming, crippling grief. The death of my mother, six years earlier, had been a different experience altogether. My grief at her passing had been tempered by my father who was intent on suppressing his own emotional responses. At the time of her death, I had come face to face, in my father, with a reaction driven by his experiences of the Holo-caust. This involved a massive suppression of emotion, a compulsive need to do things right, to move on, not to be pulled under by the impact of outside events.

When my mother died, my father's response dictated the type of grieving the rest of us were allowed. I felt strait-jacketed into an imposed way of behaving. I remember the day on which I was supposed to clean out her wardrobe. My father stood in the doorway. He said to put things in three piles: stuff to throw out, stuff to give away and stuff I wanted to keep. He then oversaw the process. It happened so quickly and efficiently that even had I not suppressed my emotions, there would hardly have been time to express them. The first two piles accounted for nearly everything. I took away with me a green mohair winter shawl, a headscarf, a silk blouse in the autumn colours my mother loved, and a worn yellow cardigan with loud brass buttons, an old winter faithful. I still have all these items. I always wonder if I would have taken more if I'd had time to unfreeze and think. With every aspect of her passing, I was not allowed to behave as though bereaved. I could not indulge in any reminiscence; I could not reconstruct her in my life in a holistic and healing way. Instead, for many years I was left with the image of her as she was at her dying: lying on her side as if asleep, curled up, grey, shrunken and comatose.

I don't blame him. His was typical of a Holocaustal response to death. I imagine that in the ghetto and camps there was no time or opportunity to mark a passing in any way. Ritual was a nicety that *extremis* could not accommodate. Certainly, one could not allow the emotion to flood one's thoughts. One's own survival would be jeopardised.

The second factor that made grieving for my mother impossible was my concern for my father. The several years of mother's decline had consumed all his energies. Now, left alone, he was immensely vulnerable. I knew I had to look out for him. Added to this was the bitter irony of her death happening before his. He had structured their lives to fit with his going first. Everything was in order; she would be looked after. With a massive first heart attack in his early fifties, and many more in the decades that followed, he was well justified in thinking that she would be the one widowed. But life has a way of coming up with surprises.

The restraint that had been imposed on me after my mother's death was not repeated when dad died. This time grief was unleashed with a fury the greater perhaps for having been suppressed before. It was doubly swollen now, doubly constituted by the loss of two much-loved parents, but there was something else as well, something larger: with their passing, their era and all that it carried, spoken and unspoken, was finished.

My father's death uncovered something else. Within months of his passing, I felt my head filling up with questions. It was as if these swirled around, eager to be released into the world, eager to be asked—at last. There was something peculiar about these questions. They were questions wanting to be asked. Certainly, they sought out answers, but the sense was that the answers would somehow take care of themselves. The pressure I felt was entirely in the asking.

These questions, some large, some small, all related to the Holocaust. Despite this uniformity, they varied enormously. There were the enormous impossible questions. How could this have happened? How could human beings do such things? How could the world have stood silently by and let it happen? And there were the smaller, but no less difficult questions, right down to impossibly finite, individual and intensely personal questions which, now that my parents were dead, there were no answers to. Did they see it coming? Did they talk about it before it happened? How did they cope in the impossibly cramped and miserable conditions of the Vilna ghetto? What did my father learn about what happened when the Germans occupied his town, Kielce, about its ghetto and the transports to Treblinka, the gassings? Exactly how was my mother able to make a hole in the side of the train so that she could jump out? How did she survive walking halfway across Poland, hiding out, trusting no one? What did my father do in the camps to keep up his spirits? Did he believe that life would ever be normal again? What soft memories of his childhood home did he wrap around himself to give himself comfort, to fuel his innate optimism? And when he was liberated by the French army, what was the feeling? With what emotions did he return to the wasteland that was Poland? Did he find out what happened to his family home? Did my mother go back to Vilna? Who was living in their vacated homes? How did my parents meet up again? How did my father tell my mother that he had cradled her dying father in the camp in Estonia? What steps did they take to locate family members? How long did it take before they realised they were sole survivors? What thoughts did they have as they looked out the train window on that last journey from Poland to the West?

Once I had recovered from the terrible sadness of having no one to put these questions to, I was struck by the oddity and 'baldness' of their sudden appearance. The fact was that I had had 45 years to have these questions asked and answered . . . and yet I hadn't done so.

I realised then, in another moment of insight, that the reasons the questions came flooding into my head after there was no one left to ask was no coincidence—it was precisely because there was no one to ask. That meant there was no interaction to be had, no discomfort to be handled, no exposure to pain so intense that it might overtake and overwhelm. It was like hiding out in the basement, emerging once the danger was over. The questions no longer had to be suppressed. Finally, it was safe to come out!

I feel that these questions had hovered below the conscious level for 45 years. I realise now that the abiding discomfort and tension that I carried for all those years was constituted of the need to know, combined with the fear of finding out. For me, the release of these questions, formerly suppressed, was an awakening of an almost visceral kind. I realised that the most tense and uncomfortable dimension of our family life was bound up with receiving Holocaust narrative, in particular, the disallowability of questions, contributing to the difficulty of communication.

It was this difficulty that as an adult, aware now of issues of source and setting, I wanted to understand. My background in applied linguistics steered me to the conviction that if there is tension and fragility in an event, it can be discovered in the language that accompanies or is used to represent the event, indeed, the language that *is* the event. I sensed that the discomfort I had known all my life was bound up with the communication of Holocaust narrative and I decided to use my research tools to help me unpack it. The first task was to locate and interview others like me: grown-up children of Holocaust survivors, whose first twenty years of life overlapped with their parents' postwar recovery.

My research and this book are about silence—the many faces and meanings of silence, the communicative power of silence as it fills the pauses and cracks and crannies of our discourse, of our relationships and of our lives. And I suppose, too, though I dislike the word, the pathology of silence. It rests on a pragmaticist's approach to silence which obliges meaning to be drawn from context. Just as words do not carry their meanings around them but are infused by their context, so too the meaning of silence is infused by its context and draws its meaning from there.

Paradoxically, this book is also about stories, indeed it is a tapestry of stories, woven through my own narrative. As well as glimpses of my own personal story, there are those of my respondents that emerged during the interviews, and the stories that my generation was not told, or that we were told only partially or indirectly. Fragments and echoes of these stories will reverberate through the writing.

It is appropriate, I feel, to end this introduction with a point of contrast. This will illustrate, literally and symbolically, both the storied nature of human existence and the nurturing role that stories naturally play in family life. They will also, through the contrast, tell another story, one that is salient to my theme.

The first story is about a man of Scottish ancestry who was born and raised in Sydney. His grandmother would sit down with him, when he was a child in suburban Australia, and tell him stories of her life in Edinburgh. Twenty years later when he went to that city for the first time, it was a kind of homecoming. Amazingly, he was able to retrace his grandmother's steps, discovering with ease the landmarks of her narratives, once passed through vicariously, now in real time. She gave him a clear map of a world that had not changed. He followed her directions, told him so many years earlier, of how to get to her home, right down to which tram stop to get off at.

From his grandmother he derived a sense of history, of tribe and of continuity. This invests his life with a meaning that brings acceptance and calm to moments of crisis. It allows him to visit a dying uncle in hospital and to bring to that visit a calm that serves both the uncle and himself. I have seen, too, how he manages to bury the aged dead in his family, with equanimity—with grief certainly, but without a distress that immobilises.

Now, in contrast, let me tell you about Susan.[5] She is one of my respondents and in many ways is typical of her generation of Holocaust survivors' children. She is in her mid-forties, a teacher and a mother of two girls. The question that opened the floodgates for this woman, as for so many of my respondents, was 'Tell me about your grandparents'. Hearing it, Susan paused for a long time and seemed to be deliberating where to start, what to say. Her tone was faltering and I mistakenly thought she was sorting through what she wanted to say. Finally she said:

> 'I know she liked knitting.'
> 'How's that?' I asked, surprised.
> A long pause followed. Susan was looking down at the handkerchief she was twisting and turning in her fingers.
> 'Because in the photo I have of her, she is knitting.'

It wasn't only the trembling way in which Susan said this that I found devastatingly poignant. All there was left of that world—the tribe of her grandmother—was one photo. And if we allow that tribe to stand for a nation of people, then the photo stands for everyone and everything that was lost. I was overwhelmed by how much work that photo had to do in making meaning and coherence for the woman's descendants; and I was also overwhelmed by the ultimate futility of the task. How could Susan possibly read sufficient meaning from this photo to sustain her need to know where she comes from, to give her the continuity that is the essence of humans as social beings?

There's a further mocking irony here. Even the statement about 'liking knitting' is suspect. After all, the fact that she was knitting in this photo does not mean that she liked knitting. At best, all Susan can say with certainty of her grandmother is that on one occasion that is known about, she knitted. There's a juxtaposition of elements here that is marked: the desire for information, on the one hand, and the paltry, impoverished resources available to address that desire, on the other. I encountered the same juxtaposition in Lily Brett's novel[6] about a Jewish woman who manages to buy back some of the photographs of her family from the Poles who 50 years ago moved into the family apartment after the Jews had been expelled. They kept the photos and other belongings knowing that the day would come when someone would come back in search of their history, and some money could be made. Like Susan, Brett's character scrutinises the faces in the photographs, making huge leaps of speculative inference based on the few crumbs of information available.

From a propositional point of view, the information gleaned is insubstantial. Certainly it is nothing like the richness enjoyed by the man with the Scottish grandmother who, apart from the recollection of face-to-face experience with his grandmother, knew so much about her world that he was able to have the visual pictures of his boyhood mind confirmed when he visited Edinburgh as an adult.

So these are two people in their forties, both with remembrance of a grandmother, a link to a foregone time. One has inherited a richness that centres and permeates his life. The other has a photo of a woman knitting. That's what I mean when I say that this research is about silence. Susan's statement, 'I know that she liked knitting', in fact speaks volumes, but not about her grandmother and not about knitting. It speaks about what is not known by one generation and what has not been said by another, and it accounts for my choice of title for this book.

From Susan I learnt that the interview prompt—'Tell me about your grandparents'—was the key to the door of my inquiry. Whenever I asked (as I'd been wont to do in the early stages) 'What do you know about the Holocaust?', the answers of my respondents would have masked the truth. Many of them knew a lot about the events of the war. Many had been driven to do their own study of the period precisely because of the lack of information from their home. But knowing about the Holocaust and knowing about one's grandparents are not the same. And knowing a few oddments about one's grandparents' lives and knowing the details of the facts of their deaths again are not the same. In my own case, I had studied the Holocaust at school, as a university student, and in an intensive postgraduate course, but I could tell you slightly more than zero about my grandparents. For the most part, even their names escape me, and it takes a great concentration of will to call them to mind. It is this bizarre disjunction—broad historical knowledge with a near-total dearth of personal detail—that is the clue to the silence in which my generation was raised.

2

The Story Begins

Arriving at understanding is not a momentary, isolated act, even if insights may sometimes have a sudden and apparently 'out of the blue' quality. In fact, understanding is the sum total and more of a gradual pathway of many, seemingly imperceptible steps which, until viewed with hindsight, may lack both coherence and cohesion. In other words, the process seems chaotic—until, finally, it makes some sense.

As I look back now, over the journey that writing this book entailed, some moments stand out as significant. Each of these landmarks represents a realisation, a mini-awakening of sorts, a sudden awareness, a new perspective, a shift of perception or judgement, a reappraisal. Let me illustrate two such shifts.

The first bears on Madeleine Albright. In February 1997, Albright, then the US Secretary of State, discovered—or, better, had discovered for her (in that the press exposed the information)—the facts of her Jewish descent and her family's Holocaust past. Up to this time, Albright had always denied any Jewish connection in her public statements, although there seemed to be a suspicion in some circles that she was in fact Jewish but not wanting to be perceived as such. Albright claimed to have a Czech Christian past and an Episcopalian present. She had said on record, as if to prove the point, that her own parents had told her of Christmas and Easter celebrations that they had had in their childhood in Europe. Also, her version of her parents' escape from Europe was that her father, a career diplomat, took the family to London for political reasons—there was no sense of their leaving because Jews were being hunted down. Half a century later, it turns out that three of Albright's grandparents died in concentration camps and dozens more relatives were killed in the Nazi occupation of Czechoslovakia. Albright appeared, in public, to have just discovered these facts.

My reason for making reference to the Albright revelations is not to ponder, though this too is interesting, why her parents told her what they did. Did they fabricate a Christian identity to protect their child in a world they had learned was hostile to Jews? If so, they were not the first. Nor is my aim to try to understand perhaps why Albright herself seems confounded by the revelations. Is she uncomfortable with a Jewish past because to embrace it would be to reject the parents she clearly loves and admires? Or is she uncomfortable because, along with stories of Christ's birth and death, she imbibed the discomfort of what was not being told?

While such questions are interesting, it is in more personal terms that I find the event memorable.

Had I not undertaken this research, I have no doubt that when I read about Albright's protestations that 'she did not know', I would have interpreted her behaviour as driven by political expediency—i.e., I would have assumed that she knew she had a Jewish past but had chosen to conceal it so as to better her career prospects. However, in February 1997 I had already been immersed in months of talking to people about how they found out about their parents' past. By then I knew that there is nothing simple or clear-cut about this process. I had already discovered a myriad ways in which such telling can happen, or not happen, or partially happen. I had become aware that there are many nuances of knowing and not knowing. I was alert to the fact that parts of telling can easily slip between the cracks, that much of it can lack clarity and be swamped in ambiguity and that, most importantly, the mechanism by which people disambiguate—by asking questions— was generally unavailable to those who needed it most.

Questions serve many functions: they help you find out more, consolidate your impressions, check the extent of your understanding, clarify any parts that need clarity, and explore and flesh out more specific information. They also turn a monologue narrative into a jointly constructed one, and this co-participation gives the person doing the telling the confidence and strength to continue, for an attentive and involved audience signals permission to keep talking.

So Albright may have suspected the truth but never sought to confirm it. There may have been evidence that she refused to confront. There may have been missing pieces in the jigsaw that cautionary voices told her were best left undisturbed. All in all, I sensed that Albright was indeed just finding out, just now putting the jigsaw pieces together. And in realising this, I also had confirmed the truth of a pronouncement by Abraham Foxman (the then National Director of the American Anti-Defamation League): 'What Madeleine Albright is or isn't, is a tragedy of the Holocaust'[1]. At a personal level, alert to my shift of perception, I also discovered what I had come to understand about the precariousness of family communication in the wake of trauma.

A second shift came about in my understanding of the home I had grown up in. For the greater part of my life I had had the view that the Holocaust was the main subject of talk in my home. Where sport and racing seemed to be what my friends' parents talked about, in my household it was politics—mainly the war, pre- and postwar Poland, and the international political aftermath of the war. I remember long discussions on the subject of democracy, its fragility and essential debility. Always, it was the ill-fated Weimar Republic and the rise of Nazism that were our case studies. Not surprisingly my favourite subject at school was Modern History. I had the perfect pair of private tutors at home!

Again not surprisingly, I was especially interested in Nazi Germany, both at school and later at university. Thus it is no wonder that I came away from such a home thinking that it had been infused with memories of my parents' past. I used to think that we found out too much too soon, that the innocence of childhood had been shattered by intrusions that no child should have to know about.

I thought of my parents as very serious-minded and I was always cautious not to be flippant or cavalier. When 'the topic' came up, it was especially important to look solemn and not say anything. I didn't realise at the time that the focus on the political and historical in fact supplanted the personal, that personal feelings were being managed through political talk. But I did know, at one level of consciousness, that whenever the subject touched the personal, conversation would veer, totter and eventually collapse. For example, if a moment of nostalgia made my father remember his parents, he would begin to verbalise his thoughts but the utterance would most often collapse under its own weight, especially if he used the word 'Mummy' or 'Daddy', and fall away to nothing. Sometimes his eyes would seem wet (the closest I ever saw him come to crying) and then there would be a moment of extraordinary effort directed at poise and composure, a reining in out-of-control elements. For a moment his face would lose all evidence of emotion, and then the crisis would pass. I certainly did not realise in any conscious way that all that family talk about the historical circumstances of war allowed everyone to camouflage the way we avoided probing the personal. Under all that talk, the wound was allowed to grow scar tissue and everyone knew better than to pick at it.

At times I felt I was drowning in the grief, and a recurrent night-mare I had through childhood was actually of drowning—sinking to the bottom of a pool and never rising again. Perhaps the worst period was around 1960, the time at which Eichmann was on trial for war crimes in Jerusalem. For the duration of the trial, much of which was composed of survivors giving witness testimony, the newspapers exploded with footage of the camps and detail upon detail of atrocity. I was about twelve and I knew, without knowing how and why, that all of this was 'about me'. I had a thousand questions but no way of asking them. The few that I voiced elicited responses that cautioned me not to try again. All through my teenage years, I looked back on this period, and regretted the old head on young shoulders, blaming my parents for not protecting me against a body of knowledge unfit for children.

The shift in perception took place when I found myself asking my interviewees what they knew about their grandparents. Then inevitably, I asked myself the same question, and I came away empty-handed: I realised how meagre was my own knowledge about our family's personal past. It was then that I understood that the sense I'd grown up with, the sense of drowning in an overload of information, was in fact less the weight of information than of the tension, and accompanying emotion, of holding down that which was impossible to tell. For example, a painful and abiding memory I have of my mother, one that has iconographic associations, is her way of biting down on her lower lip to suppress what otherwise might have emerged. I can recall thinking as she did this, so many times, *What is she not saying? What is there that won't come out?*

The perceptual shift happened when I realised that the silence of what was not spoken about was in fact the avalanche that I once thought was 'knowing too much too soon'. The memory of families snatched away. People, homes, a way of life obliterated. Cruelty and the inability to protect loved ones from it. Ashes and dust. No marked grave. No date and place. No Rest in Peace. I realised I knew almost nothing about the personal details of my parents' war. In a sense, my intellectual pursuit of the history of the period had been a monstrous camouflage: a huge amount of energy diverted, expended on public domain information, while the private domain remained shrouded in silence.

Once I began interviewing people who had grown up in households and circumstances like my own, I realised that the phenomenon that I had once thought of as peculiar to my home was in fact common to a generation that grew up in the shadow of parental trauma. I know now that the discomfort I experienced is part of the larger phenomenon of Holocaust narrative. What I have come to think of as a 'dysphoria' refers to the tension, heaviness, discomfort and frailty that accompanies and suffuses such talk.[2] I sense that the discomfort is knitted into the fabric of the phenomenon, as it were. It derives from the interweaving of two kinds of conflicted energy: on the part of the survivor, it is the attempt to tell and the accompanying suppression of telling; on the part of the descendant, it is the wanting to know, and the accompanying fear of finding out.

Seeing patterns larger than one's own home is unsettling. It erodes one's sense of agency in the circumstances of one's own life. It's not enough that our parents' lives were thrown into chaos by the political and historical events of World War II. Now it seems our lives were thrown into chaos by the reactive waves of the postwar aftermath. Such a perspective seems to reduce all one's actions to reactions, and thereby to erode one's sense of initiative and control. Certainly, it is disquieting to confront evidence of two generations tossed around on a turbulent ocean, whose waves and currents are beyond the power of the individual to influence.

Paradoxically, though, the recognition of patterns also brings some measure of comfort. It makes the commonality of response indicative of a wider paradigm. If these events are larger than the person, and the responses are larger than the individual, it would follow that we can blame neither our generation nor our parents' for a lot of the grief that pervaded our lives. It seems to have been bigger than all of us.

The research

This research emerged over time as an investigation into the incommunicability of trauma. It started out as a question: how to account for the fragility and dysphoria when parent survivors and their descendant children approached the topic of the Holocaust. No, I lie. It was even smaller, much smaller than that. I wanted to understand what had been going on in my own home. To do that, I needed patterns larger than one family. So I started asking questions of others—people like me. By the end, I realised that the fundamental question was why did I and so many of my second-generation peers know nearly nothing about our grandparents? Once I discovered the question, I felt I was as close to touching trauma's incommunicability as it was possible to be.

The main characters in this research are the now-adult children of Holocaust survivors, the group of people called 'descendants'. The domain that the research explores is what it means to grow up as the child of Holocaust survivors. It calls on descendants' recollections of the lived experience of hearing about the Holocaust from those upon whom it was perpetrated. Given my biography, the work is predicated upon a massive sympathy for the survivor generation. However, their experiences, both wartime and postwar, are backgrounded here; it is their children's experiences that are foregrounded. In particular, the spotlight is on the first fifteen or twenty years of the descendants' lives, and the focus is on 'finding out'. Essential questions are: what was it like being raised in a survivor home? How did your parents' wartime experience affect you? What did you learn about their experiences as you were growing up? Most particularly, how did you find out what had happened to them? The perspective offered is a composite of these descendants' viewpoints.

Premise # 1 *The medium of language*

This study has two central premises. The first is at once so simple and self-evident that it can be overlooked. It is the notion, proposed by Young, that 'none of us coming to the Holocaust afterwards can know these events outside the ways they are passed down'.[3] Young here is drawing a distinction between ways of knowing, broadly—knowing which is experiential, based on having lived through an event; and knowing that is found out, that is one step removed from the actual lived experience. His point pivots on the tyranny of chronology: those of us who were born after 1945 can know only by finding out.

In 'finding out', there is a medium between the event and the person learning about it. In this way, the process becomes mediated. The medium might be the written word (books and newspapers); it might be primarily visual (film and photography), or textural (displays in museums). For the descendant generation, the most immediate mediating source of information was the spoken (or unspoken) word of their parents. Young points out that knowledge acquired in this way will inevitably be influenced by the medium involved, so that a composite of medium and message together constructs meanings.

So central is this concept to my study that it deserves some clarification at this early point, along with certain popular misconceptions about language. There is a folk notion about communication that is called the 'conduit metaphor'.[4] People like to think of communication as the simple delivery of a message that is composed in the head of the sender, sent to the hearer via the speaker's voice and air waves, and then received by the hearer, who unpacks it rather in the way one does a letter or a suitcase. Meaning is delivered the way a truck delivers its load. The conduit metaphor is clear, logical, transparent, ubiquitous, but essentially quite wrong. This is not how communication works. There is a great deal wrong with it, but I will limit myself to three factors.

Firstly, messages tend to be fragments rather than full constructions. This is because speaker and hearer are able to rely on amounts of common understanding which can, and usually do, remain tacit. Such knowledge includes knowledge of the world, of the culture in which they live, of the particular setting in which they are placed, of the topic on which they are communicating, of each other and related people as participants inside or outside the message. So a message being sent from one person to another is built on an invisible bank of silent but operational knowledge. The amount of shared knowledge varies, of course. Family members share a great deal, strangers significantly less. The less well you know the person you are speaking to, the more you need to 'spell it out'. Thus in interpreting another person's meaning, you inevitably calibrate what they say against what you know about them and what you know that they know about you, in an essentially constructivist and collaborative process, a far throw from the simple delivery of a message to a passive recipient.

Secondly, the folk view of communication sees it as propositional in nature—essentially, the delivery of information. Certainly, most communications do have content in this transactional sense. However, communications are rarely exclusively transactional. Messages also carry information about the people involved: who they are, how they get on, what their relationship is, what it might become.

These sub-messages are subtly encoded, some intentional, others, not so. Our ability to recognise and interpret them is highly developed—through socialisation and acculturation—and happens at a largely subliminal level.

Thirdly, there is the optimistic belief that what is sent is what is received. We tend to apply the conduit metaphor to our own communications, and assume that our intention is as transparent as the words are audible. There is no popular sense of speaker intention being different perhaps from the actual spoken words or of the listener putting an interpretive filter on what he/she hears. The assumption is that what you see is what you (or others) get. However, communication is in fact highly filtered. When we understand the range of obstacles that impede the probability of hearing and correctly interpreting speaker intention, it is a wonder that people understand as well as they do! So the notion that our hearer 'receives' a mirror image, as it were, of what the speaker intended to send, fails to take into account either the constructionist nature of interpretation, or the fragility of the communication process.

Thus, when we come to consider the ways in which the events of the Holocaust were passed down from the survivor to the descendant generation, we will be alert to the fact that the 'messages' (stories) received by the second generation were deeply embedded in a relational and emotional context which gave them a meaning far greater than the words alone contained. And as we shall discover, the message did not need to be fully spoken. Silence and semi-silence, indeed the suppression of language, served to transmit messages as well. Indeed, it may well be that messages refracted through silence are the more powerful.

Premise # 2 The paradox of telling

Language assumes a primary place in this study because it mediates the survivor's experience of the Holocaust and the descendant's finding out. However, because the experience of living through the Holocaust and the legacy of having survived are so extreme in the demands they place on human endurance, the events are sometimes banished to a realm, as it were, outside language. Figuratively and often literally, the events experienced become unspeakable. It is no accident that we have the collocation—'unspeakable atrocity' or 'unspeakable trauma'—the very combination suggesting that some experiences are not the stuff of narrative. They can't be talked about. As the grandmother of Leah, one of my respondents, used to say when the child repeatedly asked her about the war, 'Be quiet now. Auschwitz is not for talking'.

The silencing is of course metaphoric but it is also quite literal. Because of the discomfort experienced by both parties in the telling, massive difficulties are placed in the way of successful communication. So extreme is the difficulty of the speech event—both for the role of teller and for the role of the one listening to the telling—that communication almost invariably disintegrates.

So we emerge with a paradox—the paradox of untellability. While language is the mediating influence, it also falls short of its task—it disintegrates under the strain. What is unmasked and emerges instead is the dysphoria I referred to earlier—and it is this tension that permeates the communication process and outcomes and that is so inextricably intertwined with descendants' construction of their parents' Holocaust message.

Recollections as data

Wolcott tells us that the biggest step one can take toward finding an answer is to 'begin with a well-formulated question'[5]. In qualitative research like mine, the aim usually has to do with finding out about the nature of something. This is different from quantitative research which more often seeks to measure. A key issue right at the start was how to access the narrative of trauma given that it happened in the past and was locked inside people's memories—in other words, how to use recollections as data.

From the outset, formidable research obstacles presented themselves. The biggest was the time between the events, the tellings, and the research. Investigating the language of the actual tellings, in real time, as they took place between Holocaust survivors and descendants was not possible. Not only are they lost to us now (having occurred in the first generation after the war), the moments of transmission are so private and so spontaneous (often eruption-like) that they could not have been captured on tape. Even had it been possible, the presence of researcher and/or tape recorder would have constituted an unacceptable intrusion and resulted in overwhelming contamination of data. For the same reason, taping tellings between survivors and the third generation (their grandchildren)—which was often suggested to me as an avenue—is out of the question. Though some recent evidence has emerged suggesting an easier process between grandparent and grandchild, nonetheless the research is precluded because of the intrusion factor.

What we have left is descendants' recollections of the tellings. Though subject to the ravages of time, these are nonetheless a rich source of commentary on the communication event. It is important to dwell not on what is forgotten, and outside our reach, but on what was memorable enough to be retained. There are three considerations here that support the use of recollections as a data source.

Firstly, while descendants are rarely able to recall what they were told verbatim, they often remember, as if it were yesterday, the contexts and associated emotions that surround, indeed, outlast the telling. As one respondent told me, 'I don't remember the words. But I do remember the emotions'. The fact that emotion rather than language is etched in memory is also a consequence of the tender age of many descendants when they started to find out about their parents.

Secondly, in the case of formulaic utterances which, as I show later, are a feature of Holocaust narrative, the descendants are often able to quote them decades after they were last heard. For example, 'They can't take knowledge away from you', 'Eat without liking', 'Australia has been good to us', and so on. To the researching linguist, these pre-constituted verbal packages are what artefacts or fossil findings or forensic evidence must be to the anthropologist, archaeologist or pathologist.

Thirdly, even while conceding that often the original words are lost, gone the way of most spoken communication, it is appropriate to give significance to what is remembered. There is meaning in the very fact that memory retains certain items and quietly allows the erasure of others. No doubt all recollections are to a certain degree subjective distortions. They serve, nonetheless, as interpretations and as such are part of the rich commentary that informs this study.

The research therefore concedes the passage of time and the magnitude of space—sometimes a world away—that separate the telling from the recollection of the telling. These obstacles are considered challenging, but not insurmountable. To go back in time, to capture the moment, one must be prepared to immerse oneself within the context of one's respondents' experiences, or as Eisner puts it, to know the fragrance of the rose, if not its Latin name.[6]

It is the descendants' recollections—in the form of text or discourse—that provide the primary data of my study. In the process of analysis, the language in which they convey their recollections is itself treated not merely as a conduit but as itself revelatory. As Thompson puts it 'discourse—that is, language realised in action—is already an interpretation . . . To undertake an analysis of discourse is . . . to re-interpret a pre-interpreted domain'.[7] In this sense, then, the research presents a wholly integrated approach to language: just as I concede that the message of parents' Holocaust experience cannot be separated from the ways in which it was passed down, so too I am asserting that the manner in which descendants recollect their experiences of finding out is just as firmly intertwined with and inseparable from their meaning.

The participants

The primary data set was composed of 27 Holocaust descendants. Later in the process, I began interviewing people whose stories were relevant to my research but who had no connection with the Holocaust. This came about quite accidentally. When I was looking for a publisher, I had quite a few occasions to describe the kind of book I intended to write; and very often on such occasions, I was greeted by overwhelmingly sympathetic reactions. People talked to me about experiences in their own lives or that of loved ones that resonated closely with the experience of the descendants. Through these contacts, I found I was being urged to see the wider significance of my research into trauma's aftermath. Thus, while my primary data source remains the descendants of Holocaust survivors, some of whom I will introduce later in this chapter, a secondary group of interviewees was also tapped—some came to me, as it were, and some I actively sought out. References to these subjects will also be scattered through the book; their stories will support and reinforce those of the core group, the descendants.

The primary study

All 27 descendants in the primary study lived in or near Sydney, Australia, at the time of interview. There was no shortage of population to call on, Australia having offered resettlement to large numbers of refugee survivors in the postwar era (more than any country, after

Israel and the USA). All the respondents were adult children of Jewish Holocaust survivors. The numbers were roughly equal in terms of gender and this was deliberate: it was easier to find women to interview (Are women more comfortable than men in talking about uncomfortable topics?) and I had to actively search for more men to keep the numbers roughly equal. Despite the gender difference in availability, I found that once participants had come on board, there was no discernible gender difference in the way they responded. Tears, it seems, can be quite gender-free.

Most of the participants were born in the five-year span following the end of the war, being in their late forties or early fifties when I interviewed them. Most came to Australia as infants, or were born soon after their parents arrived. The countries of origin of the parent generation included Germany, Austria, Czechoslovakia, Hungary, Poland, Romania and France. Some of my respondents spoke the home language as well as English, some only English. Most knew at least the sound of Yiddish. Only one spoke English as a foreign language, and her command of English was near-native. At the time of interview, most were married with children of their own, some were partnered for the second or third time, a few had not married, five had no children. Apart from three, all were tertiary-educated and most worked in the professions.

Their parents had all experienced the upheaval of the war; all were dislocated from their homes and countries. Some were variously and at different times in ghettoes, concentration camps or labour camps. Some were able to 'pass' on false papers, lucky to be sufficiently Aryan in appearance to get away with it. Some were on the move constantly, hunted and in search of a night's refuge, never staying long enough anywhere to be caught. Some were in the same place of hiding for long periods of time, spending years in attics, bunkers, cellars, and the like.

The parents' marital circumstances varied widely. A few interviewees had parents who were married before the war and both survived. Most had parents who had lost a partner and remarried. In some cases, the children of previous marriages had been killed. Most of the parents were survivors, with a few cases of survivors having married people who had had no direct connection with the Holocaust. There were two cases of one parent being non-Jewish. They all lost almost everyone. One man's entire family (except the grandparents on his father's side) packed up and fled eastwards as Warsaw was being invaded by the Germans, reaching Shanghai and finally Australia. Some families occasionally had 'left-over' relatives, typically someone who had fled Europe in the 1930s, for Palestine, the USA, Australia, or elsewhere. Some survivors (very few) managed to save a parent, who migrated with them, but most of my respondents, as children, did not know grandparents or even really what the word meant. Most survivors knew at the war's end that nearly everyone in their family was gone. This did not stop some of them, however, from spending many years searching for lost kin. A few subsequently discovered relatives they thought were dead or were so far removed they had not earlier known the connection. A very few never stopped searching or waiting to be found.

Definitions

For the purposes of this study, a descendant is defined as the adult offspring of Jewish parents, one or both of whom were Holocaust survivors. Such a definition is predicated on a base definition: what is a survivor? A survivor is interpreted broadly as a Jew of European birth whose life was dislocated or traumatised during the twelve-year period of the Third Reich, i.e., 1933–1945. The fact that the base definition is restricted to Jewish people in no way suggests a view that other people did not suffer in the war. The breadth and depth of destruction and devastation wrought on peoples right across Europe, as well as the official Nazi attitude toward Gypsies, Slavs and homosexuals, are matters of public record and beyond dispute. Opponents of Nazism of any race or nationality also suffered: for example, Dachau, the first concentration camp, was originally intended for political prisoners.

That said, the fact remains that the ghettoes were walled prisons for Jews, the vast majority of the camp population was Jewish and nearly all camp inmates died. Within the camp system, too, there was a rigid hierarchy of rank—the Jews were on the lowest rung of this ladder, destined to suffer the worst atrocities. The Final Solution was planned by the Nazis to end the 'problem' of the Jews, and for this peculiarly specific genocidal goal, the word Holocaust (or the Hebrew *Shoah*) has come to be used.

The base definition of 'survivor' adopts a broad time span, beyond the actual years of the war (1939–1945). It covers the era from the moment Hitler's Nazi Party took absolute control of Germany (1933), through the years leading up to World War II and including the war years. The definition therefore includes people who lived in Germany under the oppressive Nuremberg laws or in Nazi-controlled territory (such as Austria and Czechoslovakia), together with those who suffered invasion and occupation (in Poland, Holland, Belgium, France, and Hungary). It does not differentiate among those who spent the war in concentration camps, ghettoes, labour camps, in hiding, passing (with or without false papers) as Christians, on the run, or (as was quite usual) any combination of these at different times.

This lack of differentiation of the term 'survivor' is deliberate. I do not wish to involve myself in the quantification of trauma, that which Novick facetiously calls 'comparative atrocitology',[8] and Jucovy calls 'a hierarchy of survivorship'.[9] The variables are too numerous and too complex. Nor do I deal with the sensitive issue of how the persons involved see themselves or how other survivors rank different elements of survivorhood. For example, there are many people who by my definition are survivors who would not call themselves this. For example, many who fled eastward and spent the war years in Russia do not think of themselves as Holocaust survivors, and may not be thought of as such by others. Many who left Europe before the storm broke, for example, after *Kristallnacht*, and subsequently lost most of their family, may also not call themselves, or be called, survivors. I am thinking here of a young German Jewish girl whose desperate family put her on a train hoping she would be safe in England; or the couple in *Safe in America* who fled to the USA and planned, perhaps naively, to bring over their families; or Arnold Zable's parents, as represented in *Jewels and Ashes*, leaving Bialystock in Poland for the adventure and safety of Melbourne, and then losing everyone and everything, from a distance.[10] For the purpose of this research, I bundle all such people together, loosely and non-judgementally, and call them 'survivors'.

The parent generation does engage in these differentiations. My mother always thought my father's experience was worse than hers, because she had not been in a camp. One survivor I interviewed said that she does not have the right to call herself a survivor because she fled east and therefore did not herself experience the German war machine. She feels it a disrespect to include her experience with those who were left behind. Among those who adamantly reject the term 'survivor' for themselves, there may also be an element of deliberate distancing, a wish not to share the shame and stigma that they perceive to be carried, particularly by camp survivors.

As a general rule, the descendant generation seems not to concern itself with such differentatiations, largely because they see many similarities in people who came from that era and that part of the world. My view—that different people construct and define these experiences with multiple perspectives and dimensions—intentionally sidesteps these difficult questions, because attending to them is outside the scope of my research.

Profiles

Later in this book, the reader will meet all the people who were interviewed during the data collection stage of the study. Their voices will work individually and collectively to establish and weave together the evidence on which the book is based. Here I will introduce a few of these people, to set the tone of what comes later and to allow some of these voices to be heard virtually from the start.

Susan's story

I'll start with Susan, who has already been introduced: she was mentioned at the end of Chapter 1 in relation to the photo she has of her grandmother knitting. Susan is a petite and unassuming woman in her late forties. She is warm and affectionate and has a ready, if somewhat shy smile. She has been married for about twenty years and has two teenage daughters. Her husband, a doctor, comes from an Australian Jewish background. Susan is trained as a teacher and has been a teacher, mostly part-time, in many different educational contexts—such as teaching English as a Second Language to migrants and providing literacy training for unemployed youth. While she enjoys her work and is good at it, her primary commitment is to her family, and the care of her daughters. Like many children of survivors, she worries a lot, more about the what-ifs than the actuals.

Susan was born in Australia, of German-Austrian Jewish parents who met and married after the war. Her father had been sent to England around the age of sixteen with his brother and sister, in a desperate effort to save them before hostilities slipped into carnage. The three children survived, but never saw their parents again. The father was later recruited into the British army and was with the British troops who liberated some of the concentration camps, including one that he later discovered was the scene of his mother's death. Susan's mother's story has always been sketchier, eluding her attempts to find out.

My impression of Susan is that she has spent most of her life side-stepping the issue of the Holocaust for fear of causing pain for her parents, most especially her mother. She is troubled by her minimal and sketchy knowledge about her parents' past; she is aware that time is running out; but is as yet unable to establish a means of communication on this topic. What she knows is fractured and fragmented:

> You sort of only pick up snippets as the years go by, just little things. Last year there was a program on TV about Drancy concentration camp in France. My mother really never talks about these things and at the time she said 'I was there in that camp, watch it'. Just like that, a throw-away line. That's her way of telling me her story. I knew she had been in France in the war because she could speak French, and I knew it had been bad, but the details: was she hungry? How was she treated? How was she feeling? I knew nothing about this. Her explanation for being able to speak French was, 'I was there in the war'. The kind of knowledge I had didn't come about through discussion. It was just bits and pieces that you put together over time, dimly, on the fringes of your mind. You don't ever know what it is you know. Sometimes I don't know what I've heard from her, what I've read in a book or seen in a movie. The documentary on Drancy was a shock. Up till then, I'd thought of her as the lucky one: it was her mother and sister who had died.

Susan says of her mother, 'Basically she wants me to know but she doesn't want to tell me'. It is only with the passage of time that she has come to the understanding that her mother suffered terribly. Because questions are taboo, Susan's knowledge of what happened is based on odd fragments of information, or messages that she has constructed from indirect remarks she's heard or overheard. For example, she recalls her father secretly warning her to be good for her mother because she'd 'been through enough'. Her father told her that her mother's had been 'a terrible life' in a combination of out-of-context and minimalist detail that was typical of the home:

> You don't know what this 'terrible life' is. It's done in a secretive way, never in front of my mother. My father said he didn't want her to know

that I was being good because I felt sorry for her. I got the message that things had happened and some of it was really bad but I couldn't ask and you end up wondering: what was it? How bad can it be?

She picked up on other hints and clues: the fact that her parents would not write their religion on Australian census forms; her mother's over-protectiveness, pessimism and distrust which Susan understood were linked to whatever it was that happened to her that she wouldn't talk about; and the odd throwaway line, like 'I couldn't have married someone who had been in a concentration camp' or 'I wanted to go to the furthest place from Europe'.

Susan spoke poignantly about the efforts she made as a child to make sense of her world, and how fruitless these turned out to be: 'Kids only see other people's lives in terms of their own'. She recalls how she tried to visualise what her mother went through—like seeing a concentration camp as a big yard—and she recalls her horror when she discovered how wide of the mark she was. She remembers a time before she had learned not to ask, when she asked her mother 'why they didn't fight back' and she remembers the emotion of the moment, if not the answer itself. In Susan's recount of her life and in her style of speaking, there is an impression of tremendous energy being invested in the search for meaning, but this is a search that has largely taken place on the outskirts of conventional face-to-face communication.

The piecemeal quality, furthermore, never seems to advance to a more integrated stage. And if it does, it does so opportunistically: it's a case of being within earshot at a the right moment; or making the right interpretation of an obscure remark; or as a silent listener, hoping more will be said but knowing not to probe. Over time, some of the shapes in the picture became a little clearer, largely because information gained outside the home allowed her better to induce meaning out of the obscure messages from her parents.

As a child you don't really see it as so terrible, but as all the background comes flooding in from all the other things you learn, and then you apply it, then the horror overwhelms you. Even as a teenager, I had friends with parents who'd been in the camps, but I never thought of my mother in that category.

The governing fear of her life has been to avoid pushing her mother beyond the brink of composure. The maintenance of composure is a recurrent theme in her talk: it's clear that again, a massive amount of energy is invested in keeping feelings in. The failure to grieve openly, to allow emotion out, to unlock the rage, is closely linked to the suppression of story:

> Information was presented as matter-of-fact—'I don't want to get emotional about this'. I felt it was very emotional, but she didn't break down, ever. But I sensed that if there was much more, she would, and I couldn't bear that. I was so scared of that, because you see your parents as the strong ones and in charge and all that and if they break down, where does that leave you? It's selfish but it's a real fear.

Years of carefully negotiating such exchanges, erring always on the side of caution, has left Susan with a sense of being repeatedly and endlessly unsatiated. She looks back on years of 'lost opportunities'. A few years after the interview, her younger daughter, who attends a Jewish school, completed an assignment which involved interviewing her grandmother about the war. This turned out to be an opportunity for Susan, on the margins of the interactions, to put together the fragments she knew into some kind of coherence.

Susan now knows that her mother escaped from Germany to Belgium just before the war started. There she was separated from *her* mother—in what is quite clearly the most traumatic event in her story—and was taken with other children to France. There a Jewish welfare organisation took care of them, moving them, on false papers, from one hiding place to another. Then in 1942, all Jews were obliged to register and, having registered, were rounded up. Susan's mother was sent to the notorious Drancy concentration camp. She survived this and the rest of the war, but lost her own mother and sister. She married after the war and had one child, Susan, who was born in 1952. Not so long ago, Susan's mother tracked down some documentary evidence of her wartime past and found a document on which was written, under her mother's name: 'Sent to Auschwitz. Has not returned'.

The school project that required dialogue on the topic between the daughter and the grandmother helped allay some of Susan's worries that her children are removed from the family's past. She fears repeating her mother's pattern of wanting them to know but not wanting to tell. And the fact is, of course, that what she has learned about communicating on this topic from the role modelling of her own mother, does not equip her for the task. I interviewed Susan at the time when her elder daughter was the same age as Susan's mother had been when she was forcibly removed from her own mother and transported to Drancy. The significance of this is not lost on her. Susan wants her daughters to feel a personal connection to previous generations, to feel some grief, to feel appreciation of their safety and good fortune—and also, to be on their guard. However, she struggles to find an age-appropriate way to tell them enough but not too much.

She knows some of her behaviours might be construed as obsessive—like being grateful for a warm shower, for a safe bed at night. Meanwhile she still will not put a *mezzuzah* on her door (the symbol of a Jewish home), a fear that she links to being a child of survivors, her version of their denial of Jewish identity in the census forms. Susan's parents are still living, and while they co-operated to some extent in their granddaughter's school project, the family discourse was managed with considerable trepidation. Susan still kept herself on the outskirts.

The experience of interviewing Susan was like stepping around shards of broken glass. And I sense that this is how it was for her to have spent half a lifetime in the shadow of her mother's pain. It is the tension of contradictions that most strikes me: Susan is so close to her mother that the boundaries between the two lives seem to blur, yet Susan knows so little about what her mother experienced that they could be strangers.

Abe's story

Abe is a senior university academic. He is around 50 years of age, married for many years, and has no children. He is an urbane and charismatic man, intellectually stimulating and also personable, although clearly a complex character. There is a restlessness about him that suggests angst and turmoil.

He is an only child, born late to Polish-Jewish parents who were married some seven years before the war. The parents were urban, tertiary-educated, secular Jews with little religious affiliation. At the outset of war, the father was 34, mother 29. They escaped from Poland right at the start of the war, 'as the bombs were falling on Warsaw', heading eastwards.

Abe has a rich memory of finding out about his parents' past:

I have images. One is a story my mother heard afterwards. The family had had a nurse who had looked after my mother's baby brother and she was considered a part of the family. She was a *Volkdeutsch* (Polish, of German descent). Apparently, when the German army entered Warsaw this nurse was out in the streets cheering and waving a flag. And it was she who ransacked their apartment and stole everything.

Abe adds that 'one of the things that stories like this told me is you can't trust anyone'.

His reaction was the opposite of what was intended: 'The effect on me is to over-trust people. I told myself that I wasn't prepared to believe that, I was going to work it out for myself, challenge it, disprove it'.

The epic of the escape and the backdrop of war were Abe's childhood background. He says he was awake to the reality of their story from his earliest memory: 'I can't ever remember not being aware'. He remembers references to camps and death and a lot of talk about it 'because when I was a very small child, they were still looking for people'. In the early postwar years, a community of survivors and refugees from the escape trail were the family's companions:

There were layers and layers of people. People from pre-war Poland, and then people from Vilna and then people they met in Shanghai and Kobe, people from all along the trail. I'd see the numbers on their arms in summer at the beach. There were friends with their children. We were all dimly aware of being alike, but it was not talked about. We sort of knew we were part of a community, but it wasn't till later that it started to make some larger sense. There were some children—the children of camp survivors—they seemed more tortured than the others.

Communication about the past didn't necessarily depend on words. He remembers his mother hiding, terrified, under the table during thunderstorms: 'I was five or six and someone said "It's because of the war, it's the bombs"'. When they fled Warsaw she'd run from the building as the bombs rained down on them, the block of apartments collapsing behind her, floor by floor. Abe early made the equation that 'thunder is bombs and bombs is war and war is terror'. Thunder was only one of a number of triggers for panic, however: as he grew up, 'the war became a whole series of traumatic events'.

The trauma, Abe says, was in the background, suppressed and not talked of. On the surface, there was the epic narrative. What lay behind them was not called 'the war' but 'when we escaped from Poland':

> The story is one of wit and heroism and negotiating tactics, what you needed to say and do in order to make it through to the next hurdle, like hiding gems and bribing people, and not being sent to Siberia, and later, stories of what happened in Japan. I'd find out around the dinner table. Sunday lunches were a bit like Pesach. It was 'Tell me the story of . . .'. There was an undertone that this was the most exciting time of our lives because, and they said this often, 'with nothing we survived'. It was a time that they were truly stretched as human beings and everything else faded in comparison.

The narrative, though, was never other than episodic, unconnected and at times bizarre:

> I was never quite clear what it meant. I got bits of it at different times, some of it just hung there and made no sense, like when they arrived on the train somewhere in the middle of nowhere in central Asia where Stalin had sent a whole bunch of Jews and they had been told to greet the train and ask them to get off and settle there.

And there were gaps in the story:

> I only asked questions about the narrative, never about emotion, because our home was very closed off to feeling. I asked and I got told but there were bits they didn't know till later and there were bits they hadn't told me and they gave me versions that they wanted to believe, like about how my father's parents died.

In a sense, then, what Abe found out about was a peculiar amalgam of narrative richness and emotional emptiness. He associates both fascination and wonder at the details of the escape, tinged with embarrassment at parents who were so overtly different from his Anglo-Australian surrounds. His life was further complicated by his parents' decision to send him to an elite private Anglo-Australian school where his family's history 'had no meaning'. The conflicts that ensued later, he said were 'the price they were prepared to pay for social mobility'. He recalls his confusion at school:

I was scared of Jewish scripture, it was very alien, all the Yiddish and Hebrew—I was terrified of all this mumbo-jumbo, I didn't have many Jewish friends. I deserted from Jewish Scripture class and went to the Church of England group where I met 'little Jesus meek and mild'. He seemed a lot gentler than the alternative of the time.

The story of Abe's parents' war years is an epic of escape. Literally, as the Germans were invading Poland, the mother fled, together with her husband, mother, step-father, half-sister and half-brother. Abe's father's parents were left behind, being too old to make the journey. The escape took them eastward—through Soviet-controlled Poland, Russia, Shanghai, Japan—before they finally came to Australia. In Shanghai, rumours reached them of the horrors they so narrowly escaped and what until then had been an epic adventure tinged with fear became suffused with the pain, loss and grief of the Holocaust.

It was only after the war that Abe's father had his own parents' deaths confirmed, with some small comfort being salvaged in that one or both of them seem to be buried in the local graveyard. However, the manner of their deaths remained unclear, and Abe's impression was that the more horrific details seem to have been left out of the version that the family ultimately chose to live with. Abe suspects that it was beyond his father's capacity to integrate the full truth into his consciousness and that his postwar years were clouded by guilt and the impossibility of closure. 'My father never got over grieving for his parents, the guilt he felt for having left them behind, the fact that he'd not said Kaddish [the Jewish prayer for the dead] for them.'

The circumstances and implications of the escape—the fact that the mother's family escaped intact, while the father's remained and died in horrific circumstances that are none too clear but can be imagined—appears to have been an arterial thread in the family's dynamic and their postwar narrative. Abe's father's guilt at leaving his parents without protection seems to have been the central point of the home's emotional fabric. This was exacerbated by the father's later wish to return to Poland and the mother's adamant refusal: she could remember having to sit in the 'Jews only' section at University lectures, and being spat on by Polish students.

Abe knew not to ask about this or related topics for fear of triggering conflict. He recalls that there was a vested interest in the facade of harmony being preserved, and he as much as his parents colluded in this: 'It was important for me that their relationship was a good one so that I felt safe and protected'. Talk about the war appears to have been comfortable so long as it stayed close to the track of the epic escape. A clear taboo was the encroachment of emotional topics. These issues were never resolved and the emotion that attached to them was pushed below the surface of daily life, invisible yet palpable.

Over the last fifteen years, especially since his father's death, Abe has continued to explore the events of his family's past, what he calls 'something that touches me deeply in ways that I still don't understand completely'. Like many children of survivors, he feels a despairing wonderment at the thinness of civilisation's veneer and the abiding moral questions: how could people do it? What would he have done in his parents' place? What would he have done if he were on the other side? The despair derives from the fact that he has no expectation of closure: 'these are questions that are uncloseable'.

Other stories

Through the process of writing this book, as mentioned earlier, I found out about other stories of silence that are related to trauma.

In one sense, these *other* stories were accidental: they came to me, rather than me to them. From the start, I found people whose experiences resonated with the admixture of trauma and silence I discovered in my research. I had expected to find a sympathetic resonance in the broader population of Holocaust descendants. I had not expected that the situation at the heart of my research would find a wider empathetic response.

I encountered this reaction for the first time on the day that I was introduced to the man who was to become my literary agent. He listened attentively as I outlined my background, the research, its findings and my plan for a book. I expected that he would engage with the intellectual content of the book and locate its value therein; instead what I encountered was an intensely personal reaction, as he connected with the trauma and silence in his own life. He then proceeded to tell me his story, which I recount later in the book, in Chapter 8, as 'Peter's story'.

This was the first of the other stories that came to me unsolicited. Because my encounters with these stories were opportunistic; my explorations of them have been less thorough and less expansive than the planned individual interviews with children of Holocaust survivors. Nonetheless, these other stories individually and collectively provide an additional dimension and with this, a quality of universalism.

The experiences that people recounted to me were widely disparate, and included trauma inflicted by others as well as natural disasters. Generally, there seems to be the view that 'man-made' trauma is more shattering of people's belief and trust in life than 'natural' tragedies. However quantifying the impact of tragedy is nothing short of pointless.

Here are some examples of these 'opportunistic stories'. I spoke to a woman whose baby was forcibly taken from her at birth. Her family disallowed any discussion of the fact, causing a pall of silence to dominate her life for some 30 years after the event. I spoke to a woman who lives daily with the fact of her daughter's inoperable brain tumour, and struggles to find a way of talking meaningfully about her experience. Another young woman I spoke to was seventeen when her mother's schizophrenia was diagnosed, from which time the topic of mental illness was banished from the household domain, the father devoted himself to cushioning the family from the mother's influence, and the girl wondered, ever after, what had happened. I spoke to a woman in her thirties who had lived for some twelve years with the silence that followed her father's hushed-up suicide, and she talked about how this impacted on her life as she subsequently blanketed into suppression all emotion, not only grief. I spoke to a woman whose family's condemnation of her adolescent interest in homosexuality served the purpose of silent manipulation and abuse. Another woman at the age of 47 continues to be haunted by the experience of a vicious rape (by a family 'friend') some 30 years earlier, an event that remained unspoken and unpunished for all that time.

In all these cases, and others akin to them, people experience the incommunicability of trauma, the impact of an imposed silence and the suffering that is wrought in trying to forge coherence in a silent world. I have learned that silence is as complex as spoken language, as differentiated and as subtle. Sometimes it is self-imposed, sometimes, other-imposed. Sometimes it is driven by the urge to protect or salvage or cherish; other times, as a weapon of defense or control or denial. One thing that underscores all instances: it is rarely unproblematic.

Juliano's story

Juliano's story is one of self-imposed silence. I met him at a faculty meeting when I was interstate, working on a short-term contract at an Australian university. At the start of the round-table meeting I was introduced to those present as the visiting consultant and asked to talk about myself and my work for a few minutes. I approached this task by simply listing the projects open on my desk that week. One of these was *The Silence*. I mentioned briefly what the book was about and during the morning break, one of the lecturers present, a man of pleasant appearance and gentle manner, approached me and asked me more about the kind of silence my book was exploring. It turned out he had a story that he was happy to share with me. It is the story of a young boy from an Italian family going to an Australian school, obliged to function in a foreign tongue, and unable to reconcile the two languages/two cultures divisions in his life. His defence against the pressures on him became a retreat into silence; and over time, as he gained strength and confidence, the silence became also a weapon.[11]

When I returned home I emailed Juliano and asked him to write a statement about this early period of his life, including how he perceived the silence, how he thought it was perceived from outside, and his adult explanation for or interpretation of the patterns of behaviour described. This is what he sent me:

> I do not have many fond memories of my childhood schooling experience. I clearly remember marching with the other children into my lower 1 class, sitting down in the middle of the room and watching as the others recited the names on the alphabet picture cards which circled the room as Mrs T played the piano. As always, I sat mute and observed the scene as from the inside of a bubble. Perhaps I repeated the words inside my head. I must have had a passive understanding of English before I started school. My two cousins with whom I played in the backyard had started school the previous year and used English while playing. I remember scolding them for not using Italian. I couldn't join in and felt excluded. For a number of years, therefore, I remained a silent participant in classroom activities. Indeed, this continued well after my language abilities in English might have coped with what was going on. Silence or lack of verbal interaction became my *modus operandi*. Teachers who dared question me directly were met with a stony silence and quickly learned to

leave me alone. I'm sure they did not know what to make of this well behaved child whose work was on a par with or better than that of the other students in the class, yet sat catatonic through most of his primary school years. The silence became a tyranny. I dreaded school and the thought of being asked questions, having the spotlight falling on me. But my silence was also a coercive weapon. I could sense the teachers' embarrassment rise as I steadfastly refused to respond to their queries. Unpleasant as it all was, I was in charge of the situation. I coped. And I could sense their amazement when from time to time I consented to reply. A special reward for the teacher. True, my replies were concise and to the point (this fact hasn't changed to the present and I still show more confidence in writing than in speaking in public), but importantly my answers were right. It proved I was listening, I was following the teacher. It was just that most of the discourse was going on inside my head.

It would seem that Juliano's experience is an extreme reaction to the pressure to accommodate at a tender age the competing demands of two languages and two cultures. Given the dislocation of migration and the shock immersion into an alien world, one can see why a retreat into silence would have offered some balm to a troubled child. At an age when a child is just beginning to know his place in the world, suddenly the earth slips from under his feet. Silence starts off as his coping mechanism (*Leave me alone*) and evolves into a means (*You can't make me do anything I don't want to do*) by which he can reclaim some of his power.

It is difficult to know how pervasive such a retreat is for the children of migrant families who are subjected to comparable pressures; I suspect that Juliano is far from an isolated case. Clearly, circumstances vary and responses do too. I remember the shock of encountering a new language when I started school, the imperative coming from the outside which urged me to convert in haste to being a speaker of English. Those were the days before support classes were provided for children of non-English speaking backgrounds. I recall two memories from that time: first, that I had to learn English as fast as possible; and second, my belief, origin unknown, that one's head could only hold—in the sense of a container—one language at a time. I therefore believed that I needed to empty my head of Yiddish before I could take on English. This conforms with what my parents later told me: the astounding co-occurrence of the two processes—my loss of Yiddish and my taking on of English. In contrast, Juliano retreated to a silent world, and emerged ultimately, as bilingual and bicultural. Given the outcome—and I refer here to the richness of the experience of bilingualism/biculturalism—one would have to conclude that his retreat into, and later exploitation of a sustained silent period in his youth was ultimately a successful strategy, albeit an intensely troubling one at the time.

3

The Silent Aftermath of War

Trauma has great depth of reach, with little respect, it would seem, for generational boundaries. A Buddhist saying has it that after a time of killing, it takes three generations for the healing to happen.

This book is centrally about 'the long shadow'[1] that violence casts, the trans-generational aftermath of trauma. It will show how trauma in one generation infiltrates and permeates the world and psyche of the next. In this intertwining of life worlds, language has a pivotal role, creating connection, mutuality and indivisibility, providing a kind of narrative chain by which the representation of experience passes to the next generation and becomes absorbed into family memory. It is an important concept in the construction of this book and will be invoked repeatedly through the pages ahead.

In this chapter and the next, however, I want to explore the contexts of Holocaust trauma in the aftermath of World War II. We begin, in Chapter 3, very broadly with the large canvas of Europe in 1945: the politico-historical context of the jostling of new alliances and loyalties on the freshly redrawn map of Europe. What kind of world did survivors encounter when the nightmare of the war ended and the nightmare of surviving began? Still in the same chapter, our focus then shifts to the precarious terrain of the inner world, to enable us to explore the psycho-social context. How did survivors go about coping with their new reality, and how did the world cope with them? Lastly, we turn, in Chapter 4, to the linguistic context. There we will look at the kinds of considerations that shaped and constrained survivors' attempts at communication in the early postwar years of recovery and reconstruction.

Silence descends: the politico-historical context

Several years ago, at the Sydney Jewish Museum, an exhibition was
held to mark the fiftieth anniversary of Liberation—the end of the
war, the liberation of Europe by the Allied forces. In the broader
mainstream culture, of course, the end of World War II was marked
by celebration. Film footage of the period shows people dancing in
the streets and kissing strangers, jubilant crowds in ticker-tape
parades, returning troops welcomed as heroes. But it was clear from
the Liberation exhibition that for the Jewish people this was not a
moment of celebration. Simply, survivors say, it came too late.

Europe, 1945. I wasn't there, of course, but when I close my eyes
and try to visualise the scene, I see a few dishevelled, dislocated individuals. Typically, they are sole survivors of once-large families. They
come up out of the dark, blinded by the new reality. Dazed, confused,
they begin to count the enormity of their loss. It's a scene from the
film of Primo Levi's *The Truce*.[2] In my image, the new reality into
which they have tumbled is a war-ravaged landscape in which alone,
possessionless and without anchorage, they must begin to live again.
When I think of my parents in May 1945—my mother coming out of
hiding in Poland, my father liberated by the French in south-eastern
Germany—this is the image I see.

On the shelves of my local library, and certainly on the shelves of
any university that offers courses in Modern European history, there
are innumerable accounts of the politico-historical landscape of Europe
in 1945. They constitute an excellent historical resource. My purpose
here is not to replicate or supplement. Rather, I want to explore one
aspect of this period, one that is contained in a phrase that jumps out at
me from the pages of the books on the subject. I read repeatedly of a
'curtain of silence' that came down in 1945 on the world into which
survivors stepped, following their ascent out of hell. Sometimes it is
called 'a conspiracy of silence'; other times, 'a wall of silence'.

So, what is going on here? If it's a curtain of silence, who is pulling
the strings? If it is a wall of silence, who is laying the bricks? If it is a
conspiracy of silence, who is whispering and conspiring?

'We didn't know'

Let's start at the end of the war. In 1945, when the Allied and Russian
tanks rolled into what remained of the concentration camps, and took

those first pictures of filthy, dazed, walking skeletons in striped uniforms, an apparently stunned world recoiled from the evidence of a holocaust. Apparently, no one had read the writing on the wall; no one had realised what had been going on for the last six years. An entire people had been targeted, apparently silently, behind closed doors. A case of not knowing? A case of not wanting to know?

Now, let's go back further, just over twenty years. In *Mein Kampf*, written in prison in 1923, Hitler claimed that he would rid the world of the vermin Jews. In 1933 he came to power, democratically, on a platform of promises to make Germany pure, proud, strong and Jew-free. Between 1933 and 1939, events inside Germany and on her various borders—the militarisation of the Ruhr Valley, for example, and the annexation of Czechoslovakia—painted a consistent picture of a nation bent on conquest. The beginnings of a war against civilians were everywhere evident. *Kristallnacht*, or the Night of Broken Glass, on 9 November 1938 saw a rampaging horde of Nazi thugs target Jews in Germany. On the Website where I have searched for the details, there's a picture of onlookers watching a fire, with the local fire department allowing it to consume the synagogue while preventing it from spreading to nearby houses.[3]

In 1938, thousands of German Jews of Polish origin were stripped of their citizenship and expelled. Historically a hotbed of state-sponsored anti-Semitism, Poland refused to let them cross the border. So these exiles languished in a no-man's-land, both physical and spiritual, at the mercy of cold, hunger and disease. Among the Jews of Poland, there was an urgent call for doctors to go to their aid. My father, then a recent graduate of Warsaw University's Medical School, answered the call. His encounter with the suffering there was a formative event of his life, though no preparation for the six years ahead.

War began when the German war machine rolled into Poland on 1 September 1939, and nothing that was done in the days, months and years ahead contradicted *Mein Kampf*'s grand plan. The Wannsee Conference in January 1942 shaped the fine details of the Final Solution, now state policy. The invasion and Nazification of France, Belgium and Holland followed, the railway system of Europe providing an excellent facility for transporting an unwanted people to their end. The multitude of large-scale and minor events between 1939 and 1945 enacted a consistent bestiality unleashed in the pursuit of genocide.

Back to 1945. The liberating Allied and Russian tanks roll into the concentration camps. Places like Bergen-Belsen become public domain knowledge. The world sees the outcome of a policy of state-sponsored genocide. Shock. Outrage. Then silence—different nuances of silence.

Events happen. Later, those who come after, interpret them. People with rival interpretations argue and debate. I have no qualms here in stating that what follows is my interpretation of events I learned of, but did not witness. I learned about them as a student of history and through the subjectivities of my parents who survived them.

In the immediate aftermath, the posture of shock became the standard response of a world that, for over twenty years, had chosen not to see, hear or heed. Who later took responsibility for this turning away? For visas denied and boats turned back, as a captive people were denied escape and allowed to be slaughtered? Suddenly, nobody knew—or had ever known—anything. German villages, such as the one portrayed in Hegi's *Stones from the River*, were emptied of their Jews and no one seemed to wonder where they went.[4] Poles screamed, 'Get out, filthy Jews' as masses of civilians were spilled out of their homes into killing fields and sealed death trains, after which their homes and possessions were taken over: 'We weren't to know whether they were coming back'. Returning German soldiers said, if they said anything, 'We were only following orders'. An entire German nation was suffused in silence. A western bloc of nations, aware that the postwar world had borders drawn differently, conscious that former enemies were quickly becoming new allies, alert to the looming Cold War, found it convenient to let the past subside and look instead to future allegiances.

What happens when morality falls victim to expediency? The Catholic Church maintained a stony institutional silence as the descendants of the Christ-killers got what had been coming to them and then, in the chaotic aftermath of the war, organised secret escape routes for ex-Nazis bound for impunity in South America. Descendants of Jewish owners of numbered Swiss bank accounts were turned away in Geneva because they lacked the appropriate documentation—no death certificate issued in Auschwitz. Gold from the teeth of Jews filled the coffers of Swiss banks whose officials found it convenient, during the war, immediately after and for another 50 years beyond, not to ask too many questions. What of those Swiss who heard, and surely wondered about, the muffled cries from sealed trains that passed in the night? What of those border guards who turned desperate refugees back to certain death on the basis of a spurious and selective neutrality? What of those in government who were to sit righteously on such evidence for 50 years in the hope that history would overlook state complicity with civilian slaughter?

It is easy today to say, 'We didn't know'. And it is easy to say that hindsight provides a different quality of vision. But there is a consistency in the pragmatics of denial as there is in the politics of memory[5]—whether it comes from now Jew-free villages or supposedly de-Nazified Germany, or Swiss banks or Papal representatives, or German industrialists whose family businesses thrived on war-recruited slave labour. One can argue backwards and forwards on these issues *ad nauseam*, and there is no shortage of literature for fuel.

One thing I know to be true. For a year, my father was marched daily by gun-toting guards in German uniforms through a small south-eastern German village in the kind of lush green idyllic fields that are memorable from Claude Lanzmann's documentary, *Shoah*.[6] Starving and diseased, he and the men with him provided slave labour for the Germans in the neighbouring stone quarry. Each day fewer returned than went in the morning, because if one fell down from exhaustion and didn't get up immediately, he was shot (or if bullets were in short supply, he was mauled by Alsatians trained for just this purpose). Each day, walking one way and then back the next, they were watched by local villagers who kept a safe distance from the events that they were later to deny having seen. At war's end, the liberating Allied soldiers forced these same villagers to walk through the concentration camp that had existed and functioned in their midst. Eyes averted, each muttered, 'We didn't know' or 'Nobody told us'. How were they to know? No one remembered the chimneys belching black smoke day and night, nor the distinctive stench from the crematorium, nor the ashes that the breeze would carry indiscriminately through the air, well beyond the camp gates.

After regaining some of his health following typhus, my father chose not to return to his home—Kielce, a city two hours from Krakow. The decision not to return seems to have been made inside a larger decision—not to stir up remembrance of his home in any explicit or verbal way. So from him I learned nothing about that place. It was many years before I had the courage to find out the bare statistics about what had been a taboo topic.

In 1939, Kielce had had a population of 75 000, of whom a third were Jews. When the city was occupied my father was not there, having been conscripted into the Polish army and sent to the south of

Poland. During the first two years of the war, the Jewish population of Kielce swelled, as the Germans sent Jews from neighbouring towns and from Vienna, into the Kielce ghetto. The ghetto was liquidated in July 1942 and the Jews were dispersed to various extermination sites. I assume, with no evidence to the contrary, that my grandparents and aunt were sent to Treblinka. When Kielce was liberated in January 1945, there were no Jewish survivors. In the eighteen months that followed, a few hundred Jews who had survived variously the camps, the forests and the Soviets, congregated in Kielce. Less than half of them were former residents.

At war's end, my father made a decision not to actively try to find out what happened to his parents and sister. I think he argued to himself that if he didn't know the details of their deaths, he could more easily keep alive a loving picture of them in his head. On his own deathbed, some 48 years later, he talked about them to me—wondering aloud what he had kept inside for all those years. How did they die? Could he have saved them if he had been there? Surely it had been his duty to stay and protect them? What right did he have to survive and they not? Questions like restless ghosts that let go only when he died.

I'm not sure what would have happened had he chosen to return home. Kielce is not an important city, in Poland or beyond. However, it has made its ignoble mark in Holocaust history from an event on 4 July 1946.[7] On that day, hordes of local marauding Poles visited an age-old East European tradition—a pogrom—on the Jewish survivors who had crowded into former community buildings, some looking for family, most in that half-way-house state, awaiting the opportunity to emigrate. As graphically depicted in the film representation of the event, *From Hell to Hell*,[8] the Poles were angry. The Jews were back. They had caused the war. And anyway, they weren't supposed to come back from wherever they had gone to. Forty-two Jews who had already survived the war, died in this pogrom.

This is my view. The world let it happen. I concede that not everyone involved contributed in the same way or with the same degree of complicity. One could distinguish gradations of perpetrators. There are the local Ukrainians recruited by the Germans and provided with plenty of alcohol for the occasional activity of mass slaughter of Jews in the forests; their hands are actually bloodied. There are the Poles who betrayed a Jew in hiding, motivated by the reward or maybe the thrill that comes from the power of life and death over another; hands less bloodied, in a literal sense perhaps. And one could distinguish the perpetrators from the bystanders, those who were not actively involved in any way, but watched it happen from close (and not so close) quarters. And even the bystanders are not all of a kind. Some were helpless to assist; some could have done something but chose not to. Some did their bystanding at a considerable distance, such as Chamberlain in London; and the policy-makers in Washington, who precluded escape by constructing a bureaucratic maze of impenetrability. In the book *Safe in America*, a young couple tries to scale this bureaucratic wall in order to bring their desperate family to the USA.[9] The wait for a permit seems excruciatingly long. Then one day the letters from Europe stop coming. Different kinds of silences.

It is not my purpose, however, to try to pinpoint gradations of complicity. Ultimately it matters little whether the Nazis who beat my grandmother to death in front of her daughter were 'more complicit' than the desk bureaucrats who sent my grandfather to a camp in Estonia where starvation and back-breaking labour took his last breath. They both died, and they are only two of a much larger number.

Whether or not anyone knew, or what they knew, or how much they knew or when they knew it, the fact is that six million civilians were killed in a planned genocide. While the extermination of the Jews was the planned Nazi objective, their abandonment happened because there was no concerted effort to prevent it. There was no single group or alliance devoted to their rescue—not one Allied government, not American Jewry, nor even those lobbying for a Zionist homeland in Palestine.[10] A small percentage of intended victims survived, sometimes by a miracle, usually by accident. They were witnesses to events that made people uncomfortable. They returned to a world that did not feel very proud of its role, a place where survivors rarely felt people wanted to hear what had happened to them. This is the world to which the survivors returned when the camp gates were opened. This, I believe, accounts for the larger silence into which the remnants of a people stumbled, in May 1945.

A new landscape

The silence that began with the abandonment of the Jews, and continued with protestations of 'We didn't know', quickly became intertwined with the rapidly shifting political realities of Cold War

Europe. Even before the Nuremberg Trials were over, the pressure was on to enlist Germany as a bulwark against the Communists. Word was coming down from on high: former enemies were now allies and former allies were the new enemy. Remembering the past, identifying the Germans as the arch-protagonists in a war against humanity, seeking vengeance or justice or amends or reparations—none of this aligned comfortably with the new sets of allegiances that were to dominate Europe and the world for the next 45 years. The film *Judgement at Nuremberg*[11] captures this political process, as the forces of expediency gather momentum. Novick asserts that, in the postwar years, talk about the Holocaust became 'something of an embarrassment' in American public life, largely because of the massive ideological 're-tooling' that was happening in the USA.[12] The implacable foe of yesterday, Germany, had to be converted at breakneck speed into the ally of today; while the ally of yesterday, the Soviets, had to become the enemy of today. Public discourse had to be harnessed to move the minds and hearts of a nation to recast the enemy.

Thus it was that the language of 'totalitarianism' came to the fore from 1945, serving a powerful rhetorical purpose 'in deflecting the abhorrence felt towards Nazism onto the new Soviet enemy'.[13] This allowed what might seem a peculiar, even immoral backflip—serving side-by-side with Germans—to be reframed as a struggle against the enemy totalitarianism, dressed first in a Nazi uniform, then in a Soviet one or any of the Eastern European uniforms of the Warsaw Pact.

And lest we think that it was only the West that reframed the past in its own preferred colours, the communist world did likewise. Buruma's *The Wages of Guilt* exposes the postwar propaganda of the East German government, where Nazi German war crimes were reinterpreted as the logical excesses of capitalism, rather than as a German or even a Nazi phenomenon.[14] Overall, the genocide against the Jews was rewritten as the capitalist war against the proletariat: memorials to war dead spoke generically about the victim, as did plaques near the site of former concentration camps where the majority of dead were Jewish. (Wiesel writes, 'not all victims were Jews, but all Jews were victims.'[15]) The rewriting of history happened on both sides of the Cold War divide.

In the West, the new world view was not one that comfortably allowed talk about the Holocaust. Novick points to a number of factors contributing singly and collectively to the conspiracy of silence that was to move the Holocaust off the stage of public discourse for

two decades or more. One was the blatant inconvenience of the Holocaust. Framed as the war against the Jews, the Holocaust was certainly
the 'wrong atrocity' at the wrong time, as it failed to serve the ends of
the new world view. It was more in the interests of those in power to
see the Nazi evil as perpetrated on a political enemy—those that were
opposed to totalitarianism. Focusing on the early political prisoners of
camps like Dachau allowed a congruence to be drawn between the
enemies of Nazism and the enemies of Communism. In this context,
talk about the Holocaust was possible in the public domain only if it
marginalised the fate of the Jews. The abomination of state racism was
recast in political terms—as an instance of the abomination of totalitarianism. There was nothing about the reporting on the liberation
of the camps, Novick asserts, that cast these places as particularly
Jew-focused. Jews were *among* the victims, and the perpetrators
increasingly were referred to as *Nazi*, not German. In this version, the
extermination of the Jews becomes an incidental statistic in an essentially political crime.[16] Langer, too, in his book *Admitting the
Holocaust*, argues that even the term 'liberation' allowed one 'to block
out the image of emaciated bodies . . . as if a single honorific term
could erase the paradoxical possibility that survival might be a lifelong
sentence to the memory of loss'.[17] The reframing of political loyalties,
on the political front, might also explain the fact that the massive loss
of life caused by the war in the Soviet Union went largely unac-
knowledged in the Western world.[18]

Recasting Nazism as totalitarianism and focusing on the totalitar-
ian nature of the Nazi regime rather than its policy of anti-Semitism,
had implications for the way German guilt was to be construed. If
totalitarianism means the total control of a country, where terror
invades and suffuses all domains, then opposition and resistance are
rendered impossible. Novick argues convincingly that this leads to an
exaggerated indulgence towards the German people who then might
be thought of, equally, as victims of their own government's reign of
terror.[19]

In this kind of public discourse, American Jewry were quickly
made aware that their dissatisfaction with the treatment of German
war crimes was likely to be construed within the long-existing divide
taught in Sunday Schools throughout the Christian world—the
contrast between the hard Old Testament God of Vengeance and
the loving New Testament God of Forgiveness. This divide shows its
face in the letters to the editor columns of major newspapers every

time a Nazi criminal is tracked down. The hunters wanting a public accounting, but a compassion-fatigued public want no more reminders, saying, 'Forgive and forget', 'Let it go', 'These are tired old men, let them have their last days in peace'. Sensitive to their minority status in the host society, Jews everywhere outside of Israel have learned that to rock the boat is to court trouble. More reason for more silence.

The Jews that stumbled out, barely alive, from the ashes of Europe in 1945 discovered that they were witnesses to events the world would rather forget. They discovered that they were small-time players on a large world map, and that their testimony was, for various historical reasons, not one that the world wanted to be reminded of. In this way, the new orthodoxy reframed survivors' experiences, rendering them unspeakable. As we shall see in the next section, the macro-messages were matched by the micro- ones as unspeakability was reinforced at the individual level, in the homes and communities of the new Diaspora, wherever survivors sought to put down new roots. At all levels, the message was apparent: everyone's interests would be served by a renormalisation; survivors were to get on with their 'pillaged lives' as best they could.[20]

A particular instance of silence within the broader realm of the politics of forgetting is perpetrator silence and the silence of postwar generations of Germans. The writer Ursula Duba, a German Gentile, is consumed by the failure of the German nation to confront its past. In her twin autobiographical narrative poems, 'Blind date' and 'His blind date', she tells of hearing about Auschwitz for the first time when she was nineteen, when she met a Jewish boy, the son of survivors. They remained pen-pals for many years, he in Belgium, then later Israel, she in Germany, then the USA.

> They exchange addresses
> and write long letters to each other
> during the next year
> he sends her books
> by Sartre Camus Simone de Beauvoir
> they discuss existentialism
> pacifism
> a united Europe
> a world without war
> but neither has the language

to write about their anguish—
his daily life with a father
consumed by grief
silent
except for his prayers
unable to relate to his children
and she doesn't tell him
of her horror
of having grown up
among murderers.[21]

Again, different hues and shades of silence. There are, of course, resonances beyond two people's experience. What does it say of the contemporary German moral landscape that the central character of Schlik's novel, *The Reader*, is more anguished about her illiteracy being uncovered than her background as a Nazi camp guard?[22] What does it mean, as Ursula Duba notes, that German Jews are still referred to in Germany as 'Jews', hardly ever as German citizens, so continuing 'their marginalisation in German consciousness'.[23] Contemporary young Germans are surprised to learn, if they ever do, that the German Jewish community was once fully integrated into mainstream German life. What haunts Munich, as it haunts all Germany, is 'the presence of an absence'.[24] Ernestine Schlant, at the launch of her book *The Language of Silence—West German Literature and the Holocaust*, is quoted as having said 'Literature is the seismograph of a people's unconscious'. In a review of the book, Duba asks one to consider what it says about postwar Germany's unconscious that there is a distinct absence of Holocaust victims as protagonists in literature written by German Gentiles.[25] Perhaps, hollow echoes of a silence so pervasive that it has become naturalised as normal.

Considering the Allied contribution to postwar German silence, Duba suggests that the USA was negligent in seeking accountability from Germany after its defeat. Perhaps this came about because Germans were white and Aryan and perceived to be like white Americans—highly educated with enormous technical skill, organised, systems-efficient, indeed with 'all the traits of civilization'. Could there be, she asks, a certain admiration for Germans' military prowess, possibly even for their machinery of mass extermination?[26]

The psycho-social context

In looking at the psycho-social context, two questions come to mind: how did the postwar world greet the survivors and how did the survivors begin to orient themselves to 'normality' having lived for years *in extremis*. The first is an outside-looking-in question. The second one is inside-looking-out.

Outside-looking-in

Given the intense interest in the Holocaust during the last ten years or so, from writers, film-makers, educational policy-writers, playwrights, historians, it is difficult to accept that the current extent of interest and receptivity is both phenomenal and new. In a world that now sees the Holocaust as the lowest point of the century, perhaps of the millennium, it is hard to appreciate that this view of events is quite recent.

Certainly, such was not the world that greeted survivors in the postwar years. Historical events are most talked about in the decade or two after their occurrence. From there they begin to fade into the background. The Holocaust has had a different rhythm in public consciousness. Fifty years after the war, it is centre-stage in public consciousness. But for the first 30 years, the world simply did not want to know. The 'groundwork of receptivity' was not in place: there were no popular books or movies, no public memorials or museums, no one urging survivors to give testimony.[27]

The not-wanting-to-know began with a not-wanting-to-look. In May and June 1945, the world recoiled from the film footage shot at the newly liberated camps. From there, the cinematic versions found their way to newsreel screen outlets across the western world. Such visual access by a civilian population to the horrors of the war was certainly a new phenomenon—the Vietnam War's daily televised carnage was yet to come. Perhaps it was because the world was then less used to such exposure, that the visceral repugnance was so much the greater. A distressed reader of *Life* magazine in 1945 wrote to the editor that 'the stories are awful enough' but 'why, oh why, did you have to print that picture?', arguing that notwithstanding 'the truth of the atrocity', shouldn't the public be spared the horror?'.[28]

Of course, nothing happens in isolation. Politically, the restructuring of Europe in the shape of the Cold War brought the Nuremberg trials to a premature close. De-Nazification of Germany became a low priority, as did the requirement that the past be under-stood and in some way atoned for. Expediency swept conscience aside and what followed were three decades of active indifference. In an overview article about how the Holocaust was received, social worker Maria Rosenbloom writes: 'For a long time [it] was a taboo topic. People talked little about it and wanted to know even less . . . Even if [survivors] were willing to talk . . . there was no one to listen'.[29]

Even among themselves, it would seem survivors shunned words. A survivor I interviewed, Marika, spent part of the war on the run and part in hiding. Having Aryan features she could pass as a Polish Chris-tian. She lost her parents, husband, community—everyone except her younger sister, who suicided six months after the war, after being raped by a Polish soldier. Marika was then entirely alone in the world. One day, on the streets of her home city, she encountered her ex-brother-in-law: her dead husband's brother. They greeted each other with a kiss on each cheek, but neither then nor later did they ever ask each other, 'What happened to you in the war?' or 'How did you survive the war?'. Today Marika is in her mid-eighties, and when she recounts this, she still seems stunned at the absence of these questions.

As people turned away, survivors were quick to take note. The temptation to remain silent—welcome in that it allowed them to try to put the past behind them—now blended with the dictates of social etiquette. Fresco calls this period 'the gaping, vertiginous black hole of the unmentionable years'.[30]

My first recollection of this was in the late 1950s and 1960s, sensing the social discomfort of some guests having coffee and cakes while they listened politely to my father as he spoke about the war. Many of my respondents in the research underpinning this book made reference to similar feelings of embarrassment and shame. This was a complicated cauldron of emotion: we were embarrassed for the visitor and at the same time ashamed that we felt embarrassed; we wondered if the visitor would have the same difficulty in responding as we were used to in ourselves. Today, when I think back, I'm not sure how much of the tension was a projection of my own discomfort and how much was my recognition of the social inappropriateness of the topic. In my mind's eye, though, I can see where the various people were seated that day, where I was in relation to them, and how acutely I sought to avoid eye contact with anyone.

Nowhere is this turning away more poignant than in the response of the psychological community. I refer here to psychologists and psychiatrists who had contact with survivors by virtue of their professional role. It is ironic that an inability to listen touched even those trained in the craft of healing psychological pain.

It is now generally accepted that the therapy professions failed to deal appropriately with the needs of survivors. Perhaps this is because the psychological literature of the postwar period, until quite recently, was predominantly psychopathological, focusing almost entirely on the symptomology of trauma. The term 'survivor syndrome' was coined on the basis of certain clinical cases and then inappropriately generalised to apply to the wider survivor community. The label was used for a constellation of mental disorders—anxiety, exaggerated fears, failure to grieve, failure to achieve closure, intermeshed boundaries with family members, depression, nightmares, uncontrollable crying—indeed many of the symptoms that have since been associated with post-traumatic stress disorder.[31]

The evidence now suggests that individually and collectively the therapy professions failed to allow survivors to talk about their experiences.[32] At the core was an inability to hear what their patients had endured. Listening meant being up close to trauma: listening to the voice, looking into the eyes of the witness. Dori Laub, describing the intertwining of therapist–listener and survivor–narrator, says that 'The listener to trauma comes to be a participant and co-owner of the traumatic event'. For Laub, whose work with the video testimony archive at Yale University is an exploration of the intertwining roles of witness and listener, the blurring of boundaries in the telling process is at the same time crucial and hazardous. For the telling to reach a 'testimonial resolution', a common bond is needed between the two key participants:

> The professionally trained receivers of the testimonies which bear witness to the war atrocities—the listeners and interviewers whose own listening in fact *enables* the unfolding of the testimonial life accounts of Holocaust survivors—cannot fulfil their task without, in turn, passing through the crisis of experiencing their boundaries, their separateness, their functionality, and indeed their sanity at risk.[33]

Therapists no doubt had their own personal and professional crises, triggered by the need to deal with their own 'inner terror' as they confronted 'the gruesome story about when Hansel and Gretel were really pushed into the oven'.[34] Seeking to explain if not justify the failure of therapy, Krell asks his colleagues: 'Which of us wants to step into the abyss with the survivor and into such depths of anguish and rage that one can do nothing but weep?'[35]

For the therapists, keeping one's distance meant seeking refuge in technical and familiar labels that did no justice to the reality in front of them. What relevance has Freudian therapy to a sole survivor whose postwar anxiety is unquestionably related to what she witnessed and endured? I am reminded of Primo Levi's story about a man with him in the camp who was whimpering during a nightmare. Levi was about to wake him from the nightmare, but then decided not to, thinking that it was most probably more comforting than the reality to which he would wake.[36]

Little wonder that survivors had no respect for, or faith in, talk therapy as a way out of their pain. Such distrust was aggravated by the bureaucratic maze through which they had to travel for war compensation. More often than not, this meant being interviewed by German psychiatrists to whom they had to prove that their current medical complaints might be attributed to a savage beating or prolonged starvation, rather than to pre-existing conditions. To be assessed thus by a German-accented doctor, given that profession's ignoble collaboration with Nazism, was intolerable. I had a tiny sense of the indignities survivors must have felt when each year I accompanied my father on his compulsory annual visit to the German consul in Sydney: for the tiny pension he received from them, he had to go there, once a year, to prove he was still alive. I hated those visits but I didn't want my father to go there alone. I could feel the walls of something pressing in on us, but we didn't speak about why we were there.

Perhaps I am being unfair. Perhaps to expect the therapy community to have treated survivors appropriately is to ask too much. Perhaps any words at that time would have functioned as scalpels on open wounds. Mankind has achieved amazing feats in the development of instruments for the inflicting of hurt, yet we have not evolved adequate healing equivalents. The point of my highlighting the failure of those in the psychological community to respond appropriately to victims of trauma is that it allows us a window on the response of the population at large. If the very people who were best equipped to allow survivors to talk failed to do so because of their inability to confront such horror at close quarters—despite the buffer afforded by their professional role—then what chance did survivors have of their story being heard by the wider lay population or, more personally, by their own children in their own homes, where there was no emotional separation?

The wish to protect oneself from close exposure to trauma is one explanation for the patterns of therapeutic response in the decades after the war. However, by itself, it is perhaps simplistic. In offering an explanatory account in terms of a psychological recoil—therapists shutting themselves off in an act of self-preservation—we are removing the pattern of behaviour from its social, cultural and political contexts and thereby failing to acknowledge other relevant and contributing factors. These are important because the silence with which this book is centrally concerned does not happen in isolation. It is embedded in a larger network of silences, all of which constrain and shape and reinforce outcomes.

Naomi Rosh White takes a larger view, more sociological than psychological, in explaining the profession's obsession with the psychopathology of survivors as well as the media's representation of survivors as 'disturbed'. She argues that the labels 'disturbed' and 'abnormal' are themselves cultural constructs which need to be denaturalised and subjected to scrutiny. Most pointedly, she asks: 'What would constitute "normal", "healthy" non-pathological postwar responses to the physical and psychological degradations suffered by the victims of Nazism? What is the "acceptable" response from which their behaviour is seen to deviate?'[37]

Rosh White claims that the language of psychopathological accounts of survivor symptoms is a large part of the problem. Because inadequate credence is given to the past or to the current social and political conditions of survivors, it is the survivor as individual who is constructed as having the problem. Undoubtedly, this is very affirming for some people. It affirms the norms from which the patient has deviated; it raises perhaps false hopes of a 'treatment'; and, most importantly, it affirms the power and authority of those who have labelled them as disturbed.[38]

The power of language in this kind of labelling is that it can locate the problem within the individual victim, rather than with those who performed the atrocities. It is a process that puts the spotlight on the victim while the perpetrator slips from active view. It removes the event from the wider social domain and places it within an enclosed territory: inside the head of the allegedly disturbed individual. It allows the perspective of those-with-power to prevail over the perspective of those-without-power. Goffman's *Asylums* is riveting testimony to how these processes unfold.[39]

I have seen this shifting of responsibility happen with the notion of the Jew as Holocaust victim. In the latter case, I have had non-Jews say to me, ostensibly without any ill will, that perhaps there was something in the nature or condition of the Jews that 'asked for' the treatment that was meted out to them? After all, they dressed differently, they kept to themselves, they spoke their own language. Did they not in some sense 'bring it on themselves', by choosing to be different?

The unexamined assumptions that underpin this view come not only from an ignorance of the historical circumstances but also from a failure to recognise this as a recasting of roles and labels that makes the victims responsible for their fate, irrespective of the massive historical evidence that points to outside agencies and circumstances. It is the same thinking that allows the popular writer Ayn Rand and countless American government administrations to tout policies of 'rugged individualism' that locate and interpret individual circumstances outside the social, political and historical events that frame them. According to this view, people who live in abject and oppressive poverty simply lack the will to live otherwise. We see this, too, in postcolonial rationalisations about an indigenous people's conditions of life. It is a convenient ideology because it relieves governments of the responsibility of action and grants the right to *laissez-faire* policies that perpetuate the *status quo*, from generation to generation.

I am reminded here that the current Australian Prime Minister John Howard wants all Australian children to remember the sacrifices made by those who fought during the first two world wars. But he wants the Aboriginal people to stop harking back to the slaughter of their people and 'get on with being Australians', with the rest of us. For him and those of his thinking, it is only fair and reasonable to mark the anniversary of the ANZAC war dead. But the Aborigines' wish to remember their past is derisively termed a black arm-band view of history. In the politics of forgetting,[40] it is only the present realities of power and powerlessness that validates one group's right to a remembrance of the past but not the other's.

Packaging the post-Holocaust response as a medical disorder has further implications. The problem becomes removed from the wider general social world and transported into the technocratic, specialised community of medical personnel. This not only removes it from the social world but also from the public world. It is no longer society's problem but the individual's, now cared for by specialists. One outcome is that others—anyone outside the inner world of the individual 'disturbed' person—is relieved of the moral discomfort that the Holocaust tends to provoke. It takes an extreme effort of will to confront morally perplexing and destabilising phenomena; it is so much easier not to. Clendinnen's *Reading the Holocaust* is motivated by exactly this will—to confront the moral and intellectual bafflement of what she calls the Gorgon effect, that 'sickening of the imagination' and 'draining of the will' that afflict anyone who tried to understand.[41]

There is an additional implication in these events, one that is connected to the silence I am exploring in this book. When a victim group is psychopathologised in the way that has been described here, the notion of mental disorder 'robs the survivor of a vocabulary for articulating the significance to him of his experiences'. Any attempts to do so are framed by the psychopathological construct itself, and interpreted as evidence of it. This goes to the heart of why it is so difficult, once you have been diagnosed as 'neurotic' or 'disturbed' or 'insane', to prove that you are not. Once the label has been cast upon you, others filter all your protestations through the construct of your declared madness. As Rosh White states, we have the absurd situation, both laughable and tragic, of survivors who, having failed to compartmentalise their past from their present, are stigmatised 'for reacting to the attempt to exterminate them'.[42]

There is a further pressure to keep silent that has to do with the connection between public discourse and private talk. When survivors' accounts are seen, by both the therapy profession and the general public through media accounts, as evidence of maladjustment rather than as massively important historical events and personal experiences, what they have to say is rendered unwelcome. This excludes survivors from the mainstream, and means that people in general are closed, both literally and metaphorically, to survivors' accounts. As walls are erected around conversation topics, survivors are constrained in talking about the things that matter to them. As a consequence, they fail to receive the social validation that they would have received, had their communication been more welcome.

The silence, public and private, has many facets. Apfelbaum, a French Jew whose father was killed in the Holocaust, writes of the need for individuals to construct themselves in a way that links personal memory and collective public memory. She argues that societal silence, and especially official state silence, is harmful, for it de-legitimises the individual's 'private personal history'.[43] But it is not at all easy to establish these connections. Writing from the experience of being the child of survivors of the Armenian genocide of 1915, Altounian tells how silence is further reinforced by the fragile status of survivors as a minority community in a host population.[44] Contemporary French governments do not want the descendants of refugees from the Armenian genocide to compromise France's present-day diplomatic connections with Turkey. And many Armenians in France today do not want the spotlight of national attention focused on them. She claims that there are minimum codes of *bienseance* which bind survivors to keep their own counsel and not inflict the atrocity of their experience on their hosts—a kind of 'don't make waves', writ large.[45]

Novick also draws a connection between public and private discourse. After showing that the first twenty postwar years were marked by an absence of public talk about the Holocaust, he suggests that it is entirely feasible that the taboo in public discourse impacted on private discussions as well. He suggests that discussions in private tend to reflect what goes on in the public domain and that 'we rely on our culture to provide us with a menu of appropriate response'.[46] The message sent out in those days was 'this is something you shouldn't be talking about'. I am reminded here of the grandmother of the respondent I mentioned in Chapter 1, who refused to be drawn on the topic of Auschwitz ('It's not for talking'). Jennie's mother, another survivor, would turn away, saying 'It's a long time ago'. And I vividly recall my own mother, tight-lipped and minimal, turning away in response to a question from me, with her firm and non-negotiable one-liner, 'Let's not talk about that', the most efficient device for switching topics I have yet to encounter.

Everywhere I come across evidence that trauma of this magnitude, and attitudes towards it, impose a silence on those who come through and live on. This is what Hass no doubt means when he wrote about the entire survivor population, 'Feelings were kept underground'.[47] Recently I received a phone call from a woman doctor who was organising the jubilee reunion of the graduating class of doctors of 1950, at Sydney University. She contacted me because my father re-graduated as a doctor with this class. I asked her what he was like then. She told me he was 'quiet' and 'encouraging' and 'optimistic'. She said they often had lunch together on the grandstand overlooking the oval, near the Blackburn Building where they studied.

Did he talk about the war, I asked? No, she said, he never said anything about the war. I have the feeling, though, that even his young, carefree Australian-born fellow students may have wondered what was behind that silence. The 1950 *Year Book* of Medicine VI at Sydney University says of him, 'Not so well known are the two little ones that he has hidden away somewhere at home. Perhaps they can explain their father's preference for a quiet corner, a smoke and a good book'.

On the same day that I received this call, I also heard the story of Vera, a Dutch-born woman, now in her seventies, who was in Singapore on the day it fell to the Japanese and endured the rest of the war as a prisoner. She was invited to my daughter's school to speak to a class studying the play, *The Shoehorn Sonata*, by Australian playwright John Misto, a play about the experience of Australian nurses during the Japanese occupation of Singapore.[48] Overnight, Vera said, their life collapsed completely; they were behind barbed wire, subjected to appalling conditions and cruel beatings by vicious guards. As it turned out, all four members of her family survived, she with her mother in one camp, and her father and brother, who'd been sent somewhere else. At war's end they found their way back and were reunited in their home in Sumatra. She made the point that after the war neither she nor her mother, father or brother ever spoke about their experiences. It was not clear when she had begun to speak publicly about what happened to her, but my impression is that this is only recently. She was pleased to say that fifteen years ago, the nightmares had stopped.

The outside-looking-in view that I have described is, in the main, a psychopathological one. Like Rosh White, I fail to see what it offers us, apart from contributing in its own way to the politics and wider culture of forgetting. Fortunately, this viewpoint is not the only way of looking at and interpreting these events. Rosh White and Langer are two who have chosen to foreground survivor accounts and attempt to understand the world through the filter of the survivor's experience of it.[49] Rosh White's *From Darkness to Light* tracks the memories of eleven Polish Jews and shows what can be achieved when survivors' resilience is allowed to serve as the organising interpretive principle. Langer's investigation of 'the ruins of memory' constructs a post-trauma world fractured to its very core. His achievement is that he is able to portray a fractured universe without pathologising the victim at its heart. Both are examples of honest explorations that recast the pathologised survivor and enable us-who-come-after to glimpse the world through their eyes.

Inside-looking-out

There is a need to do justice to survivors by trying to see the world from the inside-looking-out. This perspective is much more difficult to recreate because in the decades after the war, there was an absence of systematically gathered information on how Holocaust survivors saw themselves and their experiences. It was some three decades before many Holocaust survivors were able to go public. By then most had raised families, put down roots in a new country, taken on a new sense of self. Thirty years gave them some distance from the trauma, some degree of healing, some capacity to talk about it. The passage of time can create the required distance that prevents the emotions associated with the experiences from overwhelming the teller.[50] Like my father, some achieved sufficient distance to interest themselves in issues of Holocaust education. Some took to writing, some allowed films to be made. Some began telling parts of their story at home, perhaps for the first time, to grandchildren. A colleague mentioned the case of a woman she knows, the only child of two sole survivors of enormous families: she complains about 'a deafening silence' from her parents about what happened to them. But these days, she hears the stories from her teenage son to whom her parents can and do talk.

When survivors did begin to tell, what they spoke of was sometimes the war, sometimes their childhood. Far less attention has been given to the way they looked at the world upon liberation. When, for example, I was working as an editor with David Kaye on his testimony *I Still Remember*, I had to urge him not to stop at 1945, but to include meeting his wife Alice, coming to Australia, having a son, reconstructing a life.[51] For survivors, the feat of reconstruction seems to fade into insignifance next to the feat of survival. Thus how survivors actually looked out at the world in 1945 is today largely locked inside the archive of memory. We can only attempt to reconstruct it.

The first thing to consider is their state of '-lessness'. They were family-less, home-less, possession-less, state-less. The temporary refuge of Allied-run camps for Displaced Persons (DP) was a euphemistic label for the state-of-having-lost-everything. Certainly, the idea of 'going home' was a nonsense. My father was one who refused to return home because he did not want to face the desolation of the loss of family. Others, like my mother, who would never be able to erase the day and site and moment of her mother's death in the Vilna ghetto, probably could not think of going back. I think this; she never told me. Like her, many sought to put Europe behind them.

In the film *Uncle Chatzkel*, Ron Freeman returns to Lithuania to try to restore what it is his family nearly lost by choosing not to look back on its painful past. He stands at the site of a mass grave: 'Somewhere [here] my great-grandparents are buried. I recall my grandmother's world-weary sighs and I begin to understand what was behind them, why she would never talk about what happened here, why we never looked back'.[52] One exile from that time recalls the rush to emigrate from Europe as 'a mass psychosis of leaving'. If people had once thought of themselves in nation-state terms (Polish, Czech, Hungarian, etc.), postwar they became at best 'European'. One of Rosh White's informants said, 'the Nazis taught me that the Jews have no country'.[53]

None was naive enough to imagine that their homes were empty, waiting for them to return, neighbours and community welcoming. In Poland, for example, where Poles had moved into what had been Jewish homes, taking over the furniture and belongings of a people hastily transported elsewhere, the message certainly was that returnees were not welcome. Recent survivor accounts abound in the portrayals of such returns. In Kaye's *I Still Remember*, the young man returns to the house where he and his parents and brother lived before the war, and there awkwardly confronts the family that now occupies it. In Reimer's *Inside Outside*, a similar scene is described when the author, on a trip to Hungary, begins a cordial exchange with the current occupant that ends sourly when the Hungarian misinterprets Reimer's nostalgia as a desire to reclaim former property. In Brett's *Too Many Men*, the encounter is vicious. More poignantly yet, in the film *From Hell to Hell*, a young couple is reunited and then searches for their child, left with neighbours as a baby. Not only were the adoptive parents hoping this would never happen, the young girl has no idea of the true identity of these strange people who suddenly appear from nowhere and seem far too interested in her.[54] The return to lost homes is the subject of Read's study, *Returning to Nothing. The Meaning of Lost Places*.[55] We can only speculate as to what it meant in 1945.

Something else was lost, apart from family, home, state. This something contributed to nihilism beyond even that of displacement. What was lost was the sense that there is a moral order in the universe, a coherence at the core of being, from which all meaning emanates. I refer here not specifically to the loss of religion, though the idea that Auschwitz could not have happened had God existed was a common one ('Don't talk to me about God. I've been where we know there is no God'). Most survivors could not escape the realisation that their survival was a matter of mere chance—not the reward for good deeds, or the result of heroism, or the outcome of wise choices, or evidence of a beneficent god, but a mere accident. A poem called 'Could have' shows the arbitrary nature of surviving:

> You were saved because you were the first.
> You were saved because you were the last.
> Alone. With others.
> On the right. The left.
> Because it was raining. Because of the shade . . .[56]

Surviving by accident destroys one's belief in natural justice. It must leave one dangling, unconnected to any sense of moral order or moral coherence. How then does one reconnect? How does one recover a sense of self, a reason for being? Like the grief for family lost, moral nihilism seems best managed not by efforts at remembrance, but by the attempt to forget.

I believe this moral nihilism, coming from the experience of the victims of a world gone mad, put survivors beyond the reach of rehabilitation. This was not, however, for want of trying. I recall a time when my father was in his late sixties, with chronic angina that had brought him close to death. I sat by his bed in the emergency room. He took my hand and fixed his eyes on mine and asked that no heroic efforts be made to keep him alive should his heart give out. And then he said what he thought was his goodbye to me. After extracting a solemn promise that I would look after my mother, he told me in words he then thought were among his last, that he felt there was more goodness than evil in the world, that he had met more instances of kindness and compassion than of cruelty. As it was, he did not die then—a bypass was to give him another thirteen years—and we never returned to that conversation. My view today is that he wanted to go out with this view, that it was a last-ditch attempt to re-establish a faith in the moral centre of humankind.

The experience of such extreme trauma separates and isolates, and silence keeps the victims self-contained in their own world. While

not everyone believes in talk therapy, it is clear to me that the absence
of talk on a topic of trauma is ultimately destructive—because it is talk
that makes us human. It allows us to intermesh. Silence keeps us
separate, enclosed behind our own barriers, wondering at our own
reality. There is a look I remember that my mother had, when she
withdrew behind a glazed mask, her lips firmly drawn together in a
tight line that was her mouth. Today I think I am closer to understanding that look. I think it is underpinned by a belief that what she
was feeling, based on what she had known, was in its most absolute
way, incommunicable. This recognition itself feeds the moral
nihilism.

Yet there is a link between silence, the passage of time and
healing. This is not a Jewish phenomenon, but a larger, human one.
The late 1970s was a time when many Vietnamese 'boat people', as
they were then called, came to Australia, fleeing the protracted
Vietnam War and a ravaged homeland. At that time I was teaching
English as a Second Language and my classes had large numbers of
Vietnamese new arrivals. I was struck by these quiet, stoical people,
so committed to 'freedom land', as they described Australia. In
particular I noted their refusal to talk about what had happened to
them, along with their gratitude for any kindness shown to them.
One evening I commented to my parents on this tight-lipped
dignity. My father said, 'Yes, they will be quiet for twenty years or
so. Then they will begin to talk'. I knew of course he was commenting as much on his generation of Holocaust survivors, some of
whom had just begun to open up, as he was on the tragedy of my
Vietnamese students.

As I contemplate the period after the war, I am struck by what I
see as a tension, in survivors themselves, between the desire to forget
and the need to remember. Erika Apfelbaum refers to it as 'the obligation of silence and the obligation to live'.[57] It is this which I believe
to be at the very heart of the survivor's perspective—the inside-
looking-out viewpoint.

The mandate to remember is as much cultural as personal: 'And
tell it to thy son' is a motif in Jewish history and religion, dating
back to the story of the Exodus from Egypt.[58] Passover as a ritual is
intimately designed (and from a discourse perspective, superbly so)
to enable the telling and retelling of the story. The Hebrew Bible,
apparently, contains 169 instances of the verb 'to remember', along
with many injunctions not to forget.[59] Eli Wiesel has said that 'what

distinguishes the Jew is his [sic] memory . . . If we stop remembering, we stop being'. Langer comments on the number of books
about the Holocaust that feature 'memory' or 'remembering', in the
title. Hass says, 'Survivors don't have a choice . . . for [them]
memory is involuntary'.[60] Perhaps because of this cultural weight,
survivors' sense of self is all too often inextricably interwoven with
their history, as in this remark: 'I do not live in the past . . . the past
lives in me'.[61]

This urge to record and re-tell is a cultural imperative, and not
necessarily universal. The Romany people, for example, have
responded to their tragedy rather with an imperative to silence. Isobel
Fonseca in *Bury Me Standing* refers to their powerful instinct to
suppress the past, an instinct born of defiance rather than denial. She
points to the difference between the Jews, who have 'responded to
persecution and dispersal with a monumental industry of remembrance' and the Gypsies 'with their peculiar mixture of fatalism and
the spirit, or wit, to seize the day, have made an art of forgetting'.[62]
Yet, despite these divergences, I find the following words of an
Englishman of Gypsy ancestry as replete with the imperative 'and let's
not talk about that' as the discourse of any child of Holocaust
survivors.[63] He recalls,

> the constant incantation of 'Now you are English boy, Milo. This is
> your country, this is your home'. But what of all the enigmas that
> remained? . . . I will never know, I will never know more than this.
> All my questions were met with shrugs or silences or sly deflections.
> My grandmother would say to me as I pestered her for more infor-
> mation: 'Milo, we have saying in Transnistria: when you eat the
> honey do you ask the bee to show you the flower?'.[64]

There is sometimes the sense that the Jews refuse to let the world
forget, as it no doubt would too easily if given the chance. I've heard
people say, 'Oh no, not another Holocaust book/film/story!'. There's a
low-level irritation with the Jews for 'harking back' to the Holocaust all
the time. The pejorative term 'Shoah business' has been coined to deni-
grate this perhaps compulsive need to represent and rerepresent
experience. Jews' not wanting to forget is marked only because it stands
out against a larger generalised will towards amnesia. This tendency is
aided by the passage of time and the desire of many, especially in
Germany, to deny through 'normalising the crimes':

When a German grandmother who is asked about . . . Kristallnacht
by her granddaughter . . . replies without any expression of sympathy
'that she heard the sound of broken glass somewhere' she tries to
turn this event into an everyday occurrence by denying [its] extra-
ordinariness . . . and by denying her own inner participation.[65]

Combined with the Jewish commandment to remember, is the
sense of duty. Many survivors gave a promise to others that they
would tell what happened, not let the others' deaths go unremem-
bered. This urge to honour those who have no voice is a constant
refrain in the testimonies of survivors. Perhaps it gives purpose and
meaning to one's life, serving in some way therefore to combat the
moral nihilism engendered by 'surviving by accident'.

Many of my generation have written about our understanding of
our parents' compelling need to remember. As a child, journalist
Elizabeth Wynhausen, daughter of Dutch Jewish emigrants to
Australia, was silently aware of her parents' fragility: 'She sensed the
desolation that words concealed. Theirs was a communication of
history beyond speech'.[66] Likewise Arnold Zable writes poetically
of what 'came down' from his parents—the 'ashes and jewels' or
fragments of history, all that remained following the annihilation of
his parents' kinfolk.[67]

I have little doubt that this kind of discourse serves a very fundamental human need, indeed that narrative itself ought to be seen as a
resource by which people and culture recreate themselves. My father
once wrote that although their lives were spent in relentless energy
devoted to reconstruction, to build a future in a new land, nonetheless
when friends 'from there' got together, sooner or later the conversation would always drift back to the war. And recently a friend reported
that his father, a returned soldier from the Pacific war, who was never
able to talk about his experiences of war, has started, at the age of 80,
to open up. He has dreams and nightmares about the war and his wife
finds that whatever they talk about, when they chat, 'it all ends up
with the war'.

This kind of talk also has powerful psychological validity. Because
the war was the crucible of their lives, the central event that dwarfed
everything before and after it, survivors need to spend the rest of their
life making sense of it. I think it was Solzhenitsyn who wrote that
people who live through extremes of experience are condemned to go
over and over it restlessly, as though this seemingly infinite energy

would contribute to the construction of coherence. Certainly, for children of survivors, there is a sense of their lives having been infused through the filter of their parents' experience. It is with bitterness that one of the people I interviewed said about his father, 'Before the war he was an engineer; after the war, he was a Holocaust survivor'. There is the sense here that his Holocaust experience was so dominant that it became the medium through which he defines himself and is defined by others.

I look at the few photos I have that were taken of my parents before the war. I try to read their expressions, to know who they were, then. Of course, this knowledge is beyond my ability to induce. But I do know that the Holocaust re-set their identities, as if they were soft clay being reformed into a new shape. A cataclysm that reshapes who you are cannot be relinquished to oblivion. It is a part of you. As one survivor said, 'I can't take it off like a coat at the end of the day. It is my skin'.

But what kind of life is it, lived in constant remembrance of anguish? My father said that immediately after the war he thought he would never forget to remember what it meant to have adequate food, clean water, shelter from the elements, a warm shower, not to be hunted—to know that there was likely to be a tomorrow. He also said that you actually can't live that way, that the quality of 'taking for granted' is a crucial component of normalcy. It was when he started to take these things for granted that he knew he had begun a new life.

Survivors must soon have decided that sanity, healing and reconstruction were not served by memory but by forgetfulness. Thus Susan Karas taught herself, 'willed herself to forget'. The tension between remembering and forgetting is captured in her, for she holds both in her head, at once. Of lost ones, she says, 'If I met you tomorrow, I would not remember your face'. Yet each night, as she brushes her teeth, she mentally recites the names of her 48 nearest kin whose remains are somewhere in the soil of Europe.[68]

4

The Context of Incommunicability

In his book *Holocaust Testimonies: The Ruins of Memory*, Langer tells of a survivor, Irene, who returned to her home village in France in 1945, having survived Auschwitz. She had been transported to the camp at the age of fourteen, at which time her mother and three younger siblings were sent straight to the gas chambers, while her father and older brother went 'to the right'. She never saw them again. Returning to her village after the war, she encountered for the first time a problem that she was to wrestle with for the rest of her life: how to talk about these experiences meaningfully to 'an audience of outsiders'.

People asked her what happened to her family. She first tried to say 'Everyone in my family *was killed*' but rejected the words as hopelessly inadequate: 'killed' is a word we use for 'ordinary forms of dying'. But to say, matter-of-factly, that 'My mother and brother and two sisters were gassed when we arrived at Auschwitz' seemed equally unsatisfactory because 'plain factuality could not convey the enormity of the event'. In the end, after sifting through a few other verbal options, she is reduced to silence, 'as the only appropriate response to such a catastrophe'.

Langer calls Irene's experience an example of 'anguished memory', the seeds of which are sown 'in the barren belief that the very story you try to tell drives off the audience you try to capture'.[1] It's a familiar refrain among survivors, who are wont to say, sometimes to the frustration of those who want to listen, 'You can't understand if you were not there'. Laub says that the experience of the Holocaust is so far removed from the realm of conventional human experience that it leaves within the survivor 'a quality of otherness . . . outside the range of associatively linked experiences'.[2] Horror beyond the reach of pity, beyond the hope of closure.

In a macabre twist, the writer Primo Levi tells of a recurrent nightmare he had in the concentration camp, one that forecast the outside world's reaction. He dreamed he would survive and return to a normal life where he would try to tell others—people he knew or people who asked him—where he had been, what had happened to him, what he had witnessed. And he would be met with disbelief.[3] In the premonition of disbelief, Levi's nightmare was born.

Perhaps even more macabre is the fact that the SS forecast this very incredulity, mocking their prisoners in the last days of the war:

> However this war may end, we have won the war against you; none of you will be left to bear witness, but even if someone were to survive, the world would not believe him. There will perhaps be suspicions, discussions, research by historians, but there will be no certainties. And even if some proof should remain and some of you survive, people will say that the events you describe are too monstrous to be believed . . . and will believe us, who will deny everything, and not you.[4]

The recurrent dream of not being believed was not Levi's alone. For Laub, it signals the 'absence of an empathic listener . . . of an addressable other' who can hear the anguish, allow it to be registered and acknowledged. Such an absence 'annihilates the story'.[5]

What is being suggested here is that certain experiences go beyond the limits of language. When I heard people ask my father questions about the war—'Did you *lose* your family in the war?' 'Did your parents *die* in the camps?'—I knew without knowing that these verbs 'lose' and 'die' were inadequate for the task. I sensed how the differential between their meaning and the reality threatened to engulf and capsize the conversation. I would cower in the expectation of a dismantling, a crumbling of composure. I feared he would drive his listeners away if he rejected their words, and he must have feared the same. Many times I saw him hesitate momentarily when asked such a question; he would seem to be quelling something within; and then he would nod silently. Of course, I was not able to put a name to the emotion I saw repressed. But I felt his discomfort, for it resonated in my own.

Linguistic constraints

The notion that trauma stretches and then defeats language's capacity to represent it is explored in a short article called 'They didn't just die in Auschwitz'. The author, Henry Huttenbach, delivers an impassioned plea for what he calls the 'vocabulary of truth'. He argues that avoidance of the stark horror of factuality through euphemisim is, even for the most benign of motives, a form of denialism.[6] In Lily Brett's *Too Many Men*, the main character takes her survivor father back to Poland on a visit. There she embarrasses him by insisting on correcting Poles whenever they refer to Auschwitz as 'the Auschwitz museum' rather than 'the Auschwitz death camp'. 'What does it matter what it is called?', her father asks, 'It is still the same place'. And his daughter responds, 'It's easier for people to believe it is something else, something abstract, if it's called a museum. They can forget that it was a place for the slaughter of human beings'. Her response has the stridence of political activism. His rejoinder—'Which people is so interested in Auschwitz?'—is sadness itself.[7]

Huttenbach attributed the choice of softer, gentler words to carelessness in expression, or to the constraints imposed by polite talk. Brett's character, and possibly Brett, imply that it is a convenient indifference. At the Holocaust Museum in Washington DC, I overheard a conversation among a party of visitors and I was struck by the inadequacy of the language used to represent the horrors—like, 'Poor things, must have been so hard, and it went on for so long, didn't it?'. I suspect that more than the constraints of politeness are at work here. Yet this is different from Irene's problem, mentioned earlier. Irene knew too much of the truth to find words adequate; the museum visitors probably knew too little of the truth. In the case of the latter, the failure in the language may derive from a failure of imagination. In a talk given in December 1996, Abraham Biderman, author of *The World of My Past*, said 'Humanity has to invent a new vocabulary'.

I want to suggest that there is something about the experience of trauma that defies communicability, that constrains the person involved in the trauma from using language to give voice to experience in a way that authentically or even adequately captures its horror. And sadly, I also want to suggest that unless the survivor is able satisfactorily to represent the nature of the trauma suffered, attempts at communication will neither serve nor satisfy.

So what is it about trauma that is not communicable? There seem to me to be three issues of importance here. The first has to do with the apparent limits on the linguistic options open to a speaker. Words, after all, are rooted in their situational context, from which they derive their meaning. They draw significance from their context, have purchase value there and not elsewhere. To use 'die' or 'kill' or 'perish' for actions that led to Holocaust death suggests a view of death, both qualitatively and quantitatively, that cannot align itself with the horror of what the survivor knows, has witnessed—indeed, has survived. Words like 'die' and 'kill' might be 'true' but they are, as it were, 'not true enough',[8] for they fail to capture fully the reality they purport to represent.

There's a macabre irony here, too, when one thinks of the statement that many survivors make in reference to their own survival—that it only has meaning if they are able to relate what befell those they left behind. What happens, we might well ask, to the survivor who is never able to tell the story in words even remotely adequate to the task? Perhaps this is why it has been said that the Holocaust had two kinds of victims—those who died, and those who survived.

This then is the linguistic problem, or, rather, it is people's interpretation of a problem, which they perceive to be linguistic. The problem is, as it were, reified, placed outside, positioned over there, as distinct from here. There is a pervasive feeling in trauma of this magnitude that language is not up to the job, that it falls short of the task. Saul Friedlander said that the magnitude of Holocaust atrocity was something that outstripped language's ability to represent it.[9] Wiesel said: 'I know we must speak. I do not know how. Since this crime is absolute, all language is imperfect'.[10] And T.S. Eliot said it too, in 'Burnt Norton', within the *Four Quartets*:

Words strain,
Crack and sometimes break, under the burden,
Under the tension, slip, slide, perish
Decay with imprecision, will not stay in place,
Will not stay still.[11]

I want to argue, however, that while people perceive this to be a linguistic problem or, more specifically, a linguistic *lack*, in fact this is to locate the problem in the wrong place. Language can do what its

speakers want it to do. It has the resources to capture complex, dissonant and immensely painful events. We need look no further than
works of great literature—drama, epic tales, poetry—to find verbal
representations of extreme and distended experience, instances
replete with pulsating emotion, life lived on the edge. Indeed, this
is one of the purposes of literature—to capture, hold in a moment,
and pass down word-accounts of extreme human experiences. This
explains the abiding attraction and durability of great works from
previous eras. But not all victims of trauma are great writers or
speakers, and therein lies the problem. Holocaust survivors were
'ordinary individuals rendered extraordinary only by what had been
done to them'. To convey a catastrophe like the Holocaust, one's
facility with language has to match the enormity of the event and for
survivors, 'the abyss between language and experience . . . must have
been close to disabling'.[12]

What is experienced by the individual as the *inability of language*
to express something is in fact the user's own lack of facility with the
language. It is not language *per se* that lacks the resources but rather
an individual experiencing an extremity that outstrips his or her own
linguistic ability. I accept that this proposition may not resonate
comfortably with intuitive responses. Certainly, it is easier to think of
the problem as a systemic lack, rather than an individual one. Perhaps
this is because language is not only an instrument of creative talent,
but also the defining feature of being human.

Let's look at this phenomenon through another artistic
medium—for example, canvas or clay or music. Here one might be
more inclined to accept the notion of an individual's resources being
'not up to the task'.[13] Why do I emphasise the point of an individual's
lack, rather than the lack in the language itself? It is to enable us to
think beyond the conventional explanation. Once we accept that the
problem does not lie in language as a resource, but rather in the limitations of an individual's facility, we are more likely to look critically
at the claim that 'words cannot express my meaning'—and seek an
explanation beyond it. We might come to see that this actually is code
for something else. But code for what?

Psychological constraints

Setting aside the perceived linguistic difficulties, the second component of the incommunicability of trauma is psychological. It has to do

with psychological difficulties faced by the survivor wanting to represent and communicate a version of his or her experience to someone who does not share the experience. And it also has to do with the communication difficulties faced by outsiders who are confronted with evidence of trauma.

The internal perspective

Telling about trauma, for a survivor, is a kind of re-living of the event. We see this, for example, in the massive outpouring of grief and pain that accompanied public tellings in South Africa's Truth and Reconciliation Commission after the dismantling of apartheid. We see this in Holocaust survivors—and I have known many—who have resolutely undertaken never ever to talk about what happened to them. This extends to not talking about why they will not talk.

Here's an example of re-telling being a re-living. Some time ago, I read the account of a Holocaust survivor who had decided, after many years of procrastination, finally to provide a written account, so that his children, and their children, would have a record of events. He asked me to read it over with an editor's eye. Now, through family associations, I already knew the outline of his story. I had heard, not from him but from my parents, that his young baby had been killed during the war. Yet when I read his account, I could find no overt mention of this. How could this be? Here, ostensibly, was a document intended to record the facts of a family's past. Why was such an event omitted? I re-read the manuscript until I found it slipped into a minor clause, mentioned almost inconsequentially, tucked away in a paragraph of descriptive detail, quite invisible, if you didn't know what you were looking for. Letting it slip between the cracks in the narrative was as much as this survivor could accomplish, some 50 years after the event.

The pain of Holocaust survivors is a complex amalgam of emotions: grief for personal losses and for the obliteration of a world that was; frustration at ongoing health problems, a debilitation originating in years of extreme deprivation and abuse; shame at what was experienced and witnessed, perhaps at what had to be done, in some cases, to survive; guilt at surviving when so many did not; rage at the experience of wanton cruelty; a learned inability to mourn, born of a survival-driven need to suppress normal emotional responses to abnormal events; and bitterness that justice was never served. In a phrase, 'a sorrow beyond words'.[14] I imagine that these are some of the emotions that are stirred at the moment of recount. The psychological constraints, then, might be thought of, in part, as the internal view, the perspective from within.

Linked to the internal view, the psychological factors constraining survivors toward silence, is their relationship with their children. If 'telling' was connected to looking backwards, being stuck in the past, then looking forward, not telling, was connected with having children and pouring their energies into the next generation. The future meant hope. And it meant another generation. Having children was a creative response to the attempt at genocide. Children meant that their kind was not annihilated from the face of the earth, it meant *am Yisrael chai*, 'the people of Israel (still) live'. Having children meant it was not for nothing they had suffered. Children, more than all else, offered a chance of healing and allowed some sense to be extracted from the inexplicable.

When, six weeks before the war, my mother agreed to marry my father, she was a young, newly graduated doctor—independent, politically conscious, feminist in orientation. Her agreement to marry was conditional: 'No children', she said. But in 1945, in the train that took them on a last journey, across the cemetery of Poland, on their way to Paris, she agreed to overturn that condition. Under the strength of my father's conviction, she conceded that having a child was the only way to begin again. I imagine that the decision to take this path included a turning away from the past, perhaps even an oath to herself to never talk about what happened.

Survivors looked to their children for a purpose in life. The word most of my respondents used to describe this bond was 'cherish'—a word that seems to blend extreme attachment, fear of loss, perhaps over-protectiveness. One of my respondents, John, called it 'being overloved'. Certainly, the children came bound up with a complex package of emotions: gratitude for providing a lifeline, revenge against genocide, compensation for so much waste. Precious beyond belief, the new generation had many roles to fulfill. In Duba's poem, 'The golden childhood', Debbie is one such child: 'I was my mother's lifeline . . . her confidante, her best friend, her reason for being alive, her connection to the outside world . . . the substitute for her dead mother'.[15] One of my informants recalls her childlike bewilderment in trying to tend to the emotional needs of her mother who on occasion would slip into her bed at night, hold onto her and cry for her own mother. The 'cherish factor' then had two sides: sometimes too much was invested in the child as symbol, while the child him or herself, the actual child, was hardly noticed. Lily Brett captures this:

> As a child, Lola had longed for silence. She envied those girlfriends whose parents took no notice of them. Lola felt that her parents were omnipresent. At the same time she felt that they were not there. She felt as though she couldn't get a grip on them. When she spoke, she felt they didn't listen. They were distracted by something. Something larger. Something Lola couldn't share.
> Things could be worse.[16]

Children also provided a powerful motivation for *not* telling the story. Let the pain stop at the parent generation. Let the next generation not be stained with and shamed by ethnic victimhood. Let there be a demarcation line drawn between one generation and the next. Some survivor families actually made the conscious decision not to tell their children. Some meant to tell, one day, and delayed and delayed ('let's wait for the children to be older') until silence became the vernacular. Some tried to. Some thought they did but in fact did not. Some went for the facts and suppressed the emotions. Some conveyed the emotion, devoid of facts. Some gave fragments of recounts that only made sense to the teller. Some sealed their sanitised and safe versions into oft-retold tales that said more by what was left unsaid than what was included. Some talked history and geography and politics but omitted personal, family detail. To help their children feel part of the mainstream, some parents universalised their history into the more acceptable and conventional genre of war stories. Some so feared their children's questions—like, Why didn't you get out in time? Why didn't you fight back?—while doubting their ability to explain, that avoidance seemed better. In all these ways survivors held back from telling but were yet propelled by the urge that their children know. 'All human beings crave empathy and understanding', writes Hass.[17]

The parents' reluctance to tell is mirrored in a macabre if predictable way in their children's own deficiency, a generation later. One of my respondents said:

> My mother told me a few snippets about her past. But there was never any sense of her talking, with me sitting at her knee, hearing

about the past. I would have loved that. But I never got that. And I don't do it with my kids, though when I do, they adore it. I feel bad that I don't do it. After all, if I was so desirous of that experience, why am I depriving them of it?

Having not heard stories through our own childhood, we are left with an associative discomfort with the notion of family narrative, but also without a language to talk about such things. And because this is an absence, we are generally not even aware that our lives are like this, that there are other ways of being, that families that have not been severed by trauma may do things differently.

The external perspective

The inner psychological constraints that propelled survivors towards silence have their counterparts in an external perspective, the postwar reaction of people to the fact of the Holocaust, and in particular to their encounters with survivors. We saw earlier, in discussing the political and social contexts (in Chapter 3), what kind of world survivors found themselves in. Societies everywhere were exhausted by war and weary of compassion. Cities lay in ruins. Whole economies had been dismantled. Borders were being redrawn. Millions were reclassified as 'displaced persons'. People, understandably, wanted to put it all behind them.

Some had very good reason to not look too closely at the past. Remembrance meant dealing with momentous evidence of complicity. As was outlined in Chapter 3, everywhere one looked, if one chose to see, there were manifestations of the failure to act decisively or effectively against undisguised aggression. Worse, as in Vichy France, there was evidence of state-level collaboration. In Germany, an entire nation tacitly agreed that it was best for everyone not to ask too many questions, like 'Where were you in the war, Daddy?'. In the postwar reshuffle of alliances, and the scramble for reconstruction, it suited many to let matters like war crimes and the pursuit of justice slip by the wayside. The silence of the Papacy, the alleged neutrality of the Swiss, the rhetoric of whitewash (as in Austria's rewriting of the celebrated union with Germany as 'invasion')—such phenomena were conveniently overtaken in the complicated politics of forgetting. This was a world uncomfortable in the presence of survivors.

This turning away, this not-wanting-to-listen, was a global phenomenon, reverberating wherever survivors went. Wiesel sums it up thus: 'People . . . refused to listen; and even those who listened refused to believe; and even those who believed could not comprehend'.[18] Even in Israel, where the majority of survivors fled, their stories were not welcome. Here the image of the Jew-as-victim did not sit easily with an already overburdened new nation for whom strength and 'never again' had become the hallmarks of rebirth. The fledgling state preferred to disassociate itself from the image of sickly and emaciated 'memory-haunted survivors', preferring the healthy, bronzed image of locally-born youth working the land, making the desert bloom.[19] In a fascinating account of 'straight talk', a phenomenon of modern Israeli Hebrew, the linguist Tamar Katriel expounds the historical context in which the 'New Jews' sought to distance themselves from the old.[20] The new nation of agrarian, socialist pioneers, typified in the *kibbutznik*, living and running their own land, was based on conscious and explicit rejection of a Diasporan mentality, with its tradition of perceived subordination and vulnerability. It was a radical attempt to 'normalise' a people who had been dispersed and marginalised, the Holocaust being just the most recent attempt to wipe them off the face of the earth. So Yiddish was replaced with Hebrew, and the intolerable image of six million passive victims drove a nation to take up arms to defend itself against new enemies. It is not difficult to imagine, then, that survivors failed to find willing listeners in a land that had recast 'Holocaust' to mean passive victimhood. One survivor who emigrated to Israel and found a home on a kibbutz was asked by author Theo Richmond why she had remained silent. Speaking of people on the kibbutz, she said:

[They said], 'You went to the slaughter like a herd of cows'. They couldn't understand how it had happened; those who had not been through it—people with faces bronzed from working in the sun. They looked at us, with our white faces, and somehow they could not understand.[21]

Thus in Israel, as elsewhere, survivors were admonished not to dwell on the past, to think of the future. They were counselled, often by their own kin and often with the best of intentions, towards an enduring silence.[22]

Langer argues that in this era was born a discourse that of itself constrained the way the Holocaust was to be perceived. He calls it a 'discourse of consolation', a language 'designed to console instead of confront'. Langer argues that people everywhere had not yet caught up with the inconsolability of mass murder, using 'a familiar discourse' based on old models of seeing the world. He cites Russian poet Joseph Brodsky's reflection on the disbelief that greeted Alexander Solzhenitsyn's *Gulag Archipegalo*—that the reason these things don't seep through may be found in people's need for mental self-preservation, a 'quest for mental comfort'. Langer suggests that the need for mental consolation leads to a split that is at once verbal, emotional and intellectual. This was the case even in Israel or perhaps especially in Israel, where the subtitle of the Holocaust Memorial Yad VaShem, 'Heroes and Martyrs Remembrance Authority', was to foreshadow a tradition of avoidance:

> When we speak of the survivor instead of the victim and of martyrdom instead of murder, regard being gassed as a pattern for dying with dignity, or evoke the redemptive rather than the grievous power of memory, we draw on an arsenal of words that urges us to build fences between the atrocities of the camps and ghettoes and what we are mentally willing—or able—to face.[23]

Ursula Duba asks whether, perhaps, 'nature' has built in a mechanism to protect offspring of traumatised parents from knowing the full extent of their parents' horror so that that this knowledge does not crush them before they are ready 'to carry the burden'. She then counters this with the awareness of 'the havoc that the not-knowing creates'.[24]

All of this happened at a societal level, but it happened daily at a local level too, in face-to-face reactions of people to survivors in their midst. They were fobbed off with platitudes like 'let bygones be bygones' or 'look at the positive side of things' and they were admonished to 'get on with their lives'.[25] This contributed to 'survivors' uncanny foreboding that they were not wanted anywhere.

> People were wary of survivors. Some thought there must have been a secret reason why these people had been persecuted . . . Terror was evoked by [their] stories . . . and the prevailing feeling was that they should forget the unspeakable past and learn to look toward the future . . . Survivors learned to be silent and to avoid evoking anxiety and guilt in others in order to be accepted . . . they had to be cautious in a world that did not want to hear what they had to say.[26]

Danieli describes the reactions survivors faced as 'comprised of obtuseness, indifference, avoidance, repression, and denial', much of which was fuelled by varying degrees of 'bystander guilt'. It suited people to develop myths about survivors that would relieve them of the obligation to reconcile with the past, acknowledge the present and respond humanely. These myths were various and absurd, like the notion that Jews had participated actively or passively in their own destiny by 'going like lambs to the slaughter':

> This myth implied not only that they could have fought back and that they should have been prepared for the Holocaust—as if anyone could have been—but it also assumes that [they] had somewhere to go had they chosen to escape, and that the rest of the world wanted them.

If one myth blamed Jews for going to their deaths willingly, another blamed Jews for surviving and it accomplished this by projecting onto survivors 'the suspicion that they had performed immoral acts in order to survive'.[27]

Social constraints

I said earlier that there were three reasons for the incommunicability of trauma. The first was linguistic, the second psychological. The third factor, which I will call the *social*, offers an explanation which in effect subsumes the other two, and is in my view, the most important, if indeed the most difficult to excavate and analyse.

To discuss the social dimension of trauma's incommunicability, I need to return to an idea I mentioned earlier when I said that words do not carry their meanings around with them. I wanted to suggest that language does not have a one-size-fits-all quality, a kind of four-wheel-drive capacity to function wherever you want to take it. Meaning is not an absolute thing, transportable to any place and applicable whenever and wherever you feel like. There are limitations to the fit between language and situation. Language comes packaged, with an intimate fit between 'the talk' and 'the place' where that talk happens.

If we think about this in broader terms, as behaviour, it is less abstract. We all know, as sane, socialised adult members of a society, that there are limitations on behaviour—even without being consciously aware of the rules and restrictions that we obey. For example, we know we can be naked in the shower, but not on the tennis court. We can poke our head around the bathroom door and signal for a family member to bring in a toilet roll but at the workplace we'd have to find another solution to the same problem. We might wave and call out 'Taxi!' to hail a ride, but if we stand at the side of the road and wave when there's no taxi in sight, or if a passing taxi driver responds by waving and calling out 'Pedestrian!', there's a risk that this behaviour will be deemed funny, odd, even mad.

Certain behaviours are conventionally and invisibly differentiated into roles. For example, at my daughter's single-sex school, girls sometimes surreptitiously and with an acquired dexterity slip out of their regular uniform into their sports gear in a corner of the classroom but if the teacher were to change attire in the same manner, eyebrows would certainly be raised.

These behavioural and role dictates are culturally driven. Over time, the conventions are tacitly agreed upon within the boundaries of certain communities. So, for example, kissing, sneezing, spitting are not *per se* value-laden. Rather, it is the context and the specific cultural meanings attached to each context that are significant. Often it is only when the rules are broken, that any notice is taken and the circumstance becomes literally remarkable. It is as if pathology renders visible what is normally not seen. Walking down the street munching on your lunch while window-shopping is allowable behaviour in some places, but frowned upon in others. Going barefoot in a beach-based culture like Sydney's is perfectly acceptable, while in other locations it might be deemed an outward and punishable sign of vagrancy. The display of grief following a tragedy may be fitting or taboo, depending on the circumstances of who, where, how, etc. Such conventions are not fixed in stone and may shift or be differently regarded by different groups within a society. Consider, for example, the divided public response to Queen Elizabeth's stiff-upper-lipped behaviour in the wake of Princess Diana's death.[28]

If it is at first difficult to see that behaviours come packaged in context-specific packages, as it were, this is no accident. We are socialised into these beliefs and act them out almost unthinkingly. In fact, it is in our own best interests that these behaviours are naturalised, automatic and subliminal. It would be quite dysfunctional to spend a lot of time considering the boundaries of what is socially possible. It's much more expeditious to just get on with what has to be done. This very point was made by Hume, writing on causality: 'if we walked around wondering whether effect follows cause, we'd trip over ourselves in the process!'[29] Nietzsche said, 'Wisdom sets bounds even to knowledge'.[30] In the end, social life is possible because the boundaries of the allowable are known and assumed to be known, taken for granted in oneself and in others. As a result, things work smoothly for the most part. But another result is that people have difficulty seeing what it is they know—or, in other words, seeing themselves positioned in the social world. For the social is, as it were, invisible, and what leaps out in the way of explanation is a sense of language's lack or a folk notion of psychological pain.[31]

Once the point is made about behaviours being context-bound, we may proceed to think of language in the same terms. It may help here to consider language a delicate form of social action, as venue-bound and as meaning-encoded and as ritualised as any of the behaviours mentioned above. Clearly, we cannot talk to anyone about anything at any time. Venues or settings are circumscribed arenas of action where there are rules—we know these rules, we are expected to know them, and we expect others to, too. Talking about troubles with a friend on the phone is a very different venue from a job interview. What we might say to a doctor in the confidential environment of the surgery is certainly different from the talk that happens at the supermarket checkout. Even gossip, as a particular genus of talk, has its own appropriate conventions, with its own comfort and discomfort zones (for example, OK in the back seat of a taxi with a co-worker but not OK in the boss's office in the context of a performance appraisal meeting).

Language venues or contexts, then, are places where certain kinds of language work and others don't, where certain kinds of talk are appropriate and certain others aren't. Our lives are replete with differentiated venues, each of which comes coded with particular conventions and verbal rituals. Competent, *bona fide* members of a given culture know this and are able to navigate and manipulate the conventions with facility and dexterity. Indeed, an integral part of being considered 'sane' is understanding what venues furnish opportunities for what kind of talk. Consequently, if you raise a certain topic in an inappropriate venue, you will be deemed at best inappropriate, perhaps socially uncouth, and at worst unstable or deviant. Sometimes, certain allowances are tacitly made—in the case of overt foreignness (manifested by accent, appearance, attire), age (children can get away with more) or perhaps disability (where some rules will be bent in accommodation).

My central point here is that these are not free choices. A social injunction, albeit invisible, is in operation here. It may only become discernible through a rupture of the norm or the threat of such a rupture, that is, through the threatened discomfort of some or all participants when the rules are broken. We even have expressions for such a circumstance—'This is not the time' or 'This is not the place'— which can be invoked if someone oversteps the boundaries. This helps forestall a threat to social poise.[32] Conversely, one might engineer particular outcomes because we can know in advance that particular venues come replete with their own cargo of nuance, and that this knowledge is shared. When the boss says, 'Can you step into my office for a moment, please?' one can almost predict the script of what is to follow. Sometimes the venue-groundedness of a speech event can be exploited to an individual's advantage. There's a man I know who asks his boss for feedback on his work performance when she is a in a public space, within earshot of others, knowing that any critique she might offer will be constrained by the circumstances of the encounter. Venues, then, come pre-packaged—equipped with understandings about attached scripts and stage directions. In this sense, we might say that very little that happens in a particular venue is accidental.

This is relevant to the notion of the incommunicability of trauma, for not only is there, as we have seen, a perceived linguistic difficulty and a set of psychological barriers that point one toward the benefits of silence; there is also a social constraint—in this case, the absence of a social framework or locale that would allow the communication to happen. Most children of survivors would remember occasions at which, in a public context (that is, when more than the family was present), they cringed to hear their parents allude in some way to the war. I want to suggest that if there is no place where it is appropriate to talk about a particular topic in a particular way, no acceptable roles for the participants to engage in, then the lapse into silence might be seen for what it is: the only option.

With this notion of venue in mind, let us ask what venues are available for talk about tragedy such as the Holocaust? It would seem immediately to be a highly restricted topic area with very clearly demarcated boundaries. Only three venues seem to me to lend themselves more or less comfortably or manageably to this kind of talk. One is very private talk between or among insiders or occasional close others; a second is the public domain of a formal lecture or symposium; a third is the confidential context of therapy. I will explore these three.

Insiders

Survivors found solace in a community of others like themselves. This is not to suggest a total insularity. My parents made many friends in Australia—local people, other immigrants, Anglo-Jews, European Jews, as well as a group of mostly doctors, Polish Jews, Holocaust survivors. They felt most able to be themselves when they met up with other insiders and talked about that other time they had known. My father's writings refer to 'people who have been there' and 'people who haven't been there' and the communication abyss that separates and divides them.[33] In the company of insiders, words would flow freely—as would the tears, at other times kept so firmly in check. Many of my generation recall the backdrop of these encounters, the loud voices, the sobbing, as we played on the floor nearby or lay awake on a bed in a nearby room.

Significantly, silence was also a feature of these interchanges, but here, silence is not due to the absence of options but is an active choice, even a comfortable one. Here the trauma does not need to be communicated because it is shared; whereas the insider–outsider exchange is haunted by the belief that the trauma being unshared cannot be communicated. These twin faces of silence are echoed in Jensen's taxonomy of silence's communicative functions (linking, affecting, revelational, judgemental, and activating), in each case both positive and negative.[34] In survivor get-togethers where words and tears flowed freely, silence, when it happened, clearly served to link and bond people, not to separate and divide. All this is to suggest that neither silence nor words offers absolutes, but each derives meaning from its context.

Lectures

A second venue that may be deemed appropriate for talk about tragedy of this kind is a lecture or one-way talk held in a public place.[35] Such a venue is bigger than the individual and therefore enables the individual to be safely and anonymously enveloped within the mass. As a public domain, it comes equipped with all the restrictions that exist for public discourse, such as formal usage, prescribed roles and public poise. Poise is an important ingredient because it suggests a suppression of affect and a restraint on what Goffman calls 'flooding out'—that is, the public display of emotions more appropriate to the private domain.[36] The other defining feature

of the lecture that makes it an appropriate venue here is the role relationship between speaker and listener. The listener in a lecture is not
required to respond verbally. This is a prescribed monologic framework that precludes the listener from taking a speaker's role, other
than the optional question or so at the end.

Cast in these terms, the discourse of the lecture hall is not unlike
that of writer to reader. The talk can happen and no response is
required. There is a removal to safe quarters of the producer and the
receiver of the text that effectively extinguishes the response function.
However, public lectures of the kind described here usually offer an
intellectual attempt to understand the tragedy, and not many can find
lasting consolation, let alone any personal closure, in the abstract. In
the view of Dori Laub, healing and closure are closely interconnected
with the intimacy of telling and being heard.[37]

It is worth noting that many Holocaust survivors resorted to
writing to their children, often in the form of an extended letter. Like
a lecture, this mode of communication removes the producer and the
receiver of the text to safely different zones. This way the text does
not require an immediate response and does not collapse under its
own weight. In 'A letter to my children', a biography of my mother's
life written by my father through her declining years, I found out for
the first time what had been excluded from the domain of talk by
some 40 years of her silence, most significantly, the horrific circumstances of her own mother's death.[38] But I also discovered
elements—soft, loving, nostalgic—of the connections between my
parents, between them and their parents, and the bonds that linked
them to others with whom they shared those terrible times. These
had rarely been spoken of at home, and never without discomfort.

Therapy

A third venue that, in theory at least, might provide opportunity for
talk about tragedy, is the context of therapy.[39] In the privacy of the
office of a psychiatrist, psychologist, counsellor or grief therapist, a
role arrangement exists for participants. It is possible, in theory at
least, for the person who has experienced trauma to speak of it, for he
or she knows that the listener has the safety of a prescribed role. In
the case of Holocaust survivors, this is a largely theoretical option as
very few sought therapy in any conventional sense, as I mentioned in
Chapter 3.

In these venues—insider talk, the public lecture, and private therapy—someone talking about the personal experience of large-scale tragedy could have found an audience. In theory at least, here is the possibility of a participation framework that allows people to know how to behave with the topic. In these venues, the topic might find an ecologically sound social milieu that allows such talk to exist, in some circumstances it might even offer some healing. One could argue that the very existence of therapy is predicated on the lack of the right kind of listening audience in normal social life.

There was one audience—their children—to whom survivors yearned to be able to tell their story. But if ever there was a venue devoid of a role framework, this is it. The notions of 'unspeakability' and 'unhearability' will be treated later in this chapter when we explore the face-to-face pressures of this kind of talk but, for the moment, consider this. Within the perspective of language as a delicate form of social action, as a way of 'doing things with words', what is the child listener *to do with* what the parent-teller hands over?

Imagine that someone throws you a ball but you have no idea what game is being played. All you know is that to do anything with the ball could mean you'll be breaking the rules. Yet you know that something is expected of you, some appropriate response. There's no time to think, no one to ask. The gaze is on you. Should you throw it back? Should you hold onto it? Should you walk away? Should you throw it somewhere else? And what happens if you do nothing?[40] It is exactly in these terms that one of my interviewees, Ella, spoke about listening to her mother's stories: 'I didn't know what to do with it. Should I take the information to school and tell the other kids about it? I knew that was out. But then what was I to do? Should I ask questions about it? I needed to know what to do with it'.

The child listening does not know the rules of the game and does not have a role that tells her how to respond. Ella spoke about 'an inner prudence' cautioning her to be absolutely still, to freeze her emotions, to make no response. Julie Salamon's *The Net of Dreams* records the same constraint: 'I felt a tightness in my chest from the pressure of holding back my desire to cry. Crying would violate the unspoken agreement between us—that we would not spare each other these details, the way we had always done before'.[41] In the face of such immobility, the parents, themselves urgently in need of understanding, may see indifference or disdain and then themselves revert to silence. So the pattern continues.

The pressure of this kind of face-to-face encounter is tremendous. One way that parents found to deal with it was to shift to the third person, telling about someone else, rather than about themselves. This distanced the topic and permitted the roles of raconteur and 'racontee', allowing the drama to unfold in the wings, as it were, not on centre stage. This is an example of how the incommunicable is managed.

The difficulties in the exchange between parents and child about the parents' experiences are best explained in quasi-dramatic terms. It seems to me that the difficulty experienced by many in this kind of situation is that the topic (talking about massive personal tragedy) becomes, as it were, a participant in the drama. As there is no proper venue for the talk, no social domain in which participants can slip comfortably into pre-constituted roles, the topic itself appears larger than life. It fills up the available space left void by an absence of roles, participants and scripts. It takes over, turning into an *over*-presence. It's as if the space becomes monopolised and swallowed up by the topic. And the listener is overwhelmed—not knowing what to say, where to look, what to think, how to feel, how to respond; wanting to make it go away. A surprising number of people I interviewed referred to the emotion as turning you to stone. Others talked of being swamped, of drowning.

It is not only among children of survivors that there is the sense of being swallowed up by something too immense to contemplate. We see it too in survivors like Eli Wiesel—'Had we started to speak, we would have found it impossible to stop. Having shed one tear, we would have drowned the human heart.'[42]—and among outsiders, like commentator Clive James, who writes of standing at the site of a concentration camp: 'Nor was there any point in self-reproach for not being able to shed tears. If we could really imagine what it was like we would die of grief'.[43]

A collision of goals

The survivor with whom this chapter begins, Irene, struggled to find the right words, and ultimately receded into silence. Given the restricted options available to survivors as venues for talking about their experience, it is no wonder that silence, with all its hues and nuances, became a preferred way of communicating, a vernacular in its own right. The primary function of my research is to explore these hues and nuances, so that even within the discourse of incommunicable trauma, we may be able to track what is being communicated, albeit obliquely, or even at times perversely.

Irene's case is one of wanting to tell but being unable to find the right words. It is the archetypal scenario of the survivor of massive trauma. The task with which she wrestles is to do justice to the reality she has experienced by choosing words that will also be meaningful to the listener. Ultimately, this is a task which Irene will surrender, for it becomes, in her estimation, unrealisable. What she senses is the insider's view of what we might call a collision of goals. This happens when a conflict arises in what the words are 'doing', that is, when there is a tug-of-war between directions that are mutually incompatible. For Irene, as we have seen, there is no solution: her immobility translates socially into silence.

What happens in this collision course? As I have indicated earlier, language is a form of social action. We do things with words. We pass on information, we ask for help, we express condolences or sympathy, we exchange goods and services, we give and obey orders, we collaborate on joint productions, we make inquiries, we give advice, we maintain friendships, we make new associates and so on. We could think of all of these uses of language as having two primary (though by no means exclusive) macro-functions: the function of representation and the function of communication.[44] This is not a binary relationship: it is not the case that language *either* represents or communicates. Rather, we are dealing with different degrees of these functions as realised across all kinds of talk.

Let us deal with the macro-functions in turn. In representation, the words are chosen to represent a particular understanding. This is a way, for example, of allowing the experience of one person to become known by a second person. The second person does not 'live' the actual experience. He/she is one step removed from this and discovers it vicariously through the narrative of the first. Let's say I go to see a new film and afterwards I run into a friend in the street. There I talk about the film. It is clear that a primary function of my talk here is to represent my experience of the film.

The main thrust of a representational text is to transmit information from one person to (an)other(s). Talk that has a high representational function would typically include lectures, news reports, workplace memos, a shopping list, and such like. This is not to say that such texts do nothing else apart from represent and transmit information. There's room in an office memo for some social chat. Many a lecture begins with a joke or anecdote. News reports vary from bald, top-down, information-laden texts to light, pseudo-chatty, interactive bites of infotainment.

If language as representation might be said to be language in the service of *information*, then language as communication might be said to be language in the service of *relationships*. In talking to my friend after the movie, I am not only transmitting information about the film; I am also nourishing and maintaining the friendship between us. I am all the while thinking about his role as listener, and I will endeavour to provide him with a socially acceptable role within which he will feel competent and comfortable. All of this happens seamlessly, below the level of conscious awareness.

The danger is to think of language at any time or place as unitary. It isn't. It is plural, complex, relative and dynamic. The act of communicating, for instance, is a highly differentiated phenomenon. Sometimes it is face-to-face and one-to-one, as in a conversation between two people. Sometimes it is face-to-face and one-to-many as in a lecture. It can also be one-to-many but removed to a distance, as when a writer addresses the readers-to-be of the book he or she is writing. Whatever the channel or medium, language may serve its user representationally and/or communicatively.

My role, your role

The role we choose for ourselves in a conversation has significant implications for the role we create for our listener. Our choices for ourselves open up or close off choices for the other person. In the case of Holocaust narrative, it is actually the listener's rolelessness that most impacts on the story's 'hearability'.[45]

Most of us know someone who is highly transactional, minimally interactional. Such a person, by this very choice of role, provides a reduced opportunity for others to communicate with him or her. Sometimes there isn't much scope for changing roles. In Sweden there was an attempt to introduce more relaxed rules of behaviour in courtrooms, as a response to the claim that restrictive rules were dehumanising.[46] The attempt backfired: researchers found that defendants with either a criminal record or earlier contact with judicial institutions tended to interpret as sarcastic utterances actually intended as friendly. Here is a case of language roles being so intertwined with the venue in which they nest that an attempt to sidestep them, even with the best of motives, is likely to be misconstrued and

4

stiffly resisted. In other words, social distance in a rigid situation such as the courtroom is not readily negotiated.[47]

Most of the time, the representation of experience and its communication to another person or persons is a set of compatible and parallel processes. Running into a friend after the movies involves for me no collision of representational and communicative goals. I can do each and both comfortably and naturally, without a lot of effort entering into the event. That is because there is a compatibility of goals here and even with a different emphasis among the functions, they sit comfortably alongside of each other. But in the case of trauma, where the survivor wants to tell about the event, we see a tension between the functions that language has to perform. Here there is an incompatibility, even a collision of goals. The teller needs to represent the event so that the hearer will understand but, if the representation is accurate, the teller risks failing to attend to the needs of the hearer, hence failing communicatively.

When we communicate, as we have seen, we must take the role-needs of our audience into consideration. The words we choose to represent what we have experienced have to be within the range of acceptability for the receiver; and there has to be a role into which that listener can step. Yet when the trauma is massive, and beyond the experience or imagination of the ordinary, the speaker is confronted by an impossible choice. If the event is accurately represented, there's a risk that it will be non-communicable. If the narrative is adjusted to be more communicable, it risks being less than properly representational. If Irene were to say her family was 'gassed' or 'exterminated', she would achieve a representational goal, but probably not her communicative goal. If, on the other hand, she opted for something softer (like 'died' or 'perished'), she might keep her listener engaged, but feel that she has failed adequately to represent the truth.

When there are competing discourse goals, speakers are forced to choose between them: to compromise, to modify, so as to salvage something. If like Irene they give their priority to representation, what they say will fail to communicate—triggering disbelief and incomprehension in the audience. If they give their priority to communication, they must compromise the accuracy of representation—leaving them with a sense of failure and inadequacy. The collision of goals leads us to understand why silence perhaps presents as the only satisfactory option—so long as we realise, with Langer, that the 'reluctance to speak has little to do with the preference for silence'.[48]

The Holocaust is not the only kind of trauma that precipitates this kind of language crisis. Indeed there is ample evidence to suggest that all kinds and shapes of the tragic qualify here. In a sense, sending in the grief counsellors has come to be a litmus test of extremity. Within hours of a highway bus crash or shopping mall massacre, a small team of counsellors is dispatched to do what otherwise can't be done—handle the immediate psychological fallout of trauma.[49] The tragedy need not be massive in scale: a stillbirth in a maternity ward, a suicide at a high school, an industrial retrenchment may trigger the call. It's as if there's a need to cordon off the participants in the drama, to protect them from the extremes of their own emotions. There's an abiding perception that this special group of professionals—counsellors—is uniquely equipped to offer something constructive in the wake of tragedy. This special 'something', apart from a secluded moment in time and space, may be a kind of language, a repertoire of strategic verbal tools, perhaps, that can reach out to victims and 'bring them back' within the orbit of normal society. We believe that counsellors can engineer a special social venue in which appropriate speaker and listener roles are made available.

This perspective on counselling casts the victim of tragedy as alienated from and urgently in need of a way back to ordinary life. It would seem that the function of the counsellor is as a bridge or an interpreter between normal daily society, on the one hand, and that domain of extreme emotional distress, on the other.

Silence and healing

One difficulty of silence is that it is not a conducive environment for processing trauma or accomplishing healing. A survivor of trauma needs to process the event, make sense of it, and the way to do this is through the *representative* function of language. Words must be found to represent the event. At the same time, for the survivor to heal, there is a need to break out from the isolation that trauma imposes. This is the *communicative* or interactive function of language. Clearly, when representation and/or communication is denied, processing and healing are rendered impossibly difficult. Survivors are then cordoned off; insiders and outsiders occupy separate zones. The walls between these disparate worlds are impermeable: words, left behind, lapse into silence.

Survivors of the Holocaust illustrate this dilemma: whether to communicate their trauma, albeit inadequately, or to choose not to portray the event other than how it was experienced, at the price of non-communication. It is my belief that most survivors opted, in varying degrees, for the retreat into a version of silence. The price they paid, in anguish born of a failure to heal, defies calculation. The price paid by the next generation is only beginning to be understood.

Some examples will illustrate. Earlier I mentioned the woman whose daughter had an incurable brain tumour. Her every response was motivated by the wish to console, protect and nourish her daughter. In her conversations with me, she called the experience a 'brutalisation', one that reduced her to a quivering heap of fear, pessimism and depression. It is apparent that her faith in life and God, and her belief in justice had been shattered. At all times she was desperately afraid that her daughter would see her fear:

> I felt it really was my duty to inspire her, and in talking about it I would probably give myself away in less than half a minute. Sometimes she talked about how dying meant she would not get to do all the things she had dreamed of doing. I felt that naming and talking about it would have confirmed that. But I found that not naming it inhibited me from raising the topic. I deliberately embarked on a campaign of appearing to be normal and OK and coping because I wanted to be strong for her. I knew I couldn't just talk about trivia—she would see through that—so I used to check myself and make myself, consciously make myself, talk about [the tumour] but still not call it by its name.

In Isabel Allende's *Of Love and Shadows*, a character whose past is wracked by tragedy caused by political turbulence is described in this way:

> Through a long and gentle process of purification, she had succeeded in erasing most of the privation of the past and guarded only the happy moments. She never spoke of the war, the dead she had buried, her accident or the long march toward exile. Those who knew her attributed her selected memory to the blow that had split open her skull but . . . she had forgotten nothing. She simply did not want to burden herself with ancient woes, and for that reason she never mentioned them, nullifying them through silence.[50]

These examples of post-traumatic behaviour feature silence as a coping strategy. Between talk and silence, however, fall many notches on the continuum. One such might be thought of as disfluency, or the tendency to stumble over words. This is what I myself experience when my children ask about their grandparents. In the final lines of *Where She Came From*, Helen Epstein mentions a friend to whom she is very drawn, not least because that friend 'has never been able to correctly pronounce the name Auschwitz'.[51]

At times I have noted silence being used, sometimes quite deftly, as a weapon of control and negation. I noticed this in Adele, a woman I once worked with. I saw that her habit of withdrawing, saying less than was required and sitting quietly, non-responsive, served her at key times: she seemed to be recouping her strength, rallying herself, readying her spirit for the next onslaught. Choosing my moment, one day I told her about my research into silence and invited her to tell me her story. We set a time and met for that purpose. She recalled a brutal childhood at the hands of a tyrannical father and compliant mother. The father's domination of the household was primarily achieved through his physical presence, but also through his domination of the discourse. Quite simply, he controlled the talk space in the home. Topics considered important by him were allowed, others were disallowed. All the feuds and frictions and conflicts were swept away into silence. Nothing was ever resolved. The girl's emerging lesbianism enraged him, all the more as he had no power to change or influence her. As she got older, and his power over her became less, he resorted to silence in her presence. He ended up never talking to her and this became his mechanism of control. By not speaking, he ensured that the topics which infuriated him would not be broached. It is perhaps no surprise that Adele today makes strategic use of silence in her workplace relations. Most particularly, she uses the threat of silence (which equates with the withdrawal of support and affection) in order to coax subordinates into the behaviours she wants.

These examples illustrate some of the diversity of meanings that silence can realise in different contexts. Whatever its form or its purpose, silence is the invisible, inaudible, lowest common denominator that links protagonists in otherwise unconnected traumas, in a commonality wrought by incommunicability.

Incommunicability

So far in this chapter, I have outlined a framework for incommunicability. The component strands—linguistic, psychological and social—provide the backdrop against which I will 'unpack' the prag-matics of silence. I now want to explore the constraints which shape the transmission of Holocaust narrative, parent to child, survivor to descendant. The central concepts here are what cannot be spoken and what cannot be heard.

What cannot be told

The word 'unspeakable' exists. Look up a standard dictionary and it will tell you something like 'unable to be spoken'. As an adjective, 'unspeakable' goes with nouns like 'crime', 'atrocity, 'pain', 'grief'. It means that some things are so huge, so massive, so deep, so all-encompassing that words can't be found to describe them. The sense is that words, being finite, would place limits on the phenomenon, perceived as non-finite, and thereby betray its enormity. Words, it is felt, are cursed in that the representation they offer is at best a medi-ation, more likely a mitigation.

For some people, however, a contrary motive reigns: their with-drawal to silence comes from the belief that to express themselves—to name, label, give voice—is to return the power to the trauma, making their survival even more tenuous. I sensed this in the woman we met above, who spoke about her daughter's brain tumour. Her discourse was replete with euphemism and evasion, as she skirted around naming the terrible thing that had come into her life:

> I was afraid of giving it more validity . . . I had a superstition that if I talked about it, it would give it more power. I didn't avoid refer-ring to the circumstances but I never actually called it 'a tumour'. I often called it 'the diagnosis' because that means it is still subject to fallibility.

However, she remained unsure of this strategy:

> In one sense I'm reducing its power by not naming it but there is the thought that you are giving it *more* power by not naming it. You're not exorcising it so it goes inside and gets stronger, goes into hiding, depletes you . . . because a lot of energy goes into camouflaging.

I have encountered a similar motivation in an entirely different strategy. Here we see neither euphemism nor attenuation but its very antithesis, calling a spade a spade, confronting brutal reality by explicit naming. One of my respondents, Dan, refers often to his father's passing and at such times tends more often to stress the slow decline into dementia that preceded the death than the actual death. 'Dementia' and 'senility' are hard words because of what they denote and connote in our society. It is no surprise that the language has developed a host of softer ways of expressing this grim reality: 'fading', 'withdrawing', 'declining', 'going downhill', 'not him/herself', 'ageing', 'limited', 'less active', 'dependent', 'frail', 'confused', among others. Dan avails himself of none of these opportunities to take the edge off his reality. In social situations in particular, his usage is very marked: he tends to say, 'When Dad went senile'. He seems to refer to it more often than is needed; in other words, he could often get away with not mentioning it, but he seems rather to seek out opportunities for making mention of it. He also often refers to the decline that preceded his father's death when in many instances he need only have referred to the death itself. Even the choice of grammar—'went senile' as compared for example to 'was going senile'—is a choice of the brutally direct (the finished event) over the perhaps mitigating alternative (event as process). This is particularly marked because in fact the decline into dementia *was* gradual rather than an overnight event. Dan's way of referring to his father seems to me to be indicative of his struggle to come to terms with what happened, to refuse to allow himself the opportunity of evasion. It is the opposite of the strategy of refusing to name, but it derives from the same source.

Survivors had many reasons not to talk about what had happened to them. At the core of their silence is the notion that their attempts at representation are not respectful of the dead. This is the sense that their language won't do justice to the enormity of their experience and that if they are to fail in representing what happened, then it is better not to try at all. This constraint applies especially when survivors try to explain or answer questions about their experiences. Here they are defeated by the experiential divide. Hass claims survivors kept silent because of their belief that 'the unmarked' could neither imagine nor understand their ordeal.[52] My father wrote:

> We feel that people who were not there simply could not grasp the extent of the horror of those years. They would listen, or they would allow that we were telling the truth, but they would claim (in a nice

way) that our fear had exaggerated the events. They would put forward their opinions as to what actually might have happened. We from 'there' were never able to conduct a reasonable discussion with the 'non-theres', maybe because we resented their silent pity when they listened quietly, as much as their voiced arguments when they dared to talk. At the same time, however, we needed their pity and we wanted to talk.[53]

Many survivors believe that if you weren't there, you can't know. And they resolutely repeat this line, sincerely believing that telling is pointless. In one sense, however, in taking this line of 'unshareability', they not only alienate a genuine listener who sincerely wants to try to understand; they also fulfil their own prophecy: if the story is not told, belief is not even at issue. But, like Primo Levi, many feared they would not be believed, that the story would sound exaggerated, far-fetched, so extreme as to defy credibility. Some even said that, if roles were reversed, they themselves would not believe it. The alienation they feel from those with whom they cannot speak extends sometimes to themselves: Langer refers to 'an estrangement even between one's present and past *personae*'.[54] Laub writes that 'the "not telling" . . . serves as a perpetuation of [memory's] tyranny' leading ultimately to a state where 'the survivor doubts the reality of the actual events'.[55] Related to this is the sentiment, not often voiced, that to attempt to understand such bestiality is itself a transgression, even an act of violence. This is premised on the view that the attempt at explanation requires a distancing from the victims and as a result, perhaps, an empathy for the perpetrators.[56]

Survivors wrestled with the question that their very survival posed—'Why me?' No doubt those with faith in God asked them-selves—and God too—different questions. Then there are those who started the war with faith, and lost it by war's end. And those who began their time in hell as secular Jews and emerged with faith. All, however, must have wondered at some time, whether their survival meant someone else's death. This was completely outside their power to influence. If the Gestapo came into the ghetto to take away 100 people, it was any hundred; if your neighbour was taken, that meant a smaller chance that you would be taken. So in a sense you survived because he didn't. This is how my father saw it and it was a burden he carried for the remainder of his life. Did he also wonder whether others would wonder about how he survived?

From survivors one hears a recurrent refrain: the promise they made, to others or to themselves, to let the world know what was done. One way to do this was naming a child for someone lost. This meant a sustained, if unspoken, remembrance of loss and grief. Eli Wiesel captures this when he says of the dead, 'They have no cemetery; we are their cemetery'.[57] Another way, more direct and overt, was to tell the story. Indeed, as Des Pres writes in *The Survivor*, sometimes survival and bearing witness become 'reciprocal acts':

> Where men and women are forced to endure terrible things at the hands of others—whenever, that is, extremity involves moral issues— the need to remember becomes a general response. Spontaneously, they make it their business to record the evil forced upon them. [58]

No doubt, a large part of the pain of surviving when others didn't comes from the imperative to give testimony. One may ask, when is 'bearing witness' complete? Or is it, as I suspect, never complete, a process that merely ends at the time of the survivor's death? Perhaps this is why the next generation may be overwhelmed, as I was, with things Holocaustal when a survivor-parent is laid to rest. At Jewish cemeteries, too, when the survivor's grave is consecrated, often a plaque is added, naming family members who died during the Holo- caust. There's a sense that whatever else one may be after 1945, the core of one's identity is 'survivor'. One of the people I interviewed, Jules, makes this point with bitterness, when he likens the Holocaust to a bulldozer, flattening people's lives literally or, in the case of survivors, metaphorically, reducing their identity to 'survivor'. There is the sense of this same frozen reality in Epstein's description of her mother:

> [She] saw herself as a soldier. She had forged that *persona* in the camp, held on to it in the difficult postwar years . . . and arrived in America disciplined, authoritarian, and rarely carefree. Her soldier *persona* froze out emotion and focused on the next task at hand . . . It was a *persona* that gave her the illusion of control over a life that had been buffeted by forces well beyond her control.[59]

There are reasons not to tell and reasons to tell but, clearly, the former abound and become a dead weight and, in the end, we have silence. Some felt they lacked both the authority and the competence to speak. The feeling that one is 'unworthy', not only because 'one is only one', but because having survived, one is not entitled to speak for those who died. A woman who is herself a child survivor from Holland told me recently about her mother, who had been in the Resistance: 'My mother was reluctant to speak about her experiences . . . she didn't think she did anything out of the ordinary'.[60] Yet if they do not act as witness, who will? Some wanted not to invest their fearful legacy on their children, yet feel that safety requires eternal vigilance; with time, however, they discover that talking about the lessons of history in fact offers little defence against the excesses of injustice. I often heard my father say, 'We have to speak out so that it won't happen again'. One day I plucked up the courage to ask him if he really believed that the words of a few frail, ageing survivors would make much difference on the world stage. He said, 'No, but I need to believe it will'—a kind of knowing self-delusion. Some resist telling because they fear that once their story is out in the public domain, it then becomes a story; it is no longer real. One said, 'To talk is to desecrate the memory'.[61] Most discover that telling does not bring consolation, but re-opens wounds that beg to be allowed to heal. Perhaps one of the saddest outcomes is their discovery that silence is in the end more a prison than a refuge, and indeed can turn out to be 'as risky as speech'.[62]

Survivors, then, were 'hostages to the impossible obligation . . . of talking/not talking'.[63] There is little comfort either way. The imperative to tell is in stark contrast with the actual impossibility of telling. It is well documented that no amount of telling ever quietens the compulsion from within.[64] I am reminded here of the eternal labours of Sisyphus. So those survivors, like my father, who try to tell are left with a perpetual sense of incompleteness, while those who like my mother resort to silence, not trusting the adequacy of words, condemn themselves to a different kind of tyranny, like Eurydice, condemned forever to roam in hell. And whether the story struggles to find form in the words of the telling, or fails to find form in the unspoken universe of those who choose silence, for both there is the ongoing interplay of memory and testimony that sows doubts, even within the survivor, that what happened, happened. Charlotte Delbo, a survivor who later wrote about her experiences, elucidated the paradox and doubt. Commenting on her own written memoir, she said, 'Today I am no longer sure what I have written is true, but I am sure that it happened'.[65]

One of the few stories we heard about my mother's experiences was about her jumping off the train that took the last remaining Vilna ghetto inmates to certain death. Three others, young women like herself, decided to make the jump as well. She remembered what my father had written in a letter to her during the early months of the war, that if you ever have to jump off a train, don't actually jump, but rather let yourself fall. She told the other girls this and they decided (by what means, I don't know) in what order they would jump and how much time they would allow between each of them, having calculated where they were, what direction they were going, and at what speed. The plan was to meet up at a certain point in place and time. Of those four, only two survived: two died either under the wheels of the train or were shot in the back by the Germans, who by this time had been alerted to the escape. My mother was the last to jump and her timing was right out—she hadn't been able to get through the hole in the side of the train because she had too many layers of clothing on. This meant she had to go back, take off some layers, and try again. Meanwhile the train was hurtling through the night, making a mockery of the mathematics by which the meet-up place and time were calculated.

I don't remember the circumstances under which I found out about the scissors. I think I asked her how they made the hole in the side of the train. One of the girls in the carriage was a seamstress and was clutching to herself her bag with her tools of trade, one being scissors. But, having just experienced the ghetto's liquidation and who knows what else, she was in shock, numbed into immobility, and on the point of hysteria. She refused to lend the scissors for the purpose the women had in mind, and threatened to alert the guards about the planned escape, if she were forced to give them up. 'What did you do?', I asked, breathlessly, captured by the narrative. Long pause. 'I did what I had to do', my mother responded, her chin resolute and defiant. It was a look I knew well enough to prevent me from questioning any further.

I may have heard that story a few times, but the picture in my mind remained the same. I went away and thought about it—what did she 'have to do'? As I grew up and re-visited the story through a more mature consciousness, with more fragments to put the picture together, a little more sense was created. I found out over time that my mum was the doer, my dad the thinker; my mum would survive at all costs, my father was resigned to what appeared an inevitable fate.

(Once a possibility of escape from the ghetto came up, through Polish friends of my mother's who were prepared to get her false papers, and she urged my father to escape with her. But he would not leave the ghetto hospital, which was both a hospital and a refuge-cum-hideout, so she stayed. When, at liquidation, they were separated—he taken to a camp in Estonia and she put on the train to the death camp—he was relieved, knowing that she had a better chance without him.) But I never let go of that inner question: *What did you have to do to get those scissors?* And even asking it silently made me feel bad: *who am I to ask, to want to know, or to seem to judge?* What mattered was that she escaped, she lived.

Of course, the image I had of that train ride also changed over the years. Children make sense of what they hear about in terms of their own experience. The kind of train ride that it must have been was so far removed from what my mind could have conjured up then, that as an adult I am quite sickened by the disparity. I am reminded here of the nausea Susan described when she discovered what Drancy, the camp her mother had been in, was really like.

The disparity between the representation of the event and the memory of it can be overwhelming to survivors. This is evident from their varied responses to films like *Life is Beautiful* and *Schindler's List*. It seems that the film representations of the events have to be tempered so as to render these events manageable.[66] Inga Clendinnen's comment on the success of such film representations of the Holocaust is that they are far too glib and easy:

> Morally, they allow us an out. Ultimately, they give us only a whiff of the horror and then they come in fast with the redemptive message that, as in *Life is Beautiful*, love can conquer all, or, in *Sophie's Choice*, that happiness is possible, or even . . . in *Schindler's List*, where the dead are shown resurrected, redeemed. The horror, the truth is that life in the camps was bleak, not redemptive. The moral understanding of the Holocaust is horrific . . . and we must learn this, know this . . . History matters . . . We must learn what history is telling us, what kind of social pressures brought this thing about, what we ordinary human beings do in certain circumstances, so that we can recognise them again and see them for what they are.[67]

While many viewers will realise that representation is not pure mimesis—a film depiction of a concentration camp *is not* the experience of the camp—we can understand the reaction of those affected by the Holocaust to diluted, sanitised and managed renditions of their history. There may be a curious parallel here with the behaviour described in Brett's *Too Many Men*, non-Jewish tourists becoming fascinated by a tour that delves into the making of *Schindler's List*, thereby distancing themselves from the historical reality.[68]

These disparities go right to the heart of the communication problem. Survivors had difficulty with the telling because it was so hard to have it make sense. In another world, with a different landscape, climate, world view, how do you make the story coherent, when the knowledge and experiential chasm between teller and listener is so enormous? How do you describe moral anarchy and the breakdown of law, order and decency in the context of peace, democracy and a naturalised respect for human rights? How do you describe invasion, occupation, deportation, extermination? And how do you tell all this and cope with your listener's silence? Because there is no sound, no response that could be given that would be satisfactory. And how do you answer the questions—'Didn't you see it coming? Why didn't you get out?' and, worst of all, 'Why didn't you fight back?'. If you start up an exchange, what will you do with the questions that you are asked? What if you can't make the listener see? How will you feel if he or she argues and remonstrates with you? Isn't it safer to stay silent?

Some of the most emotional arguments I have heard relate to the question of 'fighting back'. My father had very strong views on the topic, and as a result I had a long history of exposure to the emotion surrounding it. Eventually, though, I came to understand that fighting back has many meanings. He preferred to call it 'resistance', and it meant refusing to die, willing yourself to live one day more amid the most appalling conditions, refusing to be seduced by the relief and release that death would offer. Fighting to stay alive one more day was both a literal act of resistance and a symbolic one.

With time, I came to understand the emotion that this topic generates and survivors' frustration at people's inability to make the leap to understanding. It is a micro-instance of the larger difficulty of telling one's story. So much emotion wells up that the topic overwhelms the interaction. As an interesting contrast, I recently read on the Internet a response to the question 'Why didn't they fight back?', written by a survivor's son, Dan Berger, who leads tour groups at the Florida Holocaust Museum.[69]

The discussion thread 'A teen asks a question', was initiated by a girl called Lisa. Berger thanks her for the question, asks some details (her age, family background) and then gently and factually takes her through the steps towards understanding. He starts by overturning the 'lambs to the slaughter' assumption, and explains that because most of the resistance attempts failed, they are not well known: 'If they died resisting, which was the price one often paid against the Nazis, no one was around to tell the tale'. He gives her a reference on the Internet where she could find more information. He gives many examples, not just the famous ones (the Warsaw Ghetto, Treblinka) and along the way he mentions books she could read to get a better picture. Then he turns to describe what they were up against—the systematic, planned, state-sponsored extermination, and the means by which it was achieved. He gives geographical detail, showing how running away across borders, especially in land-locked countries through hostile terrain and with no identity papers, was madness. He points out that Partisan groups and local people could not be trusted not to betray someone on the run. Once he has established the context, he then gently redefines what resistance means, using a personal anecdote about his father, who said that when he was in a labour camp in Germany another Jew quickly stole a sandwich out of a Nazi's knapsack and gave him half. Berger adds, 'To me that was resistance'. And he reminds her that, anyway, there was nowhere to go and no one to help.

Berger's response to Lisa's question is masterly. It is straightforward and unemotional. He does not start with the assumption that Lisa would have had to be there to understand. On the contrary, he is confident that once she is equipped with the facts, she *will* comprehend. And he gives her the facts, in digestible doses, in age-appropriate language. Every step of the way he tailors the information to suit her, working inductively through examples and illustrations to make a larger point. And in his account, no emotion rises up to capsize the language. It works. He has worked as a museum guide, so perhaps he has heard the question many times from many people and does not take it to be malicious or accusatory. His response is crafted as an answer to a genuine wanting to know. He seems to comprehend the very nature of incomprehension. He is a child of survivors, so he's one step removed. And no doubt electronic distance also helped. It's the kind of interaction that would be impossible between survivor and child speaking face to face.

Survivors not only feared impossible questions, they also dreaded revisiting their pain, which is what retelling entailed; so some learned to tell a version that was manageable, and devoid of emotion. Although they had to steel themselves for even the effort of the sanitised version, and suffer for it afterwards, this version was still unsatisfactory. So they found ways, a myriad ways, to manage the discourse. Salamon writes of her mother:

> Sometimes I think she has carried on so well because she sees her life in cinematic terms, as a 'story'. She responded best to questions that advanced the 'plot', providing remarkably detailed descriptions of events that she hadn't discussed at length since they had happened. It was only on points of emotional detail that she became sketchy and discursive.[70]

The first time I spoke about my research in public was to a gathering of children of survivors, with a few survivors as well. I talked about all the things that prevented our parents' generation from talking freely to us about their past. At the end, as everyone was leaving, one elderly survivor approached me. 'This is all true, what you have said', he commented, 'but one thing you left out'. 'What's that?' I asked. He said:

> Shame. We couldn't speak because we were ashamed. They reduced us almost to animals but one human thing they left us with, was shame. Who we were. What we had become. What we had lost and suffered. After this, you cannot hold your head up again. Shame made us silent.

I have no way of knowing how widespread this feeling was. Certainly, many survivors did not want to burden the next generation with the onus of their memories. A new country meant a safe haven; a second chance; a fresh start.

There were some advantages in a ground zero approach.

What cannot be heard

There are as many reasons to explain why listeners turned away, why the story was as unhearable as it was untellable. Here I want to describe what the constraints of unhearability were, first in a broader contextual sense, and then more locally situated, in the perspective of the listener in a survivor parent–child encounter.

Outside the home

As we have seen in Chapter 3, listening to survivor accounts was not what a postwar world wanted to do, and that included the Jewish elements within the postwar world. In Israel, with its newly launched ideology of the 'New Jew', stories about what happened in the past were unwelcome.

It was a comparable situation in the West. By 1945, American Jewry, who hailed from immigrant waves in the late nineteenth and early twentieth century, had lost their sentimental attachment to 'the old country'. Philip Roth encountered a 'wilful amnesia' when he tried to find out about life in Europe: 'they'd left because life was awful'.[71] Many American Jews, comfortable with a relatively assimilated, low-profile 'make-no-waves' minority presence in a wider Gentile society , were increasingly concerned at the visible stigma of victimhood newly attached to the influx of Jewish refugees—fearful lest this new image remind the Gentile host society of other ways of treating Jews. They were accustomed to maintaining a safe public face and this new dimension of what it meant to be a Jew may have unsettled a tribal identity that, above all, wanted to be safe. In their midst, survivors learned to avoid evoking anxiety in others, their silence the price of acceptance in a 'foreign humane society'.[72]

I have seen some of the discomforts that minority status invokes. The adult writing of Peeters about her experience of having been stolen from her Aboriginal parents and forcibly institutionalised resonates with the sadness of a people whose story other people don't want to know:

> We have people always telling us to forget and get on with life—this happened two hundred years ago ... They say, 'You have to go forward'. I do not dispute this, but I needed to go back before I could go forward.[73]

Urging a survivor to take stock, to move ahead is of itself not unusual. Well-meaning kin often think that the way forward is to not dwell on the past. In Mahmoody's story about her escape with her daughter from Iran, she recalls that her family, with the best of intentions, imposed an unwitting silence upon her: 'When I made some reference to my life in Teheran, they would gently brush me off, saying "That was a bad time. You're home now. Why can't you just forget about it?" '.[74]

When issues pertaining to Jews 'go public', some within the Jewish community in Australia cower in embarrassment and urge restraint and a low community profile. This happened during the controversy regarding the granting of an entry visa to Holocaust revisionist writer David Irving on a public tour; again during the 'Demidenko affair', when public plaudits were lavished on a blatantly anti-Semitic book; and during the War Crimes controversy, when Australia chose to bring to an end war crime prosecutions. I saw it too, in the brief time I lived in Buenos Aires. One night there was machine-gun fire in a well-known Jewish shopping area and following this a great deal of debate among the Jewish community about what it meant and what the appropriate response was. Some factions argued that the attack was not targeting Jews and that any response other than lying low and waiting for the trouble to go away would be to invite the very anti-Semitism that was feared. Other factions said that Nazi Germany had begun with isolated, sporadic attacks on Jews in the 1930s and the community had an obligation to respond strongly to make sure nothing more systematic was allowed to happen. When Jews face this dilemma—to make waves or not to make waves—they are reminded, in their heart and mind, that they are a minority people in a larger society. And they feel unsafe. When Holocaust survivors joined the western Diaspora, those in the Jewish community who favoured a low profile, who had in many ways assimilated in dress, custom and lifestyle to the host majority, were dismayed at the attention they attracted and the consequences that might follow.

The sense that 'one can only fail' applies as much to those who were listeners as to those who were tellers of Holocaust narrative. Carroll argues that the listener or spectator is 'stripped of any authority' in responding to talk about the Holocaust or commenting on the way the talk was conducted. In the end, hearers become accomplices in the turning away from talking about 'that'.[75]

Dori Laub has analysed the impact on the listener of Holocaust testimony.[76] He claims that the story of Holocaust survival is 'a very condensed version of most of what life is all about [involving] the many existential questions that we manage to avoid in our daily living'. He catalogues these as the notion of death; the passage of time; the meaning and purpose of life; the discovery of the limits to one's omnipotence; the loss of those one loves; the great question of 'our ultimate aloneness'; our 'otherness from any other'; our responsibility to ourselves and others; and our relationships to parents and children. Within this frame of reference, Laub then casts the vicissitudes and hazards of being a listener to a narrative of trauma. He details the defences that a listener tries to erect against the 'flood of affect' that seems to be unleashed; paralysis, to avoid merging with the recount of atrocities; anger directed at the narrator; withdrawal and a diminished capacity or inclination to feel; distancing, sometimes expressed in holding the narrator in awe, a response that sidesteps 'the intimacy entailed in knowing'; hyper-emotionality masquerading as compassion, intended to flood out even the narrator's emotion; and the tendency to foreclosure, such as giving cues that you have heard it all before, thereby reducing the discourse space that is allowed for the teller's story. Children of survivors may wince as they recognise some of these defences, from their own interactions with their parents or from witnessing their parents' encounters with others. The recollection is never pleasant. Underpinning these various responses is a common thread: they each contribute to the unhearability of the story and by doing so, fail to giver the teller permission to continue. Thus silence is yet again the less abrasive option.

In the home

The not-wanting to listen was even experienced within the extended family. Survivors who were sponsored by a relative and began life in a new land often felt that their own kin did not want to know, as in Ursula Duba's poem 'Family portraits':

> His mother used to complain
> that aunt Gella never once asked
> *what happened*
> and
> *what was it like*
> She was angry that nobody over *here*
> was interested in knowing
> what happened
> over *there*.[77]

There is a constant juggling between raising the topic or keeping silent. Duba captures another aspect of this in her poem 'Missing—

medical history', which tells of a middle-aged child of survivors, who
has no easy answers to her doctor's questions about her medical history:

> she feels the dreaded deadness
> inside
> quickly weighs
> the pragmatics of the long answer
> *you know the Holocaust . . .*
> remembers puzzled looks
> embarrassment and unease
> in encounters
> with previous doctors
> wonders
> whether she shouldn't just settle
> for the short answer *no*.[78]

Within the nuclear family, the dynamics are more intense. Simply
put, you don't know what to do with the enormity of what is being
handed to you. One child of survivors puts it this way:

> I didn't know how to block out (the) stories. I couldn't cover my ears
> or turn away my face or even still the turmoil the words created in
> me. When my mother talked, her words came at me in wave after
> wave of pain and rage. It was as though her voice and face, driven by
> energies that did not belong to every day, were disembodied and
> filled all the air around me. I would have pushed them away with a
> huge physical thrust of my arms, to make a cool and quiet space for
> myself. But I couldn't. I sat immobile. Not until I was well into high
> school did I tell my mother that I couldn't listen any more, and then,
> not seeing the pain I had suppressed, she accused me of not caring
> about her and left the room.[79]

You know that there *is* an emotion you have to respond to but
how to do so, appropriately and safely? And you are intensely uncomfortable with the palpable emotion of the one telling you, even if this
is suppressed. Especially when the listener is the child of the teller,
boundaries blur and there is no protection:

> I became the child in every one of [my mother's stories]. I was the
> child my mother had been when her mother and father and sister

were torn away from her, the child whose parents fled and abandoned it, the murdered child mourned by its mother, and the child who, just by being alive, murdered its parents. I betrayed and had been betrayed.[80]

Eva Hoffman finds out as a young adult about the tragedy her father has carried with him all the years since the war: the way in which his sister and niece were betrayed and killed:

I see that my father has gone slightly pale. 'Let's not talk about these things' he says, lowering his head, and I want to stop too, right now. All this time I've done my father the injustice of not knowing this story, and now I can hardly bear to hear it. This is no longer a frightening fairy tale, as it would have been in childhood. I have a flash of my sister and my little niece in that room, and I shut it out as if even a flicker of such an image were indecent. Indecent to imagine, indecent not to imagine. Indecent not to say anything . . . indecent to say anything at all: pity is too small for this. We stop and go on to talk about something else, in normal tones. Later in the upstairs bedroom . . . I see the scene after all, and thinking of its weight on my father's soul, I allow myself to cry.[81]

It is not possible for a child listener to be dispassionate in the face of such narrative. In Dubarsky's *The First Book of Samuel*, 'Theodora hated it when they talked about the past, about Nazis and Hitler and rows and rows of dead Jews. Children like herself. She hated it.'[82] One child of survivors expresses it this way, when at age forty-two, married and with her own children, her mother died: 'It felt as though I had been left in the world alone . . . So intense was [my relation to my mother] that I was never sure . . . where I ended, and she began'.[83]

Most people, untutored, lack the strategic skills to manage extreme emotion in another. This applies most certainly to children. You quickly learn that some questions ('Why didn't you run away?') trigger an incomprehensible rage and you acquire skilful avoidance behaviours. Apart from this, a lot of it fails to make any sense. It may even seem bizarre. The terms of reference—history, geography, culture, language—are alien; and there are so few shared assumptions out of which to forge mutually understood meaning.

Susan says:

I remember asking, 'Why didn't you run away?' She said, 'They had guns and we couldn't run away.' I couldn't understand how they couldn't get away. I had this vision it was just one person with a gun. Why couldn't they run away? That really bothered me.

And, anyway, what you can glean tells you that it's all about suffering and being made to suffer. A child does not want to hear about their parents being weak. Your parents are your first line of defence, your 'protective envelope';[84] if they can't protect themselves, then they can't protect you. As well, if that could happen to them, what could happen to me? Further, you don't want to hear how Jews were humiliated, shamed, degraded, because it interferes with your ability to forge your own positive identity. The horror of it intuitively makes you recoil: this is a morally nihilistic world where evil reigns and innocence is trodden on. Few hearers want to learn about a world gone mad.

5

Born Knowing:
The Descendants' Experience

Friends as Family

The world that we children of survivors grew up in was a very particular one and it is this world that I want to paint here in broad brushstrokes.

Some years before I began the research that led to this book, I joined a self-help group of survivors' children who came together through the common wish to explore their Holocaust heritage. At the first meeting, the group leader asked us to introduce ourselves. As I listened to other people's summaries, I was struck by the way everyone present defined themselves overwhelmingly through their parents. It was brilliantly clear to me in that moment that, in our collective consciousnesses, our boundaries with our parents had long ago blurred. Epstein sums this intertwining in her relations with her mother:

> I wore the clothes my mother made for me, read the books she read, valued what she thought good. I shared my life with her, half understanding that I was her anchor and that through me, she lived out alternatives to what had been her own life.[1]

I too began my interviews with children of survivors by asking about their parents' biography: where they were from, how they spent the war years, how emigration took place, and the early years in Australia.

From these discussions, a pattern emerges of a community of survivors. The children either knew from the start that they were 'different', or they found out at school. Abe says of his own childhood perception of his parents, 'They talked funny and they ate funny food and they mixed with people who were funny in the same way that they

123

were'. While these experiences echo the more general migrant experience, the fact of the shared traumatic past made an unmistakable imprint. A common refrain is a remembrance of being a young child, playing on the floor, against the backdrop of parents and survivor friends and the emotions that those get-togethers generally evoked.

Immediately after the war, survivors regained some of their health and then, in DP camps or on the move or in transit, they waited for permission to leave Europe. This meant being accepted by another country, preferably as far away as possible. For distance, Australia was a clear winner, and it became the third most popular destination for emigrant survivors, after Israel and the USA.

The people I interviewed were born in these years, some in Europe, some on the way, some after emigration. They all have stories about how they came into this world, stories that have become part of the transmitted culture of their home. The stories, of course, vary, as do the attitudes and thinking, but over it all hangs the shadow of the Holocaust. I know one survivor who had remarried (she had lost her husband in the war), but refused to leave Poland until she was safely delivered of a child. She left the Old World for the New with a toddler. I have never been able to clarify her logic. Whenever I have tried, it is not reasoning I hear but emotion. Perhaps her feeling was that the rebirth of life had to begin there. Others did not want to have a child until they were a long way from Europe. In any case, many women were fearful of starting a family, or pessimistic about their chances of creating life, given the physical vicissitudes that their bodies had endured. This fear of further loss is hinted at in the final pages of Brett's *Too Many Men*.[2] Some could not think of replacing what had been lost, but many, like my father, felt that 'children were the only way to start again'.

When I was young, around ten maybe, my parents on occasion used to visit an elderly couple called the Genzels. They lived in a small dark flat that was filled with emptiness. It was bleak and dank and it filled me with dread. I hated going there. The man rarely spoke and had a lost, haunted look. On occasion he shot me a sad, fleeting smile. The woman was bent over. She'd converse quietly in Yiddish with my mother, and when her eyes fell on me, they would linger too long, way beyond my point of comfort. I couldn't work out who these people were, or what the connection was; I was too scared to ask; and I looked for reasons to get out of going or to leave early.

I suspect that my parents were their only visitors, the fresh fruit my mother brought the only freshness in their lives. I don't remember when I realised it, or whether indeed I was told that the Genzels were a childless survivor couple. I don't recall if they lost children in the war, tried to have children after the war but couldn't, or chose not to bring a child into a world like the one they had known. I think my parents visited them for many reasons: love, duty, caring, remembrance, charity, community. Maybe they served as substitute parent figures, a place where my parents might express their own starved filiality.

Survivors' loss of their own parents and their failure to say Kaddish in the traditional way is a grievous wound that knows no healing. The majority of survivors were in their twenties and thirties at the time of the war (young children and the elderly were eliminated early), and few survived with their parents. Many survivors later carried feelings of failure and guilt for not having saved their own parents. Helen Epstein, a child of survivors, writes about her feelings as her mother was dying: 'That night, I lay in my mother's bed feeling that I had failed to protect her just as she had failed to protect her parents'.[3] I had the same thoughts when each of my parents died: is this what it means to stand by helplessly while those you love die? I felt this even though my parents died naturally and peacefully, while theirs died unnaturally and violently. My loss tapped into my inherited sense of their losses. My belief now is that my parents' attending in the way they did to the Genzels, that tragic childless couple, alleviated in some small way their feelings regarding their own parents.

My parents were married a few weeks before the Germans invaded Poland. Each survived the six years of the war and, amazingly, met up again after the war. This was as miraculous as it was rare. Much more typical were the circumstances of a survivor family whom we knew well, where both the mother and father had been married to other people, each of whom had died; both had lost children, as well as their parents and extended families. Typically, too, the new partners had known each other prior to the war: many ended up marrying a cousin, a friend's wife, the sister of a spouse, a schoolfriend, someone from the same town. In the years after the war, as the remnants of Europe's Jewry came back from where they had been sent and perhaps found some respite in DP camps, or temporary lodgings, new unions were forged, sometimes on very tenuous foundations, and steps were taken along the road to reconstruction. There was an 'intense and overwhelming wish to create something new. To replace, to refute, to undo and go on . . . the survival of the species [was] at stake'.[4]

In the new world, survivor communities quickly grew up, providing the solidarity and warmth and loyalty that families might have done. Many spoke of the bond that held survivor families together and the resilience that gave them. Leah says, 'We had a very positive attitude. [My parents] were survivors and therefore we could all survive. They survived not to crumble, but to go ahead, and we derived strength from their strength'. She recalls:

I remember that they mixed with other survivors. They sat around tables and talked. They had parties and get-togethers. There were non-survivor friends too, but they weren't so close. I was very aware of the bond that tied them together. My memory is of friends as family, of people who were a lot closer than they would have been if there had been family.

Edna's recollections are comparable:

They were really happy times. Lots of laughter, people coming over to play cards. Not much family. The friends were a kind of Clayton's family, the family you have when you don't have a family. There were things to celebrate, like Passover. Food was a big thing. They were always in each other's homes.

Rachel says, 'They were all Jewish, all foreign, they all seemed to have only one child. There was a bond. I never formulated what it was until much later. I kind of knew that it was linked to some big experience but I didn't have any words for it'.

I am not aware of the statistical validity of this comment about the one-child family, but certainly it seemed this way. Indeed, in hindsight, the poignancy of the lack of grandparents, aunts, uncles and cousins seems to be rendered greater by there being usually only one child.

The sense of community is a common refrain among my respondents' recollections of their growing-up years. Jill's remembrance is of people who chose not to think of the sad times and forced themselves to celebrate life. 'It was if they knew that to dwell on it meant they were just not going to get on'. As a child she was taken along to these gatherings and while she understood Yiddish, she recalls the emotion of the time rather than the topics talked about. There was a strong sense of obligation and loyalty among the group, and this was transmitted to the child generation.

Recollections from this period suggest an intensity that carried over to ordinary daily matters. Bergmann and Jucovy say that where people in normal circumstances generally take life for granted, survivor parents frequently 'remain incredulous that they are alive', an idea that they transmit to their children. It's hard to know at what point the child moves from feeling special to a sense of needing to 'pay for the privilege of being alive'. The acculturation process is gradual and mostly subtle; the message is that you are to replace what was lost, and through your life 'heal past injuries'.[5]

Friends replaced family. Hannah Arendt argues that it is no wonder that fellow survivors play such a central role for exiles: in some metaphoric and emotional sense, they replace the lost homeland.[6] Most survivors' children recall 'aunts' and 'uncles' who were not actually related by blood or marriage. In fact, I spent some years of my childhood believing that the word 'aunt' meant 'a close female family friend'. And I did not know, really know, that I actually had a real aunt, my father's older sister. There was someone called 'Tanty Tetsha' in Israel, but I didn't know that 'Tanty' meant 'aunty'. I never saw the words written down. I thought it was a four-syllable name: Tantitetsha. I met my real aunt for the first time when I was seventeen, and the experience, along with that of having cousins, was bewildering. She had a framed photo of a handsome man who looked a lot like my father, though taller, slimmer, somehow more distant and elegant. I asked who he was; she explained that it was her father, my grandfather—the photo had been taken when he had come to visit her in Palestine, just before war in Europe erupted. She never saw him again. I hadn't known that he'd made that fateful trip, that he'd nearly got the family out. I'd never seen a photo of him. I'd known his name was 'Chaim' and I wondered if it was linked to 'L'Chaim', and to the shadow that flickered over my father's face when he raised a glass and said a toast. My aunt must have wondered why I knew so painfully little about the family.

Children make sense of the world in gross and simplistic ways. I spent some years believing that all Polish men were doctors, because my parents mixed closely with a group of Polish Jews who together had re-qualified in medicine at University of Sydney, sharing their limited English, their lecture notes, their anxieties about exams and their dislike of certain examiners, while holding down factory jobs at night and swotting in between times. I thought that's what people did. When later, it was my mother's turn to redo medicine, my father would spend more time with us and many evenings we'd go for a walk and he'd buy the bar of chocolate that we'd later give to Mum to 'help' her study late into the night. I thought that's what people did. One worked, one studied and the one who studied ate chocolate late into the night. Years later, when my father performed examination duties for the nurses' *viva* test, the overseas nurses liked to have him as their examiner rather than an Anglo-Australian, because they knew, both from his own accent and from his empathy, that he understood and wouldn't penalise them when they mixed up 'pure' and 'poor'.

Constructing home

As will become increasingly apparent through this book, children of survivors had great difficulty making sense of the world in which they were born. This derives in part from the difficulty the parent generation had in telling their children where they had come from. This is a defining element of the Jewish post-Holocaust refugee experience, making it qualitatively different from the more generic migrant experience. This said, I don't wish to suggest that 'the migrant experience' is one monolithic homogeneous phenomenon—clearly it isn't, as a reading of the stories by second-generation immigrant women in *Who Do You Think You Are?* attests.[7]

It is in the construction of home that some major threads of difference emerge. Children of Greek, Italian or Yugoslav migrants, for example, grow up with a sense of 'the old country'. The word 'home' is multi-dimensional: there is talk about grandparents still 'back there'; there is mention of aunts and uncles and cousins; of a place that the parents want to go back to visit or even retire to. Money is sent back to support family. Presents are sent and received on birthdays and festivals. Christmas is a time of connecting the present and the past, the new and the old, those who are 'there' and those who are 'here'. The old country and the new, it would seem, are connected through multiple, invisible bonds of love and family. Such children of migrants remember having had childhoods in which 'home' is lovingly and richly constructed. There is a sense, as Epstein puts it, of having a history rather than a 'martyrology', of being able to respond to a phrase like 'It's in your blood' with the neutral meaning of blood as associated 'with people, place and history, not with extermination'.[8]

A beautiful illustration of this richness may be found in the writings of Gandolfo, who explores the experiences of second-generation migrant children growing up 'in a land that does not hold the history or the spirit of their ancestors'. She tells the autobiographical story of a woman who returns to Sicily where her parents come from and has the sense of 'going back' to a place she has known only vicariously:

> She feels a sense of belonging the moment she arrives in the village—a familiarity . . . She walks the village streets, talks to people who ask her not 'Where do you come from?' but 'Who is your family?'. They know she belongs here.[9]

The construction of home in Gandolfo's life and fiction is strikingly different from that depicted in Lily Brett's *Too Many Men* and Arnold Zable's *Jewels and Ashes*, each the story of a 'return' to a Poland that holds terrible memories for survivors and descendants. Here we begin to sense the discontinuity that plagues the child whose ancestral links have been severed by war, loss and dislocation, leaving people for whom there was no 'back home'. Lily Brett's main character, no doubt a loosely autobiographical portrait of the author, is a child of Polish survivors. As an adult, she travels to Poland without really knowing why: 'Just to see that her mother and father came from somewhere. To see their past as more than an abstract stretch of horror'. She travels to Poland with 'a long list of . . . unanswerable questions about that time'.

Zable's trip to Poland is irredeemably sad. It is a journey into absence, a *Juderein* ('Jew-free') landscape, where all that is left of the once 3 000 000-strong Jewish population is the oblique reminders of stones and plaques 'in forest clearings, within open fields, on busy city streets, in village squares, by roadside shrines . . . in a land stalked by smouldering sorrows'. Eventually, he arrives at Auschwitz:

> In recent months I have come to know many levels of silence. It is a language with an extensive vocabulary. There are silences which echo ancestral presences; silences in which it is possible to observe the slightest movement of dust, an insect in hiding, a pod floating from a dandelion with the faintest promise of rebirth; and the awesome silence of forest clearings where mass executions took place against mute backdrops of stunning beauty. Yet here, in the headquarters of the Reich terror network, the vocabulary of silence reaches beyond its

own limits. It overwhelms with the sheer force of numbers; and the fact that here, lived and worked a company of technicians and bureaucrats who went about the task of efficiently and quickly annihilating over a million human beings.[10]

If home is the ancestral place from which you derive your core identity, then people like me had no such construct. I grew up knowing that the strange and incomprehensible language my parents spoke was Polish and knowing, too, that they hated (nearly) all things Polish. There was no forgetting that Polish was what they were—the accent was an ever-present reminder—yet I sensed that attached to the label 'Polish' was something bad and foreboding. This is no easy juggling act for a child. To this day I can recall the discomfort of trying to hold steady the tension I sensed in acknowledging that my parents, whom I adored, were 'Polish'. It was problematic and it remained so until at long last, as an adult, with a grown-up's knowledge of the world, recent history and my parents' place in both, I realised that what they were was 'Jews from Poland'.

Children of migrants have one foot each in different worlds. But children of postwar Jewish refugees have that extra complication, which is described in intricate psycho-analytic terms by Altounian, herself a descendant of Armenian survivors of the Turkish genocide of 1915, whose parents fled to France. Her experience in the wake of her parents' trauma foreshadows that of children of Holocaust survivors, a generation later. In Altounian's case, a further complicating dimension derives from the ambivalent relationship of the migrant family to the host country, which has failed to acknowledge their experience of injustice.[11] For Altounian, not only have the ancestral roots been severed; integration with the host society is precluded. People like her can never be fully grounded in a community which does not share or empathise with their experience of persecution. Nearly 100 years after the event, ongoing French government reticence on the subject—failure to condemn Turkey's persistent denial—perpetuates the alienation experienced by descendants of the Armenian refugees, lending a twisted irony to Hitler's later rhetorical question: 'After all, who today remembers the destruction of the Armenians?'. The state of limbo between two worlds, a state of being 'lost in translation' is nowhere better captured than in Hoffman's book of the same name, narrating the postwar dislocation of a family of Polish Jews who emigrated to Canada.[12]

But what does 'severed' mean in this context? It means the inability to make connections with what has gone before you. Brett's story of a Jewish woman who visits Poland with her father some 50 years after the Holocaust shows her pathetic efforts to establish these links. She manages to 'get back' the coat that was her grandfather's and with it she tries to forge a connection between herself and the family she never knew:

> She could tell so much about Israel Rothwax and his wife Luba from this coat. She could see how big he was, and she could see in what beautiful condition Luba maintained his clothes. Not one part of the lining was marked or torn. Maybe tidiness and order were inherited traits. She kept most of her formal clothes in plastic clothes bags . . . If something tore, she had it mended. She cleaned every item straight after it was worn. Maybe that was a Rothwax quality. A thrill ran through her. The thrill of being able to link herself to a family. To be part of someone else. She had only ever been part [of her parents].[13]

Language and acculturation

In the early years, the contradictions and ambiguities of growing up in a survivor family were endlessly replayed—every time, indeed, that the home accent provoked the inquiry 'Where are you from?'. So formulaic was the exchange that followed that I knew the script very early (and sometimes silently mouthed the words as the speakers uttered them). This was exacerbated, it seemed to me, by the way Polish-accented speakers say 'Polish' and 'Poland'—with a short 'o' (as in 'pot') rather than, as in English, the long 'o' (as in 'pony'). Thus when asked where they were from, their 'Poland' rhymed with Holland, and that's often what people would hear, offering the rejoinder, 'Oh, so you're Dutch, are you?' So frequent was this mishearing that I recall my mother gritting her teeth as she repeated, 'No, POLand, not HOLLand', increasing her volume and her stress on the first syllable but, regrettably, not the length of her 'o'.

The language of Polish was anathema to them. Not surprisingly, English became the home vernacular. They didn't want my brother and me to speak or understand Polish so they switched to English in our presence. Our early impression of this swift code-switch was that there were secrets not meant for our ears. We didn't probe into corners where we sensed bad things lurked. I recall being told that

'Poland is a cemetery' and trying to make sense of that at a time when I had no real-life experience of what a cemetery was, let alone a metaphor. The fact that this was at the height of the Cold War, with Poland 'behind the Iron Curtain' (which I thought was a real curtain) simply added to my imbibed sense of Poland's being remote, 'off limits' and un-visitable in any way, at any time, ever. Thus it was that names of places that I heard—Kielce, Vilna, Warsaw, Krakow—had no tangible reality. They were funny names; foreign, hard to say in English; they were suspended in space; and they resonated with something that I could never quite identify. I have learned that this peculiarly alienated response is common to many children of survivors; many report the surreal quality of discovering that Dachau is today a suburb of Munich, that Auschwitz is a few hours from Krakow. In Dobies' account of his visit to Prague, he is horrified to discover that Teresin, the main transit camp for Czech Jews like his parents on the way to concentration camps, is a bare 'one hour by bus' (the title of the story) from the capital. He finds it appalling that 'everyone is helpful with directions and totally unfussed when I ask for Teresin camp'.[14] There is something stunning in the normalcy of what descendants discover when they 'go back'.

Thus while Gandolfo's links to history and ancestry nourish and nurture her and make her feel welcome in Sicily, we had no such well of goodness from which to draw strength into our lives. It is possible, too, that along with a severed ancestry, we imbibed a suspicion that the soil we sprang from was somehow contaminated: was there some impairment here, a stain, something shameful? What was it that was better not spoken of? Bergmann and Jucovy cite instances of the secrecy surrounding the pension money that some survivors received: 'one boy thought it was money . . . from the Germans to keep quiet about [his mother's] wartime experiences'.[15]

Over time, as the following chapters will illustrate, we became adept at reading euphemism and locating allusion. In explaining how her character, Ruth, knows so much about a neighbour, Lily Brett writes:

> It is possible to tell a lot about a person without being told things . . . Ruth had known that Mrs Watson was thinking about someone . . . someone she had loved . . . who was no longer alive. Ruth had a lot of experience in identifying that sort of longing. She had been exposed to so much wishful, wistful thinking'.[16]

This mastery in reading indirect meaning, however, never came with the comfort or surety of trusting one's understandings. You never knew whether what you knew was all there was to be known.

While the absence of connection with home marks it as different, in many other ways the survivor community was typically migrant. A key feature here was how hard people worked to build a new life. John felt this from his earliest years: 'We were together and we were all surviving and rebuilding. We were very oriented to the future. I was very aware of this, that they were working for me and I was working for them'. His role, he recalls, was 'to explain Australia to them'. He did this by writing letters in English, paying bills, interpreting, explaining everything to them, from the mysteries of cricket to the wonders of democracy.

The degree to which the parents acculturated to the new land, with its own climate, culture and conventions, varied—and did so along a gradient of 'hardly at all' to 'as completely as was conceivably possible'. Given the link between language and culture, the degree of adaptation could often be measured in their mastery of English. A few arrived as near to native-like fluency and accuracy as an adult learner of a foreign language can be expected to reach. Others managed the basics but always with thick accents. I recall my mother being jubilantly boastful that a New York policeman, some fifteen years after the war, recognised an Australian accent in amongst the dogged strains of her Polish. I also recall her giving up on some vowel nuances such as 'bad' and 'bed'—saying, somewhat defiantly, 'They'll bury me with my accent'. Between the extremes of mastery and failure were many points on the gradient. A few learned receptive skills (listening and reading) but did not converse or write. When I think back to my parents' survivor community, now largely deceased, I recall that there were some whose voices were scarcely heard in English. Growing up, of course, I had no sense of what this must have meant.

One wonders, too, about the possibility of communication when the parent and child do not share a common language—or when their language-to-think-in is not the same. Many of my generation did learn to speak their parents' first language, but the Polish or Hungarian or Czech or German or whatever that they spoke rarely improved beyond the domestic language such that a young child might use. In my case, the language age of the Yiddish I recall is even younger, echoing the age at which I lost it. The words I recall, for instance, revolve around food, play, body parts, etc., and all the nouns have diminutives, so it's not the Yiddish equivalent of 'stomach' that I know, but 'tummy'. One reason I still know these few words is because I continued to use odd words as I grew older, at first unaware that I was mixing two tongues and later unaware of their inappropriateness; the little-child language must have sounded quaint to my parents who would quote them back to me, ironically cementing them for ever more in my memory.

It's a deep sadness when parent and child lack a language in common. I was told recently of a girl from an Australian Chinese family. Her Chinese never progressed beyond a functional home-and-hearth language; and her mother's English never developed to the point of meaningful conversation. Years later, when the girl's life was in danger from drug abuse, the mother's tragedy was made much more painful by her inability to talk to her daughter. The lack of a language in common gives a particular edge to the notion of 'the generation gap'.

While language is quite a reliable barometer of acculturation, sometimes there can be a bizarre discordance between the different levels of mastery. My father reached an uncommonly high level of mastery in English, a tongue in which eventually he could write, create, joke and be playful in (even while never quite mastering the present perfect tense), yet he could not accept with equanimity that my being barefoot—even in the Australian summer—didn't mean material and moral impoverishment. In some cases, perhaps, nouns, verbs and clauses are easier to master.

Survivors' journey toward acculturation was one in which their children often played a pivotal role. Children pick up a language they are immersed in with an amazing agility that is often galling to the parents. Being born here, they were of the land in a way that the parents never could be. However, this sometimes led to burdensome responsibilities. One of my respondents attributes his largely dysfunctional life to the survivor home in which he was raised. It is only in recent years that he has come to see his parents in a wider context and find forgiveness for what he once thought was malevolence, admitting, 'they were lost souls, both of them'.

Reaction to parents is not always quite so extreme. As I have indicated, many survivor children admit to feeling 'cherished'. Some say that this feeling comes out of the family's history of losses, requiring the child to fulfil too many hopes, and blurring too many boundaries. Others say that it was both a defining and a positive element of their childhood. Rena, for example, who has had a difficult adult life, and carries the scars of two failed marriages, recalls the love with which she was raised by survivor parents as the fulcrum of her life.

Finding Out or Born Knowing?

In answer to the question, 'What is your earliest memory of finding out that your parents had been through something terrible?', my respondents seemed to answer in one voice. The overwhelming sense is that as a generation, they were born with and into a state of awareness. Rachel says:

> I didn't find out. I was born knowing . . . can't remember being told. I just always knew. At about the age of five or six I already had fantasies about what I would do to Hitler, knowing that he and the Nazis had hurt my parents. But I can't remember them actually telling me.

Dreams figure prominently, especially nightmares. Elsa remembers 'dreams in which there were Nazi officers and people chasing people but I can't remember consciously how I arrived at that knowledge'. Rena had recurrent nightmares, re-runs of the same scene. Her home would become the setting for what sounds terrifyingly like a Gestapo raid. In the dream, she is woken from sleep by loud banging on the front door. Suddenly she finds herself alone. She runs out the back door down the back path to the outside toilet. And as she creeps down low, frozen in her fear, and tries to become invisible, the toilet bowl next to her overflows with excrement and she realises she has to get out. Just then, she hears loud footsteps, shouting and then the same loud insistent banging, this time on the toilet door. The dream never moves past this point. She wakes up terrified. Rena has no recollection of knowing this narrative outside of her own dream—she started having the dreams long before she read any books or saw any movies that might have triggered it. To her, and many children of survivors, these dreams seem to act out their parents' past; they underline the intermeshing of lives between the two generations. Varga's autobiographical *Heddy and Me* recalls her resentfulness in adolescence, her wanting to have nightmares like her schoolfriends, dreams with greater parallel in her own reality.[17]

What is this 'kind of knowing' that seems to have started almost before birth? Certainly it is an oblique knowledge, more a sensing at a visceral or subconscious rather than a cognitive level. This is captured in the language descendants use to talk about how they knew what they knew. Abe says his parents' epic escape from a Europe exploding into war across Russia to Shanghai was part of the fabric of his childhood: 'I can't remember not knowing'. Dan says, 'I knew something horrible had happened but I couldn't have told you what it was'. Maurice remembers, 'There was a visible shadow there all the time. But I was never actually sat down and told'. Rebecca says, 'I can't picture the process of finding out. The feeling is that it permeated the atmosphere, infused into our lives'. David says that for a long time, 'It just seemed to me like some faraway historic event that I couldn't possibly understand. I knew it was horrible, something not meant to be talked about. I knew talking about it was painful for my parents so I tended to avoid it'. Varga writes that she was 'born into an earthquake'.[18]

The finding out is by accretion, the laying on of thin layers of awareness that ultimately become a kind of knowledge. In the early years, the picking up of multiple sensory cues is probably more important than language. So infused are the early years with these sensations that one woman blurs the distinction between foetal and newborn perceptions. Born of Polish-Jewish refugee parents on the run, Julia spent her early years in DP camps, first in Poland, then Germany, then Belgium. There is fearfulness in her eyes when she recalls the tensions, insecurities and upheavals of her childhood. During the interview, she talked about a moment she had experienced as an adult in regressive therapy (intended to take the subject back to the moment of birth). She started screaming that she did not want to be born. Her comment in the debriefing afterwards was that in that moment, she had sensed a terrible fear, heaviness and foreboding: she did not want 'to come out'.

Among survivors' children, there is a discernible pattern of trying to find out more. One person described it to me as driving slowly in a fog; then gradually as patches of the fog lift, shapes start to become distinct and discernible. After a while, it's impossible to determine when the fog engulfed them and when it lifted. What might be called 'finding out' is more like the accumulation of sensory cues. For Jennie, for example, it was like constructing a whole out of fragments that don't seem to fit. The central event in her parents' history was the never-healing trauma of their two little boys being killed. I asked Jennie how she was told about this, and she replied, 'I accumulated details'.

So subtle and gradual is the growth of awareness that when there is an actual telling event, usually in adolescence, it comes as a jolt against a background that is self-constructed, an already-knowing-by-sensing. 'We were on holidays when I was about twelve', says Maurice, 'and they sat me down and told me that my grandmother was not my real grandmother, but in fact my grandfather's third wife. That was the beginning of the puzzle'. Maurice's experience—of being sat down and 'told something startling'—was not an isolated one. In many cases where it happened, the parents seemed unaware of the already-aroused perceptual state of the child. The child finds out, supposedly for the first time, but the revelation fits rather neatly into an already partially constructed jigsaw puzzle, one that the child has been putting together, albeit largely subconsciously, since early childhood.

Revelations of this kind were common across survivor families. You hear that that boy's father is really his uncle. A woman we call 'Aunty' is not in fact related to us. That man we call 'Uncle' came from the same town as your father. Your mother is actually your father's first wife's sister. Those children are that couple's second family. The children they had before were lost in the war . . . The global sense is indisputably of families put together by whatever means; of absences and loss; of gaps being filled. A garment of sorts is patched and reworked with squares of different materials. Makeshift, hastily put together, and not talked about, it's a stopgap that becomes permanent.

Aware of the significance of these revelations, even of the likely times of the year when they would emerge, some children tried to avoid situations when they thought they were more likely to happen, such as holidays when daily routines were broken, or 'family' occasions. For the children these were times when they could expect 'eruptions' in the fragile surface of their lives. For the parents, these moments of pause in a life that otherwise spurned memory must have turned thoughts to absent family members. Whenever they wanted to share a landmark—a child's first step, a glowing report card, the coming of age—with someone who would have shared the pleasure, they are reminded of what is no longer. Many children of survivors only begin to realise what this might have meant when they themselves raise their own children and pass through these family milestones.

I came to some of my own insights in this fashion. For example, on the Passover following the death of my father I was very aware, for the first time, of being parentless at Passover. Suddenly I realised something of what they must have felt, at this time, every year since the war. Each Passover my father, not a religious man, used to say the Jewish prayer of thanks, 'Blessed art Thou . . . who kept us alive and preserved us and enabled us to reach this season'—which he had said in May 1945, at the time of his escape and shortly before liberation. Each year he gave renewed thanks and for me this was just a part of Passover, as normal and predictable as the *matzot*, salty eggs and chicken soup. I remember the tear that my mother would shed as my father said the prayer, her eyes downturned and the tear rolling down her cheek. As a child I did not know where the sorrow came from or what it meant, but I had a sense of its perennial inevitability. I knew not to speak or interfere. The tear would roll down her cheek and be absorbed, ultimately, in her silence.

A picture emerges of a state of knowing without remembrance of having been told, often without understanding what it is that is known. And what is known by the child is re-interpreted in adult-hood. Thus when I interviewed the now grown-up children of survivors, I was often witness to the process of re-interpretation, as they sifted through their recollections and came to new insights. Often this had to do with recalling cues that had previously made only emotional sense.

The most uncanny realisations were in fact triggered by what was not there, by significant absences. Rebecca said:

> Look, there was no family, no relatives, no one. Where were they? There were grief messages in the emptiness, in the absence. I knew all these people who weren't there had gone up in smoke. I don't know how I knew. It was so ingrained in me, there was no need for words.

Absences or omissions furnish bizarre cues to the growing child that something is amiss. The message is: something here is not quite right. 'I was the only one at kindergarten without any grandparents', was a line I heard many times. Leah smiles sadly as she remembers thinking of the other kids at pre-school: 'having four grandparents seemed like an awful excess'. She recalls her defining idea of a grandparent: 'I thought all grandparents didn't speak English and everyone only had one'. Jill remembers absences too, because of 'stand-in aunts'. Erlich recalls that he dealt with the absence of family by 'inventing' his own, 'adopting' friends of his parents who frequently visited his home and calling them 'Grandma' or 'Aunt' or 'Uncle'.[19]

Absence casts its own shadow. Rebecca recalls that children's birthdays were celebrated, such as they were, in the context of a kind of anniversary taboo—in her family, any kind of anniversary was shunned because it triggered remembrance, not of birth but of death, and hence absence, loss and grief. Remembrance could not occur without the accompaniment of loss. She says the home she grew up in was 'nothing like' the homes of her Australian peers:

> For a start, all the Australian kids had extended families. Nearly all of them had grandparents, some even had two sets. They certainly all had uncles, aunts and lots of cousins, whereas it took me a long time before I understood the concept of what a cousin was.

The sense of aloneness seems to be woven through the generational boundaries. Indeed, descendants often used the word 'alone' in describing aspects of their parents' experience: left alone when loved ones were forcibly removed, left alone by a world that turned its back on them, then at liberation, alone in the world, alive but alone. There's something very primary here that has been transmitted. Despite a large and happy family of his own, Dan says, 'I feel lonely in the world', and there's no question in his mind that this is linked with his parents. Rena has a recurrent dream in which she is alone on the planet—it's dark, cold, and when she calls out, she hears only the echo of her own voice. She's the last person left alive. Rebecca sat by her mother's hospital bed after she died, long after the nurse urged her to go: 'I had to stay with her. I had to do that for her. I did it for me. I wanted her not to be alone because they all died alone. I didn't want her to die alone'. Death of parents is acutely resonant of the Holocaust.

Other cues carried meaning too. 'I remember the feeling of people feeling sorry for us, trying to help us', says Dan. A number of respondents recall the 'refugee experience'. Paul said, 'We were wogs, we were different, lots of the kids at school were children of survivors, we stood out'. People remember being marked as foreign—because of their clothes, their sandwiches, their parents' accents. One man, John, recalls an awareness in himself that was deliberately sidelined to the margins of his mind:

There were lots of us at school. We didn't talk about it. There were footballs to throw around. I'm not sure I wanted to know. I felt like I knew enough already. It was pretty simple: Jews had had a hard time; we were Jews. So I knew the broad strokes. I didn't feel I needed the details. I thought it had nothing to do with me, with my future.

He also remembers being struck by the sense of having an old head on young shoulders. 'At an early age I knew things that other kids didn't'. He knew about the Hungarian Revolution in 1956 before his peers had any such inkling of a world outside their playground. He was struck, as were many survivors' children, by the naiveté of their Anglo-Australian friends, who by contrast seemed the very epitome of innocence. Jane captures this in her line, 'I was the adult even when I was four'. It is the stuff of alienation when the developing child, especially the adolescent, is unable to connect with peers. Rena recalls that her efforts to 'blend in' and be 'one of' the crowd were finished once the Eichmann trial brought knowledge of the war to a new generation. She remembers the reactions of her schoolmates to the revelation of Nazi atrocities. She has no words to describe the naiveté of her classmates, combined with almost voyeuristic interest they had in the newspaper reportage. It was their first contact with the word 'Jew', outside of Biblical references in Scripture class and Christian fellowship clubs. The landscape of war-devastated Europe must have looked nothing like the rocky barren, yet somehow idyllic, landscape of children's Scripture books. Rena herself was perplexed by the stark dichotomy: Jews were the ones who killed Jesus; and those heaps of skeletons in the newspaper pictures, they were Jews too. Were they the same Jews?

The sense of growing up among innocent peers in an innocent landscape is one shared by many children of Holocaust survivors, even though in their growing up years they'd have been hard pressed to articulate the thought. Sometimes, the same feeling revisits me in adulthood. Let me give some examples. The first draft of this book was read chapter by chapter almost as it was written and printed, by a non-Jewish journalist friend of mine. She was a perfect choice: highly literate but completely outside the experiences I describe. I needed her to advise me where and how I was making inappropriate assumptions in my reader. She'd return the manuscript with comments scribbled down the margins. It was one of these that occasioned my thinking about the gulf between people who inherit the trauma of the past and people who seem to be born *tabula rasa*. In a section where I wrote about one of my mother's earliest experiences, fleeing from a pogrom, she wrote 'What is a pogrom?'. The question, 'What is a pogrom?' stayed with me in wonderment: for days I thought, here is a person who does not know what a pogrom is. What must it be like to grow up in a world where there is no need for a word like 'pogrom'? Would I have been a different person if that word were not in my vocabulary, or at least, not from so early an age?

The feeling re-emerges when good people who would never harm another soul fail to understand political processes by which democratic institutions may be abused. Recently I discovered that the online book company Amazon.com distributes a copy of the notoriously anti-Semitic and influential *The Protocols of the Elders of Zion*, and (clearly in the interests of further sales) advises buyers that readers who have ordered this title also ordered Hitler's *Mein Kampf*. Amazon's explanation was (and I quote from the letter they sent me):

> As a bookseller, Amazon.com strongly believes that providing open access to written speech, no matter how hateful or ugly, is one of the most important things we do. It's a service that the United States Constitution protects, and one that follows a long tradition of booksellers serving as guardians of free expression in our society . . . Amazon.com believes it is censorship to make a book unavailable to our customers because we believe its message to be repugnant.

A comparable argument is offered by those who believe that the so-called historian David Irving ought to be granted a visa to visit Australia, as he wishes, so that his views may be heard freely and widely. Here is not the place to offer an argument for limiting the freedom of speech of those who vilify others. My point is that the 'freedom of speech' argument seems, often, to derive from that innocent landscape where reside people who have no personal scars or who have little relevant historical knowledge.

Of course it is not as simple as one group of people that 'knows' and another that doesn't. Part of being a child of survivors is the difficulty of 'taking it in'. Epstein wrote of the family photos her parents showed her: 'These photographs . . . were documents, evidence of our part in a history so powerful that when I tried to read about it in the books my father gave me or see it in the films he took me to, I could not take it in'.[20] Eighteen years after Epstein wrote these words, Hirsch interprets the repetitive, indeterminate 'it' as an indicator of Epstein's inability to understand and incorporate the knowledge.[21] For many of us, this experience resonates as a discordance in our lives between the up-front impact of extreme emotion and the pushed-back, far-away, impoverished quality of something that for years we were only able to think of and refer to as 'it'.

Part of the survivor's child does not want to know, does not want the whole truth to emerge, does not want to discover, finally, that it is as bad as it seems. There's a part of us that looks for another truth. Paradoxically, this accounts in some way for the voracious appetite for information about the Holocaust that some survivors' children have. Lily Brett's character Ruth is one of these:

> She had read hundreds of books on the Holocaust. Books by survivors. Books by historians . . . Part of her could still not imagine the truth. Part of her still wanted to believe that it couldn't have been that bad. That her beautiful mother hadn't really slept in the middle of corpses . . . Part of her wanted to believe it was all a bad dream. [22]

Yet, even here we can't generalise. There's also a repulsion, and sometimes it co-exists in the same person who has the fascination. Jules recalls that his early life was suffused with a knowledge he didn't want to have. He says, bitterly, 'It seems I've always had the Holocaust. I would have got my first consciousness with it as soon as I started talking'. He has a sense that his life was spent finding out about his parents' war-time stories again and again and again.

It was only in discussion and analysis of these stories that he came to a late realisation that rather than being bombarded by information overload all his life, he was in fact told very little—just the same story or two over and over and over and over. Hass calls this 'emotional knowledge' rather than historical or cultural or informational.[23] Even in what appears to be a torrent of words, repeated endlessly, the effect is as of silence, 'all the more implacable in that it was often concealed behind a screen of words, again, always the same words, an unchanging story, a tale repeated over and over again, made up of selections of the war'.[24]

A young psychiatrist I know (I'll call her Kate) tells a similar story, of spending a few hours with an old friend of her parents, a woman now in her eighties, whose war years were in Auschwitz. It was a social context and in their time together, the survivor talked for 90 minutes about the very issue of *not* talking about the war.

The experience was distressing for Kate. She told me later that she had had no intention of interrupting or asking questions: she was there as a friend, not as a psychiatrist; the survivor had always said that she absolutely did not wish to talk about her war years; and Kate knew about the other woman's fear of psychiatrist's questions.

Kate left and, once alone, burst into tears—as she put it, 'from the sheer pressure of the silence, the enforced silence, deafening in [the elderly woman's] constant pressured talk that left no spaces for [me] to talk, or worse, ask questions. *Despite all the talk, silence*' (my emphasis). While Kate is used to listening to people in distress, she felt out of her depth at this level of anguish. She subsequently wrote to tell me that afterwards she told another therapist, experienced in working with survivor communities, about the event and was told that this precisely was 'the space that a lot of . . . therapy (with survivors) happens in'. Kate wrote to me later:

> I felt multiply trapped and there wasn't the airspace to defend myself, to change the topic, not even to think about whether she was actually wanting me to ask questions etc. It was the distressed barrage of talking about not-talking that I found so puzzling and upsetting, and I felt attacked in a way I couldn't understand.

What she describes to me, however, as the child of survivors, is not new. The phenomenon of enforced silence in the listener's role, of disallowed questions, is a core feature of growing up in a Holocaust survivor household.

John's story illustrates the contradictory nature of much of the experience of growing up in a survivor household. He claims that in his house no topic was taboo and that he knew it all when he was growing up. 'I knew what they got in the soup they were served, I knew that on the retreat from Russia thousands and thousands of people died, I knew it was the pits, I knew.' While he was growing up, he said, he tried to avoid the topic because he felt it had nothing to do with him. In his early twenties, after he finished university, he went to the USA where he happened to read Epstein's book on children of survivors.[25] At that moment, he was catapulted into a way of knowing that he had not experienced:

The tears started. All these stories about descendants. I realised they were me. It was all so familiar. The people were just ordinary regular people, trying to grow up and get on with their lives, and there was all this background baggage. It was the first time I had ever felt any connection with any group of people. I had had trouble relating to Jews on campus because I was too left-wing for them, but I didn't fit in with the left either, because they were anti-Semitic. Sure I had tennis buddies, but that was all about tennis. After that I went into therapy and I spent all the time crying. I had never cried like that before. I didn't know if I was crying for me or all the dead relatives. I think it was tears for myself. I was recognising a me I had never known before. There was something in me that just came tumbling out and I knew that the healthy response was to get it all out.

What John pushed under, Michael spent his boyhood also trying to escape. He recalls that he spent his childhood always trying to run away:

From about five, I was aware that something was going on. I didn't ask questions. The signs were there: 'Serious Losses Happened Here!' I only knew that I didn't want to be in that space. It was too intense. I was always trying to run away. I didn't want to be there. Anywhere but there.

As they grew to adulthood, a generation of survivors' children would seek different means of escape, both literal and metaphoric, from a situation of intense psychological discomfort. Born knowing, they were caught between a rock and a hard place: should I try to find out more and make sense of it, or should I get as far away from it as I can? Of course, different pathways were chosen at different times by different people, and many of us were steered by forces we did not fully comprehend, not realising until many years had passed that our 'flight or fight' choices were for the most part not choices at all.

Feelings, not words

Many different emotions were stored together: loss, grief, guilt, shame, fear. Zable says he has come to understand the many faces of his mother's silence. 'At times it resonates with defiance; at others it suggests an irredeemable loss. Sometimes it is softer, a surrender, a letting-go. Yet the anger and rage I knew in her as a child can flare up, without warning'.[26]

Survivors' children grew up with many emotions so mixed up together that whenever one emerged, the others were triggered. Because they were all invisibly linked to a phenomenon much larger than themselves, which was itself incapable of closure, the emotions were trapped in a vortex, spinning about, sometimes out of control, triggering untold amounts of pain. Over it all hung a cloud. Leah said that every time her parents heard of someone new from Poland arriving in Sydney, they would go to meet him/her, to ask questions:

> I don't remember the words. I remember the emotion attached to that time. There was a searching, a yearning, a longing. My earliest memories are of my parents looking for people. Always searching. Who's alive? Who survived? Who's left?

I remember encountering a similar angst in Israel when I asked a man why his father, a Holocaust survivor, had never adapted his Polish Jewish name to Hebrew, as is the immigrant's custom there. He said that his father, who died over 50 years after the war, never lost hope that a kinsman from his once-large family, of which he was in fact the sole survivor, might still be looking for him. He kept his original name so that it would appear as such in the phone book, where it could be found by someone who was looking for it. He was always waiting for those who went away to come back; and he was always searching, never giving up the hope that not everyone was lost. Probably he knew the minuscule likelihood of ever finding any survivors of his family, yet he hung on to the name as a vestige of the hope. It was important symbolically: a refusal to accept the annihilation.

I have heard similar stories elsewhere. Abe recalls a lot of talk about the war in the early postwar years because then 'they were still looking'. And poet Ursula Duba recalls living among Holocaust survivors in Brooklyn; twenty years after the end of the war, Mr and Mrs Berkovitz, were 'still looking'. She notices Mr Berkovitz peering closely at her, as if there is a resemblance that bothers him. Eventually he approaches her and asks about the distant relatives on her father's side. The wife apologises for him, whispering 'My husband is still looking for lost relatives'.[27]

Children of survivors have often had difficulty managing the disparate and at times incompatible emotions that they experienced.

This ambivalence was etched in memory and proved to be a dominant refrain through the interviews. Abe's situation is a telling one. It encapsulates both the child's attempt to marry discordant elements and the driving need to put a positive spin on the story that was enveloping him. His parents' story is the one referred to already as 'the epic', where a bedraggled family of three generations escaped a besieged Europe, fled across Russia, spent some six months in Kobe, Japan and finally stopped for five years in Shanghai. He cannot remember a time when he didn't know about it. In a sense his life has been one long experience of finding out all the little stories that hold the big story together. Like any epic, it is made up of episodic narratives, as the heroes encounter obstacles and setbacks and achieve small victories on the grand march to freedom and survival. Abe's sense of his parents' narrative being made up a set of discrete stories is echoed again and again in my interviews, where descendants refer to 'the potato peel story' or 'the school teacher story' or 'the escape story', underlining the way in which information was told to them and stored by them.

What is significant, here, I believe, is the meaning with which Abe today attaches to his own boyhood attempts to invest his parents' tale as epic: 'I always found the epic of the escape quite extraordinary . . . there was the wonder at the accidents that allowed it all to come together'. Most pointedly, he realises that in him was the need to dramatise and find heroes: 'there was a pursuit of anything that would make the story heroic and give the entire event the status of epic'. Today he is less concerned with the heroic stature of his parents' journey from Europe to Australia than he is to understand his own former need to perceive and construct it in these terms. I am reminded here of my own realisation that Peter Weir's film *Gallipoli*— a recasting of the traditional ANZAC story—says more about Weir's contemporary Australia and its rejection of uncritically accepted national and colonial myths than it does about the events of World War I.[28]

Built into the fabric of one's interpretation of past events are clues to the etiology of one's perspective. Abe today can think back sadly to his own boyhood attempts to render his family history heroic, seeing within it evidence of the discord and ambivalence that he felt growing up:

I was a little boy who wanted parents to be proud of. I had ambivalent feelings about them. Yes, they survived, but they were funny refugees. The school I went to—very exclusive, very Anglo—gave their history no meaning. I wanted to be part of the kind of history that other boys had. I wanted the heroic thing, the Anzac thing. It wasn't so much shame I felt, as embarrassment.

A recurrent refrain in the interviews is, as with Abe, the management of discordant emotion. This is illustrated too in Jennie, who was driven by two incompatible urges. One was to do well, to strive towards achievement, to make up for losses already suffered. The other was to stay out of the limelight, to cower, not be herself ('whoever that was'), to keep silent 'about who we were and where we came from'. In her adult life, Jennie today is like many survivors' children, driven relentlessly towards the accumulation of achievement. She is the mother of two small children, has a full-time job, cares for an aged parent and, at the time of writing was undertaking part-time doctoral studies. That she might 'allow' herself to stop, to take a break, seems out of the question. This story is not a single case; it repeats itself. At a conference for the children of survivors, held in Sydney in July 1993, a speaker referred to her own pursuit of achievement as an 'addiction'.[29] This drive is akin to, but in my view, extends far beyond, the well-documented urge of the migrant's child to prove himself or herself in the country of adoption.[30] Thus, if children of migrants are driven to forge a new identity in a new land, children of survivors have both to construct themselves and fulfil the expectations of others that they will replace lost lives. This renders their lives both driven and (too often) discordant. Dori Laub captures the impulse at the core of the relentless drive to rebuild lives: 'In the centre of this massive, dedicated effort remains a danger, a nightmare, a fragility, a woundedness that defies all healing. Survivors . . . keep up this relentless, driven productivity, this fierce *undoing of destruction*'.[31]

While the impression so far may be of children raised in emotionally charged environments, sometimes the reverse seems the case. Perhaps because the emotion was so strong as to threaten to engulf, some survivor households struggled to 'keep the emotions out'. David was raised in this kind of environment. He speaks of being 'excluded from the emotion of it'. While his parents' motivation was no doubt protective, they could not have foreseen the consequences:

Once I started to discover more about what happened, the best word to describe my response was disbelief. I couldn't imagine that my parents as I knew them could have experienced what they did. I tried to imagine it but I couldn't. It was the same with some aunts . . . who had numbers on their arms. My reaction was disbelief. I could not imagine it.

David later had to deal with his own disappointment in himself, that he was unable to visualise his parents in the contexts from which they had come. Jostling also with these emotions was anger—towards his parents, for excluding him, towards those who perpetrated the hurt on his family. Mixed in with the anger was embarrassment. 'These people didn't fight back. After all, in Australia, everyone's father fought in the war. Sheep to the slaughter seemed to me then, in my child's mind, an embarrassing lack of bravery.' With these thoughts comes shame that they are even thought.

About ten years after they came to Australia, David's parents put in writing an account of their wartime experiences. It is a detailed chronology of what happened to them. What characterises the work and to this day still disturbs David about it, is the tone of the writing. It is written as a factual account. All emotional investment in the experiences is bled out of it. One understands the rationale: a written account of the events stands as a historical record. The emotions of loss have no place therein. It's as if survivors who write such accounts fear accusations of exaggeration. The nightmare of not being believed.

The editing out of emotion in emotionally charged circumstances resonates in the literature about postwar refugees. Epstein writes:

> Whenever I asked her what it had felt like to arrive in New York, [my mother] invariably replied that the trip had taken twenty-six hours, that the temperature was over 100 degrees, that she was sweating under all those clothes . . . She never mentioned any emotion.[32]

Memory and Naming

The discordance, the uneasy co-habitation of incompatible emotions, is present in survivors' naming of the children born to them after the war. By tradition, Jews have always tended to name children after family members who have passed on, akin to the tradition in the Anglo world except both parties can be alive at the same time. In the context of the mass slaughter which was the Holocaust, the Jewish naming ritual takes on enormous significance. Children were named for dear ones lost. They were born to replace beings who to them were just names. Sometimes, so many were lost that the naming ritual was bypassed, because, one supposes, it was impossible to decide which name to choose. I was told that the reason so many girls were named 'Eva' ('mother of life') after the war was that the name came to symbolise all Jewish women—'there were too many female dead relatives to memorialise', so 'Eva' stood for them all, a cue to the preciousness of life. I was told of a woman who is the only child of two sole survivors, both from very large families; she always felt she had to be 'the renaissance of them all'.

Sometimes, one child's name remembers one parent's family, the next child remembers the other parent's losses. Sometimes so dreadful was the sense of loss and grief that parents could not bring themselves to force such a daily reminder into their lives. Then a neutral name that had no associations was chosen, the choice itself, ironically, saying more than it seemed, betraying itself. Sometimes a very Anglo name was chosen, sometimes even with Christian associations.

Nearly always, with the name comes a story, or a set of stories, that are conveyed over a lifetime, in fragmented reminiscence. John is typical. He knew that he was named for his father's brother, who died in his father's arms, during the Hungarian army's retreat from Russia. He was intimately aware of his father's grief for the lost brother, and what it meant to carry his name. Like many other survivors' children who have now buried their parents, he also understood the significance of a marked grave at which to bow one's head. Jane, for example, said, 'The fact that I can go to the cemetery and stand by his grave, I recognise that this is something that he could not do'.

Death, burial and memory are intertwined in the survivor. Wiesel captured this in his line, 'We are their cemetery'.[33] In Brett's novel, a young woman survivor of Auschwitz gives birth to a baby boy so frail that death in the current circumstances seems inevitable. The midwife recognises this as a tragedy, knowing that the young woman had already 'buried too many'. The woman's husband returns with, 'She did not bury any', but the meaning is lost (or appears to be lost) on the midwife. To give the baby a better chance of survival, he is adopted out and then buried, metaphorically, in the parents' postwar silence.[34] Children of survivors intuit early that the culture they were born into is not one of peaceful exits.

The drive to remember and the urge to forget are each born of the same pain and are intertwined so closely that sometimes what appears as contradictory can only be understood as different faces of the same emotion. John recalls that so diligently had his mother suppressed the name of her beloved brother that she actually forgot it. Only on her deathbed did it come back to her. And Paul recalls the moment that he understood what it meant for his mother not to have any photos of her parents and sister: 'What hurts me most and I can't remember when I picked up on this, is that my mother doesn't have any photos of those she lost. The only memory she has is what's locked in her brain'. 'Can you imagine what it must be like,' he asked me, 'to have to hold that in your mind, for fear of losing it, because if you lose it, it's gone forever?' These imperatives—not to lose the memory and yet to get on with one's life—constitute the central discordance of survivorhood; and it is a discordance into whose vortex children of survivors were inexorably drawn, being, as they were, both reminders of family gone and symbols of continuing life.

Hirsch's book explores what it meant to survivors to have only a few photos left from that period. Of particular relevance to this book, she writes about what it meant to the children to infer the sanctity of these objects but not to be able to invest them with meaning, hallowed or otherwise. She distinguishes between what she calls 'memory' (the survivor's) and 'postmemory' (that of the child of survivors'): 'Family pictures depend on . . . a narrative act of adoption that transforms rectangular pieces of cardboard into telling details connecting lives and stories across continents and generations'.[35]

An article in a monthly newspaper for parents of young children urges parents to share their family history with their children. There is an innocent, unspoiled exuberance in the exhortation:

> Children have a natural curiosity about the past and a hunger to know about their family's history . . . It gives them a satisfying feeling of connectedness and continuity . . . Family history is documented in simple things like birth announcements and old letters; in a piece of furniture or jewellery that has been passed from one generation to another; in family recipes and holiday traditions and in wedding dresses, medals and trophies stored away in boxes. Recalling where these objects came from, when they were used, or to whom they first belonged can open up a treasure chest of memories.

Of course, the writer of this article is addressing a reader whose family lineage is normal and whole. Indeed there appears to be no awareness that there is any other way to be. How else could she add, 'Sharing your history can be as easy as saying "This is a song my grandma always sang to me"'.[36] For children of Holocaust survivors a lot of her suggestions for maintaining continuity are simply absurd.

Embedded in an entirely different circumstance, Hirsch's work is an intimate interweaving of family photographs, narrative and post-memory. She deftly compares two Holocaust photographs: the one archival, of the extermination camps; the other a stiff, static, domestic household portrait, as was the fashion of the times, with faces front-on to the camera. She writes:

> These two photographs are complementary: it is precisely the displacement of the bodies depicted in the pictures of horror from their domestic settings, along with their disfigurement, that brings home the enormity of Holocaust destruction. And it is precisely the utter conventionality of the domestic family picture that makes it impossible for us to comprehend how the person in the picture was, or could have been, annihilated. In both cases, the viewer fills in what the picture leaves out: the horror of looking is not necessarily *in* the image but in the story the viewer provides to fill in what has been omitted.[37]

The work that the viewer does—imagining the story that surrounds the image in the photo—is closely akin to what the children of survivors did with the fragments of the stories they heard. They tried to fill in the gaps, to join fragments together, to make meaningful connections between disparate, sometime bizarre episodes. Indeed, if the one form of 'work' is visual/imaginative, and its point of departure is absence, the other is acoustic/imaginative, and its point of departure is silence. What both forms of work have in common is the requirement (on the viewer/hearer) to embellish the minimalism of what has been given with information that has been gleaned from the contextual cues of living in a survivor family. Sometimes the reconstructive process interferes with one's sense of one's own boundaries—like when Brett's character, Ruth, discovers family photos of a little girl who looks just like her. She thinks it is her, until she realises that the dates and places don't add up. Then comes the blinding realisation that this little girl, who so resembles her, is her mother's niece, her cousin, born a few years before her, formerly one of the millions of faceless, nameless ones, now a part of herself.

There are survivors' children named after lost relatives, who see the name they bear as oppressive, a tiny symbolic representation and a constant reminder of the burden of duty they bear. This is wrenchingly difficult to admit, and some only do so relatively late in life, often after a great deal of angst and only in the most private and confidential of settings. In public, and for the record, so to speak, they maintain that it is an honour, something of a solemn, unspoken oath to family, present and past. Of course, others are proud of the name and the associated meanings. Some arrive at something like pride after many years of feeling differently. For those for whom the name has been a tyranny, it is one often rendered the more painful by a silent acquiescence and a suppression of discordant contradictory emotions.

From the perspective of the child of survivors, you become a 'memorial candle' to people you know only vicariously.[38] The most intimate and personal thing about you—your name—carries overwhelming emotional significance to others but try as you might, you cannot make yourself authentically connect with such emotions. There is a sense that your life is only ever going to be once-removed. And these discomforts don't stop with you. Descendants inevitably find that the significance of naming takes on another layer when it comes time for them to name their own children. In my interviews, I learned quite early that an effective way to tap into my respondents' emotions and thought patterns was to ask them about names—their own, their siblings', their children's. There is an expectation that the memorialising will continue and sometimes, in tension with that, a yearning for an end to the legacy.

Yet, even without the name as a reminder, children of survivors know theirs is an obligation to make up for lives, talents, a mass of promise lost. Features of family members are remembered in you. Ancestral links are tenuously constructed. Jane says of her father:

> He was always telling me I was like his sister (that I looked like her), and I was like his mother (she was a good person and I am a good person and that's where I got my talent for languages from) and I was a good listener (Who did I get that from?).

You are told that you have your father's sister's nature or your mother's mother's eyes, or a cousin's fiery temper, or a brother's way with words. These remembrances are pressed into your consciousness. Talents remembered in lost ones—'He was the musician', 'She was the mathematician'—are nurtured in you, as you become the opportunity for others to resurrect threads of lives lost and scattered, even if you are musically or mathematically quite ordinary.

And then there are homes where these connections are not made, studiously not made, because the links were severed before the children were born. No one ever told my brother or me that we looked like someone in our parents' families. Any resemblances noted were limited to parental features. The notion of inherited family traits was not one that I had any understanding of until I was grown up. When at age seventeen I saw for the first time a picture of my grandfather, who looked so much like my father, I was completely untutored in the taken-for-granted skill of making generational parallels. In our home, grandparents were rarely mentioned; when they were, it was only by my father, and even then I did not register that his parents were my grandparents. So there was no context in which parallels, analogies, comparisons could be made. None of my very few talents were connected with anyone; the fact that I was tone-deaf and mathematically inept was linked to no one. Today, I'm not sure what's worse: being linked to people you cannot connect with; or being suspended in ancestral space, with no connections further back than one generation.

Jane recalls a period in her life, while her father was still alive, when she obsessively tried to write the family tree. He was the sole survivor of a very large family, with parents, aunts, uncles, cousins and three siblings, all of whom had been married with children—all of whom perished. When the family tree was completed, there were some 500 names, of which over 400 were marked 'died in concentration camp'. The entire endeavour she conceives today as an exercise in memory. A number of survivors whom I have helped to write their memoirs include in their books a family tree and each time I am overwhelmed anew by the annihilation of a family and of a people.

Out of ashes like these are forged some amazing lessons. Jane says, 'We were always told as children what tough stock we came from, that we could handle anything that was dished out to us in life'. Her mother, in particular, told her repeatedly that in life you always have a choice—you choose how to respond to your experience. She now finds that she passes down the same lessons of tough determination to her own children. This is a not uncommon refrain. I found it in my own home, in my father, for whom every day seemed to be a gift of life. Despite everything they'd been through, Leah remembers something distinctly celebratory in her parents' demeanour: 'Their attitude was—we were lucky to be alive in this wonderful country. I remember them telling us about sailing into Sydney through the Heads. After everything they had endured, they felt just so lucky to be alive and everything flowed from that'. Edna recalls with a laugh a favourite line of her father's, one that suggests a touch of the discordance that Yiddish seems so peculiarly adept at conveying: 'It's a pleasure to pay taxes in this wonderful country'.

'Grieving was not something they did, it was who they were'

A major thread in the emotional tapestry of the survivor home is the feelings that attach to grief. The people I interviewed had ageing parents, or had recently lost one or both parents. My approach to exploring the impact of their parents' grief on their lives was by asking them about their own pattern of grief for the loss of their parent(s).

Let's go back a generation. For the parents, the grief experienced for the losses endured in the Holocaust remained an ulcerating wound that defied closure. The losses seem infinite: loss of loved ones, parents, children, siblings, grandparents, extended family; loss of home; loss of neighbourhood and community; loss of liberty; loss of a place in their world; loss of education or the possibility of it; loss of material goods; and loss of a legacy of culture and family memory. There are other deprivations too, some more abstract, though no less devastating: loss of childhood, of youth, of innocence, of promise, of hope.

As abstractions these words seem remote but not when I think of a friend's mother, a woman whose adolescence happened in Auschwitz and Bergen-Belsen. A pretty woman, even in her seventies, she is still somehow locked into a stage of development that never went beyond about sixteen. That's when time stopped.

There is another level of loss, subtle yet pervasive. Arendt writes:

> We have lost our home, our *foyer*, that is to say, the familiarity of our daily life. We have lost our profession, that is to say, the assurance of being of some service in the world. We have lost our maternal language, that is to say our natural reactions, the simplicity of gestures, and the spontaneous expression of our feelings'.[39]

I don't know whether such devastation *per se* is beyond the reach of grief, or whether perhaps the circumstances under which the trauma was experienced, together with the impossibility of responding to the losses at the time they occurred—because to respond in the moment jeopardised one's own survival—meant that any delayed attempts at grief were doomed from the outset. Absence of the evidence of death—a document, a grave, memory of having said Kaddish—means there is no start or end time to mourning.[40] Another interpretation of the grief without end has more to do with duty to remember those who died. Hass writes, 'Mourning in the end means allowing yourself to forget. Holocaust survivors cannot do this because to forget is to betray. The duty of the survivor is to remember. Therefore they cannot achieve closure on their grief'.[41]

My own parents made a decision to live: to have children, to study medicine a second time, to make a home in a new land, among new people, to start again. My sense of their losses is rather like an archaeological dig site. Different strata reveal the detritus of different civilisations. For example, in Israel, the remains of the Arabic civilisation lie atop those of the Romans which lie atop those of the Greeks and underneath all are the Biblical Hebrews. It's layers like these that I think of when I think of the grief of our parents' generation. I see that my parents had intact a layer of consciousness that was the devastation wrought by the Holocaust, and atop this they built their postwar lives. For the most part of those 40 years of reconstruction, not a lot poked through from the lower layers. When it did, though, it was stark and strident, a bone suddenly appearing in the topsoil.

I recall that in the late 1980s and early 1990s, newspapers were replete with the issue of war crimes trials. Letters to editors said, 'What's the point of hauling sad old men before the courts for crimes committed half a century ago?' or 'When will the Jews simply learn to forget and let these old men live out their lives in peace?'. Some even suggested that the Jews ought to take on a little Christian forgiveness and let bygones be bygones.

With comments like these, I imagine there wasn't a survivor alive whose reaction was qualitatively different from my father's. I noticed a lot of movement in the topsoil around that time. Anger erupted from that contained place inside him. Normally a very gentle man, he wrote letters to the newspapers, ripped them up and then redrafted them with furious energy.

Crime and justice have no statute of limitations—this was his argument. Rhetorically, he asked if forgiveness were such a Christian concept, why had Christianity failed to practise it with the Jews, for their alleged deicide, over the past 2000 years? In any case, he said that with respect to people's losses in the Holocaust, neither forgetting nor forgiving were possible, a view I note that Salman Rushdie echoed in a newspaper article about ethnic cleansing in Kosovo.[42]

As a child I heard these words 'forgive and forget', and the reaction to them, many times before I ever knew what they referred to. I remember the flash of anger that leaped from my father when he said, 'We can forget but we can't forgive'—or was it, 'We can forgive but we can't forget'? The fact that I can recall the two words but not his meaning is evidence to me today that at that time, for me, the emotion (rage) was powerfully present but the referential sense (the coherence) was missing.

Because of its complexity and because it is outside the purview of this book, I won't explore further the grief of the survivor generation, nor the issues they encountered in their own ageing process. What is relevant to this study is how their grief, or their failure to grieve, was communicated to their children and with what meanings their children invested the messages they received. These messages themselves were highly differentiated. In some homes, there were overt signs of mourning. The lighting of Yiskor (memorial) candles on Yom HaShoah (Holocaust Day) or on Yom Kippur (The Day of Atonement) was one such event.

This was not a feature of my home. In 1965, twenty years after the war, I was a seventeen-year-old visiting Israel, staying with my aunt. I noticed, on Yom Kippur, the three candles she had lit. Nothing was said. Everyone seemed to know what it meant Unfamiliar with such a custom, as my own parents' grieving was largely invisible, I innocently asked what the candles meant. She pointed to each one in turn and in French, our only language in common, and a voice from which all emotion was removed, she said, '*Mon père, ma mère, ma soeur*'. I did not know till that moment that my father had had a younger sister. I found out that she lived at the moment I learned of her death. And she died at the age I was when I found out about her.

Different survivor families chose different days to mark their grief. The day may have personal significance. Jane's father, who lost 400 family members, used the day they were all taken away as their memorial day. Some seek comfort in the rituals associated with religion. Of course, religion and, more personally, God, have particular significance post-Auschwitz. Many lost their religion after what they experienced. Some found religion. Some had not considered themselves Jewish until thus defined by the Nazis. John remembers that his mother went to synagogue only once a year, on Yiskor, the day of remembrance for the dead. With the black humour that is characteristic of his generation he said, simulating the group names that Jews are often given, after the twelve tribes of Israel, 'I used to call her a Yiskarite'. Today John has his own ritual with his wife and children. He explains:

> On Yom HaShoah we light the six candles (for the six million) and then we name the 33 members of our family taken in the Holocaust. Last year was the first time my middle child had seen me cry. It struck her then that 33 was a lot of people. But she has to know. They all do. They'll find out—in fragments. It comes through at the school. There are the tapes I made. Look, nations fight and people die and killing is never pretty.

Lighting candles, attending services and such like are instances of structured grieving, often public. The private side also emerged in the interviews. Rachel says, 'What is not visible is [my mother's] private grief and she shows that to no one, but to this day she doesn't sleep every second night—there's too much past stuff that's irreconcilable and this sits with her'. Edna recalls that her parents worked hard all week and that Saturday afternoon was when her mother retreated to her bedroom. It was clear to Edna that this was a time of crying and private suffering. She knew at an intuitive level that this was when her mother withdrew into a place inside herself where she could not be reached. In the literature on Holocaust grief, I discovered that the word 'opaque' is often used to depict the child's sense of that unreadable side of their parent's face.

Echoes of the Holocaust resonate in the way survivors' children themselves respond to death. I knew this from my own experience and I explored it with my respondents. At the time I interviewed Elaine she was some ten months into the period of mourning following the sudden death of her husband and having enormous problems coming to terms with her situation. Both her parents were Holocaust survivors and neither of them had properly grieved. Elaine worries that with this kind of role modelling she may be haunted for many years to come. Dan, too, senses that his own protracted grieving for his father, deceased more than six years earlier, is related to the model of protracted grieving in which he himself was raised. Edna speaks in like vein of her parents: 'I think they were always grieving and I think it's the same for me, I'm always grieving'. Rebecca quotes a character from a book she had read:

> My name is Dolores Durer. I'm a Professor of English at Emmings College in Boston. I specialise in the Renaissance. Actually I specialise in grief. I was apprenticed to it early by my mother, who was apprenticed to it by hers. You might call it the family business.[43]

Rebecca sees patterns in herself and her mother, recalling her own emotional dislocation, a kind of affective numbing: in situations when an emotional response would be appropriate, she seems to become separate and aloof, numb to all feeling. Varga describes this in her mother as 'the bleak into-herself look she gets as she shuts the gate on me'.[44] This like-mother-like-daughter parallel reappears many times. Jennie says that her mother seemed to have disconnected from anything that was likely to cause anguish in the attempt to create an affect-free world:

> Mum tried to protect me from the bad things in life. She thought it was better not to know about such things. I learned not to go into things, not to feel other people's pain, to remove myself from things that could affect me. I felt dead inside. But those things are real, they are out there! If you don't have the feelings, you don't have a way of working out what to do with them.

Jill said that when her father died, she spent years being angry at him for 'leaving her', and then later when her mother died, she was overwhelmed with the sense that 'another one's been taken away'. The notion of death as abandonment seemed to have been well transmitted. Leah lost her mother when she was eighteen and her mother 48. Wistfully she said, at age 51, that it was only when she was herself 48, with teenage daughters around the age she had been when her own mother died, that she realised the enormity of her loss and allowed herself to grieve properly for the first time. At the time of her mother's death she now realises she fell automatically into a Holocaustal response to death. She said, 'I didn't grieve for her when she died. I knew I couldn't afford to crumble. I carried on. I knew I was the child of survivors and I had to survive'.

Descendants have lived apprenticed to grief since childhood; when they actually come to grieve for their own parents, many automatically slip into the patterns of grieving that they have imbibed. More, it seems they also tap into unspoken, pre-existing grief. Rather like a bush fire, unleashed by the wind, the recent grief ignites other, dormant losses, and they compound each other. Julia, for example, was never able to get close to her father for he had cordoned off his past and made it forbidden territory. He had lost his first family—wife and children—in the war, something that Julia only discovered when she was a young adult. When he died, not only did she grieve the loss, she grieved for the father she'd never had. Grief for him became indistinguishable from grief for his children by his first marriage:

> It upsets me terribly that I'll never be able to ask him questions. I always wanted to and never got close enough to him to be able to. I wanted some connection to his children. I wanted to know about them—not just that they existed, some emotion from him as their father which connected me to them because he was my father. I'll never know now, I'll never have that connection.

What Julia seems to be mourning here is not only the immediate losses and the loss of what could have been, but something more primordial, the link that binds us to previous generations. With her father gone, so too is her last chance for such a connection. If part of our identity is bound up with our sense of who we are and this derives in part from our sense of our forebears, then Julia is grieving for far more than the passing of her father. A part of her knows that she has never been whole and now probably will never be so. When I think back to the waves of bewilderment that overtook me at the time of my father's death, I am now well aware that Julia's experience is also mine.

Earlier I referred to the silence of host communities towards refugees from Europe after the war, and what this silence did to the migrant's sense of self-validation. In her research into cultural uprootedness, Apfelbaum claims that the disconnection with their past history is devastating for the children of survivors because they have had 'no direct access to the cultural roots of their parents'.[45] Hoffman says in her record of her family's emigration from Poland to Canada, *Lost in Translation*, 'My parents tell me little about their pre-war

life . . . as if the war erased not only the literal world in which they
lived but also its relevance to their new conditions'.[46]

Julia is overwhelmed by the sense that her life is premised on
tragedy. She says 'I was born because of the Holocaust', and the way
she says this, it is clear that she has somehow taken on responsibility for what happened before she was born. The fact is that her
father was previously married to her mother's sister, a marriage that,
but for the war, would most probably have continued through the
seasons of time. The Holocaust swept away that world, leaving a
man who lost his wife and children, and a woman whose sister and
entire family were gone. They married and had a daughter, Julia.
Clearly, it is true that without the Holocaust, she would not have
existed, but equally clearly, her interpretation of that fact—perhaps
aligning herself with her parents—is just that: an interpretation. She
might have seen herself as a redemptive gift, but instead has
constructed herself not only as an outcome of but also as a living
symbol of annihilation. The result is that guilt, shame and responsibility weave a blanket of self-loathing through her consciousness
and across her life.

This story is bigger than one case, Julia's. Many such unions
were forged in similar desperate circumstances. The marriages make
a great deal of sense in psychological, sociological and historical
terms, but there is also an element of ethnic or tribal continuity.
These couplings of 'family remnants' allowed some connection to
that time before everything was swept away. The reaching back into
time also goes further than a few years, seeming to echo a custom
that has its roots in the biblical story of Onan, where it is specified
that if a man dies leaving his wife a widow, she (if she has no
children) is to marry his unmarried brother. The same motif weaves
through the Book of Ruth. Long before I ever studied anthropology,
nor even knew that such a discipline existed, I recall my father's
telling me that these rules on kinship were a society's way of taking
care of those in its midst who were at risk. Of course, these days,
with welfare and superannuation and other modern measures, the
obligation for a widower to marry an unmarried kinswoman is
anachronistic and there are acceptable legal ways of circumventing
tradition. In any case, it would seem that the many unions formed in
the wake of the Holocaust have less to do with religious practice or
anthropological continuity than with a decimated people picking up
the threads of their lives and beginning again.

Achieving coherence

By the time children of survivors grow up, they are usually able to integrate their experience of living in a survivor household with what an educated adult knows about what went on in Nazified Europe. They are able to locate into a larger context which is itself sense-making, instances and events that had no sense to them as a child.

The process of making sense, however, is arduous and does not happen in a neat, linear fashion. The very phrase 'to make sense' has an element of effort, of building, constructing something, as if sense itself has to be put together and reviewed and reinterpreted. David is an example. Aged around 50 at the time of interview, he says that for the early part of his life, what he heard had happened could not be absorbed into his understanding of life as he knew it—'I just could not imagine it'. He said, 'Now I am starting to understand more than I did five or ten years ago. I'm starting to see that it could have happened as it really happened. I can see it'.

The process involves different kinds of pain. There's the pain of not knowing and then there's the pain of finding out. In the case of my mother and myself, these two elements—not knowing and finding out—are particularly demarcated. My mother was a Holocaust survivor who at some point must have made the decision not to talk about her personal experiences, certainly not to tell her children. I had the strong notion, as a child, that she deferred to my father's experience. Unlike her, he had been in concentration camps and she seemed to believe his suffering had been greater than hers. Perhaps the apparent deference also suited her, allowing her, she might have thought, more leeway to be silent. I recall occasionally asking her questions but the answers were vague or angry or meaningless. I learned that asking questions was not only unhelpful, it could be risky, capable of turning volatile without notice. Better not ask.

It was only after her death that I found out about the event which must have turned her life around was described in a book my father wrote about their life together. This event I can only assume seems to have been the single major trauma that extinguished her belief in a just world. On the day of the liquidation of the Vilna Ghetto, as Jews were being loaded up in trucks, she witnessed, but was unable to prevent, her own mother's death. Her mother was booted in the head by an SS guard who had been watching the invalid woman sitting or lying still on the ground. My father wrote that she blamed herself:

She carried two cyanide capsules [one for] her and [one for] her mother. She threw both away after the SS man killed her mother, but she never forgot that her mother had been killed by an SS man's boot when she could have died a quiet cyanide death.[47]

When I recall this moment of finding out, it unfolds in slow motion. I sat on the edge of the bed, turning the page, reading the words, being enveloped by disbelief, re-reading, and then again, then realising that *this was what she carried*, all her postwar life. This is what was being pushed down: when I saw her press down on her lower lip and hold down something, stop it from coming out—this is what it was. When I found out, definitively what happened, then I knew not only what had happened, but the fact that it had been suppressed for so long. This is what I mean by two kinds of pain.

In this inheritance of trauma, my experience of sensing but not finding out what lay beneath, is not at all unusual. Many of my respondents talk of a childhood of cues and fragments and half-messages that took on a larger meaning in subsequent years. Jennie said, reflecting the sentiments of many, 'It only made sense much later, when I was grown up'. Ella said that she read what she could in order to get information to fill in the blanks: 'They were books about people fighting the Germans. But I couldn't fit my parents in the picture. I remember, too, reading about mobile gassing units. I associated this with Jews but not with my parents'. Michael recalls his home life: 'Mine was more of a spluttering learning experience'. He supplemented the process by reading books like *Mila 18*, *Exodus* and *The Diary of Anne Frank*: 'They helped to make sense of what was happening at home'. Elaine says that children think their world is normal. She recalls 'Whatever was going on, whatever craziness there was, it was just normal, you accepted it as normal. It was only when I was about fourteen that I started to look for causes to try to make sense of the situation at home'. Edna remembers early patterns that reveal a child's attempt to find sense in chaos by generalising about the people who came to their house: 'Very early on I decided that everyone who had an accent had been in a concentration camp unless I was told otherwise. Even then, I didn't know what the camps were. I knew it was something terrible but it wasn't until I was an adult that I really knew what it meant'.

A recurrent pattern is hearing words—the word for 'camp' or 'war' or 'ghetto'—but not knowing what these words meant. Sometimes the words were heard in the home language. Sometimes the English words were used but they had no meaning that the child could connect with. *What is this war they talk about? What kind of camp is he talking about? What did they do there? Why did they go there? If it wasn't what they liked doing, why did they stay? What is a ghetto? Why did people go there? What does 'bricking up walls' mean? Why did they stay?* Unanswered questions that swirl around in your head. I recall a time in my late teens when in conversation at home I innocently used the word 'ghetto' to refer to a suburb of Sydney where predominantly one ethnic group resided. This, after all, is a way it has come to be used—the Macquarie Dictionary's first listing is 'a quarter in a city in which any minority lives'. What followed was one of the rare times that my mother's grip on what she otherwise suppressed slipped away, and her rage exploded.

Rena recalls not having any idea what 'the war' meant but visualising it as a massive black thing, like a huge wall, hanging behind and over her parents. Not surprisingly, the word 'Holocaust' was not a part of my respondents' experience of growing up among survivors. 'Holocaust' as a word connotes a more formal, outside, historical perspective of what happened in mid-century Europe. Children of survivors, as one would expect, remember words in Polish, Yiddish, Czech, Hungarian, etc., all of which connoted an insider's perspective. Abe's memory of trying to make sense of it is vivid:

> There are strange images which have stayed with me. One comes from the age of six or seven, a magazine from a local barber's shop, probably 1950s soft porn. There was cartoon page with a drawing of things happening in hell. To me the war was that—it was an image of torture, burning flames, pain, creatures taking gruesome delight in hurting others—one long continuing barbaric maelstrom.

However, if interpreting cues is difficult, reading meaning from absences is even harder. Elsa says, 'I only realised when I saw my own kids grow up that we didn't have grandparents'. Leah says, 'You live with the loss of people who died whom you never knew'. Paul looks back over a confusing childhood and says:

> When you're young you can't see the big picture. All you're seeing is the end results of things—war, migration—you don't have the world knowledge to make sense of it. I had no idea why my mother to this day gets frantic if a bill is not paid immediately. I couldn't make sense

of her fear of any kind of authority, especially uniformed. All I saw was the pressure on me to do all these things, for the family, because I was the only one who spoke English. I was in my twenties before I started to disentangle it all. Once you have the big picture, it changes the way you see your parents.

John's experience of making sense is a little different. It would seem he lost his innocence quite early, for he speaks of a comfortable fit between what he gleaned from his parents and his own embryonic world view. 'Nations fight wars. People dislike Jews. I was a Jew.' Simple, black and white. John's strategy for being able to live with it was to accept it all, unquestioning, as given and then recast it all as irrelevant to himself. He asked no questions, had no curiosity: 'It was all back there. It was nothing to do with me'. When he was a young adult, he says, there was a lot of catching up to do.

Rebecca also used a strategy of distancing in order to manage the trauma that she felt could overwhelm her life. She admits that only in the latter few years, in her late forties, has she been able to tolerate images of the war in her head:

> I'm older now and maturer and I have the strength now. I couldn't face it before because I personalised it. The camps, the stokers, the Kapos. I put myself in my grandmother's shoes and saw her being herded into a cattle car and then into a gas chamber. I couldn't face it. I made the bad image go away. I didn't punish myself for not being able to do it. I knew it was intolerable and beyond me. I'm better now. I still personalise, I still step into their shoes, but I can cope better now.

Making sense seems to be a matter largely of recognising what things go together, seeing associations, making connections. In Rachel's case, the single most traumatic event that made her parents' recovery impossible was the killing of their two young boys in the ghetto. The boys were taken away, probably to the nearby killing fields, and never seen again. She says:

> I don't remember being told about the children but I must have been because I always knew. It was only much later that my sister and I discovered that what our parents felt all that time was guilt and shame that they hadn't been able to save their children. That's what we absorbed at a very close level all our lives without knowing what

it was. I only found out a few years ago just before my father died. I asked him once if he had made peace with God and he started crying that he couldn't forgive himself for not protecting or saving them, that he should have been taken away when they were. I never knew about the guilt. There's conscious knowledge and unconscious knowledge. It didn't connect for a long time.

In some cases, the experiences are so extreme as to defy sense. Bernice seems to have been denied all information regarding her family. In her case, finding out has yet to happen. She was told not even the names of close family members who were lost. Every attempt to find out the names of her grandparents was rebuffed. At school when she studied the war in history, she understood for the first time some of the bizarre details of her home life. The mother apparently had hidden in a bunker in a forest, a kind of underground cave, for many months at a time, where you couldn't make a sound for fear of being discovered; as a child Bernice was often forbidden to speak for long stretches. When finally she was able to make this connection, it represented a tiny ray of light in a very dark world. Years later after she had moved away from home, she wrote a letter to her mother, threatening no further contact unless she was told about the family. In return, her mother sent her four blank pages.

Many children of survivors have gone back to where their parents came from.[48] Some have visited sites that have particularly painful associations for their family. Sometimes it is only when they encounter a three-dimensional reality that they become aware that the image they have constructed in their heads, left over from childhood attempts at making sense, is wholly inaccurate. Sometimes, a visit to the actual places of origin is not necessary: photos are enough to trigger the discordance between inner image and outer reality. Susan says, 'I always thought concentration camps were big yards with lots of people in them. I am always amazed at pictures of concentration camps. They're like big towns, nothing like what I imagined'.

In my family, talk of places in Poland that had once been home was banished to an out-of-bounds area—cordoned off and made inaccessible. I always knew that this tabooed place was outside of a reality I would ever know. In the mind of the child that I was, I thought simply that these places were 'unvisitable'. I look back now and try to reconstruct my understanding at that time of the unvisitability that I inferred. I sensed Poland as a 'there' and my childlike construction of this 'there' seems to have been composed of five elements: distance (*'there' was far, far away*), direction (*people travelled from 'there' to Australia, not from Australia to 'there'*); allowability (*people were not allowed in or out of 'there'*); obliteration (*nothing was left of what once was 'there'*); and hopelessness (*'there' could never be known, would never be known*). And I worked this out not from anything that was said, but rather, as Hirsch says too, from the quality of their voices and from their demeanour.[49]

As an adult, bringing to bear an adult's knowledge of the world, I very slowly came to adjust the perception of 'there' to something more based in reality. In my thirties and forties, when I would hear of people like me going 'back' to places their parents came from, sometimes accompanying them, I was bewildered by a conflict between my adult sense of yes, planes fly to these places, and my child's sense of the unknowable, unvisitable 'there'. I put off any trip until my parents were dead, knowing the impossibility of explaining myself to them. Now, at this moment of writing, it is approaching ten years since I have given myself permission to make this trip, and I have not yet made the flight to Warsaw, though I have many times been in cities only a few hours away. And it is perhaps paradoxical that, now in my fifties, I am beginning to return to my child's perception of 'there': even if one day I go there, what I will find is not what was their home. Their homes are gone. So in this sense it is indeed unvisitable and unknowable. Hirsch calls the feeling I have an ambivalent and conflicted 'curiosity'. She says that the child of European Jewish survivors shares with many of their peers a 'sense of exile from a world we have never seen and . . . will never see . . . a world that has ceased to exist, that has been violently erased'.[50] This engenders a very particular kind of diasporic experience, akin perhaps to what Altounian writes of the children of Armenian refugees who fled abroad.[51] When I visited Janine Altounian in April 2000 in Paris, I asked her if she had been 'back', and she shook her head and looked away. I knew then that her parents' Armenia was unvisitable too. Hirsch calls this an exile from a completed time, 'a space of identity', and sees it as a core defining feature of postmemory. At the end of her book, Hirsch too talks about a trip planned many times and many times postponed. She suspects that the 'unbridgeable distance' of such a journey to the lost places may well have to be replaced by less direct means by which she might 'populate the domestic spaces of (her) imagination'.[52] As for myself, I have plans but

I am still not quite ready, whatever 'ready' means.

Some do make the trip, alone, with parents or after parents have died, or in fearful anticipation of their deaths. Erlich says that by the time he was 16 he'd read everything he could find on the Holocaust 'but I still did not know what actually happened to my mother and father'. Then one day he realised that his parents were ageing: 'their hourglass was slowly running out . . . Don't let them die. We have not spoken yet'.[53] Abe says that only in the last fifteen years has he been able to make some sense out of his experience of growing up in a survivor home. This was triggered by his father's illness, which was when Abe realised that time was running out: 'If he died without me knowing, then there was a part of myself I would never find'. His first step was to go to Poland to enable him to then approach his father: 'I needed to know what I had to ask him'. The tragedy of not making it in time is underlined in Salamon's autobiography:

> My father died two days before my eighteenth birthday. I loved him all the time, worshipped him most of the time, feared him some of the time—but I didn't know him. Until recently, I figured that lack of knowledge was no more than the natural gap in a child's perception of a parent, which can be eventually filled in as everyone grows older, for those lucky enough to find the freedom with age to examine together events that were once too painful to discuss. *Parents remain stuck in time when they die before their children know which questions to ask* [emphasis added].[54]

David's story is an apt one to explore here. He was raised by parents who seem to have made the decision to protect their child from the trauma of knowledge quite early. His father, in particular, didn't want his son to know: 'He almost wanted to stop being Jewish. Being Jewish meant being a victim and he didn't want that for me'. David spent a childhood picking up half-messages, knowing but not knowing. Of the world they came from, he says, 'I tried but I couldn't imagine it. It was a different life, a different planet'. The picture is of a young boy struggling to put the bits together so that they fit, to perceive the whole, to make sense of it. He recalls the pain of knowing that he was on the outside of his parents' world:

> One of the most hurtful days was when this classmate had read out this essay in front of the class about his parents' experience in the

camp and I felt so ashamed that I didn't know anything. I knew my parents must have experienced something like that but I didn't know what it was. I feel resentful that I was not a member of a family that talked. I didn't even share the emotion.

At the end of the interview, I asked him if he wanted to add anything, and he said:

I feel deprived that I wasn't told earlier, that I was made to understand only at a later age when I was much further away from it. I would have liked to have been more part of what was going on, I would have liked to be drawn into those long intimate conversations my parents had with their crowd of survivor friends. I remember those very distinctly, the talking around the table long into the night. There were tears and moments of laughter but predominantly it was very sad where people would sit together and talk on for hours and I could see my father and mother crying. I suppose when one sees one's parents crying you feel guilt especially when you're on the outside. I felt guilty but I didn't understand why and I knew it was linked to their world before. I knew I came later. But it didn't make a lot of sense.

Susan, too, was an adult before she realised the enormity of her mother's wartime experience. Her father did not speak about the war and her mother's answers to questions were minimal and evasive. My impression when I interviewed her was that she had only recently come to understand what her mother had suffered and that she blames herself in some unarticulated way for her belated awareness. In anguish, she addresses her own accusation: 'How could I have made any sense of it? Kids only see other people's lives in terms of their own'.

Susan grew up in peaceful, sunny, urban Australia in the 1950s and 1960s. Nothing that was said in her hearing, in her home, gave her an inkling of what had befallen her parents. As a teenager, she knew that some of her friends had parents who had been in the camps 'but I never thought of my mother in that category'. It would seem that she knew bad things about the war, but underplayed her own mother's involvement. She externalised the trauma: it was 'something Jewish', something that happened to 'other people', to friends of theirs, but she never allowed it 'into the family'. As a protective device, this perhaps allowed her to grow to adulthood without full awareness but sadly, it no longer protects. She says of the moment when she found out what Drancy must have been like: 'I suppose all the background, everything you know, all comes flooding in, from all the things you have learned in regard to other people, then you apply it to your mother, and the horror overwhelms you'.

Susan's ignorance of the conditions at Drancy derives, simply, from the fact that her mother had not told her. Even after the Drancy documentary, and Susan's newfound understanding of where her mother had been, there was no follow-up communication; it was stymied now as before by a role-reversing need to protect the other from further pain:

> I may have mentioned to her that I watched it but we never discussed it. I couldn't show her how upset I was. My pain would trigger hers, or would make her feel more resolved that she did the right thing by not telling me more. Any case, if I'm upset, I can't be a strength to her.

Susan is one among many. After half a lifetime of sense-making, survivors' children have reached middle age, and have their own children; by then they have generally been able to calibrate the memory of oblique and disguised messages against an adult's world knowledge. The reward is hard-earned and often comes at great cost. But at least, finally, almost definitively and with bitter brutality, it makes a kind of sense.

6

Holocaust Narrative

'a space between speech and silence'[1]

The discourse patterns of survivor homes are complex. Zable recalls the contrasting ways in which his parents fought 'to keep their ghosts at bay', his mother predominantly through silence, and his father through words constructed to make sense of the experience. Yet, he says 'the camouflage has always been transparent' and, within both parents, he has 'always known a simmering sorrow, despite their efforts to disguise it'.[2]

Despite the complexity, within the literature on survivor homes there is a reductionist tendency, a wish to simplify the elements. This has led to the notion of two kinds of homes, one in which there was an 'endless account of tribulation' and one constructed around a 'pact of silence'.[3]

In very broad terms this is true but only in so far as these two kinds were extreme points on a continuum of response. In fact, as my research uncovers, there are myriad points on this continuum, countless ways of telling and not telling. In other words, the crude division into binary categories of those who talked and those who didn't is facile and impressionistic, and does not stand up to the scrutiny of research. This view also fails to understand the pragmatics of communication, the way in which meanings constitute an 'achieved phenomenon', being co-constructed by both willing and unwilling participants.[4]

Instead of a 'homes with talk/homes without talk' view, I want to suggest that Holocaust narrative might be placed on a continuum, from homes where communication was explicit and direct to homes where the past was hermetically sealed off. To construct an analysis of the discourse of survivor homes, I will artificially create three points on this continuum. I will begin by writing about those homes where the text of the narrative was relatively unproblematic, enabling more or less direct and explicit communication to be achieved. I then explore indirect communication with meaning being constructed through a subtle interplay of text and context. Following that, in Chapter 7, I will go on to explore the third point on the continuum, unspoken communication, where meaning was constructed outside of text or with the aid of very minimal text.

Direct Communication

Our journey into the pragmatics of Holocaust narrative begins with direct communications, the least problematic domain. Communications that we call 'direct' are based in text or words, and happened in three ways: in face-to-face conversation, in written memoirs and in recorded interviews (audio or video).

Only about a quarter of my respondents reported coming from a home which featured direct spoken communications about their parents' Holocaust past. The kind of accounts that might be classified here are one-on-one interactions in which the spoken text itself was an adequate carrier of meaning. Of the 27 people interviewed, only one, Paul, a computer specialist in his late forties, reported what he called an uncomplicated discourse that was equally comfortable with both parents. While my impression of the home he described was that its circumstances were not qualitatively different from many others whose offspring I had interviewed, Paul nevertheless insisted that its communication was unproblematic.

Paul recalls life in the home where he grew up as emotional and hectic with 'a lot of stuff going on' that he was not able to interpret until he was an adult. Traumatised by the war, and never able to acculturate to the new land, Paul's parents were content to remain always dependent on the language skills of their two sons. They constructed a small Hungarian enclave of close relatives and a few survivor friends—'of course, a relative included anyone from the same town'. As a child he knew they were different but didn't know whether this was 'the migrant factor or the Jewish factor'. He remembers the defensive and highly constrained world they lived in, constructed to avoid any brush with authority, especially people in uniform. Having been swept under when their world spun out of control, they formulated life in Australia as a risk-avoiding experience: 'We pulled out of situations where there could be problems. It's like if you can't drive, you don't drive. You constrain your life into a small world that is controllable, and there you stay'.

Nevertheless, Paul insists that in regard to the Holocaust, there was a flow of information which was uncomplicated and responsive. He remembers asking questions and always being answered satisfactorily. He comments that while his parents never initiated the talk about the war, they always responded when asked. Comparing himself and his younger brother, he says, 'I liked to ask questions, so I found out a lot. My brother never asked, so he doesn't know anything, even today he still doesn't know'. Paul seems to have had an intellectual curiosity that his brother lacked.

Paul admits that as he was growing up he was complexed about the Jews as a victim people and was drawn to stories of heroism and resistance—in history books, fiction and in the tales he heard around the table at home. Of the survivor community with whom his parents mixed, he says:

> We'd sit around the table and they'd talk. Every survivor has a unique story on how they survived, about that fine line between life and death . . . I wanted to know. Those were their best years that were destroyed. The Germans took a beautiful part of their lives which they could never get back. I was interested in that. It was emotional but it didn't upset me.

He willingly re-narrates little vignettes about the miracle of escape and the myriad coincidences and feats of daring that he heard growing up. One story was about his father's escape to the forest, toward the end of the war. There he was discovered by a group of Russian soldiers. They were on the point of killing him when he called out that he was Jewish, and only wearing a German uniform because he took it to help him escape. It turned out that one of the Russian soldiers was Jewish and he spoke to him in Yiddish, which Paul's father understood but could not speak. He pulled down his pants to show that he was circumcised but the Russian officer was not impressed. Then he recalled a prayer from his *bar mitzvah* and started chanting it. The officer recognised it, and this saved his life. Stories like this clearly captured the young Paul's imagination and heightened his curiosity.

When I commented that I was surprised at the unproblematic discourse of his home, given the background circumstances, the loss and trauma of their dislocation, he suggested that because his parents were simple village folk, uneducated before or after the war, they themselves were less complicated than those who came from, say Budapest or Vienna or Warsaw, people educated into the professions, with a more urbane and sophisticated experience of life. Maybe, he adds, his kind of home was 'simpler, less analytical, more spontaneous'. And less problematic.

I explored Paul's case in greater detail perhaps than many others, because it was the major 'discrepant evidence' in my research.[5] Yet, the feature that allows me to see its compatibility with the rest of the data is Paul's statements about his willingness to ask questions. It would seem that the listener's receptivity, that is, the extent to which hearing was considered possible, is intimately connected to speakability. That is to suggest that the one enables the other. People will tell if the telling is allowed. This will be explored towards the end of this chapter, when the issue of 'granting permission' is raised.

When we think of how children of survivors found out about the events pertaining to their parents' trauma, we usually think that this means in conversation of a private kind at some time in the past. It says a great deal about the difficulty of communicating person-to-person, that so many survivors have over the years taken to taping, writing down and, in some cases, publishing their memoirs. This genre even has a name—'witness testimony' or 'survivor accounts'—mostly pursued by people who were not otherwise writers. At Yale University, in 1981, a Video Archive for Holocaust Testimonies was established. The co-founder, Dori Laub, has written extensively about the act, process and multi-level nature of witnessing. He writes:

> It is not by chance that these testimonies ... become receivable only *today*; it is not by chance that it is only now, *belatedly*, that the event begins to be historically grasped and seen ... This *historical gap* ... underscores the fact that these testimonies were not transmittable, or integratable, at the time (emphasis in the original).[6]

My father wrote a book, ostensibly addressed to my brother and me, called 'A letter to my children'. Here he recorded in roughly chronological order his and our mother's experiences from 1939 to 1947. David Kaye, a survivor from Hungary, documented his experiences in *I Still Remember*, a book written for his son and grandchildren. Genia Biggs' escape from a Poland under bombardment to the faraway steppes of Russia was recorded in a book that was written with her two sons in mind. In Henrietta Bochenek's *A Letter to Jane*, the author, again addressing her child, places her family's experience on the record. These are a few of the writings with which I have personally had some contact. I imagine there are many others, mostly known only to family members.[7]

Every case that I know about happened in English. This is not insignificant, especially in cases where English proved difficult to learn, starting as they were, late in life. What English might have lacked in ease, however, it offered in comfort. For those Jews who sought refuge in the West, English was the language most closely associated with liberation and survival. Young writes that many regarded English as 'a neutral, uncorrupted and ironically amnesiac language'.[8]

And anyway, if not English, what? Yiddish was rejected because it was too close to the experience of loss, and in any case, inaccessible to the next generation. European languages like Polish or German or Hungarian were rejected because they were too close to the language of the perpetrators. As Young points out, survivors often found that 'English serves as much as mediation between themselves and experiences as it does medium for their expression'.[9] It is, furthermore, the language of their children and the future and closely linked to their reasons for telling.

English is also a language, it was suggested to me by Elaine, one of my interviewees, that places limits on the expression of trauma. Apart from Shakespeare, she said, there's lacking in English a language of tragedy. There's richness in English, but it's not rich in tragedy. Yiddish, she countered, was well placed to express suffering. This may in part explain why English is both a good and a bad choice: good, because it placed external constraints on the expression of pain; bad, paradoxically, for precisely the same reason.

When the urge to tell is overwhelming, it is not difficult to appreciate the choice of a written over a spoken medium. Writing distances the addressee in time and space and removes the constraints of real-time communication. It offers a safety that face-to-face telling extinguishes. It allows one the opportunity to choose one's words carefully, make revisions and redrafts, amend, delete, find a better word. It distances the teller from the emotion of the audience's response, sealing off the unfolding narrative from the volatile reactions being induced. No wonder, then, that a characteristic feature of this genre, and for the children reading the work, a highly disturbing one, is the stark absence of emotion.

Yet, if writing is easier than speaking for some, it is certainly beyond the capacity of most survivors, now ageing, often frail, and hardly confident to write in a language that their grandchildren can understand. For them, two avenues of communication remain. One is a series of audio-taped recordings made by a trained interviewer. These are then catalogued and copies made—such as in the Eleventh Hour Oral History Program. In the late 1980s, a video archive for Holocaust testimonies was set up at Yale University; one of its purposes was to enable the tellers and the listeners (survivors and their children, respectively) to discuss, perhaps for the first time, 'the pervasive if wordless Holocaust presence in their lives'.[10] More recently, the Shoah Foundation, funded by Stephen Spielberg, has sought to construct a global database and video library of Holocaust experience. This is a mammoth project with a team of professional interviewers, human resource management personnel and audio-visual technicians that has swept across the continents where survivors may still be found, seeking out testimony before it is too late. The interviewing process is lengthy and arduous; the end-product is a taped testimony. A copy of the tape is given to the survivor, who almost invariably passes it straight on to children or grandchildren.

These testimonies serve a public 'on the record' function, but also a very important private family one as well. They often stand-in for the stories never told. For some children of survivors, the videotape is their first sustained exposure to their parents' story. For others, it may also be, but it hasn't yet been watched.

Indirect Communication

We turn now to the dominant discourse type in Holocaust homes, that of indirect communication.

We have seen earlier that direct communication makes full use of explicit text to carry meaning, with little left to context, inference, speculation or reconstruction. The listener's role, in other words, is quite straightforward. In the case of indirect communication we have a style of discourse where speakers no longer rely solely on text. Here meaning is made up in part of text, but also in part of the sense that is construed and constructed by the listener, who achieves this by calibrating the text heard against the context in which the text is heard.

A simple example will illustrate how text and context interweave to construct meaning. Imagine two members of a family are at home and there's a ringing sound from the front of the house. One person (whose hands are wet because she's peeling vegetables in the kitchen sink) says to the other, 'That's the front door'. It would be quite ordinary for the second person to place this text, 'That's the front door', in the context of door bell and wet hands and interpret the remark as a request to open the front door. Indeed, not to do so would be odd.

Such meaning depends on inference. What happens is that the hearer of an indirect message will assume that the speaker is rational and communicative and will infer the meaning of the text by placing it within the context of shared knowledge of speaker and listener. In the pages to follow, we will see how this co-construction of meaning operated in survivor homes: how text-in-context operates inter-connectively to infuse elliptical or dissonant messages with meaning. Thus if a message is only 'half there' or its tone is discordant, people naturally look for an interpretation that 'fits'.

This is a view of verbal communication that sees it as 'an achieve-ment', as the collective activity of social actors whose spoken production is more than the sum of its parts. This is a polyphonic perspective—one that identifies and gives credit to multiple voices involved in the production of text. In this conceptualisation of the activity of speaking, there is no single ownership: the speaker and the audience or hearer function as co-authors of the text which is jointly produced even if only one party actually speaks. This is because interpretation requires the active collusion and complicity of the interlocutor whose involvement actually, if invisibly, shapes the unfolding nature of the text. The dramatic realisation of this very ordinary everyday fact can be seen in the theatre where every night an actor can deliver the same lines but every night 'the audience has the option of creatively assigning new meanings to what is being said on the stage'.[11] Thus, the mechanics of interpretation are only partially contained in the text itself; they are also partially contained in the being(s) who serve as audience for the text. In terms of Holo-caust narrative, this view of language spotlights the role of the listener in the co-construction of text. In the case of children of the survivors of trauma, the interpretive work of the listener is so much the greater because the text with which he or she has to work is so minimal.

Fragments: a shattering of lives and memory

Because the Holocaust shattered lives, it is perhaps not surprising that what is told to the next generation is entirely fragmented. Survivor parents did not sit their children down and give them a history lesson. In any case, even had they been able to meet the emotional demands of such a task, very often the parents did not know the history outside their own story. Paul says of his parents, who came from a small Hungarian village before the war: 'They could relate what happened to them, their family, the people around them, but not what happened, not the picture, not even today. I heard about their losses but I never heard the word "Holocaust" '.

Nor did they, in many cases, tell their children about their lives before the war, about their childhood, the cultural world obliterated by the Holocaust. There are many reasons for this 'before-the-war silence', as Epstein calls it.[12] Edna refers to nostalgia as a Pandora's box: 'If you speak about the family that was, you have to share the awful things that happened. Better just to close it all off into a total void'.

At the core of the pain enveloped in nostalgia is the recollection of a world crushed underfoot. Whenever my father would start to tell me about his childhood home, it was only a few moments before his eyes would mist and he would turn away to regain his composure. I sensed that he paid dearly for every lapse into nostalgia. My mother seemed never to allow nostalgic thoughts in, rarely lost her composure and therefore rarely had to struggle to regain an outer poise.

Nostalgia was something that few survivors could indulge in with impunity. Often they spurned it, or steeled themselves against it, or as Zable says of his father, rebelled against it. It always came at a cost. The glimpses we had of pre-war life were momentary and often romantically idealised so that even in the unsophistication of our youth, we could tell that more was being suppressed than was being said. There was fragility in these rare forays into a sealed-off past that hinted at the energy spent to keep things under wraps. This of course to some extent varied: there were homes where nostalgia was managed reasonably well, allowing the parents a place from which to draw positive and nourishing memory. Nevertheless, it seems to me that nostalgia is a problematic construct for my generation.

I frequently glimpsed among the people I interviewed a very particular kind of interest in the world of their parents. It seems rather like the archaeologist's enthusiasm for relics from former times, or the social historian's fascination for memorabilia of a certain era. There's a quality to their interest that in fact speaks about the unavailability of what attracts them. This might be related to a comment Leah made which troubled me at the time and still does: 'When our parents have gone, we face this awful informational loss; what we know now is that we'll never know. But there are lots of people who have unproblematic ancestry, who have no interest at all in their past. Why?' While I have no answer to this question, I sense that Leah has hit upon something significant: ironically, memory may be the only outward marker of ancestral rupture.

Epstein's book is a reformulation of fragments remembered from childhood. With mother and grandmother as dressmakers, she weaves the scraps of stories she heard among the scraps of materials left over after a day's work. Her mother 'would sometimes pin her present onto a scrap of her past and tell me a story about my grandmother' (1997: 13). The metaphor is extended:

> It was in the workroom that I fell in love with the dead women in my mother's family. At the end of the day ... I collected threads and scraps of stories, hoarding them, mulling over them. Each one seemed cut from a different kind of cloth. Each was distinct. There were no seams, only wide gaps in the fabric. My mother would never have made a dress the way she told these stories. There was something wrong in their proportions and some disturbance in her telling that prevented them from making a whole. My mother was a master at joining parts. She would scrutinise the way a sleeve or skirt joined a bodice and if the juncture was not perfect, it would preoccupy her until she found a resolution. If necessary, she would let her mind work overnight, then rip everything apart and fix it in the morning. But she never fixed the way she told her past. The parts never fit. They remained separate and discrete. These disjunctures fascinated me. I was never much interested in the construction of clothes but always drawn to the construction of stories, to what was said and what was withheld.[13]

Epstein's story of accumulated fragments is not unlike Naava Piatka's nostalgic play *Better Don't Talk* in which the playwright/actor recreates on stage her life as the daughter of actress Chayela Rosenthal, a survivor of the Vilna Ghetto. In her one-woman show, Piatka portrays herself and her mother, moving between the two roles with a seamlessness that suggests the highly permeable boundaries of survivors and descendants.[14]

A common refrain, then, among my respondents is this sense of having heard the Holocaust as fragments, scattered over many years. They talk about it 'leaking out', about 'accumulating details', about 'disjointed' information. Paul refers to 'all sorts of pointers, as you're growing up, that your family has come through a tragedy'. Abe admits, 'It was difficult putting it all together because I was told different bits at different times'. Until his mother wrote her memoirs for her family, Dan said, 'I had no chronology, only a set of episodes and events. There was no sequence'. Jennie says 'I have an uncertainty about the chronology. Even when I go over and over it, I still remain unclear'. Elsa says, 'It's no wonder language breaks down. Language is social. Talking about the Holocaust is anything but social'. What we have here is the result of what Hass calls 'the survivor's typical pattern of fragmentary disclosure'.[15]

Among my respondents, the yearning for a chronology is palpable: 'All I've got is a few stories', says Julia, 'the scar on the leg, the story about the good German who gave my father the sausage, and the escape from the train. I desperately want a time-line'. Michael says, 'I was told nothing, but I had glimpses. The idea that they left behind whole families, that they were on the run, that something really bad happened . . . I have a sense of my mother as a young woman who's just surviving, trying to merge in with families in order to have something to eat and somewhere to stay. She kept on moving, passing as a Russian, never admitting to being Jewish, always on the lookout, trying to blend in and not be noticed'. All the episodes for him blur into this stream of being on the run. David recalls having 'snippets' and knowing early not to ask, as does Susan:

> You sort of only pick up little things as they years go by . . . you never find out really, you get little bits of it when it's offered. Like she mentioned the new laws, which meant she couldn't go swimming any more. And now I can't separate out the bits and put it together, it's too vague. I don't have the details. I'm stuck in one scene—when she was separated from her mother at fourteen. I can't get beyond that.

Even if survivors had given their children a linear biographical account of events it would still have been too abstracted from a coherent wider history and a meaningful context to make much sense to someone outside the experience. Even where the parents were well educated and knowledgeable about the events leading to the cataclysm, it is rare that they are able to see it outside of living it. In any case, there has to be a gulf between contemporary witness account and hindsight commentary. Reportage has that quality of being caught in the moment that makes it an entirely different genre from historical account.

The end result is a generation with 'almost no access to the repressed stories that shaped them'.[16] Not surprisingly, the motif of absence weaves in and out of postwar Jewish writing. Nadine Fresco calls it 'absent memory'. Henri Raczymow writes of what it means to be orphans of a world that one never knew, and the sense of perpetually seeking something beyond one's grasp: 'if the earth is turning to the right ... I must turn left to catch up with the past'. Alain Finkielkraut constructs contemporary Jewish identity as 'the acute consciousness of a lack'.[17]

Hass asks: 'How does one cut out the middle section of one's life and maintain a continuity between the before and the after?'.[18] Perhaps our own dislocation derives from the fact that we grew up in our parents' 'after' but were steered by the 'before'. It seems to me now, looking back, that the net effect of exposure to the fragmentation of our parents' stories was that we had modelled for us a kind of lifespan discontinuity.

Vignettes

The fragments that the second generation came away with at best made some kind of internal sense. Often these were stored and retrieved as small visual 'cameos', like the escape story, or the story of the train jump, or the arrival at Auschwitz. Here what the child grows up with is a constellation of intact stories, mostly without connecting links. Having been told repeatedly over the years, these become windows through which the children glimpse their parents' history.

Michael says, 'I have this scene in my head. It never changes. My mother's mother walks her to the station, gives her a few coins and a lunch pack, and pushes her onto the train'. Michael uses present time to describe the scene: the event is set and relived in the eternal present. This view that his mother had of her mother, and her little sister by her side was the last she was to have, as she was escaping, then unwittingly, from the horrors about to befall her family. The scene has been replayed endlessly in this family, blurring boundaries, and becoming, a generation later, Michael's memory as well as his mother's.

It says something about the nature of narrative that the limited access to their parents' past that my respondents achieved was largely episodic, in the form of a subset of stories. It seems that in most Holocaust homes, in the first twenty years after the war, these stories became a *leitmotif*, each unique to the particular home, but many bearing remarkable resemblances across a generation. I have come to consider these cordoned-off stories as the speech event most manageable for this purpose, providing one small way that the topic of the war could be broached and survive the distance of the telling.

Each one of my respondents, when asked about any little family vignettes that carried information about the parents' wartime experience, immediately recognised the genre and named a few. For Sam, it was the baby born with his mother's help, in a train taking them to Austria—the pregnant woman was forced to endure the birth silently, so that they would all evade detection by the guards. For Richard, it was the moment when his father, passing as a Christian Pole travelling on a trolley car outside of curfew, could have been betrayed—but wasn't—by an old school mate who recognised him. In stories like this, each unique yet resonant, the telling did not fragment but managed to sustain itself. Perhaps this was because the tension mounting in the unfolding narrative dictates its own momentum; or perhaps it was the reassuring fact that the narrator is alive and present, there with you, so there is the chance of 'a happy ending'.

These stories take on the character of myth within the family. Jane was the eldest of three siblings. The children didn't speak much about their understanding of where their parents came from, other than to refer among themselves to the stories their parents told—giving them names, like the 'potato peel story', the 'schoolteacher story', the 'pillow story'. The potato peel story was about how their mother survived Auschwitz through smuggled potato scraps. The schoolteacher story described the moment of being slapped and betrayed by a Pole (who in a former life was a much admired high-school maths teacher) recruited by the Germans to guard the ghetto. The pillow story was about the mother's first night at Auschwitz. With a group of girls from the same transport, she lay cramped together on the cold floor. They worked out that as she was a little plump, if she stretched out and lay on her back, the others could use her body as a pillow—as close to a satisfactory arrangement as they could muster in the circumstances. The fact that the stories had names meant a referencing system was established, a kind of infrastructure for one family's narrative myth. I recall that when my brother referred a few years ago to 'the train escape' in the context of our mother's survival, I was struck that he knew about that too but I have no recollection of our both being present when it was told.

If all of us have had stories told to us, we have processed the narrative event in different ways. For some, such as Richard, the allusion to the past often carried a moralistic overtone: 'I'd complain that there was no hot water and then he'd tell me the story about how they'd had to dissolve snow and ice to get some water to wash in'. For others, the stories were the thread of the fabric that held them together as a family, affording shared moments of intense belonging. For instance, Abe says 'it was usually around the dinner table, a bit like Pesach, I'd say, "Tell me the story of . . ." and they would. There was a kind of undertone—that this was the most exciting time of their lives'. Their phrase—'with nothing we survived'—becomes a refrain by which the parents reframe and editorialise their past. When Abe says it, it's quite clear, not only from the inverted syntax, but also from the slight Polish Jewish accent that he adopts for the occasion, that this was a defining moment of the home in which he was raised. It's the same for me, with 'Food is not for playing', a rebuke I would unwittingly incite by moving bits of food around on my plate rather than eating them.

However, if stories are more or less intact as individual cameos, the seeming tapestry of stories—'little survival vignettes all strung together', as Elsa calls the phenomenon—is never really a whole. The overall picture remains fractured and fragmented, resisting unity even while the individual stories in their own right have a coherence. It's as though, even when you can't understand why this might have been happening, when and where to whom and why, you can successfully hold in your mind the idea of a train trip and an escape over a wall and hiding out in a forest. Indeed, perhaps we clung to these notions because, ironically, they had some kind of storybook familiarity. We recognised the genre perhaps: a situation requiring remedy, a build-up, a set-back perhaps, a climax and then maybe some kind of resolution. So even when the events are so bizarre as to fail to make sense as a whole, there is yet something in the unfolding nature of narrative that makes them resonate with the listener and remain as memory.

In Irene's home, there was a chronic undercurrent of ill-feeling between the father and the daughter, and very few points of shared reference. Stories served them by establishing a tenuous connection:

> I used to ask my father to tell us more stories or even to tell us the ones we'd already heard. It was like an adventure. I knew it wasn't, but we could sort of pretend it was. I wonder whether we got a sense that he liked telling the stories, sharing something with us, when there wasn't much else he could share.

For Irene, stories were the one safe place where the conversation did not inevitably degrade into a traumatic moment. Yet even the stories came to frustrate her because her knowledge was never larger than the parts; it was a collection of vignettes that did not connect, one with the other. She couldn't work out where one story happened in relation to another, so she was left with half a dozen different plots and characters that could have occurred concurrently, consecutively, or in any order.

If Irene's father seems to have responded to the children's need for connection with his past, this was not necessarily typical. In other cases, a parent told and retold the same vignettes didactically, to convey a moral point or a lesson-in-life. In John's case, the father would re-tell little survival vignettes, always ending with a lesson about what one does to survive. John says, 'It irritated me because here we were in Australia and he wanted me to learn how to protect myself and be prepared but I didn't want to learn how to box or do judo and I used to think, "For what? What do I have to be prepared for?"'

My mother spent a number of war years passing as a Polish Christian. On occasion, she was sheltered by people who knew she was a Jew. Others may have suspected but did not ask; some betrayed or threatened to betray her when they found out. One lesson she learned, and passed on, was that there was no visible outer sign, like the trappings of social class, that would indicate who would be a rescuer, who a bystander and who a collaborator, though something I picked up was that she was more likely to trust poor, uneducated, country people than wealthy, urban, educated ones.

This may have been influenced by her left-wing political beliefs. It certainly stamped her postwar perspective, and this was filtered down to me in odd fragments of stories, more in little epithets, such as 'you can never tell where courage is until courage is called for'. I remember tossing that around in my mind endlessly, teasing out all the permutations and ambivalences, milking it for more meaning than probably it was ever intended to convey. One story I put together over the years was about a period of the war when she passed as a country girl, staying with a farmer and his wife, working as a farm hand, sleeping out with the animals in the shed. She changed the way she spoke so that her urban upbringing and her university education were disguised and of course, so that they wouldn't suspect she was Jewish. During this time the wife fell ill and there was nothing to be done—a doctor and medications were unavailable because the farm was very remote, because it was dangerous to move about and because, in any case, the cost would be prohibitive. But my mother was a doctor and was not able to stand by and do nothing, so when the farmer was not around, she would attend to the woman (I think this involved draining a wound). Gradually the woman's temperature came down and she improved and the farmer was delighted but somehow he found out that 'the new girl' had been spending more time in the house with his wife and he became suspicious. He ordered her to him and demanded an explanation. She said that she'd once worked in a hospital in one of the big cities, cleaning floors and there she'd seen the nurses clean the patients in this way. He looked at her long and hard, as if reviewing everything she had told them about herself, everything that until then, they had accepted at face value. Then he told her 'not to be there in the morning'. She disappeared during the night. I gather she never knew whether he suspected her of being a Jew and therefore wanted to turn her in; or whether he suspected her of being a Jew and was fearful of being discovered sheltering her. Either way, her time there was up. Wrapped up with the words that brought this story together for me was the sense of her gratitude: after all, he gave her notice; he could have simply betrayed her to the Germans.

In Elaine's case, too, the father's purpose in retelling the vignettes was to pass on valuable lessons about survival:

The point was always the same—how to be brave, how to keep up your spirits, how terrible things can happen but you *can* get through it, you don't have to be scared, you can take risks, you can stand up for yourself, or you can run away. He'd always end with a strong dollop of optimism.

Some survivors, like Elaine's father, reframed their own survival as predicated on skills like these. You can see why such an interpretation is more palatable than the other one, the view that says whether you died or lived was as random as a lottery.

If these narrative cameos impart a meaning, which they doubtless do, it is nonetheless a particular kind of meaning. It is an understanding that is largely static: it hardly grows, deepens or rounds out with time or with repeated tellings. My impression is such vignettes are snap-frozen in form at the moment of the first telling. The story of the escape from the ghetto somehow bears the same features the first time it was heard, and the fortieth. In my case, I know the story of my mother's jumping off the train just as I knew it when I first heard it as a child. Since then, of course, I have found out some of the contextual details: the train was headed for Majdanek; it was taking the last residents of the Vilna ghetto to their certain death; and my parents, who had survived two years in the ghetto, were separated—men to one side, women to another—when the ghetto was liquidated. Although I have added layers of historical fact to the picture of my mother's escape, my understanding of it is really is no deeper today, some 40 years later.

Snap-frozen in this way, the original tellings have a peculiar stillness. Perhaps it's the shock in which they are first heard, the immobilising emotion that is never allowed to resolve itself, break up and re-assemble, progress to another way of being. Each time a reference is made, even obliquely, to the event, the same emotion washes over, obliterating anything but the feeling in its wake. This perhaps accounts for the fact that so many second generationers can't remember even basic facts about their parents' experiences. Rachel says, of her parents who lost two children in the war, 'I do remember asking their names but I found them hard to remember'. I have the same experience with the names of the Holocaust dead of my family— five people in all, not many compared to the large extended families that some people lost. It took me many years to 'learn' their names— and this in a teacher who can know and comfortably use 30 new students' names after an hour's contact. Fifty years on, it remains an effort of will to bring their names into focus.

From the point of view of the teller, survivors seem to have only told the stories whose telling they had mastered, the ones that were somehow within their comfort zone, or rather, a manageable level of discomfort. It was as if they had cordoned off their emotions for the sake and duration of these stories. This accounts too for the impression their children have of hearing the stories in an emotionless vacuum. Once they were confident that they could deliver this telling without spillage, without a breakdown of outward poise, they stayed with that version. Thus it was that we came away with the impression that we knew only a small fraction of what was to be known, that what we were told was only part of the picture, and, ultimately, that this is how it would remain. We would never find out from them. I have heard of many cases where the child finds out key information about the parent only after viewing the video made for the Spielberg Foundation. Michael, who wanted to make a film about his mother, was constantly thwarted by her refusal. Later he would acknowledge that it was her inability to tell the story differently from the way he had always heard it—monochrome, bare facts, no details, no emotion. It was locked in time, shut away from her conscious memory. It would seem that for the sake of sanity, she had long before banished it from the zone of tellability.

Some respondents report the aura of secrecy. There is the sense that there were things that we didn't know about and were not supposed to know about. The cues were many: exchanged looks, swift topic shifts, a switch to a different language, voices raised in a nearby room, but lowered when we walked in. Then some of us overheard snippets of what was not meant for our ears. Some were sat down, when they were older, and told something like, 'your father is actually your uncle. Your father died in the war'. When these discoveries are made, the sense that there had been a secret all along is vindicated, and one wonders, what else is there that I don't yet know?

Apart from the outer cues to secrecy, two explanations can be found. One was the fact that the version we heard of events was somehow laminated—static and unchanging.[19] We didn't get details, different angles on the same event. It sounded pre-packaged, rehearsed. We knew we were hearing only a version, something that had been vetted and allowed through. This quality of lamination may account for the impression, somehow, of an unconvincing alibi. Second was the fact that there *were* things untold, perhaps not deliberately, perhaps not through policy, more through delay, procrastination and default. Over time, what is not told, what is kept from telling, becomes secrets. Different experiences, too, generate different degrees of willingness to talk. Survivors who had a more active role (for example, in the Partisans) spoke more freely about their wartime experiences than those whose resistance was constituted of the superhuman effort to stay alive. These latter tend to be more silent. Some heroisms are less glorious perhaps, less socially sanctioned, less able to move from the private realm of experience to the public realm in narrative.

My impression is that the worst things imaginable a human being can face—having your baby ripped from your arms and bashed to death against a wall, witnessing horrific cruelty to a frail elderly parent—these were not told. Simply, they are untellable. They may be documented in historical archives but they are not the stuff of personal narrative. We grew up knowing that there were 'other things' that happened, what was not being told. We wondered what they were—fascinated and repelled at the same time. Sam was not the only one who wondered about what brutality his parents had endured. He said he always wondered if his mother had been raped. He asked her once. The response was typical, as was its outcome: 'Her sharp "No!" told me nothing. It meant, "Don't ask!"'. In *See Under: Love* Grossman, an Israeli writer,[20] explores what it means to be a child of survivors raised in the postwar silence of Israel when 'the Holocaust was nowhere and everywhere'.[21] Grossman's main character, a child of survivors, first imagines 'the Nazi beast', that has been alluded to in the cries and whispers of his home, as 'some imaginary monster or a huge dinosaur that once lived in the world which everyone was afraid of now. But he didn't dare ask anyone who or what'.[22]

In many of my conversations with children of survivors, pivotal moments were reached when the respondent would talk about 'finding out'. These were the landmarks or crises of our childhood—moments of shock that rivet you to the ground and change everything from that point forward. In one sense we all knew growing up that one day we would find out more horror. You are always torn by needing to know (if only for the sake of the coherence of the whole); and the dread of not wanting ever to find out. This ambivalence is born of compassion for one's family plus the perhaps Darwinian urge to distance oneself, to find a less powerless and less vulnerable place in the world.

Choices

Part of the repulsion, the wanting not to know, comes from the awareness that there's no retreat from knowing: one cannot 'un-know'.[23] I remember when I was at university, at about eighteen years of age, reading a book on the Holocaust that catalogued a litany of cruelties that I had not known about. One was a set of 'medical' experiments on a young boy whose bones were repeatedly broken, then allowed to set, then broken again, until he died. Another was of a woman delivered of a baby who then was tied to a table to die and the mother made to watch the agonising process, before she too was killed. At one point, I closed the book, laid my head down on the desk, closed my eyes and tried to un-know what I had just found out. I had the sense that with this knowledge I could not go back to being who I was. I'd lost (more of) the innocence of one who does not yet know the depths of man's evil. I remember thinking, why did I read that? How can I rid myself of these images of horror? I came to realise that what one knows becomes part of who one is and, actually, one has a choice here. Since then I find myself at times avoiding sites that will lead me to the kind of information that I do not want to become part of me. For this reason, I did not read *Sophie's Choice*[24] nor see *Life is Beautiful*, and waited a long time before I could bring myself to see *Schindler's List*.

When second generationers have their own children, they are torn between allowing their parents' story to be known by their children or preserving their own child's innocent view of the world. The choice we make is sometimes an ugly, even parodic version of what our parents must have felt, postwar and in a new world, drawn to the future but tied to the past. Some get it right, not many, and never is it achieved without a struggle of some kind. Mark Baker summed it up: 'I often wonder if it is fair to break my children's hearts and tell them about their grandparents' lives'.[25]

Rena was unable to give her son a *bar mitzvah* because through the fractured messages she'd taken in all her life, the synagogue as a place and a building had become an overpowering metaphor of the destruction of the Jews. It conjured up images of people crammed inside, locked doors, Nazis outside, burning the building down, shooting anyone who tried to escape. In Bernard Schlink's *The Reader* there is just such a scene and historical accounts are replete with replays.[26] For Rena, enabling her son to go through the *bar mitzvah* rite of passage was the equivalent of perpetuating for another generation the oppressive side of being Jewish. The choice became her parents' world versus the wellbeing of her child. She opted for the latter, but not without impunity, troubled by a sense of disloyalty to her parents and their generation. There are many stories like this. Rachel chose to adopt a baby from overseas rather than have her own, believing that the grief she had inherited as the child of survivors would therefore stop with her generation. I cite these examples to illustrate how some of the postwar choices that our parents made were echoed later in decisions we had to make when we became parents. Even minor and less complicated decisions, notably whether to display a *mezzuzah* on the outside door frame of your home, is not easy or automatic for a child of survivors. It is always problematic: if you display it, you are saying, defiantly, *I am a Jew and I am proud of it*. If you don't, you are saying, *I am not a Jew*; or *I don't want to be identified as a Jew*; or *I can be a Jew without displaying the fact to the whole world*. Each choice is driven by echoes of the past.

The listener's role

Holocaust stories are fragmented in large part because of the pressures that accompany the act of telling. These derive mainly from the fact that the communication between parent and child was not allowed to do what conversation does in normal conditions, that is, accommodate and cater for a process of negotiation as the people involved arrive at mutually agreed-upon understandings of their topic and meaning. This negotiation has a very particular quality: it involves a ping-pong movement of question and answer, checking meaning, clarifying understanding, refining interpretation. The outcome is a mutually rewarding joint co-construction of shared understandings and is the exact antithesis of Holocaust narrative.

Like other forms of narrative, the act of telling about the Holocaust involves the usual three participants: teller, listener and text. The difference here is that when the Holocaust is the text-participant, the danger is that it will take over and subsume the others, the teller and the listener. And this is often what happens: the text overwhelms and the other two participants are unable to sustain themselves. The narrative avalanche threatens to sweep away anything in its path.

Any telling has a push-pull rhythm through which the teller is encouraged to keep on telling by the response of the person listening.

Even while allowing for cross-cultural differences, we might generally say that the more positive feedback, in the sense of visible listening cues such as eye contact and verbal cues, the more the teller will feel heard and encouraged. The less this feedback is forthcoming, the more discouraged the teller will become.

Thus the listener's role not only encourages the unfolding narrative; in a very real sense, it allows it to happen. When Hass interviewed his survivor subjects about their experience, he found them extremely receptive to his questions. They responded to his eagerness to know, almost recovering memories in front of him. He says: 'My inquisitivessness, my desire to know, implied *permission to remember*'.[27] And from the survivor's perspective, this indeed is how it may seem: 'I survived . . . but I regularly made the observation that people did not really want me to talk about my experiences, and whenever I started they invariably showed their resistance by interrupting me, by asking me to tell them how I got out'.[28] One of Hass' survivor interviewees blamed herself for her children's apparent indifference: 'Now I would like my children to sit down like you are sitting here and ask me all about it. I would like them to carry on the history, the memory . . . and I don't think they will'.[29]

The construction of Holocaust narrative between parent and children is after all, a collusion, a collaboration of will, from both sides, that together, in theory, allows a text to emerge. There's a choreography in the unfolding event that requires a union of two co-operating participants. It is an interconnectivity that binds the listener, as witness, to the teller whose story, when told, becomes testimony. Laub describes this interconnectivity:

> Bearing witness to a trauma is . . . a process that includes the listener . . . there needs to be a bonding, the intimate and total presence of an *other*—in the position of one who hears. Testimonies are not monologues; they cannot take place in solitude. The witnesses are talking to *somebody* . . . they have been waiting for a long time.[30]

Children of survivors were on the whole very solicitous of their parents, attentive to their needs and compassionate about their losses. But broadly speaking, permission to remember is what we failed to give them. Now, when I look back to the countless opportunities I had with my parents, especially my father, to find out and probe and understand, I realise that he, and maybe even my mother, were waiting for permission to talk. I can remember, too, the many subtle ways—avoidance of eye contact, change of topic, lack of listening noises, failure to ask questions, display of busy-ness or being in a rush—by which permission was denied. In the early years, of course, we were too young to understand the circumstances that constrained us. Later, while maturity brought some understanding, some coherence, it sadly did not bring much comfort. All told, I believe my generation has paid a heavy price for our failures.

Near the start of this book, I mentioned that my father's death triggered in me an avalanche of questions that needed him to die before they could be asked. This meant of course that they were unanswerable. The safety that his death brought was the safety of un-ask-ability. Earlier too in the book, I mentioned the Buddhist belief that after a killing time, healing takes three generations. Today I have the view that healing begins when talk is allowed; and talk is only possible when memory is permissible.

A linguistic perspective of this same view also allows a connection to be made between the passage of time and the capacity for healing. Perhaps the span of three generations is what is needed to allow private grief to give way gradually to public ritual. The crucial element in such a shift of discourse is that what is emerging is the kind of talk that does not require a listener's permission.

Socialised Messages

We have seen how the pattern of Holocaust narrative was one of fragmented disclosure, a 'story' that leaked out over the years, often despite survivors' best efforts at suppression. Even in homes where the children felt drowned in the parents' repeated references to the war, the immersion was an emotional construct—what Hass calls 'emotional knowledge'—rather than a discursive one.[31] Overall, there was not a lot of what Goffman calls, 'fresh talk'.[32] Rather, what was heard tended to be rehearsed, pre-packaged, refrain-like. Given that this pattern is so widespread among the survivors, one might conclude that the only way the accounts could happen is through being managed.

One major kind of fragmented message is what I am calling here 'socialised messages'.

This category has to do with communications that emerge out of the parents' attempts; firstly, to process their wartime experience and secondly, to pass on the results of that processing to their children. The term 'socialised' is meant to convey the sense that processing and filtering mediate the recount of the experience. Recollection of the events is socialised—that is, prepared by the speaker for another's consumption.

In that one person's experience cannot be lived by another, all recounts in human communication are inevitably mediated to a certain extent. Here, however, we have messages that are so extreme that a process of socialisation is needed to render them receivable by another. It is as if without this processing, they would remain outside the social ambit of communication.

We have seen that survivors share an abiding belief that their experiences cannot be understood by anyone who was 'not there'. In Epstein's search for her mother's history, she comes to read the letters written by her mother, from Czechoslovakia in the period after the war. She writes, 'Even one (letter) is enough to hear my mother's voice and to understand the abyss that had opened up between concentration camp survivors and almost everyone else in the world'.[33]

It follows from this that any recount of such experience will, by definition, be a compromise. In the very act of rendering the account viable for those who are to hear it, we have compromises—qualifications, reductions, sanitisations—built into the message. Inchoate thoughts and overwhelming emotion have to be confined, constrained, managed and transformed so as to make them receivable. Thus we have socialised messages—rather like the linguistic correlates of processed experience.

Such socialised messages stand in contradistinction to a category of unsocialised messages which I am calling 'dissonant'. Here, various dissonances within the transmitted message arise in large part from the fact that the messages are painfully raw, delivered without adequate processing and filtering. We will explore these in a later section.

Dicta

One group of socialised messages has to do with the way in which a culture is discursively transmitted in the sayings that are produced and reproduced within the home. These dicta are sayings or maxims that capture, in a few words or in a verbal image, an abiding truth about life or human experience. They are understood by participants in the context of use, which might be as limited as a single home or as wide-spread as the speakers of a particular language. In the latter case, such sayings are comfortably passed down from generation to generation. Where sufficient currency and endurance prevail, they calcify into proverbs.

What concerns us here is not so much sayings that are shared across, say, a nation, as sayings that emanate from a home. In my home, for example, mealtime was complicated: there was not the choice to like or not to like, to eat or not to eat what was served. This rule was not stated as such. If my brother or I protested a distaste for something on our plates, the response was invariably, 'Eat without liking'. The meaning was inferred yet self-evident There was no eye contact and the tone was a falling, no-nonsense one, delivered without expectation of negotiation or compromise. We never questioned it: we took it to mean that there was no choice. Looking back on the saying today, I can see all the meanings that emanate from it: food is a life-source; food is precious; you don't know what you will have or not have tomorrow; eating is not to do with taste but to do with staying alive; food is food and should be eaten without question; we should be grateful that food is plentiful and not consider that there are choices; you eat, you live, you don't eat, you don't live; 'today we know we have food, so eat . . .'. There are endless reverberations that ripple out in concentric circles from the clipped imperative that was always the same, said the same way, no response allowed: 'Eat without liking'.

In this section of the book, I want to suggest that a dictum such as 'Eat without liking' is redolent with meanings that not only communicate the face-value sense of the words themselves, but also carry meanings far larger and more imposing. They are replete with cues about the parents' past so that even in homes where 'there was no talk', this kind of communication spoke as much, if not more, of other things, other times, other events, other losses, other unspeakables.

I want to deal with such formulae as an anthropologist might treat a set of customs or rituals. In anthropological terms, a home, like a people, has its own unique culture. This is the sum total of the beliefs, values and behavioural conventions that characterise the interactions among its members. It is an organic phenomenon that grows out of the shared experience of people living together. To a large extent it is steered by the parents and manifested in oft-repeated, seemingly throwaway lines. These lines might be said to epitomise certain valued beliefs or tenets ascribed to by the users. This collection of sayings or dicta are crystallised verbal gems; they furnish a rich source of data that readily lends itself to analysis and provides a window onto the collective thinking of a generation.

The in-family dicta of survivor homes point, as one would expect, to the parents' Holocaust experience and their attempts to process this experience, to derive meaning and lessons from it. Often they point to values and indicate how the parent generation came to terms with the events of their past. In interviewing my subjects, I discovered an eerie similarity, a patterning that, in itself, is meaningful. I have grouped the major threads, below, using quotations to serve as headings.

'Eat! You don't know where the next meal is coming from.'

Perhaps the most dominant theme to emerge in the pattern of sayings is the one relating to food. Indeed I am reminded of what happened at a meeting I once attended of children of Holocaust survivors. We were all seated in a circle and there was a sudden uncomfortable silence as people looked about and did not know where or how to start the proceedings. At this point, a woman took the initiative by suggesting that no doubt we all had food issues so why not start with that. Everyone laughed, the ice was broken, food became the first topic of discussion and yes, she was right, everyone had issues with food. This also taps into a joke, linking food and tragedy that recently did the rounds on the Internet. It says:

> The following is a short summary of most Jewish holidays:
> They tried to kill us.
> We won.
> Let's eat.

Rebecca speaks about her father's celebratory, if somewhat obsessive, attitude to food. He was forever offering people food, she said, the fridge was always well-stocked, they could turn on a huge meal for lots of guests at the drop of a hat, they were very disdainful of the small portions that Australians ate, they always over-catered, overestimated. The picture she paints is that plenty is something to celebrate. However, within the celebration, fuelling and steering it, is the experience of starvation.

It is not hard to make the leap to where this came from. Given the deprivation or outright starvation suffered by the parent generation, the notion of food and nourishment takes on gross and pathological proportions. Many of my respondents talked about the way food was venerated with a quasi-sacred significance, its symbolic power casting a blanket on the home. Leftovers were never ever thrown out. Bread, especially stale bread, had enormous recollective significance, as did potato peel. As children, we could not have guessed the iconic value of these everyday items. One respondent, Elaine, spoke about the force-feeding sessions that would take place after she and her sister got back from school, when the mother, every day without fail, would serve up quantities of high-protein food. Another child, in what was an abusive home environment, was forced to eat any leftovers from the previous meal. Each meal the leftovers from the previous would be served up, and this continued, until they were eaten. You soon learned, she told me, to eat everything on your plate the first time. Erlich recalls that no food was wasted: stale bread was ground into crumbs, old onion was added to the soup—'the food underwent many evolutions'.[34]

Generally, the nutritional function of mealtime took precedence over any familial or social purpose. Ella remembers mealtime being treated as a matter of expediency: plain and predictable food despatched with a minimum of fuss and a maximum of speed, a philosophy of 'You eat in order to live'. To this day, she has trouble with the concept of gourmet food or mealtime as a social, interactional event. Rebecca remembers noticing the differences in the homes of her Australian friends: 'they ate properly too, not ravenously', being embarrassed when her Australian friends would come over for dinner. Abe spoke of what it was like to fight being over fed all his childhood: 'Till I was six or seven I resisted. Then at about seven my will was broken—my parents would never leave food on the table'. Leah says, echoing the sentiments of many, 'It took me years to be able to throw out food'.

Alongside the pattern of plain, expedient, no-fuss food eaten quickly and quietly, there was another factor: mealtime was mostly cloaked in tension. Rena talks of the anxiety that surrounded the evening meal in her home. Because of his experience of starvation during the war, her father was left with a very low tolerance of hunger. Food always had to be on the table at a certain time, putting pressure on the mother to manage meals by the clock. The pressure filtered down to the children and permeated the entire space of the meal; not only did you have to eat what was served you, but you had to eat it fast. She could never eat quickly enough; she was always the last one still eating when everyone else's plates were empty.

I recall what my father told me about starvation: what being hungry means, how it concentrates the mind in a shocking totality, how he ate bark from the forest trees when he'd escaped from the death march, and what hunger reduces a human being to. I tried to understand, I tried to look as though I understood or at least to look as though I was trying to understand. But my experience of food was so different: all I knew was I had to eat whatever was put in front of me, usually too much and always too quickly. I wondered, though, what bark tasted like.

Refusal to eat or, more commonly, to eat as much as the parents dictated, caused extreme distress in the parents and triggered angry outbursts. It was like rubbing the war in their faces, mocking their experience and its legacy. I remember being with my mother in the dressing room of a shop, trying on a dress for a school dance. It was a navy blue linen, with a low neck and white collar. I had always known that being thin was a problem: my lean frame seemed to mock my mother and unleash a thinly repressed rage. I always tried to avoided being undressed in her presence, a habit that my mother, unwittingly, put down to an exaggerated modesty. That day in the shop, though, my mother saw again how thin I was and predictably, poked my protruding rib-cage and hissed the 'Bergen-Belsen'. I'd often heard these words; they were part of my mother's response to my thinness; until I found out, many years later, I thought it was a Polish curse.

In the home of every one of my respondents, without exception, food was an issue between the generations. It was the benchmark against which horrors were calibrated. Sam recalls the discomfort he felt when his parents ridiculed his dislike of fish: for them any particular taste preference or taste aversion was almost an absurdity. After all, food was food; it was preposterous to refuse to eat something because you didn't like the taste! In this way, the Holocaust became the universal benchmark. When a parent said, in response to the normal minor scrapes and abrasions of childhood, 'May all your worries be so big', we knew the scratch, or whatever it was, was being compared to the Holocaust. And we felt foolish, at best. Irene speaks with bitterness of how this made her feel, especially guilt-inducing statements like, 'I survived five years without oranges, one more day is not going to matter much', if she happened to have forgotten to stop at the fruit shop. In Lily Brett's *Too Many Men*, a survivor and his daughter travel together in Poland.[35] Every mealtime is a complex and comical affair, as the father protests that he is not hungry but proceeds to eat each meal as if it were his last; and the daughter watches every mouthful of her own for fear of gaining weight, while still taking pleasure in her father's healthy appetite. On the day they take the tour of Auschwitz, she secretly packs extra fruit for them both.

For the parent, mealtime and the presence of plenty conjured up the converse: shortage and starvation. For the child, it was a time of pressure and tension, with the release of demons that made no rational sense. Many remember the event as a tug-of-war between competing unstated interests. Perhaps inevitably, it was a constant, reiterative and nagging reminder of the war's legacy, generating the same predictable exchanges that resonated with rage and frustration. The war may or may not have been mentioned; the fact of mealtime was in itself sufficient.

'They can't take knowledge away from you.'
One of my earliest memories of socialised messages in my home is the line 'they can't take knowledge away from you'. I tried to make sense of this: *Who could 'they' be? Who 'takes' things away? What is 'knowledge'? Why would anyone take this away?* The concepts were far too abstract and the experiential context so embedded and unstated, that the only meaning this had for me in the early years was that study, education, books, reading, things of the mind, were very important to my parents. Over time the message I absorbed was that knowledge was what you were left with when you had been stripped of everything else.

The urge to be educated is also linked to the urge to survive. Being portable, education is something 'you can take with you', like a passport that you always made sure was valid, so that you could leave at a moment's notice. An example of education as a portable commodity might be seen in survivors' attitude to a medical degree. A disproportionate number of my respondents, for example, were doctors. Some of them claimed they were urged to take this path by parents who said 'doctors are always needed', so that 'if you have to move in a hurry, you will still have a livelihood'. Good advice from people who knew first-hand the experience of being uprooted. One of my respondents, Robert, was quite bitter about what he sees as being railroaded into doing medicine. He says that like other survivors, his parents were mesmerised by the portability of a degree in medicine and that once his life was set along this path 'there was no way off it'. Another respondent claimed her father told her she and her sister had to study something practical (they both did Commerce) which they could put to good use as a survival strategy. Different choice, same logic. John was told 'it's good to learn languages. Languages help you survive'. Jane said, almost ruefully, that she did what she was told and didn't make active choices: 'I was a goody-goody. I ate all my food and I studied hard!'

'We are survivors and we are going to survive.'
Many respondents referred to throwaway lines in their home that tapped into the whole survival psychology. These often had to do with the resilience needed to survive. Some pointed to a strategy they use in moments of crisis, when they remind themselves that they 'spring from survivors', as a way of invoking the strength to battle on. Jane says: 'We were always told as children what tough stock we come from, that we could handle anything that was dished out to us in life. This gave us a self-assuredness (which I have) imported to my own children'. Similarly, Rena says that in moments in her life when she had to be totally self-reliant, she took strength from knowing how her parents survived the war. The same throw-away sentiment is apparent in the film *Shine* where the survivor–father preaches a Darwinian maxim to his son: 'You have to be strong to survive. Only the fit survive'.[36]

Elaine talked of the messages she got from her father about how money would buy survival. Jewels sewn into the hem of a skirt or jacket could be used to bribe a guard and make the difference between getting across a border or not making it. Not for him was there a belief in education—he'd seen too many educated Jews whose higher learning did not save them from a dreadful death. For him money in the bank was a better asset than an education, but 'if you had to have stuff in your head, it's got to be practical, something you can use'.

The current flowed the other way in my home. One of the few stories that my mother was given to repeat was her decision to throw out the family gems in a storm-water drain, when she heard the news that the Germans had invaded Poland. She did this because she believed that survival would depend on being inconspicuous: the poorer you were, the more invisible you could become. Fair-haired and blue-eyed, she knew she could pass as Polish, a chance she felt would be increased if she were a country peasant, rather than an urban doctor. She took on the ordinariness of penury and liked to believe that it was a factor in her survival. Who knows if it was? What I know is that it was important to her that she believed it was—it offered more comfort than the survival-by-luck version, an interpretation that removes choice and volition from the human condition.

Slightly different but nonetheless related to the matter of attitude, is the oft-repeated dictum that one respondent spoke of in reference to the defiant goodwill that her mother took into Auschwitz and brought out of there. 'No matter what happens to you in life you've always got the choice as to how you react to it.' Rena recalls that the overriding message in her home was 'Things don't matter. Life is what matters'. The sanctity of human life, as well as its fragility, surfaced frequently. For example, if something was accidentally broken, so long as no one was hurt, it didn't matter: 'It's only money'. The utterance became a kind of shorthand reminder that life—and only life—is precious. There was an intensity about such pronouncements that belied their surface pretence at light-heartedness.

In my home, when a toast was given ('L'Chaim'—'To Life'), it was not of the same order as 'Cheers', or 'Bon Santé' or other such cultural formulae. 'To Life' were words encrusted with heavy unstated meanings, whose message, ironically, was all bound up with death. Whether this nuance is particularly post-Holocaustal or is tinged with the experience of 2000 years of persecution and pogroms is not easy to say. I don't know how widespread this reaction is; I have never heard the sentiment voiced by anyone else. Here I speak only for myself. The look in my father's eye and the way my mother's jaw clenched at 'L'Chaim' mean that even today, when I hear it, I still feel uncomfortable. In remembering life, we remember death; in celebrating today, we mourn yesterday. Messages come tied up inside other messages.

'Don't make waves.'

Another pattern to emerge was the parents' message that safety rests in anonymity and ordinariness. No doubt this derives from being singled out as Jews in host societies where ethnic or religious identity marked one out for special treatment. Edna learned as a young schoolgirl that 'not standing out was important', so that even when she was singled out for something good, she was embarrassed 'because I had learned just to want to be like anyone else'.

Ursula Duba's poem, 'The sundial', foregrounds the thoughts of a young Jewish girl in postwar Germany. The teacher has given the little girl the apparent honour of standing in one spot alone all day outside in the sunny playground: every hour the class stepped out and marked the changes in the shadow with a rock. Then all the children would go back except the foreign girl who was told she was the sundial. After a while, hot and restless, she begins to wonder if this is a privilege or a punishment, but she does as bidden:

> she remembered
> what her mother used to say
> listen to what the teacher says
> don't make any waves
> always be obedient.[37]

Of course, there's a contradiction in urging one's children to excel and also urging them to avoid the limelight. Sometimes the children heard mixed messages and had somehow to resolve for themselves the dissonance of these collisions.

In my case, my father urged me towards achievement and excellence, while my mother, I realise now, would have liked nothing more for me than the safety and anonymity of ordinariness. Whenever I opted for the harder path, driven on by relentless ambition, my mother would look at me and gently try to coax me away from this pathway. 'What for?', she would ask, again and again; and because I didn't understand my own ambition, I had no answer. I could never fathom her failure to encourage me. I think now it partly was the sense that such things of the world could all be so easily swept away. But part of it too, I have no doubt, was cautioning me to the safety of ordinary uniformity. Aim low, better not to stand out, mediocrity was a life-giving strategy. In *I Dreyfus*, Rubens describes the refugee parents' ambitions for their two sons: 'They had not been ambitious for either of us. They were happy for us to fade into an accepting background, as they had done and earn a decent living'.[38]

Politics was another bone of contention. Most survivors had a fervent interest in things political, political discussion being standard fare in survivor households. Yet parents urged their children not to carve out a visible political presence. John's parents wanted him not to get involved, even in causes where he was fired up by a sense of injustice. This created many clashes with the parent generation when their children, then university students, joined in the anti-war movement of the late 1960s and early 1970s. Edna recalls that when students that she was with were campaigning against nuclear war and had their pictures printed on the front page of the communist daily of those times, she predicted her father's reaction: she knew he would fear being arrested and deported back to Czechoslovakia. The children saw hypocrisy in their parents' apparent apathy: while urging their children to be invisible in the political process, they nonetheless knew the amorality of political bystanding. The contradictions were a source of dissonance for both generations.

'The past is a cemetery.'

Attitudes to things past and to what was left behind are transmitted in the often articulated desire by the parent generation to forget everything about the home country. This often translates into a fervent wish for the child not to learn the parents' tongue or experience their homeland. The imperative, 'never go back', was powerfully driven by dread of stirring up the memory of terrible losses. Rachel said of her mother: 'She always said she would never go back to those places, there was no point, no good memories, nothing there for them'.

Long before the children could make coherent sense of the trauma that predated their birth, they were aware of a severed biography and a seal placed on what came before. We grew up knowing there was a place somewhere that the parents came from that they wished not ever to return to, not in their thoughts nor in their person. Thus it was that Jewish refugees could not tap comfortably into the new Australian multiculturalism which at its core is a matter of allowing new arrivals to be who they are, to remember their past and derive identity and belonging from a different sense of another place and of another way of being. Most Jews did not want their identity to be mixed up with population groups who by and large served as agents for the Nazi machine. Andrew Riemer in *Inside Outside* talks about the Hungarians who lined up to say good riddance to the Jews as they were emptied out of their homes, marched to the railway station, and deported.[39] Such memories proliferate.

When my mother was a student of medicine at Vilna University she had to sit in the 'Jews only' section of the lecture hall, was spat on by Christian students and had to provide a source for her pathology work, as Jewish students were not allowed to work on the cadavers of Christians. Thus, when multiculturalism celebrated Polish song and dance, and SBS broadcasting transmitted Polish music and film, nothing sentimental or nostalgic was triggered for her. She turned the TV off, opened a book or took out some sewing, and there was a tightness about her mouth. These pains are transmitted generationally. I still dread it when someone, in all innocence and good faith, asks me about my Polish connection. They ask 'Have you ever been back?', 'Do you have family there?', 'Do you speak Polish?'. I tolerate this from people who have no reason to know better. I no longer tolerate it from Polish Christians who have conveniently forgotten the centuries-old anti-Semitism that made them welcome Hitler's solution. Today, in their recast versions of history, they often prefer to see themselves only as victims of Hitler, like the Jews. This is neat and convenient, but a big step from the truth.[40]

If the context of what was home is sidestepped with agility, some of the rage is released in attitudes passed on about things German. The message 'Don't buy German' came across long before the connection of Volkswagen, Braun, Telefunken and Lufthansa with Germany was clear, certainly long before the revelations of how German industry benefited from slave labour. Later we understood the message was 'You don't support the German economy with your money', or 'You don't put money into companies that profited from the war'. Many of the second generation are the same, and could no more buy a German car or travel Lufthansa than their parents. As a generation we learned this early. Irene recalls that at school, around the age of seven, she had no idea why she felt guilty about using a plastic protractor marked 'Made in Germany'.

Then there are some who seemed to have missed the message altogether, as if something inside was shut off. One of my respondents mentioned that her brother, time and time again, bought a Mercedes Benz, oblivious to the pain this caused his survivor parents. When she raised the matter with him, pointing out how it hurt them, he discounted this as her fertile imagination. These two siblings may well be instances of a pattern, reported anecdotally by many of my respondents, that siblings in the same family can respond entirely differently to their inheritance: one child imbibing their parents' pain, the other maintaining a 'healthy' boundary between self and parents. My view is that it is not a case of one child did and one child didn't, but rather that the manifestations of the inheritance are different. The brother just mentioned was under no obligation to buy the latest Mercedes, other than the inner compulsion to separate visibly from an oppressive family culture. The car marked him out as different from them.

If the home country is disparaged, and Germany vilified, then the converse is seen in the unremitting thanksgiving lavished on Australia. Edna says this was background music in her home. Michael said his father's particular mantra was: 'Australia is a wonderful country, here you never go hungry'. A common refrain, one that I heard many times in my home, was: 'This country has been good to us'. And when in my rebellious, left-leaning youth I was wont to be critical of the government for this policy or that, my parents, while occasionally agreeing with my logic, could never throw off the gratitude they felt for being allowed 'a second chance'. Furthermore, whatever Australian injustice or inequity I might have pointed out, I could be sure that they would calibrate it against their experience of the world and deem it insignificant on the wider canvas of human horror. And when at one point I espoused an internationalism that I believed would address all social and political injustices, including the injustice of anti-Semitism, I quickly found out, again, what internationalism had meant for the Jews: how the Hitler–Stalin pact allowed the Germans into Poland with impunity, and how the Russians reserved very 'special treatment' for the Jews when they entered Poland. The message that pervaded all other messages was that Australia was a paradise and we should be grateful to be here.

'Trust no-one.'

Among the sayings that traversed a generation of survivor homes was one that constantly echoes the need for vigilance in a malevolent world. These are messages that add up to what Elaine described in her home: 'Trust no one, they're all alike, you can't trust them. I'm the one you can trust'. Of course, you don't always reap what you sow: sometimes the descendant generation didn't want to grow up with a cynical distrust of the world and set about to prove to their parents that the world was not a malevolent place. Today, Rena finds her closest friends are non-Jews and wonders whether she actively, if unwittingly, sought out evidence to destabilise the injunction, 'trust no-one'.

Messages about others proliferate. This can take the form of distinctions drawn between 'us and them', which is no doubt also a function of being a minority people in a host society. Tonkin writes that minorities are likely to have 'a sharper sense of their special identity' vis-à-vis the majorities 'with whom they have to share a country', a notion not generally considered by those who talk of suburban migrant ghettoes, where 'they all stick together'. Majority identities, Tonkin continues, are constructed in the same way as minority ones, 'but insofar as they are uncontested, they can become naturalised as reality'.[41]

Messages about insiders and outsiders collectively define otherness as much as they define the self. In the film *Shine*, the survivor-father almost threatens his son with the intensity of his emotion: 'No one will love you the way I love you'.[42] Coupled with this were warnings about the Gentile world: Leah was told 'Poles got their anti-Semitism in their mother's milk', and Jennie: 'Anti-Semitism runs in their blood'. Alongside this were admonitions to remember their ethnic roots: along the lines of 'Never forget that you're Jewish'. They were told that they themselves were the evidence that the war had been won. The message was that their revenge on Hitler was to keep on being Jews. Conversely, if they failed to remain Jews, then it was 'Hitler's victory'. Sometimes the warning emerged as an injunction against inter-marriage: 'How can you marry out among those who persecuted us?' and there was the belief that one day in a temper or a squabble, the non-Jewish partner 'will call you "a bloody Jew"'.

One of my respondents reluctantly discovered that her non-Jewish partner had thinly veiled contempt for Jews and she lived with this secret for over ten years, hiding the truth from her survivor parents and her children, suppressing her reactions to avoid overt conflict in the home. Years prior to this, she had had a previous relationship with a man who had openly despised Jews. Later, when she looked back on both failed relationships, and asked herself why she would have gravitated towards such men in the first place, she was stunned by the insights that slowly unfolded. At first she believed that her choices were steered by events bigger than her: in both cases, she chose as a partner someone who would effect some distance between her and her parents, something that she was incapable of achieving at any conscious level. Later, she believed that she chose men with anti-Semitic attitudes so that she could 'take on' the kind of pain that would in fact bring her closer, psychologically, to her parents, giving her a taste of what they had known, the kind of horror that effectively had benchmarked her life. Ultimately, she came to the conclusion that both forces—the need to separate from *and* the need to fuse with her parents—compelled her choices and steered the course of her life.

The attitude of Jews to non-Jews in the post-Holocaust era can hardly be uncomplicated. Messages about the fragility of trust pervaded but sometimes other messages intruded, like the time my mother quietly said to me, almost as if she didn't want me to hear, 'It's much easier not to be Jewish', suggesting that one option for postwar Jews was to let it all go. This sense that 'enough is enough' is born of world-weariness: a 2000-year-old sentence for the alleged crime of deicide, if not for the obstinate refusal to accept Christ as Lord. Rubens' book *I, Dreyfus*, explores the tragedy of trying to submerge one's origins in the effort to be counted as Christian. In the story, a child of survivors who fled to England at the time of the Nazi occupation of Paris grows up in the silent shadow of that escape—'like most of those who got away, my parents' tongues were stilled by survivors' guilt'—to become, ultimately, the esteemed headmaster of a Christian school. But the past catches up to him and he is obliged to re-establish links that had consciously been severed before his birth.[43]

In Australia, the number of people willing to declare themselves as Jewish in the national census increased after June 1967, when Israel emerged victorious from the Six-Day Middle East War. Perhaps, 22 years after the war, it was finally safe to come out.

'Be happy.'
Perhaps the most burdensome dictum of all was the instruction to be happy. In her autobiography, Varga captures this sentiment with, 'We had far too much to appreciate'.[44] Edna says: 'They placed a lot of emphasis on happiness. They wanted me to be happy. There was pressure to be happy. They'd say the only thing that is important is to be happy. That's a bit intimidating because you'd think, "Why are they saying this? Does this mean happiness can be taken away?"'. Robyn, a therapist who has herself spent many years in therapy, also speaks of the burden of being happy:

> As a child I was cherished and it took me ages to figure out what was missing, what wasn't right ... They wanted me to be happy. I got told this many times over and over again, but I always knew there was something wrong with that statement 'All we want is your happiness'. 'We only want the best for you'. It's so loaded, this 'all we want'. What's not being said is, 'We don't want anything else in life' and by implication that makes us responsible for their happiness. What a burden! I'm not allowed *not* to be happy!

The above catalogue of socialised messages is not meant to be exhaustive but to provide insight into how communication about past experience was achieved, often very minimally in verbal terms, but very powerfully in terms of the transmitted emotions. Susan captures the quality of this kind of transmission when she says of her mother:

> She told me nothing about the war, but I knew that she'd never go back to those places, and I knew that she wouldn't buy anything German, and she never wanted us to be public about being Jewish, so though she didn't tell me, I still got a lot of messages.

Susan's repeated use of the negative in her characterisation of her mother's statements reminds me of a literary critic's remark about the survivor parents in Grossman's novel—that the word 'always' crops up frequently in their association, 'suggesting that they are governed by habit or atomised behaviour, inappropriate to present circumstances'. Baum describes this as 'ritualised and compulsive (behaviour), hiding behind a façade of normality'.[45]

The socialised messages were doubtless a rich source of meanings—about the present, about the future but, most pointedly, about the past which in many cases was otherwise all but sealed off. Unwittingly, survivors' children used the sayings that circulated through the home over many years as a means of making sense of their reality. This involved re-processing the experience that had already been processed by the parents in formulating the message in the first place.

Communication, in its ordinary unremarkable form, is mostly a process of joint construction involving co-operation and intertwining of understandings, a process so normal, natural, spontaneous and dynamic that people don't even notice it. Holocaust narrative is marked in that it is a set of constructions that happen separately, even in time and space. Survivors' talk, especially their socialised messages, is the outcome of their experience having been processed. It is therefore prefabricated rather than spontaneously produced in dialogue. What they said, their discourse about their past, is itself an interpretation, a means of mediating experience. For the children of survivors, making sense of their parents' discourse is another exercise in construction, a matter of taking the little that is said, milking it of meaning, making it cohere with other messages in a larger picture. Sadly, perhaps inevitably, the actual work of these constructions—the survivors' managed discourse and the descendants' interpretations of verbal and non-verbal cues—seems to happen with a minimum of interface.

Sanitised Versions

We have seen above that a major way in which survivors were able to process and convey some part of their experience is through socialised messages. These little sayings often emerged out of predictable, situated events that for one reason or another tapped into their re-collected past experience, triggering reminders that make present conduct reactively resonant. The trigger could be as 'minor' as a child leaving food on the dinner plate or as 'major' as that child in later years going to a school dance with a non-Jewish date.

Another way in which the past was rendered manageable as the substance of narrative was through various interventions made to the story. This is said even with the assumption that telling is itself a form of intervention and necessarily a mediation. Of course, there's no way of knowing how conscious these amendments were, nor how perva-sive. However, from my interviews, there emerges a very clear pattern of descendants' belief that over the years what they heard was *a version* of a story, by no means a transparent description of the original event, if we can imagine this. The sense is that the telling is designed in order to make the remembering manageable. Of course, it was not as simple as descendants wanting to know and survivors not wanting to tell. Descendants on the whole collaborated in the avoidance of taboo topics, fearful that what they might find out was worse than what they even imagined, and, for the most part, they were right.

For all the reasons that have been discussed earlier—the unspeak-ability of traumas suffered, unresolved grief, shame and fear—survivors made interventions or amendments as their story unfolded for the next generation. To begin with, what was told was much reduced. Six years of horror are not for retelling moment by moment. As well, a major constituent that often was removed was emotion; many descendants referred to the flat, suppressed, matter-of-fact delivery style of their parents.

After her interview with me, Jane asked her mother, a survivor of Auschwitz, whether she had edited out the horror when she had told her story to the family:

> She said she did not filter anything for my benefit. I asked her again if she suffered a lot (*no*), if she saw people killed (*no*), if she saw people

die (*yes, but that was part of life there*), if she was hungry (*no, she got an extra bowl of soup for serving meals and she shared this with her mother and cousin*), if she was beaten (*sometimes*), if she was cold (*at least we had our own shoes—farm work boots*).

Jane's mother weighed 65 kilos when she arrived at Auschwitz and 45 kilos when the camp was liberated. Numbers, it would seem, are not affected by the passage of time, the difficulties of telling or the need not to remember.

There was a monochrome quality to the tellings. They were often delivered in a bare-bones style, without the embroidery and embellishment that would create background or give life to those who peopled the pages of their memory. Sam was one respondent who complained bitterly that his mother's story was fenced off to him: he always got the same limited version, and his probing and questioning reaped no reward. He was one who continually asked, despite the discomfort he knew it engendered. Years later he made a film of his aunt's life. When she saw the film of her sister, all Sam's mother said was, 'Yeah, that's true'. Interpreting this and its significance, Sam said that her remark was merely a confirmation that the events depicted actually happened. Failing to see what the point of the film was, suspecting that there may be some doubt that the story wasn't true or was exaggerated, Sam felt she was really saying, 'How much more proof do you need?'. Yet his reasons for making the film had to do with the attempt to repair and restore the severed cord that binds people backwards to their ancestry and forwards to their progeny, a desire to provide a continuity for his own children that he himself lacked. My understanding is that Sam's craving to know was typical descendant behaviour and his mother's unyielding refusal to tell more was typical survivor behaviour. Again, a rock and a hard place.

Another word that aptly describes the stories we heard is 'impoverished'. Epstein comments on how family stories derive their richness and texture from the 'multiple versions' to which a child is exposed over time. Post-Holocaust homes, however, have very few versions, because there are very few people left to tell them. The documents and mementos have been dispersed by disaster and there is nothing left to point to and tell about. And further, those who survived has each 'designed his or her own strategy for coping with the destruction of the world into which they were born'.[46]

So the stories were edited, diluted, had the horror deleted, sanitised, generally made acceptable for public transmission. There's no surprise here: the raw recollection of massive trauma simply cannot be told. A commentator who said, 'That's why we have counsellors', made this fact translucently clear to me. If post-traumatic stress victims were able to package their stories manageably for transmission, there would be little need for counselling. It is as though the period of counselling is in place precisely to bring a victim to a point past the raw hard edge where the topic can now be broached outside the therapist's safe haven. Holocaust survivors, however, by and large, did not have access to counselling after the war. Their stories, perhaps as a result, remained pretty well sealed off.

In Susan Glass' book *The Interpreter*, the main character is a simultaneous interpreter, and also a Holocaust survivor's daughter. It is no coincidence, really, that she fulfils these two roles, the one serving as a kind of metaphor for the other. She recalls moments in the bathtub as a child; her mother would 'forget herself' and begin to talk about how it was for her as a child in Nazi Europe:

> She always said 'that place'. Never *Bergen-Belsen*. Never the hell-hole. Just *that* place. She threw the words away. Mumbled them. Swallowed them almost, as though her lack of emphasis on the words might make them a fragment of her imagination and allow her to rewrite her own story.[47]

Epstein makes a similar comment about her mother's version of 'an encounter' (that is, interrogation) she had with the Gestapo in Nazi-occupied Czechoslovakia, in June of 1939: 'My mother said, in that peculiar language that I had grown up trying to decipher, that she had not been "mistreated"'.[48]

For all sorts of reasons—from being able to live with their memories, to being able to tell their children of what happened—survivors tended toward sanitised versions. Rachel referred to the shock she experienced when she saw the video that her mother made for the Spielberg Foundation. Here were stories that were familiar but they were also distinct. They were different versions of the ones she knew. She realised then that the versions she had heard

were cleaned up a bit, sanitised, put through her filters so that she could talk about them comfortably. I'd heard stories about how they'd shared soup and clothes and looked out for each other. This was true, I've no doubt, but it wasn't all of the picture. On the video I heard about how they helped a woman give birth secretly and then smothered the baby.

Rachel's younger sister, Jennie, recalls a consonant picture:

In Mum's stories we found out about things that she was proud of, she'd take the good from it, and not tell us the bad. A lot of it was like gossip, little things that a person had done. Mum went into the camp with a group of girls from her town. They survived because of the strength the group gave them. They looked out for each other. Mum told us stuff that was heroic, that pointed towards what was good in being human.

Although one of the hardest lessons survivors learned was that survival was not the outcome of God's intervention, or compassion in another human being, or strength, cunning or endurance in oneself. More often than not, survival was a mere accident. Elsewhere I have said that this is a very unpalatable tenet to live with. It is no wonder that survivors tended not to dwell on the fact. Doing so would be to remove all sense of agency and turn life into a theatre of the absurd, a memento of that world of the camps, where as a guard told a newly arrived prisoner, 'Here there is no *why*'. Hass writes that survivors' bleakness, sadness, ongoing 'undercurrent of apprehension' and worry about the arbitrary nature of life constituted 'the other side of having survived by luck'.[49]

It is not only survivors who have difficulty processing the implications of having survived by accident. Novick claims that, in part, the gradual reframing of the Holocaust in the American consciousness has had to do with the need for the wider public to 'draw lessons' from the events of history. He asks, 'And what lesson emerges if we embrace that most widespread (and most plausible) of all possible explanations—luck?'. He also accounts in the same vein for the venomous attacks by the Jewish community on Arendt's book *Eichmann in Jerusalem*. Far from blaming the Jews of Europe for not resisting, as her critics claimed, Novick suggests that Arendt was in fact arguing that resistance was impossible. The vehemence of protest against her and her book, he believes, derives from the fact that she was breaking with the 'myth of widespread Jewish resistance which had been assiduously promoted since the war'.[50]

This in part might account for a quality of many survivors' stories: they seem to seek and find agency in human action and logic in survival. John recalls a story he was told many times as a child, how his mother who had been a champion runner at school had escaped from the camp and re-invented herself as a Christian Czech until the war's end. The story as it was told focused on her running away: it was 'told as a victory', having had the horror spun out of it and having been recast as heroism.

Other respondents uncannily used the same term—'little victories'—as they reflected on the kinds of stories they were told and wondered, as if for the first time, at their very particular nature. Richard remembers being told how his mother survived because when the Nazis came to get her family, she jumped from the building's second floor. The window had been bolted in and she normally would not have had anywhere near the strength needed to unlock it. But she did, and she jumped and she survived—miraculously. Elsa said that the stories she was told were generally quite trivial but were always instances of a time spent in hell where somehow her mother had been able to salvage some element of human dignity. She mentioned one story that she heard, separately, from her mother and each of her two aunts who were in the same camp. The story each time was told a little differently, each time reflecting the perspective of the teller, and the energy she invested in salvaging her dignity. David recalls a story being told him again and again. Both his parents were in a labour camp. There were three sections, A, B and C. The third was where they used some kind of toxic acid and people never came back from there. In the story, David's mother spends months trying to bribe a guard to move her husband until, one day, she saw him coming through gate C. 'That story was all about my mother's persistence.'

Thus the versions that survivors conveyed were inevitably mediated by their need to find meaning and solace. It is regrettable that these amendments have fed so conveniently into the Holocaust revisionist claim that survivors' stories are less than truthful, are in fact a tapestry of lies. Indeed, it is bitterly ironic that the inevitable amendments made to survivors' tellings were in the direction of understatement and avoidance, rather than exaggeration and distortion. It is well to remember too that revisionists also claim, in the face of momentous contrary evidence, that concentration camps were actually transit holding places, that there were no gas chambers or crematoria, that most of Europe's Jews emigrated before the war and that a worldwide conspiracy of Jews has exploited the Holocaust to extract sympathy and compensation.

Dissonance

Over the two decades, roughly, that children of Holocaust survivors spent in their parents' home, they came to some kind of knowledge, usually fractured and partial, about their parents' wartime experience. As well as the fragmented nature of this knowledge, its quality of dissonance is another distinctive feature. I use this term to describe a malalignment or misfit among the constituent elements, the effect of which is to generate a disquieting sense of cognitive and/or affective discordance.

Simply put, parts of a story or an image don't quite gel. It's a sense, registered by the listener, that something in what they are hearing doesn't quite add up, something is illogical or inappropriate. Furthermore, because questions tend to be disallowed or are themselves problematic, the discordance is mostly incapable of resolution. Even when this is not the case, too often the teller fails to see how what he or she has said can be illogical, and if they say it again, it's clothed in the same words, a repetition rather than a reformulation, as if the problem had been one of hearing rather than of interpretation. So the re-attempt has no explanatory power. You are left with an abiding disquiet; what you don't know in your youth is that this disquiet is probably a life companion.

The dissonance is multi-layered. The purpose of this section of the book is to try to tease out some of these layers and explore what lies beneath. I will look at five layers within the communication, each of which in its own way contributes to the discordant message.

Knowing and not knowing

A sense of knowing, as we have seen, appears to be in place from earliest infancy. Yet 40 years later there are descendants who still seem baffled by their own lack of knowledge of their parents' background. Can you know and *not* know at the same time? This juxtaposition gives rise to a layer of discordance.

You feel you must know the story because you think you've been told it so many times. You don't realise that what you've been told, abstracted from time, place, context and the possibility of coherence, cannot be taken on board and therefore is like not-knowing. It's rather like a rote learning of material that makes no sense. It never connects with something more fundamental, is never integrated, truly absorbed. The bits don't compute in your head; they roll around and are unconnected to anything else in your world apart from other equally unfettered Holocaust 'bits'. Susan captures the confusion:

> All that time we had with them but so little of it was spent talking about it. It left you wondering—if you had heard more would you have come to grips with it more? Or do you end up knowing more because you've spent so much time filling in the gaps?

In any case, your imagination doesn't serve you. You can't imagine your parents young. They come from another world, which isn't like this, your world. The photos, if there are photos, are black and white, and quite alien. The background is unfamiliar. People rugged up against the kind of cold you just cannot imagine. People with names that have strange cadences, names that won't attach to faces. There are diminutives attached to names or what you work out in time are terms of endearment, but they too are alien. You can't imagine families—cousins, aunts, grandparents.

The pressure on you to make connections is massive and it hinders rather than helps. I was about 40 years old when my father first put up on the wall the only pictures he had of his mother, father and sister. This was nearly half a century after the end of the war. One day they were there, on the wall. He said nothing about them, maybe waiting for me to ask; and I said nothing, waiting for a cue from him. A metaphor for survivor–descendant silence.

Now I wonder where he kept these photos before they went up on the wall. And did he look at them himself quietly, at times when he was alone? Did he cry? Is that why he waited so long—until he could look at them without crying? For a few years, I passed these pictures on his wall, not quite oblivious to them, but not willing to look more closely (indeed, willing myself to *not* look). One day I found myself peering at them and then without realising it, I found myself weeping. This was grief: I recognised the emotion unequivocally. It took all those years for me to know that these were people who mattered to me, whose lives I should have shared, at least known about, whose deaths I should have mourned. But you can't grieve for a connection until there is one.

Could I have grieved sooner? Could I have understood sooner? Could their world have had meaning in ours? As a generation, how could we have known? We don't know what it's like to live in a country where tanks roll across the borders and suddenly you are 'occupied'. You can never get the dates right: when the Germans invaded, whether the ghetto came before or after the camp, which camp and how they got there, who liberated them and what happened after. The facts have to be committed to memory; you try out private little mnemonics, like the one I used to try to help me remember which of my middle names is for my father's mother and which for my mother's mother. These devices, skingrafted on, remain a surface device. They don't link up, integrate, take on a coherence of their own. I think back to that bureaucratic moment at my father's funeral, when there was a need for some basic biographical knowledge—place of birth, date of birth, names of kin, etc.—when my brother turned to me and asked, 'Do you know this stuff?' and now I ask myself, 'How could we *not* have known?' and 'How could we not have known that we did not know?'

It was only when I was at university, studying modern European history, in particular, Nazi foreign policy and the prelude to war that I understood how the Final Solution was planned, and later how it was engineered. Then, suddenly I had a balcony-view of history, rather than a ground-view of tragedy. I was able to place the fragments of information I had accrued at home against the wider canvas of history.

And for the first time it made sense, a cool, macabre sense but a sense nonetheless. There was even a curiously satisfying logic to be gleaned. Liquidation, I discovered, is methodical and systematic. First the media are saturated with negative and fearful representations of the Jew. Then laws are introduced to strip Jews of their citizenship and their right to work. They are cast out of the mainstream. Then unbridled power allows the injection of terror, lawlessness, fear of authority and non-conformity, the reign of thuggery. Next the Jews get identified and registered, then rounded up and herded into one place, so creating the pre-conditions of annihilation. Finally, what remains of them are packed into cattle trains and sent to another place of concentration (it took me many years to work out what this 'concentration' meant), where they are sorted according to particular categories, branded with a numerical ID, and then methodically worked and starved to death. For others, death is more immediate: their bodies are stripped of any conceivable assets (like gold teeth or hair), they are efficiently exterminated, then incinerated—effectively removed from the face of the earth. Political scientist Colin Tatz argues that of the various sequenced steps by which a genocide moves from a plan to a reality, it's only the final stage, the killing, that can happen outside of language.[51]

Given this perspective, you never again confuse or forget the logic that makes ghettoes come before concentration camps. Suddenly, the fragments that you have heard all your life begin to cohere. The *ghetto* was where they went after the Germans entered Vilna. The *bricked-up walls* defined the prison perimeter. *Liquidation* was the end of the ghetto, when the remaining population, about 10,000 Jews, were deported to *the camps*. Now I understand *concentration*. Now the story about the *train escape*—the scissors and the jump—fits in: the train was taking her—women, young, old, and children—to an extermination camp. The *beating* I heard about, that permanently injured my father's wrist: this must have happened in the camps. How many years later, was it, that I took out a map of Eastern Europe, and let my fingers trace the route to Estonia, the first camp my father was sent to, where my grandfather died; then via the Baltic to Gdansk, where the second one was; and then to south-eastern Germany near the Boden Sea, where the last one was. Lines on a map, moving a finger across a few centimetres, trying different senses, to *make it go in.*

This, however, is not how it comes down to you in the parental home. There, words and fragments of information you've heard all your life wrap themselves centripetally around foreign sounds— *Judenrat*, *Gestapo*, *aktion* and *kapo*—and roll around in your head, trying to connect but endlessly incoherent. This is what I mean by the discordance of knowing that you have been told something and yet feeling that you don't comprehend its meaning.

This failure to comprehend should not be surprising, nor should the fact of any accompanying discordance. At the Holocaust Museum in Washington DC, it was decided that the average visitor needed some way to connect personally to the extremity and scale of destruction that is displayed in the exhibition. So as they enter, people are given a mock ID card of one of the six million dead: the card provides a name and some biographical information (this part is real). People are seen fingering the card as they walk around the Museum. I view the Museum's decision here as an attempt at a touchstone, a way of grounding the abstract and infinite. Maybe this is as close as one can reasonably expect to get, connecting to a common humanity.

Perhaps it's part of the human condition that we resist knowing that which is incompatible with life, what I mentioned earlier as a need to maintain a degree of 'mental comfort'. Leah recounts this:

> Once when we gave someone a lift out to a place where we never went, my Mother kind of exploded after hearing Ukrainian spoken. I knew Ukrainians had a bad reputation but I didn't know what connection that had with my mother. She talked about it on the way home. That's when I heard about babies being smashed against walls and thrown up in the air and shot, and people being pushed out of buildings. It was horrifying but I couldn't imagine it. You just can't imagine human beings doing this. You're horrified and repulsed and you can't imagine surviving all of this and holding these images in your head for the rest of your life. You don't want to let it in'.

In Grossman's novel *See Under: Love*, the main character, Momik, holds his breath while his grandfather tells his story:

> (He) listened . . . from start to finish, and swore he would never-ever-black-and-blue forget a single word of the story, but he instantly forgot because it was the kind of story you always forget and have to keep going back to the beginning to remember, it was that kind of story, and when Grandfather finished telling it, the others started telling their stories, and they were all talking at once and they said things no one would ever believe, and (he) remembered them forever and ever and instantly forgot them.[52]

Momik's forgetting the story as soon as it is heard is no doubt a protective device, a means of censoring and keeping out that which he intuitively knows is not good for him to know, that which is not able to be integrated comfortably. The response echoes Primo Levi's recurrent nightmare in the camp, the fear that one day he would tell what happened and he would not be believed. There is something here that points to the very essence of the human condition. It has to do with the limits placed on empathy. To survive, we cannot take in an infinity of horror. Self-preservation dictates boundaries between us and others.

Rubens' *I Dreyfus* is a novel about the multiple and subtle layers of knowing, not-knowing, denial and discovery. It is also ultimately about the limits of representation, the core futility of trying to convey the experience, a futility that, as I have tried to describe, drives and fuels the silence. At the close of Rubens' story, the main character, who has spent all his life protecting the secret of his Jewishness, keeping it within the well-defined boundaries of his immediate family, confronts his ancestry at the crematoria of Birkenau. He arrives there after following the route that his grandparents took having been picked up in a Gestapo round-up of Jews in Paris and then deported east. In the museum at Birkenau, he

> saw all that he had read about. He knew about the mountain of shoes, the piles of artificial limbs, the kaleidoscope of spectacles . . . But this was a different kind of knowing. It was a knowledge from which one could never walk away. It was proof. Proof undistilled, unpolluted by metaphor or literature. A heap of children's shoes is exactly what it is, a heap of children's shoes, and the slightest simile diminishes it. They walked around in silence. The horror was beyond commentary.[53]

Discordant emotion

Another discordance has to do with the emotional overlay that accompanied the narratives. A number of patterns emerged in my data. One pattern is the high degree of emotional intensity alongside paltry factual details. There is the sense of being washed in an intensity of emotion. It has a searing, permeating constancy, alongside the partial, patchy, fragmented factual knowledge of what happened—to whom, how, when and where—most of which fails to be absorbed.

How is it possible to feel you are drowning in the knowledge, yet not to know? It seems to me now that what we drowned in was a tidal wave of emotion—grief, anger, shame, guilt, doubt—transmitted for the most part non-verbally, by a look, a clipped remark, a turning away, a biting down on the lower lip, a sudden outburst, all of which carry emotional meanings. Erlich points to the same contradiction in his home:

> It appeared that we spoke openly about everything that happened to the Jews *there*. It seemed that everything was laid out on the table . . . but in truth father never uttered even one word . . . and mother only told us whatever was convenient to her.[54]

Eva Fogelman's film *Breaking the Silence* claims that the children of survivors have inherited an entire memory of (events) which has little to do with what their parents have told them; in fact part of the problem, for many children was just this want of actual telling by the parents, an overload of behavioural and non-verbal signs that are so difficult to interpret . . . Many responses are not articulated or narrated as much as conveyed in a thousand daily ways to children as memory.[55]

Jill speaks of the home she was raised in: 'No one talked about a topic that was huge in the background. It didn't seem remarkable then that it wasn't talked about'. She is left today with only a rudimentary impression of her family biography.

She is not alone in this. Even in middle age, many descendants have no more than the bits and pieces, plus the sadness that this is how it will remain. Where people have managed to make it cohere, it is often as an outcome of devoted, even obstinate effort, usually linked to formal study or the will to research and record the family tree. These people come to the task in middle age, wanting finally to put an end to the distress of only knowing the minimal, elusive and evanescent details of their parents' lives. Jane is typical:

> They tried to tell me but I couldn't get it. I got it as stories that grad-
> ually built up, but it was always like this, disjointed. I had to piece the
> chronology together for myself. I tried to get it in order many times.
> I got my grandmother to talk to me about their pre-war lives and I
> put all that on tape, but it took me another twenty years to work out
> the chronology of the war.

As well as the absence of talk about the war, there's also an accumulating sense of what is *not* present: drop-in family members outside the nuclear unit, an easy evening meal over plentiful and uncomplicated food, a lack of interest in current events, a healthy contempt for authority, a sense of the now and a comfort in the present. One of my respondents talked about a generalised sense of unsafety in their lives and related this to lack of family. She described her perception of 'the having of family' as the 'cushions' that protected a child when elements of the world impacted cruelly on one's life—like fights at school. When on the other hand there is the bare elemental unit—the nuclear family of two parents plus child—there are few cushions. This means exposure and vulnerability. Absences, then, had a powerful and haunting impact. We were washed repeatedly in their significance without ever knowing that this is what was going on. Jules says and not without bitterness, that he 'had the Holocaust for breakfast every day of (his) life'.

That these absences are marked, and pathological in their markedness, is evident from other situations where extended family is absent but not traumatically so. One of the editors who read an early draft of this book commented that she too grew up alone in a nuclear family, her parents having emigrated from Britain to small-town Australia. Though she had no aunts, uncles, cousins and grandparents here, she knew she had them back home—they were constructed and reconstructed through correspondence and family talk. Today she can say, 'I was never aware of family being absent'. Similarly, children of European migrants (Greece, Italy, Yugoslavia) and, more recently, Poland, South America, Hong Kong and Vietnam, may have extended family present in their constructed lives, if not in their immediate physical lives.

For survivors and their children, ancestral links were severed. Letters, phone calls, photographs, trips home—there were none of these. One of my respondents mentioned that her mother was called in to see the kindergarten teacher one day, around 1950, to be told of the school's serious concern that the child's vocabulary was deficient: words like 'grandmother', 'grandfather', 'uncle', 'aunt', 'cousin' were simply not known. Was something wrong?

The experience echoes something of the stolen generations, Aboriginal children taken from their families and raised in institutions.[56] John was removed from his family as an infant in the 1940s. He talks about how ancestral and family links were severed:

> We didn't have a clue where we came from. We thought the Sisters were our parents. They didn't tell anybody—any of the kids—where they came from. Babies were coming in nearly every day. Some kids came in at two, three, four days old . . . They were just placed in the home and it was run by Christian women and all the kids thought it was one big family. We didn't know what it meant by 'parents' because we didn't have parents and we thought those women were our mothers.

Even glimpses of the parents' pre-war lives were limited: 'They couldn't comfortably tell us', said Rebecca. 'We got snippets but it was always the same snippets, over and over. It drove me crazy'. Near the end of the family history that Rebecca has written, she writes:

There was little talk about their life before the war and we grew up with none of the closeness of family life which was supposed to be traditional among Jewish families . . . There was no passing on of family traditions, family histories, Jewish stories . . . there's a few Yiddish songs I remember that give me a warm glow but little else.

A case mentioned by Hass cites an angry young man accusing his mother of 'constantly talking about it', where the mother actually believed she had consistently avoided talking of the war to spare herself distress. What emerged was 'that this boy took his mother's look in place of verbalisation'.[57] One of my respondents, Ella, who grew up in Romania, gives a first-hand account of how this happens. Here she talks about growing up in a 'culture of fear'.

When I was fourteen, I went with my mother, who was a doctor, to a holiday resort where she'd got a job. There was a beautiful walk by the sea. It was very dark there at night, but quite safe. Lots of people were out strolling, mostly tourists. We went out one night but that was all. Mother didn't want to walk there again, even though it was so beautiful. She simply said she couldn't handle the sound of the Munich accent. I accepted that right away. It made sense to me, though really, in terms of my factual knowledge, it didn't. But I understood on another level. In families like ours, fear travels like osmosis.

A corollary of this discordance between too much emotion and too little information is the constancy of the one, and the jerky, impulsive nature of the other. In some cases, the parents may have remained silent on the subject for many years until a crisis in their own life (typically loss through death of a spouse) or in their child's (typically marital or health issues) releases a sudden, seemingly unchecked torrent of information. This information, sealed away for many years, is clearly of a different order to their usual style; these occasions seem to allow for a small modicum of direct talk in language that is candid and unmitigated. Hass mentions just such a case: a survivor's son, going through a divorce, reported that his parents chose that time to talk to him at length about their wartime experiences. He understood their intention: 'They told me to console me and assure me that life would continue'. There's another reference to a son's complaining that he was having difficulty studying for his medical exams. He told his father he couldn't do it. His father then told him, for the first time, that 'he had lain for thirty-six hours under a pile of corpses in order to hide from the Germans'.[58] The message here is clear: one can do what one has to do. There's an intertextuality here among different kinds of talk about trouble where people disclose and console each other interactively.

Another type of discordance comes from the child's sense that horrific events are being relayed in a calm and rational voice. David says that on the whole his parents concealed things from him, only mentioning the war in passing 'and the thing that struck me was that it was usually without much emotion'. Leah too comments on her mother's matter-of-fact tone, adding 'I was aware of my mother trying to keep her emotions flat'. She recalls:

> I remember a visit from a woman from Melbourne who had been in the same class as Mum. When she left I asked her why she hadn't mentioned this woman before. She said they had been classmates, but not close friends. And it was then that I found out that out of her entire class (all the students were Jewish) only three survived the war. And it was all said very flat. But I was deeply affected by this and I remember thinking about it afterwards and looking around my own class and recognising what a huge thing it would be to lose everyone bar three people. But she just said it, in that flat voice.

And another time:

> A lot of the time what she said was matter-of-fact. There was one incident when someone she knew from her schooldays had dobbed her in to the Gestapo and she was taken in for questioning. It just came out like that, unemotional. Something . . . triggered a memory and she told me. It must have been terrifying but there was no emotion in her voice when she talked about it.

Ella had a similar experience. She recalls her mother's voice as 'steady and calm', a tone that was 'light, relaxed and matter-of-fact':

> I tried a number of times to talk about the number on her arm. I tried to ask her about the camps. Sometimes she would tell me stories. What shocked me was the serenity with which she talked. It sounded like she'd been away at a sanatorium. Like, the showers every

morning. Being awakened early every day and having icy cold showers. I couldn't tell from her tone what it was really like. Her face showed nothing, no grief.

Irene speaks about the discordance in her father's telling, of the effect of his 'deleting the horror':

> He portrayed everything in an unemotional way. This didn't freak me out at the time because I didn't know what the emotion was that should go with it. It does now. A few years ago I asked him about the ghetto. He talked for about half an hour and then I said, 'You make it sound like a Boy's Own adventure story' and in the same flat voice, he said, 'No, people were dying everywhere of starvation'.

When Sam was filming an interview with his aunt about Auschwitz, he had her talk while she was making dumplings. She talked while her hands worked. She gave him 'the official version', as he calls it, 'with a great deal of detail and not a skerrick of emotion', as if she were reading something out. She would stop, wipe her brow, and then continue, in the same tone. He interprets this behaviour as the effort of will needed to keep emotion at bay:

> I sensed the emotion was being suppressed. That's why it seemed shrill. She's saying, 'Don't give me a hard time about this'. It's brittle. There's a lot of tension. She doesn't want to be interrupted. She wants to get it out, and then over.

Of course, the child listener colluded with the survivor to get through the event with the minimum of fuss, disturbance or fallout. We learned ways to discourage the narrative, to divert the emotion, to get beyond the moment.

The point is that absence of emotion in the telling about such circumstances is itself very telling. Leah said of her mother, 'She didn't talk a lot. When she did it was very matter-of-fact. I didn't like seeing her pain, so I didn't push her'. Susan also interpreted the space between the text and the absence of emotion:

> It was presented as very straightforward, like she was saying 'I don't want to get emotional about this'. She never broke down but I knew it was very emotional for her. I always felt that if I pushed her, she

would break and I couldn't bear that. It scared me. Because you always see your parents as the strong ones and in charge, and if they break down, where does that leave you?

The sense is always of emotion controlled, sealed off for fear of flooding out. Bernice recalled asking her mother why they had no relatives:

We were standing near the sink in the kitchen. She was about three feet from me. I couldn't see her face but I could hear her tone. She started saying something and then stopped and I knew I could never ask that again, and then we went on as if nothing happened.

Jill said, in a matter-of-fact tone that seems to mirror the one of which she speaks, 'I knew they had lost all their families, but I never saw them get very emotional about it':

Even when she was talking about Bergen-Belsen, it was matter of fact. There was little emotion. I never saw her cry except on Yom Kippur at the synagogue, when they have special prayers for the dead. Then she'd get emotional and I'd see her sadness, but otherwise, nothing.

My sense of this phenomenon of suppressed emotion is that it is a management strategy adopted by survivors to enable them to speak, without which words would be drowned out by emotion. It seems to parallel that which I have read elsewhere of the manner of speaking of a victim of child sexual abuse: 'She spoke with uncanny calmness, as if she had schooled herself to tell this terrible story'.[59] However, there may be other explanations. In Dobbs' political thriller *The Wall*, the main character, Katherine, had carried a dark trauma over many years. When at last she spoke about it, 'her voice was matter of fact, like a disinterested observer, as if all the emotion had been squeezed by the experience and there was nothing left for the retelling'.[60]

I am reminded here of Elsa whose mother's only 'indulgence' was Saturday afternoons, when she'd retreat to her room and might be heard crying. 'But you didn't go to her. You stayed away. This was her time. There was a pattern to it, and therefore some kind of sense'. Thus, even the letting out of emotion was staged: it was as if the emotion, if allowed to 'happen' spontaneously, unstructured, unrestrained, would wash everything away in its enormity. It's hard to know whose loneliness is the more poignant—the mother within her self-constructed, incommunicable enclave of sorrow and grief; or the daughter, in her realisation that suffering was happening so close to her without her being able to do anything to help.

I recall that my own mother, who never ever spoke directly about her wartime experience, whose few references to it were oblique and clipped, had a passion for B grade TV movies. She would lie on the couch in the lounge room and tears would stream down her face, a display disproportionate to the stimulus that apparently triggered it. I'd wonder about this, not only about the discordance—silly, soppy movie, mother crying profusely—but the sheer quantity of tears that flowed. (There was also on occasion a macabre reversal: sometimes the movie was truly tragic, and then she'd find it quite amusing.) I knew not to ask her so instead, I turned to my father, who not only was devoted to her, but was more communicative. I had had the sense that he was also aware of the inappropriateness of some of her reactions.

I was sitting up on the examination table in his surgery, while he bandaged my bleeding knee, when I asked him about this strange phenomenon in our home—I'd since found out that other people's mothers didn't do this—and he said, very gently, looking pointedly at my knee rather than in my eyes, 'It's OK. Don't worry about it. When the bottle's very, very full, it's good to let a little bit out, from time to time'. I took that statement away with me, as I knew there was no discussion to be had about it. I thought long and hard about its import, and though I could not have articulated my understanding at that time, it did have explanatory power. I understood that my mother's grief needed an outlet and the silly, soppy movie served this purpose. I also understood that, for one who'd lived through an actual tragedy, tragedy in the Hollywood style may indeed be a source of mirth. It was years later that I read, in *A Net of Dreams*, Salamon's account of her survivor parents, where she mentions 'a willingness to weep at fiction without the inhibition they felt about weeping at life' and I knew exactly what she meant.[61]

For Abe, whose family travelled the epic journey across Russia, adulthood has given him the distance to see that he was 'raised in the story' which he says was an integral part of their lives. He refers to the discordance between text and emotion as an 'inevitable constant', suggesting 'the narrative itself was constructed to make sense of the incomprehensible'. The only way it could be made sense of was 'to tell the story as a Mosaical wandering in the desert'.

Emotion so contained inevitably seeks release. My respondents frequently referred not only to living with instances of emotional numbing but also to the opposite, what amounted to wild unleashings of emotion. Here the emotion in question is anger—moments of unrestrained fury that contrast so strikingly with what Krell calls 'contained rage', effectively the state of being a survivor.[62] These moments of unleashed anger erupt without warning, may be gone in a flash and are tremendously unsettling. I could never forget my mother's outburst at the sight of boys flogging fish to death; nor could Leah forget her mother's reaction to hearing Ukrainian. Hoffman calls it 'helpless rage'—the kind that has no words.[63] Elaine says:

> It was terrible. All that pain coming out. She was all over the place. She would be trying to hold back her tears. She didn't want to show her fear or weakness or vulnerability, but all her demons were coming out. It was sheer terror for her and there was nothing I could do.

A number of the respondents remarked that the few insights they achieved into their parents' past took place during family crises, when people's defences were down. On one occasion, Julia recalls, it was the day after her mother had a general anaesthetic for an operation and when she woke up the next day, she started talking about the war, saying things Julia had never heard before. As soon as she recovered her strength and started getting better, she 'closed up and stopped talking'. The crisis passed, the emotion is newly recontained and sealed off.

Moments of wild rage that seem to come from nowhere remain etched in memory. Most descendants can cite their own example. David recalls a day when he was nine or ten that he took to school a little metal comb that his father had, that came from the days in the concentration camp. When he came home in the afternoon and took it out of his pocket, his father saw that he had it and went berserk. The boy was overwhelmed by the disproportionate rage unleashed seemingly for no reason. Later his mother's words soothed and comforted him but the memory has stayed with him. It was many years before he understood that the emotion was a function of how keenly the father wanted to keep the boy separate and unstained by his parents' past. 'He didn't want to transfer any of his pain to me'. Seeing the little metal comb in his son's hands uncorked uncontrollable emotion, for the father saw his precious son tainted by his horrors.

In some homes, the emotional outbursts were less rare and in fact became the central feature of the parents' discourse on the Holocaust. The descendants I interviewed who grew up in homes like this speak about the 'noise' in a parallel way to that in which others refer to the silence. It would seem that at times this kind of discourse served as a smokescreen, a distraction, that disallowed questions as effectively as the silence. One commentator called it 'covering up with noise'. Either way, though both styles of discourse have their own communicative effect, not a lot of information was imparted by either.

That survivors experienced and transmitted an emotional discordance is not at issue. Jean Amery, the writer who survived Auschwitz and many years later took his own life, wrote that after what was experienced in the Holocaust, those who survived could 'no longer feel at home in the world'.[64]

Shame

Survivor shame is multi-layered and immensely complex. It is not only the sense I suspect of their wondering about others' wondering about the unasked eternal question, 'What did you do there that you survived?'. It is also a shame associated with victimhood. Epstein comes to understand her mother only after her death:

> I realized that her years in the camps had transformed a normal happy adolescence into something shameful. She had come to discredit her years as a teenager, to bury her memories of friends, boyfriends, adventures. It was shame that accounted for her silence in place of stories . . . Other people blamed (her generation) and they sometimes blamed themselves for not having seen what was obvious, for having denied or excused or delayed when action was required.[65]

The myth of the passivity of lambs to the slaughter is built on the premise that the Jews of pre-war Europe should have seen the writing on the wall and acted sooner to save themselves. The irony of this is that it demands of the victims the foresight to imagine the unthinkable even given that this same unthinkable remains so unthinkable to those who came afterward!

David's father's vehement reaction to seeing the comb in his son's hand derived from his wish to protect his son from his own sense of shame at what had happened in Europe. Ironically, one of

David's early emotions in relation to his parents was shame. Like many children of survivors, he wanted to know 'why they didn't fight back'. The more silent they remained about what had happened to them, the more the silence reinforced his idea of their passivity, and the more he believed that people like them went like lambs to the slaughter. This phrase itself or the notion of passive compliance in their own destiny accompanied much of the newspaper reporting of the Eichmann trial. It would seem, for some, to be a comfortable and very visual image—lines of quiet, orderly Jews, resigned to their fate. It removes both the agency of the perpetrators and the resistance of the victims. It suggests, to those brought up in another place and time, that when the trains pulled up at Auschwitz, the lambs compliantly stepped from the carriages, were neatly shepherded into the factories of death. But you don't have to have probed very deeply into witness accounts to know that it was nothing like this. Somewhere I read that a survivor wrote 'there was nothing quiet when you arrived at Auschwitz'. He was referring to the noise, beatings, blinding lights, guards screaming, dogs snarling and attacking, machine-gun toting soldiers forcing the terrified and disoriented new arrivals into the selection where defenceless people were torn from loved ones, and sent right or left, to an immediate or a postponed death.[66]

Yet I have learned that it is extremely difficult to explain to anyone how six million could have died. It's a common reaction to see this as compliant passivity. I know survivors' children who believe it and non-European Jews of the survivors' generation who see it this way. It seems to be the default interpretation, that which requires least effort. I am troubled, however, by people's willingness to stay with this view, despite all evidence to the contrary, and I found myself needing to understand it better.

My research in the notion of Jews' being apparent willing accomplices in their own destruction taps into a very sensitive area of the post-Holocaust Jewish psyche. This includes the generations of Israelis brought up since the state's foundation in 1948, raised in a strident culture of self-protection and independence which, in its own way, is a response to the Holocaust. Certainly, as a child, I knew not to ask about the subject of 'fighting back'. The question would unleash a torrent of exasperated emotion from my father. I resolved to find out my own way, one day, which is what I did through studying the events as history. Over time I arrived at the answer which itself lies in an understanding of the circumstances of the period and of previous centuries.

Few people have this knowledge or the will to acquire it. Few have the explanatory skill or emotional peace of mind to impart it clearly. So the fiction of an easy surrender to death is one that persists when, paradoxically, the truth is that giving in to death would have been far easier than enduring what it took to stay alive. A cynic might say that people prefer to hold onto this view in place of tempering their ignorance with a sustained and studied search for the truth. There is probably something here, but there is more involved, I believe, than the ease and comfort of ignorance. I sense a resistance to seeing it otherwise.

The image of passivity and compliance is one that the mind more happily accommodates. It takes the edge off the extreme anger one might feel towards the perpetrators if one saw the slaughter for what it was. Apportioning some of the blame to the victims for their own death allows one's emotional response to be more moderate—and for the outsider, moderate is preferable to extreme. We see this in people's reactions to the planned cultural genocide of Australian Aborigines by successive government policy on taking away their children. *It was done for their own good. Their families couldn't look after them. It was an opportunity for the children to break out of the poverty cycle. It was an act of welfare and was well-intentioned*, etc. The forced removal and assimilation of indigenous children is a different time, a different place, a different genocide. Still, it suited bystanders, even those bystanders who come after, to temper their perception of the appalling reality with more palatable interpretations. It seems easier to blame the victims for not looking after their own than to believe that the government could engage in such actions.

For those who came after the Holocaust, a dramatically different cultural environment prompts the question, 'Why didn't they fight back?'. The postwar generations are completely removed from their parents' cultural reality. They have been raised on a diet of heroic characters who achieve their goals against immense odds, and within a prescribed time limit. From Superman to the action-man characters played by Arnold Schwartznegger, Bruce Willis, Jean-Claude Van Damme, Harrison Ford and Steven Seagal, Hollywood has given us the endlessly replayed scenario of good triumphing over evil, an outcome predictably achieved by fighting back. Before the genre of action movies, there were Westerns, where cowboys got what they wanted from the land they invaded and they got it by fighting. And the feast of classic epic heroes in the first fifteen years after the war— *The Ten Commandments* (itself an allegory of the Holocaust), *Moses, Ben Hur, Spartacus*—also sent the message that energy, action and concerted will overcome even apparently insurmountable odds. It's an Ayn Rand universe of rugged individualism where you pull yourself up by your bootstraps and you alone are responsible for what your life might become. Adversity is something to be seized upon, for out of it will come its own reward. It's an approach centred on blaming the victim for their victimhood by which it somehow becomes possible to assert that if people didn't want to be on welfare they wouldn't be. By the same crude logic, if the Jews had wanted to live, they would have fought back. This mindset, in the child of a survivor, produces not only shame in their parents but also shame in themselves, that the shame is there at all. These days when I hear or read the lamb metaphor in application to the Jews or any other people, it is to me an indicator both of how little the user knows and how hard it is to know.

The shame that survivors' children sometimes feel is complex, like their parents', but the layers are different. There's the shame that your people—people like your parents, because that's all you know— died in their millions without, it would seem, putting up much resistance. The word 'resistance' is poorly understood; it has come to be associated not with the ghettoes and camps but more narrowly and literally—the idea of Resistance as a unit of underground Partisans attacking enemy installations, guerilla style, wherever they could. This notion is fuelled by movies that memorialise the heroism of underground fighters, while guerrilla warfare, for those with no knowledge beyond the celluloid, has an image modernised and forever romanticised by the intense, brooding face of the beret-wearing Che Guevara. It is normal to want to think of one's people like that. Missing from these images of resistance are bits of reality, like the fact that the Germans' retribution for Partisan attacks was visited indiscriminately upon civilians, or the little-known fact that some Partisan groups, certainly in Poland, were as anti-Semitic as the Nazi enemy they were fighting and would often kill or betray a Jew who tried to join them.

And there's the shame that in knowing about the deaths of family members, you are unable to feel the 'right' emotions. You don't know what you're supposed to feel or what response you're expected to show. You do know that the minimum that is needed to console them is to display some understanding and sympathy. But even this you can't muster because you can't get the story right in your head and you can't ask questions to help resolve some of the issues. It's as if you're frozen in the spotlight, unable to perform. The emotional climate in which the narrative about the Holocaust takes place is *a priori* very fraught. The parent is usually concentrating hard on holding in the emotion and so is the child, if only by modelling the behaviour in front of them. The difference is that in the child's case, the exact emotion being suppressed is not known. This came out in something Sam wrote to me following our interview:

> After our meeting I was filled with sadness for a day or two and it struck me that I, like my mother, can discuss the Holocaust in an unemotional and detached way and that only later, when I have a private quiet moment, do the feelings well up. I always feel some guilt at not being more emotional at the appropriate times.

Just as young children blame themselves for their parents' divorce, promising 'to be good so that Daddy will come back', children of survivors want to exert their own will and agency so as to make things better for their parents. They often force a logical connection between their inability to feel or respond appropriately and the fact that their parents are inconsolable. When their efforts fail, the thought becomes: *If I really cared about them, I'd make sense of it; I can't make sense of it, so it must mean I don't care.* From here it is only a small step to self-blame. This sense of bewilderment is captured in Salamon's recollections:

> We didn't . . . understand the current of tension that often seemed to be in the air or where our enchanting sentimental father went when he slipped away from us into a silence we didn't know how to interpret. We knew these disappearances were, somehow, connected to our being Jewish and to the Holocaust . . . but we couldn't identify his emotion or its exact cause. Was it rage or despair or simply disappointment at something we had or had not done?[67]

There's also the (irrational) shame born of a feeling of guilt that *you* caused all this. Children put themselves at the centre of their universe and it is through this centre that they perceive and respond to experience. Children of survivors often make an irrational nexus between themselves and their parents' pain. Rena is an example of this. For the first twelve years or so of her life, she blamed herself for the terrible things that her parents had suffered. She was enormously relieved, during the Eichmann trial, to discover through reading the newspaper, what Eichmann's role had been—this meant that she 'didn't do it'. Irene remembers feeling guilty for her Gentile appearance:

> As a child with blond hair and blue eyes I used to think: Would I have done the right thing? Would I have tried to save my father? And the answer was 'probably not'—I was too scared for my own life. I felt so guilty about that. I used to lie thinking about it when I went to bed at night.

Julia is another example. In her mind, she was born 'because of the Holocaust'. Her birth meant others died, so if she subtracts herself from the equation, she gets 'no Holocaust'. A state of 'no Holocaust' would remove her parents' pain. By a curious mathematical step, she arrives at a sense of her own responsibility for her parents' losses. That her adult intelligent self can see and acknowledge the illogicality of her equation in no way brings her comfort.

I also have the sense that just as the second generation's patterns of grief and mourning seem often to be modelled on that which they imbibed in the home, so too is it with a sense of guilt. Laub tells the saddest of stories of a survivor who was unable ever to talk about her experience of the Holocaust. The suppression of the story over time meant that 'the untold events had become so distorted in her unconscious memory as to make her believe that she herself, and not the perpetrator, was responsible for the atrocities she witnessed'. This perhaps is an extreme case. However, it demonstrates the end point of a process experienced by many survivors (and experienced vicariously by their postwar children): a blaming of self for that which they had had no power to stop. Laub says of his case: 'if she could not stop them, rescue or comfort the victims, *she* bore the responsibility for their pain'.[68] I have no doubt that my mother must have endured this for the 46 years beyond her own helpless witnessing of the murder of her mother. It remained unspoken: in Laub's sense, her witnessing was itself never witnessed. My sense today is of a wound now so removed in time and space that it was beyond healing.

The bizarre

Linked closely to the theme of dissonance is the bizarre quality of many Holocaust stories. Elsa told me:

> Sometimes when my mother was talking about the camps, her tone would be kind of embarrassed, even a bit giggly. It was a nervous titter, it's what came out because she was just so uncomfortable talking to us about it. And some of it didn't make sense. She said that in the camp, if they didn't go to work a German would jump in the window with a bit of hose and start beating them. I'd say, 'A rubber hose? A garden hose? Why didn't he come through the door, why come through the window? To me it was a comic scene, with this ridiculous creature coming through the window. It just didn't make sense. It's not just the lack of knowledge. This is what she said. I just couldn't understand it.

She goes on to say that she could never feel confident that what she knew was anywhere near adequate because 'you can never be sure that you have the whole story'. She goes on:

> Mother would say such weird things, they were quite bizarre. And there was the way she told us—she didn't start at the start and work her way through it. The really disquieting thing was that they made sense to her, and you'd end up keeping quiet because it was so insult-ing to tell her that they didn't make sense.

Another vignette she recalls was the one her mother told her about the journey after liberation. She was with a small group of women:

> They were heading home and on the way they found a derelict barn. Unfortunately they ran into a group of Russian soldiers and the big thing was to avoid being raped. They were cold and she said they warmed these saucepan lids (*where did they get the saucepan lids from?*) against the fire and then held the lids against their stomachs (*why?*). After a while, she went outside to do her toilet and that's when her sister told the Russians that she had typhus which is why she had the saucepan against her stomach (*why?*), and they left her alone.

Elsa ends with, 'That's how she told it, as if all that was quite natural. She just couldn't see that I had no idea'. For Elsa, as for many descendants, listening to a story like this, being unable to 'do anything

with it', and ultimately realising that that's as far as she would get with
making sense of it, takes half a lifetime. Most give up the quest as
doomed to fail. Elsa persisted, finding that she continued to be
bothered by her failure to make sense of some of her mother's stories.
One day she saw a documentary about liberation:

> It was about a group of American soldiers who themselves were
> remembering the moments when they liberated a concentration
> camp. One of the soldiers reported that that he walked up to a huge
> barracks and shot the lock off and went in to find hundreds and
> hundreds of bodies stacked up to the ceiling. Among them were four
> little children sitting on top of dead bodies, playing a game like jacks
> with some bones.

Elsa then said:

> That story gave me some insight into my mother's situation. It was
> bizarre. There was so much those children no longer saw. It was the
> same for my mother. There was so much she no longer saw. Not
> because of memory—it was stuff she had edited out. That's why the
> stories were bizarre. And I think I knew when she was telling me the
> stories that there *were* things I did not want her to see. I think I knew
> it was better for everyone if she did not look too closely into the
> corners of her mind and memory. Better that these things remain
> unearthed.

Elsa here hints at the complicity between teller and listener that I
have elsewhere referred to as granting permission to talk. When the
speaker edits out the parts that are too horrible to tell, the listener is
quietly grateful for the reprieve offered. It gets one through the
moment but it does nothing to assuage the discomfort.

For Elsa there was a dissonance at the very core of her relationship
with her mother. The person she knew as mother was different from
the person that the war seems to have erased. For example, Elsa saw
her mother as depressed or melancholy but, when she encountered
people who had known her mother before the war, she discovered her
reputation as 'a big joker, someone who giggled a lot and never
stopped laughing'. These features didn't gel with the woman who
raised her and, although Elsa was happy that the depressive trait was a
late arrival, a reactive condition rather than coming from within, there

is great sadness in her final realisation 'that I just did not know my mother at all'.

Many of us come to realise that the parent we always knew was a different person pre-war. When Epstein returned to Prague to track down her mother's history, she discovered that there had been piano, dancing and gymnastics lessons in her mother's childhood, and she found out about the foods she'd liked and the games she used to play, none of which she had ever been told about. 'It was as though the war had discredited all of that. It was not useful or valuable and she did not wish to pass it on to me.' She discovered that her mother at fifteen had been 'a frivolous human being, interested in dancing, skiing, boys . . .', an image totally at odds with hers of her mother: 'even her laugh—the laugh she claimed to have lost in the war—exuded tension'.[69]

Richard mentioned rare glimpses he had into his mother before the war took away everything: 'Once she told me how she used to flirt with her sister's husband'. I am struck with the fact that he recalls this, surmising that it has stayed with him either because he was told so little that it's easy to retain, or more likely, that the glimpse into the girl that was is utterly at odds with the mother he has always known. I am reminded of the strange incongruity I had sensed once, long ago, when my mother mentioned something about going nude swimming somewhere sometime in her adolescence, and I was unable to reconcile the carefreeness of this behaviour with the woman I knew.

This is captured, too, in one of the stories of a woman survivor recorded in the Yale Testimonies. Here the woman talks about why she stayed married to the husband from whom she'd become estranged:

> The man I married and the man he was after the war were not the same person. And I'm sure I was not the same person either . . . but somehow we had a need for each other because he knew who I was, he was the only person who knew . . . and I knew who he was.[70]

My impression is that the Holocaust not only took away their family, their home, their job, their community; it took too their sense of their own identity, to the point that their postwar survivor self feels like the life of another person. By the time children of survivors reach an awareness of this, it is often too late: this is one more way in which the wider tragedy is writ small again, in the inner lives of those who come after.

The parent generation, for whom the circumstances of their wartime experience are so thoroughly known, seemed not to understand how a postwar child, severed from the parents' time and place, could find it anything but bizarre. At the very least, they should have expected that their children would interpret what they heard within the parameters of their own limited experience of the world. In Glass' *The Interpreter*, the narrator's mother is a Holocaust survivor: 'I remember as a child thinking, from the snippets I heard, that we could have done with the Nazis at Brownies and Girl Guides. They were great at making fires and burning things'.[71]

At times, fragments heard are so unimaginable, given the child's reality and worldview, that 'it's easier to shut them out'. Sam recalls a story his mother related: with a few others, she had escaped from the death march, the forced retreat from the concentration camp in the last days of the war. They came to a farmhouse. They told all the people inside to get out, in fact they chased them out, then they killed a farm pig, skinned it, cooked it, ate it and, afterwards, they were horrendously sick. He says, 'I can't imagine her chasing people away, being starved, eating forbidden food [pig] and over-indulging to the point of illness. None of this is like my mother'.

Irene has a comparable experience:

> I had no concept. I remember one of the stories my father told me about what happened at the labour camp at the end of the war. Some Red Cross supplies arrived and some of them drank the condensed milk. Because it was too rich and their bodies so starved, they died. I remember him saying that some of them didn't try the milk; instead they went into a room. There were flowers in a vase and he took out the flowers and drank the water from the vase. For me that's completely unrealistic. It's bizarre.

Perhaps if the survivors had not emigrated to a distant and different land, that which seemed so bizarre to the children might have been less so. Rebecca, brought up close to the seashore in sunny Australia, said of her mother's experience in Russia:

> It just doesn't make a lot of sense to someone growing up where there's plenty of food and the sun shines every day. The idea of my mother

walking through snow up to her waist, with a yoke and two buckets of water, and then getting home and slipping and losing all the water and then having to go back and do it again. It made no sense to me.

Her mother would sometimes hop into bed with her: 'She would cuddle me, a lovely gentle cuddle. I welcomed that because I was a pretty lonely kid, but I never knew what to say. You're lying in bed in this sunny house near the beach and she's talking about snow and cold and deprivation'. Elsa said she would try hard to imagine the scene she was hearing about when her mother was talking:

and then she would say something else which would contradict it and I would ask for clarification but the answer didn't fit. For instance, she might make mention of the servants and I would think, right, so you were well-off, but then I knew my father was a butcher and that didn't fit. I kept on getting conflicting information that didn't fit in with my rational scheme of things so in the end I gave up trying to visualise because I knew it was impossible. I resolved to get the information some other way.

Sam, the amateur filmmaker, 'wanted the detail, I wanted to be able to visualise it beyond the bizarre and cartoon-like quality that it had. She never gave me any of the detail'. He adds, 'Maybe she didn't take it in at the time'. Elaine says, 'It was all over the place. Incoherent. I couldn't put it together. I always felt she'd got something wrong, in the wrong order, or she'd left something out'. Abe says, in an incredulous voice, 'Some of it was truly bizarre. They were on this train which arrives out in the middle of central Asia where Stalin had earlier sent a whole bunch of Jews and these Jews who'd settled there before all came out to the station and asked them get off and settle there too'. Ella remembers that her family got a TV around 1958, when she was seven. The kids' job was to make sure the movie was not about the Nazis, and if it wasn't, the mother would come and watch. Then during the Eichmann trial when there were repeated images of starved skeletons, the mother would say, 'Nothing can reproduce what it was like there', and Ella would think to herself, 'What could be worse than that?' Rena would often try to protect her ageing father by admonishing him not to watch anything on TV that was related to the war. It was a futile attempt, but he'd console her by saying, with a bitter laugh, something like the celluloid version was tame.

Michael believes everything about his life at that time was bizarre, from the little sailor suits he was dressed in, that were bought in Italy on the way over and were so inappropriate to the Australian climate and culture, to the kinds of things his parents were frightened of: 'Here we were in Australia, the most laid-back country on earth, and they saw threat everywhere. Any instance of bureaucracy and official-dom caused fear and panic'.

Bizarre circumstances seem to beget bizarre lessons. Ella grew up without any fear of death, but with a fear of being lost or separated from ones you love:

> Death was not made frightening for us. It just happened and it seemed natural so when my father died, it was OK. People didn't cry and my mother didn't grieve, at least not in front of us. Maybe death is better than the kind of life they had. Maybe death was a solution to the problem of life.

Faced with the bizarre, one can choose from a number of options. You can ask questions directly but in fact these rarely served to enlighten, and often caused more angst. You can learn to live with it, accepting that life has its quotient of blurry edges, incongruities and ambiguities. Or you could seek answers from other sources. A common ploy was to be oblique: ask the father about the mother; ask the mother about the father; ask an aunt or close family friend about the parents. Other sources of information were books, films and documentaries, which were effective in gradually building up knowl-edge of the historical context and circumstances, the backdrop against which one individual family's tragedies were wrought.

Cued messages

Earlier in the section on socialised messages I wrote of the need for the information about the Holocaust to be reworked so as to make it amenable for narrative. Out of this reworking, we get in survivor households patterns of sayings that relate to things from food to education and trust, and only collectively and obliquely touch on the Holocaust.

Just as important are the messages that were not managed or socialised. These were particular sayings—Hass calls them 'pointed parental pronouncements'—that were closely linked to Holocaust topics.[72] The child learned to see them as 'cued', that is, sending a meaning that is larger than their literal, face-value one. Like socialised messages, the cued ones brook no discussion and tolerate no probing. They drop into a conversation, seemingly from nowhere, and effectively extinguish it. They carry more meaning than the circumstance requires, and the child knows that more is going on than meets the eye. The result is discordance.

The cues are repetitive and predictable. Maurice said that his father was very politically conscious and easily impassioned about justice and people's rights, even when it had nothing to do with him. The boy read meaning into the fact that the father was so extreme in these views, and whenever he launched into one of his tirades, it cued the boy to the war. Jennie recalls the things her usually sedate father said when he found out she had a date with a Polish boy. She did not know at the time the source of his anger, but its extremity cued her. Susan recalls her mother saying how she had been determined not to marry any camp survivor: 'I suppose she thought that she was not strong enough to support herself *and* someone else who had been through that'. Often, when one parent was a camp survivor and the other not, the children were told by the parent who had 'suffered less' to be good for the other, because they had 'suffered enough'. Leah recalls being very irritated by her uncle, her father's younger brother, who lived with them. Her father used to say to her, 'Don't expect too much from him. There are things you don't understand. He has suffered a lot'. So she made allowances for oddities in his behaviour and never found out any more about what had happened to him.

The pattern of making allowances and involving the children to do the same, in the absence of any meaningful explanation, sent cued messages to a generation of children who knew so little about the past. Edna remembers her parents talking about a family friend, 'She was beautiful even with her hair shaved' (*Why would her hair be shaved?*). Richard's mother told him that to pass as a Polish Christian girl, she had to learn the Catechism (*What's the Catechism? Why do people learn it?*) and he had difficulty making sense of how proud she was, even to the present, of knowing it 'better than the Catholics'. Susan knew her mother spoke French because 'she was there during the war' (*Why would you learn French during a war?*), and knew somehow that this was cueing a larger meaning but, as often happens, she recognised the cue without being able to put the message together. Bernice's mother told her children that she would poison them if there was another war (*Why?*) but, apart from this, told them almost nothing. Grossman's character, Momik, the child of survivors, passes on the cues to the next generation by raising his own son 'cautiously and without love, in order to make him strong and prepare him for the inevitable disaster which is to come'.[73]

The point about cued messages is that even if the full meaning of the oblique reference is not retrievable, the cueing achieves its own ends by re-framing present events to give them a significance beyond the literal and obvious. Listeners are thrown back onto their own inferential resources, left as Sam put it, 'to fill in the blanks'.

Shifts in the participation framework

Elsewhere I have characterised Holocaust narrative as having three participants: the teller, the listener and the text. I intimated that one of the difficulties in this was that the text tended to swamp a face-to-face encounter and overwhelm both teller and listener. To compensate, the communication becomes increasingly indirect: messages are fragmented and dissonant, and meaning is so oblique that listeners' inferential skills are obliged to work overtime.

Another way in which indirectness was achieved was through restructuring the 'participation framework', a term that Goffman uses to denote the various roles that people play within an exchange. Goffman found the terms 'speaker' and 'listener' too gross and unrefined to be helpful as analytical tools. They provide too blunt an instrument to assist someone trying to understand spoken communication. He shows how subtle shifts in the participation framework can bring about effective adjustments to the structural roles available to participants, and this helps people achieve their communicative goals.[74]

In the case of Holocaust narrative, the factor that makes the telling and the listening so difficult derives in large part from the very real risks inherent in face-to-face interaction where the requirement is that the listener be seen 'to take on board' what they hear. So difficult is this, as we have seen, that many survivors looked for ways around it—through avoidance, procrastination, through writing their accounts as letters to their children, all these being different permutations of silence. Another way around the problem was to bring about subtle (and not-so-subtle) shifts in the framework of participation governing the discourse they had with their children. These moves enabled them to sidestep the painful proximity of simple speaker-to-listener discourse.

The first of these I will call 'ratified eavesdropper' (after Goffman).[75] What happens here is that the child who is the listener moves from a clearly public role (listener) into a less public role (eavesdropper). As such, the listener is still 'ratified'—meaning their presence is known about, as distinct from say, a child hiding and over-hearing—but the difference is that the eavesdropping child is allowed to be a non-participant. Being a ratified non-participant is a luxurious role in that one is able to take information in receptively but is relieved of the obligations of fully-fledged listeners, namely having to produce responses and exhibit overt, active listening behaviours.

There is a 'strong' version and a 'weak' version of the concept of ratified eavesdropping. The case of Elsa demonstrates the strong version. Her home was quite religious, with close links to the synagogue and its congregation. Friday nights were shaped by the conventions of the Sabbath. The family was always together for the evening meal, which was more elaborate and lasted longer than other evening meals. If guests were invited to the home, it would typi-cally be to Friday night dinner and then people would relax around the table—and talk. Because of the father's connections to the synagogue, they often had as guests certain religious young men, new arrivals to Australia, who had not as yet settled in. Elsa's home was welcoming; it was the congregation's way of being hospitable to newcomers. She remembers one of these visitors in particular, a young man who was keen to hear about the parents' experiences in the war:

> We would all be around the table and he would ask some questions and I would just cringe inside. I'd think, 'How could you ask that! It's so painful!', and then I would listen to the answers. They knew I was there and they knew I was listening and that was OK. They wanted me to know but they couldn't bring themselves to say it directly, so telling Michael, while we children were there, was convenient. I picked up information this way and drew conclusions. I built a picture of it in my head.

Elaine tells a similar story, this time with herself, the ratified eavesdropper, as an adult. She says that through her childhood years and later, there was no constructive way in which she could talk with her parents about the war. 'I never had any permission to talk about any of this stuff. It was a taboo.' However after she married, things changed. Her husband, who converted to Judaism when they married, was not expected to know and made an excellent listener. He was able comfortably to talk to his parents-in-law about what they had been through. Often on Friday nights, at family gatherings or on special occasions, the discourse roles were made available. The father was cast in the role of raconteur, Elaine's husband asked the questions and was a keen listener, and Elaine quietly heard it all, as if for the first time, in her role of ratified eavesdropper.

Many children of survivors have told me that they have noticed that their parents are much more comfortable talking about these things to their grandchildren than they were to their own children. In part, this could be the effect of the passage of time; by the latter years of their life, when they have grandchildren, the immediate shock and trauma have passed and survivors may gradually have found a *modus vivendi* that allows them to tell their story without the same extinguishing level of anguish. Hass writes: 'With greater distance from the Holocaust, their exposed nerves recovered their myelin sheath'.[76] The reduced reticence may also come from the awareness that their lives are drawing to a close, and a compulsion to tell it all, finally, so that the story will not go with them to the grave. It may be related too to the fact that the very existence of grandchildren suggests a continuity of lineage, and a comfort in this, that it may have taken them 30 years or more to register. It could also be that there is some truth in the folk notion that relations between grandparents and grandchildren are less fraught than those between parent and child.

Another interpretation, which can sit alongside the above, is that in fact when the grandparents talk to the grandchild, they are setting up a ratified eavesdropper role for their own child, who is often present for the telling. Michael says that he only recently found out many details of his mother's wartime experience through conversations he has overheard (where his presence was not hidden) between his mother and his ten-year-old daughter who, it seems, asks questions that he always wanted to ask but couldn't:

My daughter asked the questions. She just had the naiveté and innocence to ask, something I could never have done. I had had this blockage, and it became bigger and bigger. I always saw myself as my mother's protector. I saw her as a wellspring. Stuff would come up, heavy stuff, she would erupt in tears. I couldn't handle it without a lot of fear and emotion. I learned to recognise the trigger points and I stayed away from them and with time, they form their own adhesions. So you kind of choreograph yourself into this position and you stay there. My daughter, though, just came out and asked . . . and my mother just started talking, and I was there and I listened. Maybe things would have been different if I had been able to ask.

Michael berates himself for not having asked such questions when he was young, without truly realising that the naiveté and innocence out of which his daughter's questions arise were part of her world but not part of his. He is hard on himself, as indeed are many children of survivors who tend to attribute to themselves a great deal of the blame for the difficulty of communication in their home. Michael and Elsa are examples of the strong version of ratified eavesdropper.

There is also a weak version; weak because it seems less structured, less engineered, more an unforeseen by-product than an intended outcome. Hass' respondent Stephen demonstrates this:

> Our house was often filled with . . . survivors, and talk around the table was always loud and pained and angry about the war and the camps and the people who never made it. There were poker games on Saturday nights that were always filled with survivors and their children and we all, from our first days, were fed stories from the camps. I think I was eighteen before I discovered that there were Jews who hadn't been in a concentration camp.[77]

The scene typically is one of children on the floor playing while parents talked. This pattern is pervasive through my respondents' reports of their childhood. Leah says, 'A lot of what I remember is background. They're there talking and you're playing but you've got one ear opened to what they're saying. So you pick things up'. John says, 'Often I would overhear people talking about what it was like. They knew I was there. They were comfortable with that'. Edna says that survivors could only talk about surviving with other survivors:

> People didn't want to listen. My parents didn't even tell their relatives here who had been here since the thirties. But they talked a lot among their survivor friends and that's how I heard the word *Lager* (camp). It was often when I was playing with other kids. I remember throw-away lines that hinted at things without ever spelling them out in full.

Jane tells a similar story: 'We grew up in a survivor community. I used to hear all the conversations. They never sent me from the room. There was just a lounge room, no TV. They'd talk about who survived and who didn't. I overheard lots of things I would never have been told'. Julia remembers finding out information only when the parents had company over, when her father would tell his stock stories, usually the ones that featured his bravery or someone else's compassion. Abe talked about living within the community of Jewish refugees that made it to Shanghai, a little hiatus of time where 'not knowing' was a blessing: 'It was scary but not traumatic. They didn't know then what lay ahead and they didn't know yet what happened to those they'd left behind'.

In some cases of overhearing, it is difficult to assess whether the listener hears because of the proximity of the talk, or whether listening is a result of trying to eavesdrop. It is even harder in such circumstances to know whether the process was ratified or not. A case I heard of concerns the Pacific War of 1941–45. A young Malaysian soldier was conscripted into the army that was sent to China to stem the westward and southern Japanese invasion. He was away at war for several years. When he came home, a silence overtook him. He did not ever speak to his wife and sons—born after the war—about his experiences in the war. He spoke only to his friends whom he knew as soldiers, in whose company he had been during the war. His children knew what they did of their father's wartime experiences only by listening from the next room to the conversation that their father was having with his soldier friends.

Another example of the 'weak version' is a point that Sam makes about his mother, who seems to avoid the circumstances that might allow her son to probe more deeply into her past:

> My mother busies herself with one thing or another. It's difficult to arrange to see her alone. I wonder whether in some way she chooses to always be occupied and not to allow the quiet and solitude that might allow a sensitive and detailed telling of her story to me.

This is my life

'This is my life' is the name I have given to the second pattern in the adjustment of participant roles.[78] Here the parents replace themselves as tellers with an outside agency (such as a film or documentary) and become listeners (albeit knowing ones) alongside the child. Robert's case illustrates this very well. As a young teenager, he reports being 'dragged off' to a number of memorial services and to some documentary movies. There was never much warning or preparation. They would just arrive at the place and sit down, and 'it would happen'. He calls this 'a direct attempt to tell me indirectly'. He says, 'basically that's the way they told me'. He recalls sitting stiffly and uncomfortably next to his father, watching the film. Then they left and walked away in silence and drove home. 'They never actually sat me down and said anything. Probably they wanted me to ask questions afterwards'. But he didn't: 'I went because they wanted me to. I knew they wanted me to know what happened'. Robert's sense is that his father felt he had a duty to tell and that's why they were there. His way of telling was to enable the boy to find out. As they left the cinema, the sense was that the duty had been met. Yet the weight of what was not said must have been intolerably heavy. Of the fate of loved ones, the personal narrative, there was no glimpse. Today, some 40 years later, he knows hardly more than he did as a young boy.

Today Robert has no greater curiosity to know than he did as a child. 'These days I'd stay away. I don't want to see it and I don't want my kids to.' He is quite dismissive of the whole issue of knowing or not knowing. He seems to have imbibed the taboo and naturalised it, continuing to apply it, right into adulthood. When I asked him about any interest he might have in his parents' pre-war lives, where they came from, the families they lost, the world they were part of, he shrugged, 'Shit happens. They came here. They rebuilt their lives. That's all there is'. Children of survivors to varying degrees had their ancestral links severed. To me an indication of perhaps the most radical severing is when the descendant fails to see that the link has any importance. This will be further discussed in Chapter 7.

In taking their son to see the war documentaries, Robert's parents cast themselves in the role of listeners alongside him, and thus made themselves available for questioning, though this in fact did not happen. Susan's case is a slightly weaker version of this. I have mentioned already how Susan's mother would tell her, in a throwaway line, to watch a programme on the TV, as an oblique way of telling her the stories she was otherwise unable to relate. Susan used to look for opportunities around such events to try and open up the topic:

> I may tell her I've watched it but we never discuss it. I know she wants me to know but she doesn't know how to tell me. I can't ask her

questions because it upsets me and when I'm upset I can't be a source of comfort for her. And when I get upset, it firms up her resolve that telling me is not a good idea. This is how it's been for years.

The mother–daughter stand-off continues, even to the next generation. If Robert is averse to talking with his children about his parents' past, Susan is simply unable to talk to her two daughters on the subject of their grandmother. Partly this is because she doesn't have a lot to tell. And partly, this inability derives from the absence in her own life of the role model of parent talking about the past:

> How am I going to tell my kids? I don't know what to say or how to say it, or what's appropriate for their age. I want them to know it generally as well as the personal details. But I find it difficult to talk about it with them. I feel the same thing—if I talk I'm going to break down. So I send them to Sunday school, because someone told me this is taught in sixth class. So I'm just like my mother—I want them to know but I don't want to tell them.

Jennie is aware of similar constraints: 'I want them to know. I realise I'm trying very hard to find the right words'. Elsa has firm views on the responsibility of her generation, and her children's, to seek knowledge and to disseminate it. She insists that her children know what happened to their grandparents, that they are conscious of the fragility and preciousness of civil liberties, and the right for people to be different. She refuses to accept that her husband won't watch Holocaust-related documentaries because it's too 'upsetting'. For Elsa, to refuse to allow oneself to become upset is a kind of denialism. Elsa's parents are dead now, and she deliberately uses opportunities to feel empathy for them—for instance, by watching a TV documentary on the Holocaust. 'If I can get a glimpse of that world,' she says, 'it brings me close to them'. I suspect that here Elsa gives voice to a sentiment that is very far from being hers alone.

The 'go-between'

The go-between parent is the third pattern of adjustment to the participation framework that I want to illustrate here. This is a role set that gives a particular function to the parent who is allegedly the less traumatised by the war. This is how it was for Maurice:

I wasn't prohibited from asking but I didn't feel I could because it was like a taboo topic for my father. So I couldn't bring myself to talk about it. But Mum could, she could hint at it. So she was the go-between.

Sometimes the potential for the less traumatised parent to act as go-between was thwarted by that person's protective impulse. Maurice's mother did not experience the Holocaust directly because her family had emigrated to Australia in 1938. The father, on the other hand, was only fifteen when he was sent to Auschwitz. The couple met and married in 1957 when he emigrated to Australia:

> She tried to protect him from having to come out and deal with all the awful things that happened to him. She was the kind of person who didn't want to give expression to any negative things. For her, happiness was a very strong duty. The fact that she took on this role was a good fit for him because it meant she stopped him from talking about it. She would steer the conversation away from the war, by saying something like, 'Let's talk about something happier'. The topic of the war was a no-go zone in front of my father.

It served the children in some sense too. A pattern was established very early in the home. The children knew they could get a glimpse of their father's story through the hints that their mother would let slip. She functioned then as a kind of conduit and a relatively safe place where they could try out information. This system spared the father from the pain of telling, spared the children the pain of asking directly, and yet allowed some information to seep down over the years. Maurice's mother, however, was not sure what the best way was to protect her husband:

> I think she thought that bottling it up was bad for him and that there would be some catharsis for him by talking about it. Yet she realised it would be too hard to make him talk to us. So she did it the other way around: she tried to encourage us to approach him, draw it out of him, make him feel that we wanted to hear, which would give him a natural reason for talking

In any case, the kind of information that she passed on was very limited: generalisations like 'He lost all his family there', references to movies they'd seen or to some of the correspondence which went on with distant relatives in different places in Europe, Israel and the USA. This correspondence was made to serve a purpose in the home's pattern of indirect communication:

> Referring to Dad's correspondence with relatives . . . they begged the questions from me about how they were related and why they had gone there and not here, how they were separated, what happened to them. It was as though I could only ask about my father through other people's experiences.

I saw a similar allocation of roles in my own home: my mother deferred to my father's supposed greater suffering and at times protected him, even from himself. I can remember her pleading with him not to watch another documentary on Nazism, saying he didn't need to see it again or know more than he already knew. He'd encourage her to go to bed, and then he'd watch it and slip into bed later. Sometimes the medication she took meant she didn't hear him calling out during the night. Mostly, his nightmares woke her too. They never ever talked to us about the nightmares. But I knew about them.

So did many children growing up in survivor homes. Dan says: 'Some of my earliest memories were of my mother waking up at night screaming . . . The two of them would go into the kitchen and have a cup of tea and my father would stroke her hair to comfort her'. Jane says, 'My father used to have bad dreams and he'd wake up shouting. They explained it to me. I was told what he was dreaming about but it didn't make a lot of sense. I knew he'd been beaten and had lost his hearing in one ear. I kind of imagined that the dream was about that, always about that'. Erlich comments on the reversal of roles that characterised his home: 'I was not the four- or five-year-old, who would wake at night and shout for his mother. It was my mother who cried and woke us up'.[79] Clearly dreams were one way, not a very confronting one, that repressed stories could find an outlet.

When we analyse the subtle adjustments in the home's participation framework, from ratified eavesdropper, to 'this is your life' orchestrations, to the go-between role, it is clear that nothing here is accidental. Behind it all looms the desire for a story to be heard and a dread in anticipation of the telling.

7

The Unspoken Text

In Chapters 5 and 6, our focus was on explicit, direct communication and then on indirect communication. Now we come to the subtlest of all the communication patterns, messages conveyed in the absence of text. It is important, though, to note that their subtlety in no way suggests a loss of effectiveness. On the contrary, I suspect that because such messages slipped in, in a way, beneath the level of language, descendants did not mobilise a response to them, as they may have, even silently, to more direct messages. Hence communications received in this way may have been less amenable to conscious assimilation, interpretation or repair.

I have divided the material here into three parts. First there are the 'exclusions', communications that were actively excluded from the standard discourse of Holocaust households. Sometimes the parents excluded them by forbidding them. At other times, the child consciously excluded them in the interests of harmony and in the interests of avoiding conflict or emotional entanglement. Second we have 'iconic messages', communications carried through the iconic value of a particular object, behaviour, attitude, activity or phenomenon. Though such triggers work without text, they have nonetheless a powerful communicative impact. The third and last group is an apt one with which to finish the book because it points toward a silence so endemic that it is naturalised. These are omissions so deep, exclusions so pervasive, that there is no awareness or recollection of absence. In other words, this way of being has been accepted as normal.

Exclusions

I will elaborate on four different kinds of exclusions. What they have in common is that they refer to enforced absences of which

248

descendants were aware. As these are consciously known of, my respondents were able to talk about them in great detail.

Taboo topics

One of my respondents said: 'As soon as the topic of the war came up, [they] would just stop'. All of us knew there were some parts of our parents' memories that were barred from us. As we grew up we learned to recognise early-warning signs; we came to recognise the rough edges of topics that were out of bounds. Then as a rule we would position ourselves vis-à-vis the topic: we would studiously and vigilantly avoid it, withdraw from it or try to find alternative ways of managing the information at hand. At all times, we were sensitive to the riskiness of this kind of talk, and we would gingerly skirt the perimeter of the topic, aware that at any moment we might step on a land mine. More typically, we retreated from the points of danger and sought safety in the anodyne.

Taboo topics mostly relate to losses so intense that they continue to cause great emotional pain. Jules tiptoed around any reference to his mother's loss of her mother and sister, even to their hair colour which she once described as 'golden, with the sun shining through'. Dan says, 'I could sense my father's agitation as we got to the subject of the camps and his relief when we moved away from the topic'. Jill's father would quite happily talk about his family's life in pre-war times but nothing else; he'd stop short at the war. And she knew that she could never ask about her mother's parents and siblings. I once mentioned this pattern of taboo topics to a survivor, who said, 'But you can't talk about it and stay sane'.

Sometimes all you know is that your name or one of your siblings' names belonged to someone who was dearly loved and lost in tragic circumstances—beloved but unspeakable. Names, for obvious reasons, are potent symbols. A particularly poignant testimony to this is the case of a woman survivor, John's mother. The loss of her brother caused her inconsolable grief, to the point that through her postwar life she actually forgot his name. It returned to her on her deathbed.

Detail omitted

Where painful topics were broached, key detail was often omitted, contributing at times to the listener's difficulty in piecing the fragments

into a coherent whole. For Julia, this piecemeal quality meant that she
could never trust her own understanding of what she knew: 'I still have
the feeling that I don't know whether something was told to me or I
made it up'.

One symptom of this difficulty is that descendants are rarely sure
that they have the whole story. Julia is now in her late forties but her
confidence in the trustworthiness of her knowledge about her parents
appears to be continually eroded. Her intuition that there was more
to the stories than she was being told was vindicated when one of the
stories, indeed a bedrock of the mother's talk about herself, cracked
open, almost without warning. This happened a few years ago and it
was a devastating experience for her because it fulfilled the descendant's nightmare: finding out what you have dreaded all your life.

The story Julia had always been told was this. In January 1943,
her mother was living in the ghetto with her two sisters; at one point,
the three girls were selected to be taken to Treblinka. Julia's mother
was the youngest of the three. She worked out an escape plan: she
bribed a guard on the train with some jewellery and they were able to
get off without being shot at. Then they found their way back to the
ghetto. (Julia could never understand why they would have chosen to
go back to the ghetto, but it was mid-winter and they had nowhere
else to go.) The story she had always heard included the death of one
of the sisters, whose child had been taken from her earlier in the war.
The cause of death—'a broken heart'—was the closest she could get
to finding out how she died; this had been one of those topics that
she'd spent many years skirting around. But for some reason, this time
she persisted. She asked, 'What did she die of?' The answer came,
'She was sick'. Julia asked again, 'But what did she die of?' And then
suddenly her mother broke down, 45 years after the end of the war,
and released the one bit of detail that had always been left out. The
sister who died had been ill. She couldn't go on and she told the
others to leave her. It was the only way to survive, so they did. Julia
reports:

> She didn't even say 'We left her to die'. She said, 'We left her there
> and went'. She never actually saw her dead. She carried this huge
> guilt buried in her all these years, and in the end, she let it out.

When we discover these whole truths, as Julia did here, and as I
did about my mother's mother's death, we feel that despite the

empathy and compassion and intertwining of boundaries that has gone on with our parents, in fact, we never really knew them. This represents another loss, and at very close quarters; and the severing of another link, perhaps the most primal.

How many such memories must survivors have carried with them for the duration of their postwar lives? One of Ursula Duba's narrative poems, 'As you wish, madam', attests to this. It relates the experience of a nineteen-year-old girl who arrives in Auschwitz with her mother after three days and nights in a crammed cattle car. It is 1944, and the two had been deported along with the entire Jewish population of the Hungarian town of Munkacs. On a loudspeaker, a German guard is screaming that the new arrivals have to form two lines—one made up of those who are now to do a ten-kilometre run and one for those who are too old or sick or both. It is announced that the latter group will be taking the bus. Concerned that her mother not have to do the run, the girl approaches a man (whom she later learns is Mengele) and seeks permission for her ailing mother to go on the bus. 'As you wish, madam', he responds courteously, 'with a slight bow' and the mother boards the bus. But it turns out that there isn't any running after all. She discovers that her school-girl German had caused her to mistake a word in the screamed instructions at their arrival. The German word *laufen* means both 'run' and 'walk'. So it turns out that she need not have sought a place 'on the bus' for her mother, after all. And she keeps asking where her mother is. The next day,

> one of the guards
> points to the thick smoke
> coming out of the chimney
> and tells the nineteen-year-old
> there—that's your mother.

The girl survived the war and emigrated to America; she never ceased to blame her mistake in German for her mother's death. Of course, logic would dictate that it was not her mistake in German or her finding a place 'on the bus' for her mother that caused the woman to be selected for immediate extermination. These are incidental, albeit macabre, peripheral details. The fact is that the mother, white-haired and sick, would have been 'chosen' anyway. Decades later, logic still offers little solace for her self-blame.[1]

Quite evidently, survivors' sense of guilt is one thing that gets in the way of telling their children their story. So descendants jigsaw what they hear with what they infer. Of her efforts to piece together the facts of her parents' lives, Rebecca says:

> I spent my youth trying but failing to get details of information . . . Now I'm struck by the enormity of the fact that I'll never be able to do it. I don't know if it's my sense of history that makes me want to do this, or whether I crave this sense of history because I have none of my own.

Sam says of his mother:

> She has an official story. It's all plot, no description. I have trouble getting behind it to fill in the details. She treats my questions abruptly until she gets back to the official line. This allows her to avoid the pain of remembering. I've tried all sorts of obscure ways to get the information because I realise now that I won't get it from her.

The parents must have known that some of what they spoke of would be difficult to interpret, and in a sense they took advantage of a child's limited knowledge of the world. Sam asked his father where he was in the war. The answer was 'a labour camp'. The boy made sense of this by thinking his father went to work 'maybe in a factory, maybe making bullets'. Any questions he asked met with the same answers. Sam says: 'It was direct, but there was a lot left out. I was too young to know and they were trying to protect me'. Vagueness served a purpose.

The omission of horrific detail is, of course, a form of sanitisation. Ella asked her mother about the camps but the answers were non-specific. The family was taken somewhere; nothing was said about the grandparents being gassed or the uncle becoming sick and dying. The account given was vague, minimal and sanitised. Ella came away with a picture of Auschwitz as clean, like a summer camp. About the death march, all she gleaned was that her mother had had diarrhoea, that someone had given her some milk, and that she'd survived. The episode had nothing to do with the wider picture of what the Nazis did to the Jews. She ends with, 'Had I gone on a long trip and not felt well, it could have happened to me'.

In many cases, the parents kept the details from their children in an effort to spare them, yet, ironically, the not knowing itself was a source of great anguish. David was aware that he was excluded from some things: 'I remember the emotion. They would stop when I came into the room. I got the feeling they didn't want me to be included'. Dan's father would talk to him on the topic but tended towards a discussion of abstractions and philosophy: 'in terms of specific people and specific events, there was nothing'. Jill said, 'I knew my mother was in Bergen-Belsen and she survived as a nurse's aide. But just recently I twigged. Who was she nursing? Obviously not Jews. It must have been Germans'.

What I am describing here is a straining to know, without having the tools to find out. A metaphor perhaps would be standing in a library, blindfolded and with your hands bound. Irene captures this straining to know by an analogy to a moment in the film *Europa Europa*.[2] A tram goes through the ghetto and the boy strains to see out the windows, to fathom what it was like inside the walls. 'I was like that. I had no idea, no image. All the time I was straining to see.' When Robert's father took him to see documentaries about the war, the boy knew that the personal details of his own family were being left out. At Passover in my home, my father would begin with the prescribed text, 'Once we were slaves in Egypt' and then gradually shift to being 'slaves in Europe'. We knew what was being referred to but, as always, the personal detail was omitted.

When it came to the deaths of their own parents, our parents were so overwhelmed at their own failure to protect and defend, that on the whole, these events were unavailable for talk in our homes. Very few of my generation know the details of our grandparents' deaths. In some cases, like my father's, he himself did not know and could not bring himself to try to find out. In other cases, like my mother's, she knew but to stay sane she had to reinvent herself and, in the newly constructed frame, these memories were suppressed. In her waking hours, this was achieved by sheer strength of will. At night, she dosed herself with medication. I don't know if she was afraid of nightmares or insomnia or both. Memories came packaged either way.

Disallowed behaviours

Some of the messages our parents' style of discourse carried also bore meta-messages, messages inside messages. These referred to disallowed behaviours. One example I have already mentioned is the survivor's response to death, which may carry an endorsement of stoicism in the face of loss. Indeed crisis meant the suppression of emotion. When my daughter was born very prematurely and there was a great danger that she might not survive, my father immediately expected the worse, put forward the 'soldier on, get on with it' face and expected me to follow his lead. He was outraged that I might go daily to the neonatal ward and see her, touch her and, as she became stronger, actually hold her. Expressing my breast milk so that she could be fed with it encapsulated for him the very bonding that he was so adamant I avoid. Of course, his reactions were born of another time and circumstance. But so suppressed and locked away were these memories that for this period of our lives, there was very little communication. He could not say what he really wanted to say and I could not do what he wanted me to do and within the silence that fell on us we both stepped back, to a place of total incommunicability. Gradually through the months that followed my mother gently patched the drift between us. I don't know what she said to him. To me, she gave no verbal explanation of where his responses were embedded. Silently, she nudged me towards him and, I gather, him towards me, and silently we eventually resumed where we had been, before the crisis; of course, it was never mentioned again.

In a sense, as Laub explains, a subsequent tragic life event in a survivor may re-open the trauma of the Holocaust, forcing a reliving of terrible memories. Such was the experience of French author Martin Gray who lost his family in the flames of Warsaw and Treblinka and had to relive that memory when a forest fire in the south of France claimed his new young family. He says, 'their deaths have reopened all the graves [and they] died a second death'.[3] These responses to subsequent crises are not reflective, examined ones, but knee-jerk reactions learned through six years of horror. In those times, one's survival depended on one's capacity to hold in emotional responses, to rise above them, to stay alert for the next onslaught—in other words, to learn to respond inappropriately. To have responded appropriately at the time of the trauma would have been to court death. Such a response may have been life-saving at the time; however, it can also lead to an endless mourning, a crisis in fact that never achieves closure.

The containment of emotion is a major pattern that I found in my respondents' interviews. Elsa remembered going to synagogue on Yom Kippur, six months after her father's death. The song, 'Kol Nidre', which her father used to sing for the synagogue, was being sung by someone else and sung badly. Its haunting sound, her remembrance of her father's beautiful voice, the fact that it was not being sung well, all these were suddenly too much for her. She began to cry, the first time she'd shown emotion about her father in public. 'My mother kicked me in the shins. You don't show emotion. You are never to demonstrate a need.' Rena had a similar experience about forced public emotion. She was a moody adolescent, tending to be sullen and morose, particularly at family mealtimes which were always tense and demanding. Her mother would kick her ankles under the table and these kicks had many meanings: *Smile. Don't be sad. Be grateful that you have food in front of you. Don't make your father unhappy. Display a different face.* Susan believes that a large part of her mother's emotional response was hidden and she respects this:

> Everybody finds their own mechanism for coping and if you undermine this, you don't know what you'll expose. It's better not to upset the applecart. I never pushed too hard because I was afraid of unleashing the emotion in her and in me.

The parents suppressed their emotion and they expected their children to do so too. Many of my respondents remember the difficulty of handling their emotional response to their parents' suffering. Leah remembers her mother once trying to tell her about her own mother's death. She can see the moment today like a framed photo. 'I remember it distinctly, even where we were sitting. I was about twelve. I was riveted to the spot and very frightened. She had tears in her eyes. I didn't handle it well. I couldn't bear seeing her pain'. Rebecca's story is remarkably similar, 'I felt heartbroken when she talked to me about her own mother. I steeled myself so I wouldn't show any emotion. I'd hear a voice in my head saying, "I don't want to hear this. Please don't tell me"'.

When the text of the narrative overwhelms the telling, the listener is at a loss. Elsa remembers that she did not know how to behave appropriately. 'I knew the question of responding was dicey. That's why I opted for the low-key. Then if I got it wrong, at least it was minimal.' When Helen Epstein returned to Czechoslovakia to retrieve her maternal history she was shown the old Jewish Street, now as Jew-free as most of the country. She writes: 'I could feel my body cutting off emotion the way it did when as a child I listened to my mother talk about the war'.[4]

The blocking of emotions and the numbing must have impacted on family relations. Yet only a few of my respondents confessed to seriously damaged relations. Bernice was one of these, 'My mother has hidden her emotions for so long, it's all blocked off'. Jules is another who claims he was treated with 'emotional brutality'. The literature too is replete with reports of emotionally tumultuous behaviours. For example, there is Salamon's recollections of her mother's mask-like demeanour which could erupt without warning into something quite different: 'Her features twisted into a mask of hatred as her lips pressed together, trying, it seemed, to contain unspeakable rage'.[5] It was on these rare occasions that 'her face would reflect her actual experience'. I wonder, though, whether the troubling element of this experience for the child is less in the occasional eruption of extreme anger and more in the daily effort to conceal all emotion.

A major disallowed behaviour was the expression of nostalgia. Here refugees are very different from other kinds of migrants who move across the globe usually for economic reasons, to find a better future for their children. For such migrants, nostalgia is the almost inevitable outcome of taking up residence in a new country. Often it is a function of the trauma of dislocation, exacerbated by the isolation of settlement in a new land, homesickness for the familiar sights, smells, sounds of home. As mentioned in Chapter 2, nostalgia was a key constituent in the migrant's construction of 'home'.

Nostalgia, however, was not an emotion that refugees fleeing trauma could afford. Nostalgia is a warm and happy reminiscence, tinged with wistfulness for the past, including places and people— another time, another place. The Holocaust survivor, newly arrived in Australia, found nostalgia too painful. This is not to say it was like this for everyone; there are homes where nostalgia found a kind of place. But for many, it was impossible to corral some memories and not others, for when such emotions were summoned, they inevitably capsized under the accompanying weight of loss and grief.

Abe's story is a telling one. On his deathbed, the father confessed to the rabbi that he had never said Kaddish for his parents. The rabbi went away to organise it but Abe's father died before it could happen. Abe's interpretation of this is that once the father had achieved closure by talking about it with the rabbi, he could let go. At his funeral, Kaddish was said for him and his parents, and a plaque for family lost in the Holocaust was later placed on his grave. Graves of survivors in Jewish cemeteries frequently have this additional plaque—naming those who have no grave. In my view, these little plaques placed on top of the parent's grave are a metaphor for the unleashing of Holocaust memory at the time of a survivor's death.

Nonetheless, nostalgia was something that some survivors managed to achieve and I was interested to know why some managed it and others didn't. I have the sense that families which lost children were very poor candidates for nostalgia. Conversely, survivors who'd had a happy childhood themselves were more likely to talk about their pre-war lives, often romanticising or even idealising these times; often they would try to seal these memories off from the later ones relating to the war. Such families were fortunate, for their nostalgia served them as a form of inter-generational nurturing, allowing connections to be made across generations and continents, keeping ancestral links alive. Today for me, the sound of Yiddish carries memories of that bond, which Epstein experiences through Czech: 'It had been the language of my childhood, the code I shared with my parents, the language of lullabies and fairy tales and trust'.[6]

In my family, there were faint flickers of nostalgia, primarily from my father. He would recite verses from Horace or Ovid, an old school song or rousing youth movement anthem, and memories of his schooldays would flood in. But these were flickers, never sustained, because they were doomed to be deluged by remembrance of his home, and the loss of his parents and sister. I think he believed that nostalgia was healthy, and he persisted in the effort to manage it better. My mother, however, could not. She imposed and achieved almost total suppression. I caught a glimpse into how she did this when she forbade me, as an adolescent in the 1960s, to listen to the mournful folk songs that were all the rage then. She said music like that didn't help you 'get through the day'; it was 'not good for the spirit'. I don't know exactly what it was about brass bands but I know the sound brought her no small amount of disquiet. She loved the music and as ferociously, avoided it. Someone once bought her a record of Russian military music. She kept it but never played it. We kind of knew it was taboo.

Occasionally she would allow a fleeting remembrance of a school friend or a university mate, but nothing more. I remember many conversations that were abruptly cut short, that stopped rather than ended, because the only path forward was a nostalgic one, and there, she wouldn't go. For the most part, nostalgia was not something my mother allowed herself. Certainly, thoughts about her parents never left the hermetically sealed chamber in her mind. She would press the edge of her top teeth down on her lower lip, and render stillness from the turbulent emotions within. I remember an argument between my parents after she said that their generation had had a different (meaning 'higher') notion of friendship than my generation's. My father retorted with what I guess to be a rough translation of: 'You can't blame the children for living in normal times'. At the time, I didn't know what either of them meant.

From her I have inherited an inability to cope with nostalgia in any form or context. When it catches me unawares, I feel an intense something (anguish?) within and I find myself pressing down on my lower lip, causing a localised pain, even sometimes drawing blood. Is this a distraction from a much worse inner turbulence? Repeated experiences like this have left me with antennae that are nostalgia-hypersensitive. Television commercials, for example, achieve a lot of mileage by playing on these emotions and in so doing, wreak havoc on people like me. I remember being reduced to tears watching a telephone advertisement that played on the reunion of loved ones and a jeans advertisement evoking a sentimental yearning for lost youth. Such aural and visual triggers are a constant trial. So are certain kinds of music: 'Auld Lang Syne', most national anthems, a great deal of opera, Christmas carols and choral and ritualised music, all evoke in me an intense wave of nostalgia. Certain formal occasions which operate along very conventionalised routines, like graduation and wedding ceremonies, have the same effect. I realise now that this is because they are actually frozen moments of nostalgia and now that I understand what is happening, I do my best to avoid them. Certain moments in interaction do the same, like saying goodbye to someone leaving or saying goodbye when I myself am leaving. I understand that I am not alone here. In the film *Left Luggage*, the lead character, a 20-year-old girl, tells the little child she babysits never to leave without saying 'I love you'.[7] One of my respondents has a ritualised leave-taking with her young children which involves their knowing (they find out anew each day) that their mother loves them wherever they are, even when they are not with her. She knows this is separation anxiety handed down from her parents, and on to her children, but she is caught within it.

A number of my respondents reported, as Elsa put it, 'a struggle to maintain control' in the face of the many nostalgic triggers one encounters. Edna recalls that nostalgia was a taboo emotion in her home, and as in mine, music, a great evoker of emotion and remembrance, was virtually banned. She concedes that nostalgia was a great Pandora's Box. And yet her father had a need to express nostalgia, so the credo in the home seems to have become a kind of ground zero one: life began with her birth, in Prague just after the war. An exorbitant amount of time and care was spent on baby photo albums, with pictures taken in Prague and later in Australia. These albums became an outlet for her father's nostalgic needs.

Edna's ultimate response to this kind of home life was to be attracted to history and the past and to gain strength and pleasure from these pursuits, leading her years later to a fascination with museums as places which restore and nurture memory. Today she has revived memories of events in her family's history that could have made for positive nostalgia, that could have been told and retold and thereby celebrated. There's the story about how the family became religious: a fire in their street, their house ablaze, all eleven children saved, 'and after that, grandfather became religious'. Such tales are for her like putting a foot in the door before it shuts forever on our view of the past.

Rebecca is another who struggles with nostalgia. Her own yearning has been sublimated in a love of oral history.

> My mother adored her mother and she told me snippets about her. But there was never the sense of her telling me about times past with me sitting at her knee listening. I would have loved that but I never got it. And now I can't do that with my own kids. Even though when I do they love it but somehow, because I didn't have it and craved it, I am unable to give it.

Clearly, in the baggage of emotions that survivors brought with them, nostalgia was often a problematical one, requiring sensitive management, a sense that everyone is aware that it needs to be handled with care. It is not surprising, then, that over time such fragile cargo encountered some breakages.

Unasked questions

Paul was the only one of my respondents who said that asking his parents questions about their past was uncomplicated. Yet even Paul did not start asking questions until he was grown up. As children, all of us sensed that questions were unstable, something to be deployed sparingly and tentatively. Few of us would have been able to articulate our reluctance then; even now, it is difficult to put into words the difficulty of putting things in words. It's as if the message consumes the medium and there isn't a language to talk about not having a language.

I am interested in how we learned not to ask. I imagine from the experience of having our fingers burned. Glass' protagonist in *The Interpreter* recalls these memories:

> Just once I heard my parents' friends talk about camps and I . . . asked if they were as much fun as the place we went to on a bus for the school trip. But no one said anything. No one answered me. And I began to feel this awful shaky panicky feeling . . . I never mentioned 'the camp' again at home.

That such a reaction is possible even where there is no comprehension of events, is remarkable. This same child later asked her teacher 'if we could have those bluey-green numbers stamped on our arms at summer camp like mother's Maman and Papa had done at theirs'.[8] In understanding the fragility of a question in this context, we have to remember that the asker is a child—with all the innocence, ignorance and imaginative scope that we associate with childhood. Elsa said that it was only as a married adult, with her own children, that she had any success talking with her mother about these things. Sometimes when her husband was overseas, Elsa would stay with her widowed mother; in the evenings they would talk and she found out a lot, having the confidence now to know 'where a door would be opening and where I could ask questions'. Children don't have this finesse, so an effective strategy is to shut down and not ask.

Questions were dangerous turf. This motif weaves its way through my data. I asked people when this had begun for them. Michael said, 'As far back as I go, I couldn't ask'. For Susan, the impossibility of questions governed her relationship with her mother. I asked her how she learned not to ask, and her response was 'you wait to be told'. The parent often had particular phrases: 'That was a long time ago', 'Let's not talk about that', 'I can't remember'. These were potent signals to the listener that enough is enough. David says, 'There was this overriding feeling that we had come to this country to make a new life and a new start and it's important not to dwell on what happened back there'. Often the tone that greeted questions— implying 'What would you want to know that for? Why would you want to go visit there?'—was disparaging and dismissive, shutting down and extinguishing further questions in its wake.

One of the dangers with questions was that the survivor often misinterpreted their motivation and they became inflammatory. Instead of recognising a child's curiosity to know more, sometimes parents reacted as if they were not being believed. This then cast the child as inquisitor, an impossible role to sustain. John felt that when he asked questions it was interpreted as a cross-examination. It would infuriate his parents to think that their own son didn't believe them. Often, he was simply trying to work out a chronology or make sense of something bizarre or clarify something that was unclear.

These episodes had a rhythm that tended to simulate an interrogation. One person asks; the other answers. In other words the roles of asker and answerer are clearly differentiated, unlike in casual conversation where these roles are shared. Paul, for example, reports that in his home, the parents 'responded to questions but did not initiate'. Nor did they elaborate, so the discourse that unfolds appears interrogative: question, short answer, next question, short answer, next question, short answer, etc. This is not a discourse that is self-nourishing or easily sustainable.

Sometimes the child's questions were so inappropriate that instead of being seen for what they were—indications of just how hard it was to understand—they were recast as provocations. Parents of course are not trained, as teachers are, to interpret question-asking behaviour diagnostically. Sam once checked a fact with his mother—Was it only a year that she had been in Auschwitz?—not realising what his 'only a year' might have meant. When I was about twelve, the son of one of my parents' survivor friends, asked my father (probably, I think now, to avoid asking his own!) whether they were given chicken to eat in the camps. I didn't know the answer to the question but I already knew not to ask and I cowered in apprehension and anticipation when I heard the question voiced (*Oh my God, why did he ask that?*). I remember the moment to this day, the room we were in when it happened, where we each were standing or sitting, as if the picture has been freeze-framed or laminated into perpetuity. I recall with acuity the eerie stillness that followed the question. Then my mother's voice cut through the long pause like a knife. 'They ate worms', she said, and then, after a few angry muttered exchanges in Polish that I didn't understand, the silence in the car all the way home, while I turned the notion of worms over and over in my mind, wondering *why, what sort, where from* and *how come?*

I experienced an uncanny parallel of this episode as an adult with my own daughter when she was about eight. We were in Amsterdam, and I had taken her to the Anne Frank House which is restored as a museum. I was pleased at how Anne's story is lovingly and clearly laid out for the visitor because, for one thing, it relieved me of the need to contextualise or explain. I didn't feel like giving an age-appropriate history lesson, especially in public as there were a lot of people there. As we left, my daughter asked me a question which betrayed that she'd actually had no idea of the circumstances or significance of these events—no idea of who Anne Frank was or why she is memorialised in this house or in this way, or even what 'an attic' was. Suddenly, I was overcome by a level of rage that was wholly out of proportion to the literal sequence of events. The question was innocent and well-intentioned but I was out of control. I pushed the girl into her father's arms and ran up the street, away from the museum and the crowds of people, until I could find some seclusion in a park and there I tried to recover some composure. I have no doubt today that the episode was a re-enactment of a script from another time and another place, with another question asked, all stored in my memory, with myself in the role of child.

Of course it is not only children of survivors who have difficulty matching up their reality with various others' representations. It is not for nothing that 'innocence' goes well with 'childhood'. Duba's narrative poem 'Carpet bombing', recalls her childhood experience of the Allied bombing of the German city of Cologne:

> . . . she caught the word
> carpet bombing
> again and again
> and couldn't understand
> why this word
> was causing such terror
> while she tried to figure out
> what kinds of carpets
> were going to fall
> from the sky—
> long narrow carpets
> also called runners
> like the one in the hallway
> staircase carpets
> firmly held in place
> by shiny brass rods
> small carpets

like the one
in front of her bed
or large carpets with intricate designs
like the one in the living room
which was treated with such reverence.[9]

Another problem with questions asked of the survivor is that they destabilise the rhythm of the story that survivors have learned to tell, the official line, the one that they know they'll make it through without dissolving, if they just keep to the script. Questions do not serve this enactment for they provoke and distract and unbalance. So many survivors give the impression that questions are not welcome. Some interpret questions as the listener's attempt to seize the direction of the talking and steer the topic another way, perhaps because of their own discomfort. Michael sat behind his daughter, out of eye contact with his mother, as the child innocently asked probing questions of her grandmother, questions about her great-grandparents that he could never ever have asked. He held his breath and dared not move a muscle, let alone interrupt, as the answers came, almost comfortably, some 50 years after the war.

Thus the atmosphere that surrounded questions was *a priori* brittle. Sam says, 'If I push it, it will break'. Susan talks of the delicate tug-of-war she had with her mother: 'I took what she gave me, I never probed, I'd back off when it got dangerous, I'd always err on the side of less'. So the listener's discourse rights are severely circumscribed, giving very little space and manoeuvrability:

As a child you just accept what you're told and as you get older you re-interpret it and you want more detail, more nuance, but if you've missed that moment, there's never a time you can raise it again, because you can't ask, you have to wait. Maybe the opportunity will come again.

My belief is that children in these households become quite expert at reading between and around the lines. Susan says, 'You don't really know what the other person is thinking, but you can never ask just in case you are right; and you're making inferences all the time'. Jill, her parents now dead, looks back on her life and laments the fact that she couldn't ask questions and they wouldn't tell, and so she knows very little. The absence of questions for her is the source of this problem: 'I tell my kids never to be afraid to ask. You'll only miss out if you don't ask'.

In my child's mind, knowing nothing about wars and life, my parents' background was an immense black wall that loomed behind them. I asked my respondents what it was like for them. Elsa said it was a blackness, a horrible unknown; the only way through it was to find out what happened, but the obstacle to this was their pain, and questions always came up against this. So she waited. In her recognition of pain and the fear of going there, she is typical. Over and over again I heard variations on the same refrain: 'I was too scared to ask them'; 'I knew it hurt them so I didn't ask'; 'There were too many dead relatives, I didn't want to be told about all these dead people'; 'I didn't want to hear the answers'; 'I learned it's better not to ask'. Julia believed that if she asked her father about his first family, of which he never spoke, it would kill him. So she planned to get the information from her mother and it took three years before she could find the right moment and summon up the courage to ask. Some learned to navigate the waters with dexterity, knowing which parts to avoid. Abe says it was safe to ask about the narrative but not about how they felt—'never about the emotion'. He said that there was a façade of non-conflict in the home and 'untoward questions might fracture that'. Many learned not to ask about immediate family, and especially not to ask about the people whose names they bore. Others saw the entire terrain as closed off: 'I never asked because I knew I would not get an answer'.[10]

Thus in this way, what develops is a collusion, a conspiracy, where each party tiptoes around each other. Just as the survivor wants to tell but also doesn't want to, so too the child wants to know but at the same time is fearful of knowing. Maurice recounts an incident that captures this family dynamic of tiptoeing around each other's sensitivities:

> When I was about 19 I went skiing with some friends for a week. The night we returned my parents went out somewhere. Only a few days later did I hear from friends that on this night my father had spoken at a meeting of Holocaust survivors. My mother told me he was very hurt that I hadn't gone. But I didn't know it was on! He hadn't said anything, nor had my mother. He expected her to tell me and she must have thought it was an imposition on me, to go the night I came home.

When Leah looks back at the frozen moment she remembers of her mother trying to tell her about her own mother's death, she says

'I don't know whether the stopping of the conversation was my own doing or hers'. Elsa summed it up beautifully when she said, 'It was almost a game we played: I'll let you protect me by not asking'.

It is easy to forget that to ask questions is a linguistic act, one that requires some skill, and at least some contextual knowledge. I sense that children of survivors struggled with a lack of procedural knowledge to cut through the opaqueness they encountered. This was a sense of not knowing how, a realisation that there are rules but not being sure what they are. Julia says: 'There are questions that we don't know how to ask'. John said, 'If I asked the right question, I would have got the right answer, but I didn't ask the right question, so I got an indirect answer'. Edna says, 'I was daunted. I didn't have enough information to ask questions in the proper way. I didn't have the words to ask the questions and they didn't have the words to tell me and I guess there was nowhere to start'. And later she reflects, 'Maybe I didn't want to know what my parents had really been through'.

What emerges then is a picture of impossibly tight constraints placed on communication in the wake of trauma. Though my data set is largely derived from the trauma of the Holocaust, it would seem that there are universals here that are generalisable to other places and times. I was interested to read, for example, in D'Orso's book, about the town of Rosewood, Florida, USA which in 1923 visited upon its black population a devastating pogrom the outcome of which was to disperse its black population forever. The story focuses on the character Arnett who

> never heard much more from his mother about Rosewood than what she told him and his sister that Christmas. It became their annual ritual, (the mother) sitting the children down on Christmas Day and telling them the Rosewood story. It was always the same, nothing new added, and no questions allowed. None. Arnett's mother spoke, and the children listened.[11]

In the end it is small wonder that questions become disallowed, and the child stops asking. The tragedy is that this sinking into silence, this acquiescence, was often misinterpreted by the survivor parents. Jennie sums it up thus: 'When I couldn't get my answers, I stopped asking. Once I stopped asking, it would have seemed like I wasn't interested'.

Iconic Messages

Iconic messages refer to the meanings embedded in certain tangible objects, certain distinctive behaviours and attitudes, and certain formal occasions that resonate with Holocaustal significance. These are most typically part of the parental home, and include the behaviours encountered there and the experiences shared as a family. No doubt the intensity of the iconic meanings is diluted over the generations. In the children of survivors, for example, the icon most usually generates not so much fearfulness as much as the recognition that it would have done so for the parents. Paul knew that his parents were fearful of anyone wearing a uniform. So the sight of a uniform, for him, takes on its own kind of meaning, reminding him of his parents and of himself as their son. This is one step removed, a vicarious experience, part of the curse of being a generation that carries, as Erlich puts it, 'memories not its own'.[12]

For convenience, I have divided iconic messages into the three categories—objects, behaviours, occasions. Some icons of course overlap categories. For example, the significance of food touches all three: a loaf of bread, even stale scraps of bread, are precious (object); parents can't waste food (behaviour/attitude); formal ceremonial events celebrate freedom from hunger (occasion). In this way a single icon might resonate through three different avenues.

Tangible objects

Let's take an example of a tangible object as icon. Long before I knew about crematoria, about bodies in concentration camps being burned in death factories, I knew there was something ominous about industrial chimneys. My brother and I grew up about 2 hours' travel time from Sydney. A few times a month we would go into the city as a family for a meal out or a movie. On the way home we passed through an industrial suburb where there were some chimneys spewing out black smoke at any time of the day or night. Industrial chimneys they were. Without knowing why, I used to dread passing them. Something happened to my father's demeanour. He tensed and then went inward somewhere in his own mind, and I knew to keep out of sight and earshot for the interim. Industrial chimneys therefore served iconically to remind me of the horrors my father knew in his lifetime. The remembrance is vicarious—it's not crematoria I think of but my father's remembrance of crematoria.

It's not dissimilar to my experience with dogs, especially large dogs, especially German shepherds. My father was in a camp where trained dogs did what the Nazis wanted, saving on bullets and providing

macabre pleasure for those who took relish in cruelty. To my knowledge, he was never attacked or mauled, but he witnessed such scenes.
When as a child I went walking with my father, he would hold my hand.
This was in the countryside and there were many more dogs than in the
city today. I was vaguely aware that he sometimes grasped my hand
quite tightly and that he often steered us across to the other side of the
road for no discernible reason other than the sight of a dog on our side
of the road. So I knew, at some level, that there was an association of
fear with dogs but it was never spoken of. I certainly was not aware of
investing these behaviours with significance. I was in my forties when
my son one day attributed to me his fear of dogs. He said when he was
little I would grasp his hand very tightly when a dog came near and
often cross the road to avoid our passing one, leaving him as an adult
with a vigorous suspicion of the canine world. Only then did I realise
that I had echoed my father's behaviour in my own.

In an article on authenticity in discourse, Widdowson explains
why a transcript of authentic language is so difficult to understand for
anyone who was not there as a participant.[13] It is because what is
actually said is only a small part of what is understood, as shared
knowledge. For example, a tape recording of a family having breakfast
might be a collection of elliptical utterances containing half-uttered
phatic sounds which are comfortably understood by everyone present.
Because the script is known, the situation routine, not much needs to
be said. A look in the right direction may get the jam passed your way.
A grunt might serve as thanks. Widdowson, in fact, refers to the
linguistic fragments as a 'discourse trace', indicating that this is where
people had interconnected, even if the voiced utterances are few and
fragmented. The objects that send iconic messages of the Holocaust
serve a similar function. While I don't recall having been told about
the chimneys or about the dogs, I must have found out at some point.
Much later, the language of the telling was lost (was it intolerably
heavy to maintain intact?) and the object or 'discourse trace' remained.
The icon then serves on its own to ignite the connection.

In interviewing my subjects, I told them about my experience
with chimneys and German Shepherds and how these had evolved
into icons for me, and I asked them if they had any parallel experiences. A few of the respondents had difficulty with the concept, but
with the majority, it took no more than my citing my examples and
the icons came tumbling out. A common one was dogs. Bernice's
mother has a scar on her face from having been bitten by an Alsatian.

Dan told me his mother has scars on her buttocks where she was mauled by a dog in the camps. Leah remembers being told how her mother hid her Jewishness and got work in a German household where there was a man who had been in the Hitler Youth; he told her his German Shepherd 'could smell a Jew a mile away'.

Another common icon is stale bread. The notion of bread, of course, is long established in language and myth as symbolic of sustenance and therefore life. However, for Holocaust survivors, this has transmuted into stale bread, for this is what often meant the difference between life and death. In many Holocaust households bread could not be thrown away, even when hard and inedible. You kept it and you ground it into breadcrumbs and you used it in cooking; you did not throw it away. We grew up with people who might have risked their lives for a scrap of bread or a piece of potato peel. For them, after the war, living among plenty was never ever an entirely easy thing. For example, it was distressing for my father to see the bread that people would leave out for the birds after a picnic. Such waste must have been a constant reminder that freedom from hunger is a right, like other rights, that can be removed.

I wonder, too, whether these iconic objects in a macabre way also link back to the memory of those who were lost. In Glass' *The Interpreter*, the little girl finds her survivor mother in the middle of the night 'sitting in the corner of the kitchen by the bread bin, stuffing pieces of hard dry bread into her mouth'.[14] Some survivors become hoarders, keeping linen closets full of towels and blankets that, as Michael says of his mother, 'you couldn't go through in a hundred years'. These symbolise safety and comfort. This is the legacy of years of hiding out and being on the run, having only what you could carry. Whenever I see pictures of long lines of refugees, mostly displaced civilians—women, children and old people—evacuating a place that has been consumed by war, I think of another time, other people. *Plus ça change, plus c'est la même chose.*

Other icons that repeat are trains and train tracks. Edna said, 'Not long ago I took my son to the train station because he was off to a Jewish holiday camp. I looked back and waved. There was the train, loading up one hundred Jewish children, going to camp. The associations were too strong for comfort'. Another is arched doorways, resonant of the notorious entry into Auschwitz, inscribed with the ironic 'Work makes you Free'.

Another is the sight, as much as the notion, of a marked grave, which signifies the millions who were never buried. The idea of graveside emotion, usually suppressed, is a motif through my data and through much of the relevant literature. Epstein writes, after discovering her great-grandmother's grave:

> If I had grown up in Prague, if I had had a simple family history, . . . I would have come here to tend my great-grandmother's grave. I would have come here when I quarrelled with my husband or was frustrated with my children or just needed a quiet place and time to think things through.[15]

Lily Brett's main character, Ruth, visits the Polish city of Lodz where her parents came from. There she goes to what remains of the Jewish cemetery, where 'a large calm descended on her', triggering introspection:

> What had pacified her?, she wondered. Was it her proximity to people she had always felt close to? . . . They weren't her dead. She knew that. Her dead weren't buried like this. Her dead were burnt in outdoor ditches or baked, like roast meats, in ovens. But these dead, the dead in the Jewish cemetery, Lodz, were the closest to her dead, her family, that she would ever get.[16]

Another icon is lice. So when their children come home with a letter from the principal warning about lice in the school, the reaction can be disproportionate, evoking memories of conditions of filth and degradation. The tattoo some camps' prisoners had on their forearm (or the scar that replaces a tattoo that has been removed) has immense evocative power. Edna says that as a child she tried very hard to make sense of all these people who came in and out of the house — who was family, who were close friends, who came from Europe, who was local. After a while, she developed a system: 'I worked out that if they had accents, then they probably had tattoos'.

Patterns of behaviour and attitude

Another form of iconic message is displayed in certain patterns of behaviour, including attitudes. In winter, as my father sat in the lounge room watching a TV movie or the evening news, he would often bump his feet together side-on. I knew this meant he felt cold, the way others might rub their hands together. But I also had an ominous apprehension about this foot-banging habit, partly because it was outside the normal way of expressing cold. I don't remember being told, only of sensing that cold feet were linked to the war. At some point, I don't remember when, I must have found out about the ice and the snow and the frostbite.

I also knew never to come up behind him or to bang a window closed suddenly or honk the car horn unexpectedly in his earshot. Sudden, loud sounds gave him a start and left him shaken. I knew too, when I took Dad's hand, to take his right one, not the left, because when I grabbed the left he would suddenly wince in pain, and when I looked closely I saw some scars and malformation on the inner side. I don't know when I found out that this was from a severe beating in the camps. I think I sensed the link to the war long before I knew the specific detail. This perhaps was because the dramatic pulling away and momentary pain across his face happened repeatedly, without explanation. As it was with the dogs and the cold feet—strange behaviours that remain outside the province of talk. So, like many children of survivors, I became adept at filling in the blanks.

These are examples—I imagine most children of survivors have their own—of iconic behaviour, where a recurrent pattern of doing things triggers Holocaustal associations. For Abe's mother, the sound of thunder evokes her memory of fleeing Warsaw as bombs rained down and an apartment building collapsed behind her, floor by floor, while she escaped literally in the literal nick of time. While Abe was growing up, thunder would force his mother to retreat under a table, and he remembers at age five or six, someone saying to him, by way of explanation 'it was because of the war, it was the bombs'. Bernice's mother had a habit of eating raw mince: 'in the war we were so hungry we couldn't wait to cook it'. This is an extreme example of intolerance to hunger that remained a legacy for many. For example, Dan knew that his father's amazing capacity to devour a huge bowl of potatoes at any time derived from the ghosts of deprivation past. John could hear his father's nightmares from his bedroom. Elsa knew well the Saturday afternoon sobbing that could be heard from her mother's bedroom and knew 'there was no consolation'. For many, the sight of parents' crying was itself iconic—for only the war could bring that on. For Michael, language-switching was a cue: 'When they switched to Polish, I knew—Polish was the language they used to veil the truth from me'.

Most survivor families were left with some physical disabilities— like my father's wrist, and Dan's mother's scar from the dog mauling. My mother had a tiny scar on her forehead, from the jump off the train. For many there were digestive issues, often related to the experience of starvation. One respondent said, 'When you see that your father can only eat blended food, you have to start to wonder'. Many survivors had severe dental problems after the war, again due to years of deprivation. As a child, Edna inquired about the hearing problem of a family friend to be told, 'She was beaten around the head by a guard'.

In all of these experiences where descendants find out about war-related frailties or disabilities in their parents, a core commonality prevails. We encountered the outcome of brutality and violence, indeed we lived our lives in their shadow. This is the exact opposite of children raised on a diet of Hollywood-style action movies, where all manner of violence is displayed, but rarely ever the outcomes of brutal acts, physical, psychological and social.

Other behaviours are less visible because they are themselves acts of avoidance. Michael says that the discourse in his home was governed by the wish to step around the mother's 'maelstrom of emotion that was always there, just a second away'. Things like separation would trigger it, so typically he would leave the house by stealth and come back the same way, rather than tell her he was going out for a few hours. For a similar reason, children of survivors learned to be hyper-punctual, because arriving home even five minutes late could trigger an outburst of parental rage. As adults, some of us try very hard to be late or at least on time, rather than compulsively early; and we try not to revisit our inherited fears on the next generation. Other avoidance behaviours relate to the suppressing of emotions like nostalgia, as discussed earlier. Elsa recalls that in the place of nostalgia, what she saw was 'a tendency to bring down the shutters, throw up the defences, become quite distant'.

Because survivors had endured such hardship, their tolerance of pain was perhaps unusually high. When Sam had the usual anxiety of a child his age about the doctor's injection or the dentist's drill, his mother taunted him about being a wimp: 'She'd gloat about her pain threshold. I related it to the camps'. Rena also felt uncomfortable ever complaining of pain or ill-health—she felt she had no right to bother her parents with anything that was less than life-threatening. Other respondents reported that they were more likely not to tell parents of any symptoms to avoid the inevitable fussing and fretting that would follow.

Another icon was simply that our parents tended to be serious-minded. There was a gravity about their demeanour, a 'non-specific heaviness' as Maurice recalls it. Jennie says her father's attitude could be read from his physical demeanour—hanging head, hunched shoulders—which cued her to a whole range of emotions. When I encountered for the first time the French term *joie de vivre*, I knew that I already knew it, by its absence. There was a gratitude for life, a reverence for life, but not a *joie* for life. I recall when I was about 23, studying with a new friend, who made me laugh like I had never laughed before; I was aware of muscles in my face being used for what seemed the first time. Could it be that I didn't laugh, really laugh, till I was in my early twenties? Dan remembers that his father had great difficulty in any contexts that were happy or light-hearted: because he believed he'd survived by accident, he felt that he had 'no right to be happy'. As a little girl, Rena dared not ask her mother for the usual things that little girls turn to their mothers for—ribbons, dress-ups, cakes for the school stall, and such like: 'I didn't want to bother her with petty things because she was so serious all of the time'.

Susan's mother told her very little about her experiences and in the absence of text, Susan inferred meaning from many of her mother's attitudes: her distrust of the world, her protectiveness of her daughter, her pessimism, her fear of people knowing she was Jewish. Today, all grown up with a family of her own, Susan cannot put a *mezzuzah* on her front door. Dan's parents' overprotectiveness cued him to their former losses: 'You knew that you were cherished. You were aware that you were horribly precious to your parents'. Abe's parents made sure that their son was not circumcised or bar mitzvahed; they sent him to a private boys' school and generally tried to keep his Jewish profile very low. Elaine's parents protected her 'from anything and everything, so I concluded that the world was malevolent'. She was anxious about ever getting sick, because even when she had a minor cold, her mother would stand next to her bed, beyond the scope of reassurance, and drive her 'to distraction'.

Most of the iconic messages were patterned, tending to repeat and resonate over time. Occasionally, there were single events that happened, with minimal text, but where the child picked up the cues to the Holocaust; memory of these remains decades later. Jane recalls once being at high school and her mother being with her when suddenly the school siren erupted. 'It was just like an air raid siren. Mother went hysterical. She screamed, "It's an air raid!" and started running about. I was desperately embarrassed. I immediately linked it to her past'. Leah recalls that her father's younger brother, who lived with them, often fell asleep with the TV on. She crept in one day to turn it off and he woke with a start of fear, his hands in front of his face, instinctively in protection. Sam recalls the time his aunt believed the gas heater was leaking and no one would believe her. She called the gas people who'd installed it and they reassured her that it was her imagination. She got a second opinion, and it turned out, she was right. It was leaking. 'I remember wondering,' Sam said, 'about how come she was so good at smelling gas'.

Special family occasions

In recalling triggers that had iconic meaning in their lives, my respondents often referred to family gatherings on special occasions. Dan remembers Yom Kippur as a massively emotional ritual moment in his family's life. Everyone fasted, the mother attended the prayer for the dead, the father blessed the children. He says:

> It was spine-tingling. There was a very intense feeling. It was as if he were saying 'This is very important, this is what we are here for'. It was a time he took out every year to review his spot in the world. There was enormous emotion. It was all bound up with people lost. It was uncomfortable but also good.

In other homes, the occasion most evocative for the family was Passover. Certainly this was the case in my home, where every aspect of the ritualised meal was delineated with twin references, one to the Pharoah's Egypt and one to Hitler's Europe. The former had a script, a literal one, that we read in the book in front of us. The script of the latter was more blurry; though spoken, it was alluded to in undertones, and we made our own meanings. It wasn't until many years later that I experienced a non-Holocaust-infused Passover meal in Israel—I was staying on a kibbutz and there was lots of dancing, singing and general merriment while I looked around in astonishment. I realised then that the way it had been celebrated in my home carried a particular set of marked meanings.

Perhaps the difference might be captured by understanding the difference between public ritual and private grief. In non-survivor homes, the celebration of the Exodus from Egypt is a public ritual. There is no personal connection, every aspect of the experience is symbolic, from the food to the tablecloth, to the strange rituals. And the discourse of the evening is one long, staged answer to the question, 'Why are we doing this?', which the youngest asks and the oldest answers. Each Passover this recurs, so that we come to know and re-know the event in a routine, predictable, systematic, public, and most importantly, non-traumatic way.

However, when Passover is celebrated through the lens of the Holocaust, as it was in many survivor homes, it is no longer a moment of public ritual but one of private grief. The iconic associations are of the Holocaust rather than of the Exodus. It is a cataclysmic event that happened not millennia ago, but in our own lifetime, or just before. Smooth ritual gives way to raw nerve.

Any formal family occasions where absent family members were notably missing became iconic sites. My brother's *bar mitzvah* was one of the most emotionally difficult occasions I can recall. I was twelve. I don't remember if my father listed the names of the dead not with us. I do recall that he talked, standing up, formally, to the hundreds of guests, formally attired, all looking at him—about his own *bar mitzvah* and what it meant to him and his relationship with his father. I remember sitting at the main table, being weighed down by the emotion of the occasion, terrified that I might put a wrong step forward in a game for which no one had told me the rules, knowing that there was more going on than I could take in. The anguish was a magnified version of the moment in our home when nostalgia was suppressed or side-stepped, and 'let's not talk about that' may have been the only spoken trace of what was left unsaid. At the *bar mitzvah*, from my young perspective, here we were, secular Jews, with no link to any Jewish institution, suddenly out of the blue, having this enormous event, in a synagogue (*What's a synagogue?*) with more serious-looking people than I had ever seen together in one place where everyone, except me, it seemed, knew what was going on. On the day of my brother's *bar mitzvah* was born in me a foreboding, a sense that one's understanding of anything could only ever be incomplete. Certainly since then, ritualised occasions—the graduation, the wedding, the funeral—trigger in me at best discomfort, at worst, a flight response. Family occasions, says a person interviewed in the film *Out of the Ashes*, were times when you saw people choke up because of who's missing.[17]

It may, however, be more complicated than the simple stark reminder of who's absent and dead. Some analysts, like Barocas and Barocas, point to the difficulties that survivors have in accepting the normal 'autonomous strivings' of their young adult children.[18] The steps of individuation by which a child grows up, gradually separates from the family of origin and becomes independent are interfered with in multiple and complex ways by the fact of Holocaust survival. Parents may have invested their relations with children with an energy derived from a sense of 'you are all we have left'. Letting go, allowing the bird to fly from the nest when the time is right, can be a highly traumatic event for the parents, especially when the child has been seen more as an extension of self than a separate individual. As a result, parents may unconsciously obstruct the pathway to independence, preferring to keep the child safe by their side. This may manifest in overt warnings about the general malevolence of the outside world and reassurances about the safety of the home. In any case, separation—such as when the child leaves to go to a distant university, or overseas, or get married—can re-trigger associations of loss with other separations in the past, where loved ones wrenched away were gone forever. The threat of another loss contributes to the litany of unfinished mourning. Thus even happy occasions like *bar mitzvahs*, graduation ceremonies and weddings can signal individuation, separation, ambivalence and thereby may tap into the wells of sadness.

Whatever the manifold emotions that permeated ritualised occasions, it was not only these that carried iconic meaning. It could be times in the family that were out-of-the-ordinary. Richard, for example, recalls that his father worked from dawn to dark, that he rarely saw him, even more rarely talked to him, and certainly not about family or the past. But when on occasion they would go away on a family holiday, and his father and he would spend some time together; then he might find out a little about what happened. He came to expect to find out on such occasions, and with the expectation was dread.

And then there were benchmarks by which people measured their age. It's been noted that because they didn't get to see their parents grow old, survivors encounter difficulties beyond the usual when they themselves age. I can recall that over the years on my father's birthday he would mention, in a tone of voice that I rarely heard, as if talking to himself, 'I am now three years older than my father was when he died'. At the time, the maths of this calculation was beyond me, if only because the constituents in the equation had an unknown value. In any case, children don't distinguish among gradations of old: old is old. My father's age didn't have a lot of meaning for me. My grandfather, never seen, hardly mentioned, even less. How could I relate to numbers associated with the circumstances of my grandfather's death when I knew nothing of the circumstances of his life? So the annual benchmarking of my father's life against his father's death was at the time quite beyond me. At a literal level it was meaningless, but at an iconic one, it was resonant.

Omissions

In this chapter we have looked at communication that was actively excluded where text was suppressed; and then at iconic communication where the text is of the nature of prefabricated, non-verbal, built-in meaning. The third and last point on the continuum is the one that comes closest to pure silence, one I am calling 'Omissions'. Here, the absences are *so* absent, the reference to the past *so* muted, the ancestral background to a family *so* obliterated, that the child grows up unaware even that something has been left unsaid. My interviews with three children of survivors illustrate this most aptly.

I'll begin with Richard. He was happy to be interviewed and launched into his story very enthusiastically but, very soon into it, he began quite dramatically to cry and he continued crying through the whole interview, sometimes sobbing loudly. I usually am not discomforted by people crying, and had become used to having a box of tissues nearby when I interviewed my subjects, but with Richard there was something different. He seemed not to realise that he was crying, and certainly not to appreciate that he was in a deeply emotional state. He insisted on continuing, even though at times I could not make out his words through the sobbing. It was not so much his tears that unnerved me as the discordance between his non-verbal and verbal language. Despite being wracked by sobs, his words were mild and unmarked.

One incident that Richard referred to betrays how little he knew about the family his parents lost. It furnishes a hint of what Apfelbaum calls 'deracination', or uprooting. Richard was told precious little: what he knows of the lives and deaths of his grandparents on both sides amounts to fragments at best. He does recall, however, a moment from his own youth when he might have had a momentary glimpse into the enormity of what he did not know. He remembers being at the football and running into an elderly survivor from the same small town as his father. Richard must have grown taller since the man had last seen him for he was suddenly struck by the boy's resemblance to his grandfather, long dead. He remarked on this, referring to the grandfather using the term of endearment by which he had been affectionately known back then—*Avram hagavoa* ('tall Abraham'). Richard recalls: 'That was when I found out that he was tall. It was the first time in my life I had any indication of what he looked like'. But even as he said this, Richard did not seem to register how paltry this fragment of information was. It reminded me of Susan's saying, 'I know that she liked knitting' because the photo she has features her grandmother knitting. Ironically, it is in the significance with which children of survivors invest these paltry titbits of knowledge about their grandparents that one comes closest to hearing the silence of their homes.

Thus at the same time I was struck by two impressions: how little Richard knew about his parents' pre-war lives and wartime experiences and how unaware he was that his knowledge was so paltry. He seemed not to be aware that key absences were significant. Simply, there 'wasn't a lot of talk' in the home about such things:

> It wasn't taboo. It wasn't that we weren't allowed. Just that I didn't have any questions. And they didn't volunteer anything. Sometimes on holidays my father would tell us stories. My role was to listen. And that's what I did, I sat there like a kid listening to a story-teller. There wasn't any puzzle. It was like going to the movies or listening to a serial on the radio. I didn't try to avoid it and I didn't try to seek it out. I don't know why I didn't ask questions, I just didn't.

At another point, he said, 'I didn't ask because I wasn't inquisitive. I didn't know there was anyone missing and anyway, it was two generations away, it was too remote'. I asked him what he knew about his parents' lost families. Just that both sets of grandparents were lost, and four siblings on his mother's side, eight on his father's, he said. He wasn't sure those numbers were right. He didn't know their names. He didn't know where or how they died. He didn't know the circumstances of his grandparents' deaths, and nothing about their lives. He knew his paternal grandfather was tall because someone who survived from the same town told him that.

In all this, what is important, I believe, is not so much that he didn't know these things—very few of us do—but that he seemed to be unaware that he did not know, all the while sobbing relentlessly. This is a case of silence so pervasive that it does not register as such. The taboo—and there must have been a taboo—has been naturalised and recast as erasure in a kind of affective numbing that spreads to fill all the available space.

Two things have happened here. Firstly, of course, vital information about the family biography has not been passed on. Secondly, the omission has been constructed as normal. The end result is that the son, now around 50, does not know how his grandparents died and does not know that he does not know; and when it is pointed out that not knowing is odd, he seems to have considered this for the first time—all the while sobbing. When I asked about the profusion of tears, he said, 'Don't worry about that. I tend to cry easily, especially when there's any link to my father'.

Richard was one of the last people I interviewed, and ironically it was through him that I fully realised that my very elaborate interview protocol had been quite unnecessary. The main question I actually needed to have asked my respondents was about their grandparents. I discovered that I could tell what kind of home it must have been if the person sitting opposite me knew something about their grandparents' lives and something of the circumstances of their death. In addition, I realised the significance of how they themselves reacted to their state of knowledge—whether they accepted this as normal, as Richard seemed to, or railed against it in fury or frustration, as Susan and Rebecca and Jill did.

It has often struck me that after someone dies—I mean a normal death, of old age, in peaceful circumstances—the close family needs to tell and retell and retell the circumstances of the death, and this is what they do as people come to offer consolation. The same story gets told many, many times. Perhaps this is what grief needs to do to enable the bereaved to reach acceptance. If the bereaved in normal circumstances need this, would not the need be just so much greater when the deaths occur in abnormal and horrific circumstances? Wouldn't it take many *more* tellings, not fewer, to reconcile oneself to the reality? What happens when there is no re-telling? Where does grief untold go?

The difference between exclusions and omissions is an important one. In 'Exclusions', the terrain of discourse that is not entered into is part of the landscape of people's lives, albeit fenced off. There's an elaborate conspiracy of avoidance enacted to enable people to get on with their lives. They know it's there and they know not to go there and they can talk about what this means to them. It's as if the class of 'Exclusions' lies within a person's visual field: he or she knows it's there and chooses not to trespass. 'Omissions', on the other hand, lie outside the visual field. They are therefore non-existent, not part of one's world. The terrain registers as absent.[19] There are no edges, no perimeter; it's a seamlessness that encourages oblivion. These absences have long been established as normal; naturalised, they remain unnoticed.

A trusty sign that omission has taken place is where the respondent sees as unproblematic something that is inherently complex and fraught. For example, when I asked Paul questions about the discourse patterns in his home, he obliged with answers, but in a tone that suggested that this was all a lot of fuss about nothing:

> My parents responded to you if you asked them. They didn't make an issue of it. Take my brother and I. He didn't ask so he doesn't know very much about it all, and I liked to ask so I know a lot.

Paul attributes the patterns in his home largely to personality differences between himself and his brother rather than to forces larger than individuals and families. For me this is indicative of an insularity of thought and experience: it echoes the fact that as my generation was growing up in the shadow of the Holocaust, few of us had any awareness that the same drama was being played out in survivor homes around the world. This tendency to 'see as unproblematic' is shared by the three respondents I discuss in this section—Richard, Paul and Robert—who also were among those whom I invited to be interviewed rather than those who approached me independently. They also had varying degrees of reluctance to talk, certainly in comparison with those whom offering their stories for interview, approached the interview as a potential learning opportunity.

Robert revealed a similar unawareness of what he was not seeing. He was the teenager who was taken by his parents to see documentary films about the Holocaust, specifically about the liberation of the concentration camps. He concedes that they wanted him to know but were unable to tell him directly. As with Richard, I was struck by the paucity of the replies to my questions, replies that had a shut-down effect rather than, as with most of the interviews, an opening up one. Robert said, 'They wanted me to ask them questions about the war afterwards'. 'Did you?', I asked. 'No', he said. I asked whether he had had to struggle to piece it altogether, as many of the respondents had done. He said, 'No. What was there to make sense of? It's understandable as history'. I asked him if he had ever asked them about their pre-war lives. 'No'. I asked if he had ever asked about their experiences during the war. 'No. I knew they had a tough time'. I asked if he thought the war had changed them: 'I didn't know them before so I don't know. I think they gave it their best shot here'. I asked if he had any sense of what the world was like that they came from; he said, 'No. It was probably difficult to be a Jew there'. I asked how he felt when he was taken to see the documentaries. 'I went because they wanted me to.' I asked why he didn't ever ask questions; he said they probably told him everything he needed to know. I asked him about iconic things like stale bread; he said it was 'logical to keep stale bread' as it was handy for breadcrumbs. I asked him about his own struggle to keep weight off; he said 'I happen to like rich food. It's got nothing to do with *all that*'.

Robert's answers were minimalist. His utterances ended with a falling tone, sending the message that this is how it was, making further discussion difficult and clearly unwelcome. He knew that I too was a child of survivors but didn't engage me in comparisons, as many of my interviewees did. The interview had a staccato effect, with clearly defined roles of who asks and who answers. Whereas most of my interviews were like digging in fresh soil, with Robert I hit rock very fast and then there was nowhere to go.

However, as with Paul and Richard, the interview left me troubled. Again I was moved both by the number of negatives in the responses but more so by the lack of awareness that I had confronted. What troubled me was the fact that in these people's lives, the state of not-knowing had been allowed to become ordinary and unmarked, the act of not-asking questions had become construed as normal. There was no recognition of the ruptures and disjointedness of family lives, nor that they themselves had reconfigured the unusual as straightforward. It was as if they had disavowed any concern for what was not apparent, being committed to believing that surface reality is all there is. So for none of these three respondents was it a case of severed ancestral links. It's as if such ancestry never existed. I am reminded of Rena's recurrent dream from childhood—of being the last person alive, alone on the planet. In my imagination, there is no silence more silent than this.

And I am still troubled by a question Leah asked me. She said, 'When our parents have gone, we face this awful informational loss; what we know now is that we'll never know. But there are lots of people who have unproblematic ancestry, who have no interest at all in their past. Why?' While I have no answer to this question, I sense that Leah has hit upon something significant: the yearning for connection may be simply the outward marker of ancestral rupture.

8

Other Voices

This chapter is dedicated to presenting the recounted stories of a number of people who shared with me their experience of a sustained silence in the context of trauma. As I said in Chapter 2, these stories were more happenstance than sought out: however, because of my interest in aspects of incommunicability, once they came to my notice I tried to explore the details and circumstances of each story, as far as the people involved were willing to co-operate.

The stories in this chapter are less homogeneous than those detailed through the previous chapters. There, despite the differentiation in response, the one unifying feature is the parental experience of the Holocaust. All of the 27 respondents grew up in survivor homes and faced a similar task—making sense of their world with very little sustained explanatory input by the parent generation. In those cases, the primary trauma was experienced by the parent generation and the silence of the home was a reaction to that experience.

Compared to them, the current group of stories displays fewer overt signs of homogeneity. For example, the primary trauma may be, but is not necessarily so, the parent's; more often, but again not always, it is that experienced by the person who told me their story, with the silence being a feature of the reaction of their family. Another difference is in the nature and function of the silence. In the Holocaust-related data, the silence is the outcome of a vice-like set of impossible choices, themselves the result, as we have seen in Chapter 3, of a collision of discourse goals. The first is the parents caught between the desire to tell and the desire to refrain from telling. The second is the child caught between wanting to ask but being fearful of finding out. If the first and second are intrapersonal, the third is interpersonal—the clash that comes about between parents who want to tell and want the child to ask, on the one hand, and children, on the other, who do not know how to hear or ask or generally cope with the demands of the interaction.

In the data set with which this chapter is concerned, there is greater diversity of nature and function when we consider the silence vis-à-vis the trauma experienced. The stories here have been organised according to the function, in each case, of the silence that was experienced. Through the differentiation of experience and response, however, the thread of silence in the wake of trauma appears to be the dominant motif. Generally, the pattern is of a trauma, which is then masked by silence, within which some kind of regrouping or inner reconstructing occurs. Through all these stories, silence carries its own messages.

Peter's story: growing up inside a secret

Peter's story is about growing up in an externally imposed silence. He was raised in the Midlands in England, an only child in a low-income family. Now in his late forties, married to the same woman all his adult life, he is a warm, gentle and empathetic man who seems to have achieved an enviable degree of centredness and calm. He opens himself generously to and connects comfortably with others.

Peter's father was a machinist. Both sets of grandparents had had their homes destroyed in the Blitz, and never again were able to own their own property. He was born in the early 1950s, not long after the war-related rationing policy had ended. Indeed, the impact of war—both the First World War that involved his grandparents, and the Second World War, in particular the Blitz—emerges as the major backdrop to Peter's childhood.

Peter had some awareness from an early age that his family was different, partly because he was an only child (unusual before the era of birth control) and partly because his was a tightly-knit closeted family that did not comfortably welcome others into its midst. He was not allowed to form close relationships with people outside the nuclear family, either in the extended family or in his peer group. There was always some reason given for why such people could not be let in:

> It was a very private family who never spoke with anyone else about personal matters. Everything had its own place and was spotless and immaculate. The feeling I had was that if we let anybody in, it would

upset the order. As I grew up I realised that other people did things differently, that they had other people coming in and out of their lives. But not us. People were talked about a lot: there was always something wrong with people, a reason for why they couldn't be let into the inner sanctum. And the key thing about my early life was that I *never ever* spoke to my parents about why I was an only child.

The sense is that his safety is severely curtailed by the fact that 'there were only three of them'. Peter's parents today are very elderly and his own family grown up, but even now there is in him a tangible apprehension when he imagines life beyond the time of his parents' deaths.

For Peter, 'the silence' is the fact that he was born into a secret milieu of baby death. He actually grew up inside a secret, intuiting that there was something unstated going on, but not knowing what it was. He eventually found out: before his parents had him, they had had multiple experiences of miscarriage and neonatal death, usually still-birth. He was about twenty when he found out; even then, it was indirectly conveyed (his mother told his wife), that there had been about fourteen pregnancies in all, of which only he had survived. There was no mention, ever, of these facts in the home in which he was raised.

I grew up fairly lonely. I desperately wanted a sister. I fantasised about this. I wanted someone to tell me what was going on. I used to think *someone must know* what is going on. I figured that people who are older know, so you either have to get them to tell you (that's why I wanted an older sister) or you have to wait until you grow up.

Peter married his childhood sweetheart whom his mother had long before informally adopted as an honorary daughter. She says that a clairvoyant once told her that she would have a son and a daughter; to Peter, she said, 'when you married, that was when I got my daughter'.

He was aware at an early age that his mother was needy—the onset of epilepsy had resulted in periodic and dramatic personality changes—and indeed, needier than him, that he was 'going to have to take care of her', that from her, he could not expect any emotional nourishment. In other words, no mothering. Rightly or wrongly, he grew up associating her disease with his birth, and nothing that happened consequently disassociated these two facts. His father talked to him about his mother's erratic behaviour. Peter grew up knowing that he had to make allowances for her: 'the message I got was that I was on my own'. He speaks about reaching emotional independence by thirteen, when he, metaphorically at least, could 'leave home'. It would seem that the first thirteen years were the site of a tremendous struggle: coming to terms with the state of being unmothered.

Peter is at a loss today to explain the taboo that shrouded his childhood home. He suspects that his parents were trying to protect him from the trauma and the perceived shame. He recalls that he was overly protected in other matters too, for example, there was never any mention of money, as if they did not want him to share in the burden and stigma of being poor. He remembers that he never knew what a loaf of bread cost; this and other deficits were his parents' way of protecting him. Certainly, in regard to the economic status of the family, he recalls that 'the priority of always being clean, well fed and taking the two weeks holiday' was adhered to 'to the point of neurosis'. He adds, 'My parents never acknowledged that they were poor, and by the local standards they were better off than some'. It would seem that issues related to trauma—the loss of the babies and the loss of the family's economic status through the war—were dealt with by silence. Not talking about something was his parents' way of shielding their son from the pain and shame that they themselves felt.

> There was big resentment of anyone who had made it good and displayed their wealth; it was a kind of reverse snobbery about displays of wealth. We were different. Maybe I felt it because I was continually told we were different like, 'they bought their car on hire purchase. We would never do that'.

Neither the subject of the miscarriages nor the sustained silence that surrounded the topic has ever been discussed within his family. Today, an uneasy truce exists, with Peter in close contact with his parents, yet as fearful as ever of raising 'the topic' with them. There is a sense that this is qualitatively the same fear as that which he carried around as a child, one that he is still ill equipped to handle. He is fearful of triggering an eruption whose impact he might be powerless to control, and in this his story reminds me of children of Holocaust survivors who tiptoe around the volcano of their parents' pain. There's an uneasy amalgam of emotions in Peter: a wishful desire to resolve the past; a regret that his parents might pass away before a resolution is reached; alongside a 'sleeping dogs' philosophy of leaving the unsaid alone. It is within this uneasy constellation of emotions that 'the silence' remains unbroken.

Today he attributes to this environment a large part of what he calls in himself 'the deep ache'. This is a reference to an enduring emotional pain—a sorrow at the inner core of his being—that has no overt external reason or event with which it can be linked. It is remarkably akin to the feelings I have heard expressed by the children of Holocaust survivors.

Gillian's story: preservation of the family's public face

The next story is also one about secrets in the family, this time of a whole family bound by an oath to keep silent about the truth. At the centre is Gillian, a woman in her early thirties, who told me the story.

Gillian is bright, slim and attractive. She has a mass of curly blonde hair and she exudes a great deal of energy. She works as a teacher and loves being in the classroom, which she finds both creative and satisfying at many levels. Gillian has a radiant smile and a loud infectious laugh and these features are closely related to the way people perceive her. You always expect her to be bright and bubbly and she invests a lot of energy into creating 'a happy place', whether that be in the classroom, the staff room, at home or with friends. She says that she's always been like that and that people have always commented admiringly on her 'beautiful smile': she was rewarded through her growing-up years for the happiness that could be read on her face. Gillian appears to have the perfect life, being happy in what she does and who she is. Yet, there's something brittle there, something too good to be true, something indeterminate and fragile.

That all is not so perfect is apparent in what Gillian says about her growing-up years:

> We were only allowed to be happy. I was so rewarded for my beautiful smile that it became second nature. But it wasn't real. People didn't know that sometimes I was weeping inside.

Gillian speaks about the energy invested into the happy image of her family. This no doubt was a kind of 'emotional labour', a term that refers to the work that has to be done to force one's exterior self to disconnect with one's inner self so that the one is not a reflection of the other.[1] This is the kind of work that airline stewards do, and increasingly in marketing and the hospitality industry, people at the interface with clients become skilled at the public presentation of self.[2] Emotional labour refers not only to the projection of a happy

face. Other occupations—for example people who work in the funeral
business or as debt collectors—have to learn to project a dour solemnity irrespective of their real emotions of the moment.

Gillian's parents were British migrants from families who experienced a great deal of hardship, who each came to Australia in their
early teens. The work ethic and the drive to be successful were the
engines that drove their families forward and when they met and
married and established their family of three children, the lessons
they'd learned from home steered their adult lives. Gillian says:

> We were taught that we always had to put our best foot forward. You
> were never to expose any weaknesses. You were only allowed ever to
> be happy. Happiness was obligatory! They started from nothing and
> had to struggle really hard to make a life, and were really successful
> and did a fantastic job and that was just so important, having the
> image of success. But it wasn't all about image—they actually wanted
> to give us everything and make everything be great for us, but in
> doing that, they imposed this image thing on us: everything had to
> be squeaky clean.

When Gillian was 21, the single most influential event of her
adult life happened: her father, an engineer in a private building firm,
experienced a bout of economic decline and committed suicide. He
was taken to hospital where he remained on life support for three days
at which time the decision was taken to allow him to die. She remembers clearly the scene in the room allocated to family of patients in the
intensive care unit. When Gillian arrived there, her mother and
brothers had already been at the hospital for some time and had been
present during the discussion with doctors about the state of her
father and the prognosis. She recalls that she asked, 'What can they
do for Dad?'. Her mother replied that there was 'not a lot' that could
be done. At this point her middle brother, who was very shaken and
angry, blurted out, 'Don't you understand? He's gone!'.

It was in that little room that the decision was made, by Gillian's
mother and middle brother, to keep the fact of the suicide a secret
within the family.

> They said, 'We'll just tell people that he's had a brain hemorrhage'.
> I just accepted it. This was just the way our family had always been.
> We'd always strived to keep a good image to the outside world.
> That was really important. It was a large part of the family culture.

Gillian believes that this family culture which determined the way the family responded to the death of the father was also responsible for his suicide:

> He was not willing to admit to the world that he was in trouble and needed some help. There's no way he could say to anyone, 'I'm not coping'. So it meant that couldn't help himself or even ask for help from others. He just ploughed on regardless.

For ten more years, Gillian kept the family secret:

> I told people the line about his brain hemorrhage so often that I almost believed it. At first it felt like a lie, but then I started to believe it and it lost the edge of being a lie. Deep down you're aware that it's a lie and this really affected my relationships. It kept me at a distance from people: the one thing that was so important to me was the thing I couldn't share with anyone.

The lie was easier to maintain than expected. Death is a delicate subject and people tend to veer away from the topic in discomfort; certainly no one interrogates the bereaved to 'check the story', as it were. No one had the indelicacy to question the official line. Even within the family it was not discussed. There was talk about the father but only ever the good things. As a result, it was not properly processed. Gillian believes that her mother today would like to tell her friends the truth but is afraid that they would be unforgiving of the fact that she's lied about the event for so long.

I asked Gillian to describe what the silence meant for her. She said in fact it began in the months prior to his suicide. She was very aware then that there were problems; there was an economic decline and his job was threatened. He was under more and more pressure. He was actually seeing a psychiatrist and was on medication but 'I knew it wasn't working'. She describes the weeks prior to the suicide as frenzied:

> I was desperate. I was ringing psychiatrists to try to understand what was happening, to get some advice, to tell them that he wasn't getting any better. I knew the way he was going, he couldn't stop himself. Something was going to happen'.

Afterwards, there were many emotions. There was anger towards her father 'because he wasn't strong enough to admit that something was wrong'. There were guilt and self-blame 'because I could have done more'. She was lonely and isolated because 'we weren't even able to talk about it within the family'. And she felt repressed: 'I never cried because if I started I wouldn't be able to stop'. When Gillian actually shed tears, some ten years after the incident, there was, as she had predicted, no stopping: 'these days I cry all the time', she said, laughing. Around the time that she began confronting the past honestly she found an old diary and, in reading it, for the first time she allowed herself to feel compassion towards herself: 'I could see the strong sense of how hard I was trying to hold it all together, always trying to do the right thing, to keep up the pretence and not be able do anything'. She speaks of the isolation and alienation she experiences with girlfriends—being unable to participate in 'deep and meaningful conversations', and therefore always 'living a lie' and setting a limit to her friendship:

> I couldn't talk about what I really wanted to talk about. And at the same time I had to field conversations. You'd be surprised how often the topic of suicide comes up. And in any case, people generally have no idea how to handle a death. People were uncomfortable surrounding me because my father had died. People have no idea what to say. I found *I* was trying to make *them* feel better—I was more concerned about their discomfort than my own feelings at the time!

There are echoes of Gillian's story in another's—Catherine Bowe, whose story was reported in the news. At the age of eight, Catherine discovered her father had hanged himself. A Vietnam Veteran, David Bowe had struggled for eighteen years to come to terms with the trauma of war as he encountered it. At first she blamed herself for his death: 'She couldn't be worth much . . . if her father preferred death to living with her'. Then came a denial stage where she expected him to come walking through the door at any time. The silence that dominated his trauma—both a wider societal silence and a personal one—in the aftermath of the Vietnam War combined to set the seal of silence on Catherine's life. There came a point, however, when she decided to break the seal. As part of a school project for her HSC subject, Society and Culture, Catherine investigated her father's past, interviewing other Vietnam Vets, researching Post-Traumatic Stress Disorder, and writing up her report, all of which constituted a deliberate act to break the destructive pattern of silence in her family.[3]

Brendhan's story: silence as a tool of oppression

In the next story, silence moves from the family to the institutional arena and then back to the home and community. Brendhan's story is set inside the novitiate of the Christian Brothers, a Catholic missionary order, where he spent a short period of his life between school and university. The experiences he had there over 30 years ago still make him tremble and he is unable, and probably never will be able, to recount that period of his life with equanimity. As he talks about it, he seems to go inward; he looks at the ground and his eyes dart about nervously; it's as if he were looking for something but has forgotten what. An exceptionally articulate man, his own disfluency in this situation seems to bewilder him. Aware that the experience was a thoroughly negative one, he apologises in advance for his halting narrative: 'I can only tell it in fragments. That's how I make sense of it'.

Brendhan offered up a fragment of his experience to illustrate 'what the Christian Brothers were like'. The training period for the novitiate was three-and-a-half months, but after three weeks, something happened. They were in a group of 50, and one of them, a young man called Chris, suddenly left. No one knew in advance that he was going: he just wasn't there one day. After he left, there was no comment from the Master of the Novices. Chris simply ceased to be. There was quite a lot of grumbling from others that this was a weak thing, not to comment on the departure of one of their own. The sense was that the event absolutely required comment. 'We needed to be told and to have an opportunity to say goodbye', but there was none, and the silence that loomed loud when Chris left set the standard for the rest of Brendhan's time there. As if in explanation, Brendhan adds bitterly, 'That's the Christian Brothers, that's the way they do things'. My sense is that this failure to acknowledge the needs of the individual in even the most minimal way has come to represent for Brendhan the overwhelming 'erasure' that he felt among the Christian Brothers.

It was Easter Sunday in 1968—Brendhan still remembers the exact date—and his parents had come for their 'first real visit'. This is how he tells the events, in short sentences, speaking slowly, concentrating on the sequence of events, and I can sense the effort being invested to keep the emotion out of the recount, to keep his feelings at bay:

I had written to tell my parents that I was unhappy. They arrived and I said, 'I'll show you around'. My mother said, 'I have a terrible headache. If you're leaving, then can we do it straight away?' I said, 'Yes, OK', and I went and packed. My brother helped me carry the bags to the car. Then I went to the Novice Master's door. He was in his room, not out ready to say hello to families. On reflection I find that quite odd. I knocked on the door. He opened it. I said, 'My parents are in the parlour downstairs. I'm probably leaving today', and I walked away. I said 'probably' to take the edge off it. I went to find my brother and together we walked out the back door of the building to where my parents had parked the car. On the way, I passed a member of the group and I remember the shocked look on his face when he saw me put my bags in the car. He knew what was happening at that moment. I said nothing to him. I walked into the large study where a friend I'd made was spending the day—he was from interstate so he had no visitors that day. He said, 'Are all your family here?' I took all the books out of my desk. I saw the same shocked look on his face. I didn't say goodbye. I went to the car and put the books in and then to the parlour where the Novice Master was standing with my parents. He said, 'I can see things are more serious than I had realised'. I said, 'Yes'. We shook hands and I said goodbye.

According to Brendhan, the young novices were meant to be 'nurturing their vocation' and 'anything that departed from that had no acknowledgement of the most minimal kind'. It seemed to him in retrospect that there was no language to discuss difference of view-point or to allow an individual perspective. It's as if on arrival you renounce not only your worldly connection but also your former sense of self. You allow yourself to become a collective in which the individual has no place:

> You have to say 'here we all are, we're all together, we are one'. There was never any such thing as 'one less' because we were considered—and had to consider ourselves—as a mass entity, not a divisible unit. As such everyone moved together in harmony and conformity.

In these terms, Brendhan says he is able to make sense of the behaviour of the Christian Brothers and the behaviour forced onto the novices:

> As soon as you acknowledge a departure of one person, you have to acknowledge 'one less'. But in that context, anything that detracted from the identity of the entity as a whole was incomprehensible. There

was no language to attach to it, to articulate or describe or explore it. And so there was no language to validate it. There was only silence.

Referring to Chris' sudden departure, Brendhan says:

> I only knew Chris as a member of the group. I had no inkling that he was about to leave just as no one had any inkling about me. I spoke about it with no one before I left and later I found out that, as with Chris, nothing was spoken of me afterwards. I was not referred to, my departure was not mentioned, as if I had not been there, as if I did not exist. Years later I started to hear rumours about the response to my departure. Apparently it sent a wave of shock through the novices, greater than Chris', because it must have reinforced his. One day I actually met up with one of the group. He apologised for not having seen my distress. He had the sense that he should have known, should have seen it. But he couldn't have. There was no language there to think or talk about such things.

Brendhan remembers as clearly the trip home that day and what happened immediately afterwards and in the weeks that followed. It is of interest that he also refers to a silence in this period, but this time the silence denotes not a raw abdication of self but a soothing balm, a healing space in which he was allowed to have made a mistake and allowed to repair.

> I got into the car and we drove away. We stopped at a friend's place on the way. My Mum had told this friend not to bother visiting me that day because I was probably leaving and we might all pop in on the way back. We called in. My friend said, 'Was it like a messy divorce?' and I said, 'Yes'. Then we went home. I unpacked. Half an hour later this same friend turned up and he and another friend took me out to the city. We went and had a coffee and there was a jukebox there—they played some of the songs that they thought I wouldn't know 'because of my absence'. Other than that, we didn't talk about what had happened.

This day set the tone for how people reacted to Brendhan, and through this period the silence he perceived was a positive and calming one:

> No one asked me why I left. My parents never asked. No one asked what it was like there. Some months later my great-aunt asked a

simple factual question about whether the beds we slept on in the monastery were hard. I said, 'No, beds are beds'. That was the only question anyone asked. I suspect they said nothing out of deference to my feelings. The view probably was that Brendhan had made a big mistake but we weren't going to rub his nose in it. After all, we all make mistakes. It was as if it hadn't happened.

I asked Brendhan how it was that he had entered the monastery in the first place. I wanted to understand why the experience had been such a devastating one for him, and it turned out, rather as I expected, that this was intimately connected with the destruction of his own illusions:

> I was ensnared. It fitted into my emotional landscape very congruently. There was a nice fit between what the Christian Brothers purported to offer—security, safety, the promise of salvation—and my emotional needs of the time. I was a believer through all of that so when I left, I felt like a failure, someone who had walked out, who wasn't good enough. For a long time I felt a sense of absence about myself, as if I had no identity. It wasn't only the time at the monastery. For so long I had built the image of myself with the Christian Brothers and it turned out to be just a romantic delusion. In reality what they offered was depraved indifference or culpable neglect. The best you could say was that it was benign neglect. There was no mentoring, no care. They only respond within the tiny perimeter of their view of the world. They had no language for anything other than vocation, faith, God. Anything that was not that, was the negation of that. So you were either this or that. It was the most intense experience of the absolutes of Christianity—good and evil, God and the devil. It was religion in its most severe and forbidding form. My leaving them was leaving God. If I was not of them, I was the antithesis of them. It was an utterly exclusive landscape with no shades of grey or breadth of interpretation. It took several years to recover. At university, I built from nothing but I built on solid rock, whereas with the Christian Brothers, I had built on illusion.

In Brendhan's story, as we have seen, silence has two faces. The first is the silence of the Christian Brothers which functioned as a tool to extract obedience and conformity, to shape behaviour into an enforced 'as oneness' in which the individual was subjugated to the collective. The oppressive silence of the novitiate positioned Brendhan into a role for which he was wholly unprepared and unsuited. The silence therefore proved wholly destructive and caused him tremendous suffering at the time and beyond.

The second silence is the response to his escape by family and friends. Apart from the friend's 'Was it like a messy divorce?', and the great-aunt's 'Were the beds very hard?', it would seem that those who cared for him—as one person, as Brendhan—must have realised that the best way to treat his suffering was to create a space where he could heal. That space was provided by absenting the kind of words that might have rubbed salt in wounds still fresh and raw. It would also seem that his recovery, which he attributes largely to a new start at university, was made possible by the healing space created for him in the months after he came home.

Indeed, Brendhan speaks about the second silence in a different tone. With the Christian Brothers there is a sense of outrage at their betrayal, being 'seduced' by false promises, and then battered into acquiescence through psychological cruelty. With the silence of family and friends, there is a sense that they had saved him from 'that terrible place', and brought him back into their midst where, at a respectful distance, they could keep a non-intrusive but watchful eye on his gradual healing. Here he is not positioned into a role but rather is allowed to recover his former self. The way in which the two experiences of silence are differently invested with meaning indicates that silence, like words, is not an absolute, but derives its meaning from the context of occurrence. In Jaworski's words, 'Silence is an activity . . . subject to interpretation in the same manner as other instances of linguistic communication'.[4]

Frances' story: silence as negation

The next story returns to the home for its setting, this time focusing on a husband–wife relationship. Frances is a middle-aged woman with a grown-up family. She is intelligent and well read, loves the performing arts and fine art, and has strong opinions on anything from a daughter's boyfriend to government policy on education. She and her husband are as happily married as any couple is that has been through a series of crises and traumas in their lives together. When I told Frances about the book I was writing and about the kind of silence I meant by the title, she decided to tell me about a dimension of her relationship with her husband that she has not previously mentioned.

The man to whom she has been married for nearly 30 years never uses her name—not once in all the time she has been married to him. It is a taboo and as with most taboos, there is no overt discussion of the fact of the taboo. The taboo is the more tyrannical for not being spoken. Because communication requires some kind of referral system, he has developed a host of alternative expressions with which both to address her (e.g., 'my dear one') and to refer to her (e.g., 'my better half'). What is unusual here is not the apparent terms of endearment, but the proliferation of these in her husband's lexicon alongside the absolute absence of her name on his lips. When Frances spoke to me about this, she was clearly affected by it—she found it demeaning, but couldn't quite explain why. I had to admit I found it an instance of quite marked usage. Most people in intimate connections use their partner's name at least from time to time. Indeed, couples often go one step further in personalising their system of referral to each other by inventing terms of endearment that are exclusively theirs (when others hear them they tend to cringe). The fact that Frances' husband does not use her name and indeed has generated a host of alternatives to make the use of her name redundant, suggests that more is going on than may be apparent.

In the taboo on her name, it is as if there were an inner prohibition that manifests in his avoidance of 'Frances'. The prohibition is visible only insofar as one notices the absence of her name. Were no one to notice, the prohibition would remain invisible. In trying to 'unpack' this pattern of usage, two processes appear to be significant: one reflects the husband's view of Frances as wife; the other reflects the husband's view of Frances' non-wife identity.[5] These two perspectives are comfortably compatible and as equally denigrating. It is not a surprise that they combine to make Frances feel 'lessened'.

First, the view of Frances-as-wife. It is not without reason that Frances feels detracted by the fact that he won't use her name. There's something about a name that is unique. While a descriptive term, for example, 'my other half' or 'the good wife' can be reference-free but meaningful, a name depends on its referent for its basic meaning. If I say 'Henry', you have no idea what it means unless you know who Henry is. By subtracting his wife as uniquely referred to and replacing her name with the member of the class or type, the husband in effect opens up a grammatical space. Into this space, another individual can slot without any inconsistency. In other words, linguistically she has been demoted from being a person to becoming a position. As such, the grammatical machinery is in place—ready and prepared—for her replacement. The usage suggests that in one part of his mind, not necessarily the conscious part, he wants to be married but not to this individual. By creating the grammatical space and by thinking of it in generic not personal terms, he has in Frances a token rather than a real wife. He can fool himself by pretending that she can, as it were, be cashed in for someone else.

Second, the view of Frances as non-wife. In linguistic terms, Frances' husband's style of referring to her is using a particular form for a very odd purpose. Terms like 'the wife' or 'the better half' are instances of 'membership categorisation devices', Sacks' term for a class of things, but not an individual.[6] In using these words where in fact a person's name would be far more apt, he effectively brings about some dissolution of the individual within the class. Frances is identified by virtue of her membership of the larger group. Thus, Frances is an instance of the class of wives. So in retreating from the identification of the wife as the unique referent of her name, the husband effectively appeals to the general type and his wife becomes just that— a wife, another half. This brings with it a certain anonymity but it is not the positive anonymity that goes with brand names. Within this referral system, Frances has no existence outside the domain of being her husband's wife. So she loses out twice. In the first place she is a stand-in wife, able to be cashed in at any time. In the second place, though her status is only ever token, she still can have no identity outside of being her husband's wife.

To consider how such a system of referrals evolved, what motivates it—*cui bono*, or who stands to gain—would take us from the domain of linguistics to that of psychology, well beyond the perimeter of my concerns in this book. It is worthy of mention that Frances has intuitively credited the absence of her name as marking an absence of engagement; she feels sure that the attendant emotion of negativity is justified; but beyond this, she had been unable to connect this micro piece with the larger whole of their relationship.

Her story is included in the pages of this book because what we have here is a micro version of a silence—one word only, but a very important word—in which Frances has operated for 30 years.

Carmen's story: silence as stoicism

Most homes would have some taboo topics, and I imagine death is a frequent one. The next story arises from the way in which one family managed the topic of death.

Once again I happened upon the story opportunistically as I was answering Carmen's questions about my research. Her story is about how the tragic death of her younger brother was managed in her home. She was twelve and Mal was ten when the cancer struck:

> It was never ever spoken about in our family. He was sick for about five months. The cancer was very quick and a lot of the time none of the other kids were involved. The way I knew he had the big 'C' word was when I overheard my mother speaking on the phone. When he died it was never actually said. We were sent to other people's places, friends of the family. This was the way it was done, we were protected from death, this is how they saw it. At the time I just put it aside. I didn't talk or think about it. Ours had always been a stiff upper lip family. When things happen, you just cope and get on your life. That's how we were raised. One day he was an active little boy playing sport. He came home with some ache in his leg which didn't clear up. I have no recollection of how it unfolded. We didn't sit by his bed and talk to him. It was just like he had a cold. It was 'Oh poor Mal, he's sick', not 'Oh poor Mal's got cancer and he's dying'. I didn't even know the word 'funeral'. It was so secret that we didn't know that he'd died. And afterwards, we didn't note the anniversary of his death. He was never mentioned ever again. It was only years later when we married and had our own children that we realised what it would have meant to our parents.

Yet, as we have seen with the children of Holocaust survivors, the ways of knowing are many and subtle. Years later, Carmen opened up the 'tight cocoon' of her life when she wrote her autobiography. In it she included the following words:

> My mother . . . tried to protect us from his approaching death, but the hushed tones and unannounced visitors warned us without words that something was terribly wrong. We lived in an atmosphere of knowing but not knowing . . . avoiding questions about something that was too painful to articulate . . . Our parents had no training in how to talk about this loss, even though my father (as a doctor) had

told countless numbers of other families about approaching death. One minute we have a brother and the next minute we don't. There is an immense chasm in our lives that is there but not there. Nothing is said and his death goes into the deep recesses of our minds.

Carmen attributes this stoicism in the face of grief both to prevailing attitudes of the time and to the influence of her father.

He was in the war and he saw terrible things. He was a doctor and he was there for a long time. He never ever talked about the war. We just knew it as 'the war'. I don't know how we knew he saw terrible things but we did. It must have been through his silence.

Later she wrote:

He had tended shattered limbs and deranged minds and seen savagery and death, but he never once spoke of such things. In my teenage years I found a simple poem he had written about the unspeakable things he saw in the Middle East and in the jungles of New Guinea and on reading it I grieved for him and for the silence that these events had forced upon him.

The same stoicism attached to Carmen's mother's death:

Again, he didn't talk about it. I was 18 and away at boarding school. On the day she died, he went back to his rooms to conduct his regular afternoon surgery. I came home for the funeral. He never spoke about her. She'd been the centre of his world and our lives and the home and family, and he never spoke her name again. Two years later he took his own life. It was a long time after that until I could unlearn these lessons, stop being stoical and allow myself to weep for my mother and to learn to talk about her.

Linda's story: silence as conspiracy

The site of the silence in the next story switches between institution and family. It is wrapped around a teenage pregnancy and forced adoption.

Linda was seventeen and very much in love with her boyfriend, whom she planned to marry, when she discovered she was pregnant.[7] The second youngest of seven siblings, her mother's reaction was shock and she was immediately parcelled off to a Church of England home for pregnant unwed teenage girls. This institution had arrangements

with government social workers and church authorities who conveniently managed the 'problem' of teenage pregnancies alongside
the problem of infertility in married, church-going couples, adopting
out the 'unwanted infants' to the 'more deserving' married parents:

> It was all hush-hush. It had to be. They couldn't have got away with
> it if it were all public. It started by making the mother of the girl
> ashamed of the problem and duping them into believing adoption
> was in their daughters' best interests. And then making the teenage
> girl believe in her own badness and unworthiness.

Before she went to the home and while there, Linda was never
part of any discussions or plans that were made. She thinks 'shame'
and 'scandal' were motivating thoughts in her mother's mind but she
never heard these words voiced. When she was in a room with a social
worker and her mother, she was not included in their discussions.
'Nobody ever asked me. It was just decided. And I was obedient'.

At first only her mother and her boyfriend knew what was
happening and where she was. Some time later, her two older sisters
found out and sided with the mother in urging Linda towards giving
up her baby for adoption. Throughout the pregnancy, their voices
urged compliance and silence. At the home, she was kept isolated and
subjected to an ongoing campaign of verbal mind-bending designed
to make her compliant to the wishes of the authorities. She was
coerced toward the viewpoint that if she loved her unborn baby, she
would know that the best thing for the baby was to give it up for
adoption. She was meant to feel 'bad' and 'unworthy' and it is therefore no surprise that she emerged with this self-perception after the
ordeal of the birth was over.

The public face of these proceedings was to 'help' unwed mothers
find an option other than abortion or 'keeping it'. Linda was encouraged to put the whole experience behind her and pretend that it never
happened, in fact, get on with her life as if the baby never existed.
Linda argues convincingly that what was done to her, and hundreds of
thousands of others like her (300 000 girls over a 40-year period),
could not have happened without the collusion of people in positions
of responsibility and power, people who also had a duty of care
towards people like her. No doubt there were some instances of
teenage pregnancy where the girl involved actively and independently
chose to give up her baby for adoption, grateful for the opportunity
either to avoid a scandal (these were the 1950s and 1960s, after all) or

to get on with her life and put 'her little mistake' behind her. However, the evidence that Linda has collected would rather suggest that in the majority of cases, girls in this circumstance were abused and deprived of their human rights.[8]

In fact, there is not one silence in Linda's story; there are many. The first kind of silence involved the denial of her right to information about her situation, her entitlements by law, her options and what was secretly being done to her. The reality was that this home for unwed mothers was an efficient mechanism to achieve a particular outcome: adoption. Everyone at the home was motivated by these ends. The parents of the girls who had their daughters admitted there also wanted this outcome, as 'giving the baby up' meant a neat and tidy resolution of the problem of their daughter's unwanted pregnancy.

Another kind of silence is that imposed on the girls at the home. They were discouraged from speaking with each other, from speaking about their babies, and referring to the babies as 'our babies'. They were called 'the infants' and 'we were just carrying them for more deserving people, married people'. They were treated as unworthy of raising their own children; it was better to give the babies to total strangers than to leave them with their mothers. There was a subtle kind of mind-bending quality to the discourse that the girls experienced:

> They used a kind of questioning that requires a 'yes' answer. 'You know the right decision, don't you dear? You know what's best for the baby. You want it to be loved and cared for and looked after properly, don't you dear? You're not capable of doing that, are you dear?' You have the impression that they are the professionals and they want what's best for you. You are coaxed into trusting them and distrusting yourself. And you hear this all the time. You're isolated there and there's no one to say you'd cope, you'd be a good mother.

The birth itself was indicative of the absence of care and compassion and underscores Linda's isolation. There was no preparation for the event. She was not told what to expect. For most of the nineteen hours of her labour she was alone. She was expected to be stoical, and she was. She was not told that the baby would be taken away from her the moment it was born. She expected to be able to hold it and secretly nurtured a plan to go home with the baby and set up a home with her boyfriend as they had planned. She remembers a pillow or white sheet being put up in front of her so that she never saw the baby; she saw a nurse quickly leave the room carrying a bundle, no doubt the baby. The rest was lost to the barbiturates she'd been fed.

After the birth, the girls were discouraged from exchanging addresses or making contact with each other. They never met anyone who had been there before them or who had been through what they were experiencing:

> You were made to think you were the only one. They wanted you to think that if you were not feeling right about things, it was because there was something wrong with you. Even later after the birth when girls would ring up to inquire about their babies, they were given no information; they were told, 'It's very unusual that you're not over it yet, dear. You have to put it all behind you now. Everyone else has done so. It's only you who hasn't'.

There is another kind of silence here, the silence of the girls themselves. Linda says, 'In a way we were part of the conspiracy, by staying silent and not seeking each other out'. She adds that only a few have become vocal or politically active. Very few have successfully integrated the experience into their subsequent lives. Now in their forties or fifties, perhaps married with a family, they often have so submerged their teenage nightmare that it must feel like someone else's life. These women still follow 'the party line', still believe that theirs was an independently made decision. They say, 'It was my choice. I signed a consent form so I gave my baby up'. It takes them years to see that something unnatural happened to intervene in the mother–child bond, to recognise that their human rights were infringed.

The aftermath plays out in different ways. but two profiles seem to have emerged. There are some women, like Linda, who are never able again to achieve the trust and intimacy that having a child entails. And there are others who quickly marry and have children, often quite a few ('they kept churning them out to replace the lost one') but are never able again to bond with a child.

A further silence is that imposed on the babies. Linda found her son a few years ago but there is no happy resolution to this story, at least not yet. She has been unable to establish a relationship with him. Now 27, he is unable to reconcile her story with the one he was raised with—that his mother willingly gave him up, that she was unworthy to have him, that giving him up proved her unworthiness, that they rescued him, that he should be grateful to them for the life they gave him. Linda says that her son knows, in his adult mind, that she had no choice in the adoption process. He was actually happy that she sought him out and found him, but 'the infant in him' needs to remain the way he has been all his life. It's easier not to rock the boat, easier to shelve whatever is confronting and uncomfortable. There's safety in silence even if it's illusory. She refers to 'the silence of his life'.

Another silence is the silence of officialdom and bureaucracy. This meant that she was unable to find out about her baby. She went back to the home twice within the 30-day period of revocation with her boyfriend to try to get her baby back. Each time she was told a tapestry of lies, which in effect created an impossible obstacle to her finding out the truth, let along doing something about it. Many years afterwards she found out that the second time she went back to the home, when she was told he'd been adopted out, her baby was actually right there. He'd required further medical attention, having been born, she later discovered, with a long list of birth problems.

After Linda returned home, another silence took over—this time imposed by her family. Only her mother and two elder sisters knew the truth and from none of them did she receive empathy or compassion. She was expected to maintain the public story that she had been away working interstate. 'Not only did I have to block out the grief and the madness that was taking over me, but I had to make up these cock-and-bull stories about where I'd been and what I'd been doing'. An elaborate system had been worked out whereby the letters she'd written were sent interstate, put in another envelope and postmarked from there. She was actively discouraged from speaking about her ordeal and 'advised' to get on with her life. The message remained, 'Don't wallow. Get over it. Put it all behind you'.

The silence was everywhere: 'There was nothing. If I started to bring it up, I'd get the look. And after a while the look was enough'. She describes the look as 'wincing' and the message was 'No, don't, I don't want to be reminded'. Silence here was used as a weapon to deny her reality, deny her pain and loss, and demean her into a powerless party in a much larger collusion. She was forbidden from speaking about it with her father, having been told that 'it would kill him'; he died four years later, without ever knowing what had happened. Her impression was that 'it's more comfortable for people if you remain silent. People don't want to feel your pain—it's just easier'. Linda believes her well-being was sacrificed on the altar of public propriety: 'it relieves others of the obligation of dealing with your pain if you hold it in stoically'. The enforced silence also meant for Linda that she was 'bad' and that the rest of the family had to be protected from her. For the next twenty years, the experience was entombed in silence. Linda says, 'I didn't put it behind me. I numbed. I buried it so deeply so that it couldn't hurt me'. During that time, she managed to dissociate from the way she was. On the surface she appeared to be fully functioning but she remembers it as being numb, barren, 'without essence'.

The most important change in Linda's life is her decision some five years ago to break the silence. She is now one of the public voices of the group called 'Origins', which strives for government recognition of past injustices and she no longer allows other people's discomfort with her truth to stop her from speaking.[9] Her family makes it quite clear that she is not welcome among them if she wants to talk about the topic of her child: 'It's alright to talk about their children, but not mine'. She embarrasses them, makes them uncomfortable, and so is excluded from family gatherings, weddings, Christmas. One of her brothers, a lawyer, refuses to give her any help ('When are you going to get over it?'). So she continues to encounter around her, both in family and in bureaucratic, legal and government circles, a desire to let the past go, to explain what happened in societal terms ('after all, people thought differently back then') and to whitewash motives ('they were only trying to do the best thing for everyone concerned').

If for so long she was silent and compliant, today she is angry and highly articulate. She counts her losses. She lost her baby, her mother-hood, her boyfriend and intended husband, her family of origin, more than twenty years of her life, her innocence and sense of her own integrity ('that I allowed myself to be so horrendously abused'), a core sense of safety and 'faith in a world of fair dealings'. As if to sum it all up she says, 'I lost the potential to be who I was meant to be'.

She also lost her silence.

Sharon's story: silence as denial

The next story is something like the mirror image of Linda's: it is, if you like, the adoption story told from the baby's perspective.

Sharon was adopted at birth and discovered the fact by accident when she was about eleven. She recalls that it must have been tax time, because she and her parents were sorting through papers and documents on the lounge room floor.

> I saw something that interested me. I peeked at it and couldn't believe my eyes. I disappeared into a locked bathroom to read and re-read it. Finally I put it back where it had been. No one knew. I was

in shock and denial for weeks afterwards. Whenever I was in the house alone after that I would re-read the document and burn the words into my brain. And then I'd put it back. I was terrified they would find out I knew or that I had any interest in the matter. I still have a fear of being discovered knowing.

When she was twelve, Sharon tried to find out how to search for her birth mother. A friend discovered what she was doing and Sharon feared she would be found out—her friend would tell her mother and the mother would tell Sharon's. She took an overdose of Valium, antibiotics and whatever else she could find in the medicine cupboard. Her mother found her with the bottles around her, took her to the doctor. Fortunately, she'd only taken enough to be very sleepy for a few days.

I remember being half-asleep and really groggy in the head. My mother was sitting by my bed and she wanted to talk about IT. She was saying, 'But you knew about your adoption. We've talked about it!' But I wouldn't allow her to talk. Now it was my turn to drop the curtain and not allow anyone in and that's what I did. The next day everything returned to 'normal' and it was never spoken of again. But from then on the adoption issue was out and I knew I wasn't supposed to know.

The silence in Sharon's story has different facets. Before Sharon found out about her adoption, there was a silence of which she was not consciously aware. Once she found out, the silence was one imposed on her by her adopting parents. After the suicide attempt, Sharon herself imposed a silence, not only on herself but on her parents. Perhaps part vengeful in motive, it was also no doubt steered by the fact that she had no language to talk about what had been rendered absent.

In the years that followed, sometimes the topic of adoption came up in relation to someone else and Sharon would feign nonchalance. She was unable to bring herself to talk openly about the topic, scared of hurting her parents, even fearful that they might discover that she had an interest in it. She refers to the way she would 'drop the curtain' if the topic came up. It would appear that most people in the family and community knew she was adopted but the topic, certainly in personal terms, was largely absent from the home.

When Sharon was 41, married with children of her own, she made the decision to live overseas. Her mother was helping her pack her things: 'I felt she was trying to talk with me before we left. She never said anything but I could just sense that she was trying to organise time alone with me, so I made sure that never occurred'. A few years later Sharon came back for a short spell to help her mother sell her house. Again she was aware of her mother making forays towards the topic. One day her mother organised for her cousin to be there and Sharon walked into a room where her mother and cousin were seated side by side, virtually in expectation of a dialogue they had rehearsed. He said, 'Aren't you interested in finding out about your birth mother?' Unable to ask Sharon herself, the mother had arranged for someone else to do the asking. In Goffman's terms, the cousin functioned neither as the author (the one who wanted the answer to the question), nor the principal (the one responsible for the question), only as the actor (the one who delivered the question).[10] We saw this mechanism in Chapter 6, as used by some Holocaust survivors: there the framework of participation was altered to enable the children to eavesdrop legitimately on talk that the parents wanted them to hear but were unable to deliver directly. Here in Sharon's case, the cousin functioned as the mouthpiece or proxy for her adopted mother, to enable the topic of the adoption to be broached. That the topic was fragile is evidenced clearly in Sharon's response. Typically and dismissively, she brushed the question aside—saying that she knew everything she needed to know, that 'she was obviously very beautiful!'—and then swept out of the room.

Sharon also internalised the taboo, forbidding herself for the most part even to wonder about her birthmother:

> No one allowed me to wonder about her and I rarely allowed myself to. It's only when I was hurting or in trouble I would hide in the dark in a closet and think 'Why would anyone love or want me, when my own mother didn't want me?'

There is an interesting intergenerational dimension to my research into people exposed to silence in connection with a trauma. I referred to this in the opening chapter of the book where I detail my own sense of being 'lost for words' when it comes to trying to tell my children about 'what came before'. It seems to me that the issue of disallowability in aspects of talk in the home may only surface as visible when that child becomes parent and faces otherwise inexplicable barriers to communication. Sharon confirms this in her comments about how she responded to her children:

I now realise that it was easy for me to communicate with them before they really began to communicate. Once they needed any depth of communication I was unable to provide it. Seems now it was all so superficial. I wish I could do it all again.

It is uncanny how Sharon's words seem to be drawn from the Holocaust survivors' children data set: 'I had an anger that involved them but had nothing to do with them'.

Her sense of her life of 47 years is that she has lived with a festering secret in her heart:

No one knows the real me, not even me. I've always told friends I was adopted as I didn't want people to find out from others, but I never told anyone how I *felt* about it. I encouraged people to think I was fine about it. That was my secret. I couldn't share my feelings about it with anyone. I always felt I was hiding a bad part of myself from the world. I concentrated on making other people happy and not rocking the boat. I spent all those years protecting my secret. And now I feel like I want to take out a full-page advertisement in the daily paper and tell the world!

In her paper on cultural uprooting, Apfelbaum cites Arendt's perspective on the influences which determine how a person is able gradually to construct and to live their identity. One of these is 'filiation', the genealogical link that explains why adopted children can find *le non dit* ('the unspoken') dimension of their life so painful and destabilising.[11] In reading Arendt's words and interviewing Sharon about the impact of 'a silent adoption' on her life, I am struck by the parallels with the ancestral severance among children of Holocaust survivors.

Sharon today expresses great regret that she 'missed out on so much and gave so little of herself in trying not to be' but also an amazing exuberance as she seems finally to have allowed herself to start again.

The Stolen Children: silence as cultural genocide

This chapter has been a collection of individual stories of people who in different circumstances and settings have encountered and had to deal with a sustained silence of some kind, usually associated with a trauma. The silence may be theirs, or another's; it might be self-imposed, externally imposed, or either/both at different times. In the case of the stolen children, we have generations of indigenous Australian children forcibly removed from their families as infants, sometimes at birth, and raised institutionally or fostered out. Apart from an incidental mention of a rare kindness by an individual here or there, the records, especially the oral history of this period, show an almost unrelieved wasteland of racial abuse which was legitimised in its day because it was sanctioned as government policy and implemented often by or with the blessing of the Church.

In the widely publicised report *Bringing Them Home*, the multiple nuances of silence are heard everywhere. Sometimes silence is a noun: here the sense is almost of a benign absence. Sometimes silence functions more as a verb and here we may see an element of choice, where the non-speaker is actively opting for the pathway of silence. But more often, and nowhere more clearly than among the stolen generations themselves, silence is a passive verb: people who *were silenced*.[12]

A feature of the assimilationist policy of child removal was the totality of the separation. Children were told that they were unwanted, rejected or that their parents were dead. They had their identities completely and forcibly transformed: 'They changed our names, they changed our religion, they changed our date of birth ... That's why today, a lot of them don't know who they are'. Letters from home were destroyed and letters the children wrote were never sent. The links were severed.

The policy had a particularly cruel dimension of mind-bending. Despite their colour, the children's Aboriginality was denied: 'It was drummed into our heads that we were white. It didn't matter what shade you were. We thought we were white. They said you can't talk to any of them coloured people because you are white'. This 'don't talk to the natives' policy was endemic. They were taught that Aboriginal people were bad, lazy, drunk, stupid, dirty—all the epithets of racist propaganda. No wonder one said, 'I wanted my skin to be white'. Some were told to pass themselves off as 'from an island somewhere' or from Southern Europe. Sometimes, years later, a family reunion was set up, with no prior counselling or preparation of either side: usually this was the first time the child's Aboriginality was admitted, leading to an agonising moment of shock and self-loathing when the child, brought up in a racist climate and told all her life that she is white, meets a stranger, a black woman, who she is told is her mother. One wonders how any government, past or present, can refer to this period in terms of 'welfare' or claim that in any way it was well-intentioned.

A core aspect of the cultural genocide was the obliteration of the Aboriginal languages the children spoke. The children were told not to speak 'the devil's language'; if caught, they had their mouths washed out with soap. Enforced Bible-reading 'sorta wiped out all the language that we knew'. The end result is 'language death'.[13] The outcome at the individual level is the tragedy of family members who, decades later, can only communicate in the language of the oppressor. At the wider collective level, we have a generation with their connection to the past severed. This is cultural genocide.

In later years, some reunions among separated families were successful, if immeasurably sad for what the intervening years had taken away. Peeters' autobiographical writings refer to these as 'the years that never were', suggesting an obliteration of time as well as of identity.[14] Some stolen children finally relocated their family, but the ensuing relationships were tortured by self-blame on both sides: the children blaming themselves for having been taken away (because they were 'bad children') and the mothers blaming themselves for losing their children (because they were 'bad mothers'). Some have never reconnected. Parents and grandparents have passed on, siblings have been dispersed, identities have been lost in dusty archives.

The experience of Karen is one of many documented by the *Bringing Them Home* report. A part-Aboriginal woman adopted at birth by a white Australian family, Karen went to live in New Zealand at the age of six months. Her experience was not in the same category as those who were institutionalised; she was told that she was adopted from Australia and was part-Aboriginal. She had a good relationship with her adopted family, but as a teenager at school was teased for her dark skin, and became withdrawn and confused about her identity. Eventually she married a New Zealander and had two boys. One was dark like her and was interested in knowing his family heritage. Karen said, 'I was unable to tell him anything as I didn't know about it myself'.

Karen's experience shows that, like children of Holocaust survivors, the legacy of silence is passed on from one generation to the next. In her case, it was brought about by her having been deprived of knowledge about her cultural identity. In other circumstances, fear erects a wall of silence and is passed on even though nothing tangible is spoken about. Peeters wrote about what it was like to have been forcibly removed from her family and brought up, as many girls were, in Cootamundra girl's home. Particularly poignant is the effect of these fears on her own child-rearing and on her children. In her adult years she lived in constant terror that her children would be taken away by welfare in the same way that she was. The habit of silence also meant that she was not able to share her fears with her husband or children. 'I kept my children and home clean at all times, just in case [Welfare] would come'. Resonating the experience of Holocaust survivors who tried hard not to stain the next generation with their victimhood, Peeters was also afraid of traumatising her children if she shared with them her childhood experience of being brought up in the home. As a result she chose only to speak about the positive moments there. She now acknowledges that her choice to remain silent about her past did not spare her children from the trauma and shame imposed upon her: 'People think the suffering stops with me. But I have passed these feelings, teachings, on to my children not realising what I was doing.' In fact, she was unable to speak freely about her past with her children or grandchildren until a public event—attending a reunion at Cootamundra in 1994—so legitimised and validated her reality, that she was able subsequently to confront for the first time the rage and pain within her. She then set out on a path of healing, a major discovery along the way being the importance of 'just simply knowing our story'.[15]

There are, of course, tremendous differences between the government's policy of forced separation and of the Holocaust. An obvious one is that the silence among the stolen generation derived from the forced negation of self and cultural identity imposed through institutionalisation, while the silence experienced by children of Holocaust survivors was the aftermath of incommunicability of massive violence having been perpetrated on the parents. Nonetheless I am struck by echoes and parallels: in the dispersion, fragmentation, loss and severance, and most significantly, in the silence. Clearly, to be whole, people need to know who they are, and a large part of that 'who' comes from the past.

The silence experienced by the children stolen from their homes and by the families from whom the children were abducted is paralleled in the silence of the Australian history books about the treatment of indigenous peoples after white conquest. It is only now at the turn of the century that a growing number of white Australians is beginning to acknowledge the frontier violence that has been an integral part of indigenous life in white Australia. Like a state secret, the truth about our history has been carefully shielded from all 'except those at the ragged edges of society'. Author and historian Henry Reynolds has documented how one ignorant schoolteacher, himself, came to know the history that had been systematically denied him: 'It was never mentioned and therefore in theory, it never happened'.[16] His latest work, *Why Weren't We Told?*, tells this story.[17] Reynolds reserves his most bitter attack for the historians of the nation. He asks 'how historians would handle the subject if 20 000 Europeans had been killed within Australia in domestic conflict or civil war'.[18] He refers to the 1969 Boyer Lectures of the anthropologist Stanner, which included a sustained attack on the nation's historians. Stanner argued that the systematic intellectual and academic 'inattention' to the treatment of Aborigines was not a matter of absentmindedness but:

a structural matter, a view from a window which has been carefully placed to exclude a whole quadrant of the landscape. What may well have begun as a simple forgetting of other possible views turned under habit and over time into something like a cult of forgetfulness practised on a national scale.[19]

It is not without significance that the title of the lecture in which this critique appeared is 'The Great Australian Silence'.

9

An Emotional Landscape

I could have chosen to end this book in the academic style appropriate to a work of research. Had I done so, I would have returned to my original research questions and tried to address these anew, this time in the light of my findings. I would have trawled back through the work, seeking alignment and continuity, promoting the fiction that research is a comfortably linear pathway from question to answer. I would have been at pains to bring all the threads together, neatly to snip off any unruly ones, or at least tuck these behind the main fabric so that they were less apparent from the front. I would have laboured again over my language, ensuring it was appropriately cushioned and tentative. I would have made overtures to the research community among whom I would want to have been counted as a member. And then I would have ended.

Such an approach, however, is entirely out of keeping with this book, the emotions that were present at its inception, that motivated its progress and that accompanied the journey to this point where we have now arrived. The story of 'the silence' sprang from my own personal experience and I have deliberately sought to foreground the intuitive and emotional dimension, the feminine side if you like, as a conscious attempt to give credence to the intuitive and lend legitimacy to research that is driven by emotion. I suspect that much research is equally dipped in the emotional and personal, but takes great pains not to appear so. So-called rational, objective, value-free inquiry, in its various masks, has no place here.

It is entirely appropriate, then, that I conclude in a manner that is consonant with the tone and demeanour of what has gone before. I am dealing here with an emotional world and I am unable to reduce my ending to a set of neat conclusions as if I were writing up a laboratory experiment. Out of this research comes not an answer but another set of questions, which perhaps might be reduced to one: if now we know that out of trauma emerges traumatised talk, how can we find a language to talk about these things, other than silence?

The end, then, is broad strokes on an emotional landscape, unpeeling the layers, recognising the hues and shapes. With this perspective, I will try to paint these as I see them today, knowing that as the day passes and the shadows lengthen, shifts will inevitably occur.

The past is a different country

One shape on the emotional landscape is the view from the present onto the past. I place myself now on a metaphoric balcony which itself represents the coming to an end of this book. I look out now on the past, my past, the past of my parents, and try to see the terrain anew. Perhaps, after all my ceaseless exploration, I am able to 'know the place for the first time'.

I remember that in Jerusalem, there is a memorial to John F. Kennedy that takes the form of a tree cut off before having reached its prime. The symbolism is poignant: the sense is of a future unfulfilled. I am reminded of it because of the notion of severance that it evokes.

Children of Holocaust survivors have a past cut off. The links to our ancestry are rarely made known to us. We are raised in a land that has present and future but no past. Not only is there an absence, it is one that often translates into a taboo—a 'somewhere' condemned to remain unknown and undiscovered. Zable puts it this way, when he talks of 'our elders':

> What was it they were trying to convey . . . when they told us their stories? . . . their tales petered out into an infinite darkness they called the Annihilation. They left a legacy of fragments, a jumble of jewels and ashes, and forests of severed family trees.[1]

Here the image of the forest is one of a wasteland of ancestral death, reminding us of the killing sprees and mass graves as Eastern Europe was emptied of its Jews and rid of its 'Jewish problem'. But trees and forests are not irremediably negative marks on this land-scape.[2] The forest was also often a hideout, a place of relative safety. My father holed up in a forest after the escape from the death march and before being found by the French army. Starving, he ate bark from the trees. I was told that but for a long time knew it without understanding.

It is the severed family trees that children of survivors often seek to restore. Rebecca explains her need to write her parents' story:

> I want my children to have something that I never had and that has haunted me all my life. I never knew who my family was, where we came from. I want to leave them this legacy so that they can carry on because I feel I am the only carrier. It's no accident that there's a historian and a librarian and a conservator in me. I want them to have a sense of history that I never had.

A yearning overtakes them after they have buried their parents. It's a yearning to know where they came from, and where their roots lie. Epstein's book is the record of one such personal odyssey, spanning one hundred years. To construct it, Epstein used the raw material of a twelve-page chronicle of her mother's plus the skills of an investigative journalist to track down the biographies and life-worlds of three generations of women on her mother's side. When she writes about wandering through the university library, in the months after her mother's death, browsing through books on European history and its Jews, I am reminded of myself, and suddenly my own apparently aimless behaviours of that time make sense. Epstein says, 'I was mourning my mother and if you had asked me what I was looking for in that enormous tomb of books, I would have said that I was looking for her'. Epstein found that her journalist's skills—the well-known verifying tools of who, what, where, when and why— were largely closed off to her. She writes: 'A person whose family has remained in place inherits possessions—a hat, a cupboard, old diaries, a prayer or recipe book—that transmit personal history'.[3] For her, however, as for many of us, the past was annihilated, and with it all the official documents, photographs and mementoes that are passed down mostly without fanfare among the generations of people who have not been dislocated.

Like Epstein, I too found that the 'dearth of a tangible past— people, objects, a physical context' was made intolerable by the passing of my parents. I recall days spent at Macquarie University Library, purportedly researching in teacher education, yet somehow finding myself in the Modern European History section, touching books, browsing, absorbed and directionless. Days spent with nothing to show for it, other than an inner disquiet.

The images I have used here are ones of severance and erasure. They constitute a diachronic perspective, one that sees identity in longitudinal and ancestral terms. There are, of course, other ways and other images that are possible representations. Some of these are to be found in Fresco's interviews of eight children of survivors, one of whom reflects that it's like having had a limb amputated, but a limb that one never had. She calls this a 'phantom pain'.[4] This is a somewhat confused image, I think, because it is the actual amputee who experiences the phantom pain. If the analogy is to hold, the child of survivors is yet another step removed—experiencing the phantom pain of the amputee—rendering the suffering as a kind of 'twice removed' angst. Laub cites another way of seeing these matters, one he calls 'the empty circle', drawing on a dream element of a patient of his, herself the child of survivors:

> Children of survivors often grow up in an environment which is mysteriously permeated by the traumas of their parents, yet in which the harrowing events are never spoken about . . . They are faced with the task of assimilating such realities into consciousness through their own imagination.[5]

The paradox that descendants face is to live simultaneously with the dominance of their parents' experience while its enormity itself constrains the imaginative capacity to visualise or comprehend: 'at the centre remains a hole, an emptiness caused by an event that defies representation and is experienced as a profound absence'.[6]

Such descriptions indicate that children's responses to their parents' experience of the Holocaust are unavoidably complex and fraught. To suggest otherwise is to ignore the overwhelming evidence of dissonance in the lives of children from survivor homes. We have seen through this book that there are those who know almost nothing about their parents and grandparents and the losses sustained in the family. Some of these people know that they don't know, and know now, that there are things they will never know. There is an abiding sorrow—akin to the dull ache of which Peter speaks in Chapter 8— that accompanies this awareness. Even sadder, though, from the perspective of a people obliterated, is the fact that there are those who don't know that they don't know. Here we have more than genocide. This is annihilation, because even the memory is extinguished.

Lessons from the dysphoria

Remember that my point of departure for this book was my ill-defined sense in my own home of a dysphoria that I had carried with me since childhood, unchanged and unresolved. I started out without a language in which to think about this, with only a vague sense that the dysphoria was linked to talk about the Holocaust. It is opportune now to contemplate this anew, this time from the vantage point of having spoken with so many people about comparable experiences. My understanding now operates at two levels, one local and essentially linguistic; the other more general and essentially interpretive.

The realisation that the dysphoria was a feature beyond the parameters of my home was grounded in patterns of communication I recognised across the homes of the people I interviewed. In one very real sense, this book has been an investigation into the pragmatics of communication in uncomfortable contexts, using the aftermath of the Holocaust and a handful of other trauma-related circumstances as the various settings from which the data were collected. I entered the research aware of the dysphoria, suspecting that it was located in the language, but entirely ignorant of the mechanisms by which this actually happened—how the messages were encoded, in text and in silence. Of course, I did not begin with a lay idealisation of communication as a conduit, as a simple process of message encoding, delivery and decoding. Yet I had not imagined anything as complex as the organic patterning of tributaries that would emerge—for this is how I see it now, rather as an aerial view of a complex waterway.

As yet I have not decided whether the image of these waterways is one of fragility or of resilience. When I think of direct spoken text as the most economical and powerful vehicle of communication, then I tend to view alternative routes as evidence of fragility: I see that a pathway has splintered, some might say pathologised, and messages are marginalised, squeezing themselves into niches and corners and ending up in places where they weren't supposed to go. At other times, I am aware of the pragmatic shortcomings of direct, explicit speech and it is then that I am in awe of the robust and diverse nature of my communicative waterways. No longer is it a matter of splintering or pathologising, but of having a natural survival instinct and resilience that allows for messages to be carried in many different ways, as well as enabling the passage of some which could not otherwise have been transmitted. Here diversity is strength. In some ways, these alternative viewpoints serve as a metaphor of the survivors themselves, sometimes perceived (and perceiving themselves) in terms of victimhood, sometimes in terms of resilient endurance.

The second level at which my new understanding operates is more general and interpretive. It relates to how one might now perceive the dysphoria from afar, whether we can say, after all this talk about talk, whether, or to what extent, 'the general resides in the particular'.[7] Without doubt, the major shift in my understanding was the realisation that the determinants of the discourse of my home lay well beyond it. By this I mean that the discourse was a construct of something larger than the speaker–hearer relationship within one immediate physical context.[8] Indeed, it derived both its nature and force from factors beyond the personality of individuals in any particular setting. Not only are the individuals almost irrelevant to the processes; it would seem they are powerless to prevent or influence their determinants. This discovery leads me to a larger, interpretive statement, one that now permits the view that Holocaust narrative in the homes of survivors was not an idiosyncratic, family-based, private, mental process but 'a pattern of a public event'.[9]

There is an exquisitely delicate balance of elements here: the data collected from participants caught up in the process are grounded in the *insider* perspective; but these meanings must be framed, contextualised and interpreted from the *outside*, if we are to be able to construct a larger sense. With this twin perspective, we see that the talk of one household was the talk of all households affected by the Holocaust. The story survivors told their children was not the tale of one set of circumstances as opposed to others. The private was the public, and the public was the private. Each story was its own teller's story and at the same time everyone else's story too. Like a roll of film shot at the same time and location, survivors' stories are both individual and collective. Like their styles of telling, not-telling and partially telling, they are at once unique and all the same.

The interpretive level of understanding comes with another dimension. Attendant upon such an interpretation is that the dysphoria of any particular individual within the parameters here described is not of their doing. They should not be mistakenly blamed, for example, by the parent generation, for the appearance of indifference; nor mistakenly blamed, by themselves, for their perceived failure to respond appropriately to that which in fact has no appropriate response. In relocating responsibility for these events outside the purview of the mere individual, it is my wish that this research realise a palliative function among those for whom the Holocaust is 'a grim inheritance'.[10]

In this ocean of sorrow and regret, if there is any consolation, it is that, like our grandparents and our parents, we had few choices in the directions our inner lives took. This is one of the lessons emerging from the intertwining of the general and the particular. After all this, after all the talk about talk, after stripping away all the outer membranes of this talk, after laying it bare for scrutiny, finally it makes a kind of sense. Despite its tardy coming, I suspect that within this realisation, there lie the seeds of comfort.

The face of indifference

We have now identified the dysphoria that surrounds the communication of Holocaust narrative from parent to child, and we have seen that the attendant miscommunications are legion. We have seen how in the context of silence and half-messages, children of survivors put together meanings that were altogether a product of their medium.

On the other side of the coin, many survivors misread their children's responses. They saw their children turning away. They saw the disengagement and avoidance behaviour, the lack of involvement and the face of indifference. When we didn't ask questions about their past, they were wont to interpret our silence as indifference—not for example, as a protective measure, itself an outcome of a pattern of unsuccessful communications that had left a family history of discomfort with this topic. They were quick to interpret as indifference that which—it is entirely (and tragically) possible—was actually the face of their own silence, reflected back to them. They did not seem to consider that the face of indifference might conceal something else, something more problematic. Laub writes this of a survivor whose testimony he witnessed: 'Her own children she experiences with deep disappointment as unempathic strangers because of the "otherness" she senses in them'.[11] I believe this disappointment, often based on misunderstanding, itself based on miscommunication, is experienced by many survivors, perhaps as their last tragedy. Like the others, it is rarely if at all spoken.

I want to suggest (and I explore this further, below) that it was convenient for them to opt for the less problematic interpretation (indifference) rather than to explore the more complicated one (silence). I am not surprised that they mistook the cues of our silence, nor that they preferred not to deal with it. But I want to contest their conclusions with a statement that I deliver with the solemnity of a universal truth: it is simply not possible to have an attitude of indifference to the suffering of one's parents.

I know from two sources about the discordance of the child's pained participation and their mask of indifference. One is the many descendants I have interviewed who are fully engaged with their parents' past but are unable to demonstrate this to them. These people worry about their parents' misinterpretation of their discomfort. The second source is survivors themselves—the many times that survivors have commended my interest (made apparent by the research and writing of this book), adding sadly, 'My son (or daughter) has no interest at all in any of this. He (or she) doesn't care'. They of course may not know—and in not knowing, will not see the significance—that this book was possible precisely because my parents are now gone.

I have already suggested that the seeds of the miscommunication were sown in something larger than the participants in the dialogue. However here I want also to suggest that the survivor generation as a whole unwittingly contributed to the constellation of misinterpretation that surrounded their discourse with their children.

Survivors who spoke about the past, and those who didn't, invariably sent the message that they predicted that none of us who came after could understand what they went through. The literature is replete with these statements and any conversation with survivors produces the same line, often identically formed: 'You can't understand'.

This is not to say that survivors did not want people to try to understand. They were caught in a bind, as we have seen earlier, between wanting to speak and not wanting to speak; between seeking permission to speak and looking for a reason not to speak; between wanting to pay homage to those lost and not wanting to revisit the memory. Silence was rarely an active, reasoned choice; it was more like a compromise between impossible options.

They were right, of course: we could not and cannot understand. However, the prediction was peculiarly unhelpful—and unhelpful in many different ways. First, it gave a superficially easy way out to those of us for whom trying was too hard: after all, if understanding is impossible, why struggle to get there? Second, it told those of us who *wanted* to try that we were doomed to fail; and given the disparity of the world of survivors and their children, failure to comprehend seemed very likely. In other words, it became a self-fulfilling prophecy. Third, the prediction was irritating because we were not operating on a level playing field. The prediction was too easy to fulfil—after all, there could never be a point when any one of us could say, with full faith and confidence, 'Yes, I now understand'. Even if we could, how could we convince them that our understanding matched theirs and fulfilled their criteria of what it meant to understand. Fourth, for those doggedly determined to understand or steered towards understanding by forces larger than themselves, the prediction of impossibility did not help. For in order to understand, we needed to build a bridge to the past, a bridge rendered possible through open channels of communication. Just as survivors may have sought permission from us to speak, we sought permission from them to ask. To ask with impunity. For this, communication would have needed to be opened to us, not as it too often was, closed down.

There's a peculiar paradox in survivors wanting their children to have been interested but adamant that no-one could understand their experience. It only makes sense if one 'unpacks' the 'you can't understand' and appreciates how it functions in the discourse of Holocaust narrative. This is not a talking style that encourages participation and involvement, that opens up talking opportunities; on the contrary, it is an instance of extinguishing behaviour, an utterance that closes down rather than opens up conversation.

Now when I consider this in the light of the communication patterns that this book has uncovered, I see that there is a comfortable fit between the discouraging prediction that their message sent and the silence of our homes. If it's impossible for anyone else to understand, if I tell people that it is impossible, I will so deter them that they won't press and probe in all the places that resonate in pain and grief. 'You can't understand' extinguishes questions before they are even thought of. It sends the message that this kind of talk is unwelcome. It is a pre-emptive strike that creates the very conditions of its own failure.

Misinterpretation: one case

The complexity of these spoken interconnections is best illustrated through an example.

One elderly survivor, a widower in his eighties, came to me for help in writing his memoirs, a task he had started and stopped at different times over the previous ten years. In many ways, he reminded me of my own father. I found his accent lilting and beckoning, the way today that Yiddish sounds to my ears. In between other matters, he told me of his rather fraught relationship with his only child, a middle-aged daughter, to whom he'd tried, over the years and in different ways, to communicate his history. Unbeknown to the man, I actually knew his daughter from other contacts and knew that she was particularly interested in the Holocaust and what it meant to be the child of a survivor.

The man told me that when the Spielberg Foundation was in Sydney to prepare filming survivors for their testimony, he had seized on the opportunity and had arranged to have his story recorded. The process, from appointment to interview to filming to finally receiving the video, took several months. When he received the video, he rang his daughter to invite her over to watch it with him. She said, 'Look, this is a difficult week, can you get another copy made, and I'll watch it when I can?' 'Sure', he said, and rushed straight out to have a second video made. When it was ready, he picked it up and dropped it off at his daughter's place on the way home. The following weekend he rang her to ask her what she thought of it. She said, 'Dad, I haven't had a chance yet. I'll get back to you when I've had a chance to watch it'.

At this juncture in the narrative, he leaned across the table to me and whispered in a rising tone, 'So, have you heard from her?' Startled because of the switch from third person narrative to direct talk, I said, 'Who, me?' I was put off balance, wondering why he'd ask me that. Ignoring my discomfort, he went on, sadly. 'I haven't either', he said. This was nearly a year after the original video was made. There was sadness and bitterness in his words and in his eyes. He had almost resigned himself to accepting that what he went through and what he lost were of no significance to his only remaining family member. I sensed a tiny fraction of the desolation he was feeling—that his story would die with him.

What could I have done that morning that would have been helpful and appropriate? Perhaps I should have concurred with his pronouncement and expressed sympathy for his situation; but I didn't, as I was sure this is not what he wanted. Perhaps I should have tried to convince him that he was wrong about his daughter, that what he had taken for a lifetime of apathy is not what it appears, that what he took as indifference was in fact a learned mechanism of defence by a child of a survivor who may not know the details of her parent's story but has lived her own life in its shadow. But I didn't, because to do so would have been presumptuous. Perhaps I should have aligned his experience to that of my home, shown the parallels, explicating the perspective of the child of survivors; but I didn't because I judged him to be well beyond making parallels for a learning purpose, and I saw that his mood was not one of listening but of telling. Perhaps I should have told him about this book, the evidence I had collected and the larger picture that had formed about survivor homes but I didn't, because the sadness enveloping him was all wrapped up in his home and I judged him to be unamenable to appeals of the general. Perhaps I should have urged him towards more positive communication strategies with his daughter so as to help repair their relationship; but this would have been inappropriate; it was not what he came to me for. In the end I listened to him in silence. Not long afterwards, he took his manuscript and went away.

He may have interpreted my silence as indifference.

Silence

The failure to communicate authentically across the wall of silence built by trauma has been the substance of this book. It is fitting, I think, if perhaps a little ironic, that I have constructed my perspective on silence through the voices of the people I interviewed, interweaving their stories with my own, so that together, along with my mediated commentary, a larger picture has been jointly constructed. As a research genre, this might be termed a polyphonic ethnography—a writing up of a view of a particular world, starting from the inside, constructing the meanings of participants, enabling multiple voices both to speak and to be interpreted.

In this way, as I have suggested, the particular and the general intermingle and the stories, like squares in a quilt, become, in an interpretive sense, larger than the individual case, forging a pattern of a public event. Thus ending now with one of the stories of one of the participants in this journey is at once personal and more than that.

The woman who told me this is a child of Holocaust survivors, with all the intertwining of boundaries and histories that this means. In her mid-forties, she discovered that her father had himself just recently found out that a woman he had loved during the war, in the most horrific of circumstances, had given birth to their child, and the child had died in the concentration camp. The sadness of one more personal loss, and of discovering it so long after the event, was over-whelming. Given the difficulty of communicating about his past, she had no ready way of responding. After half a lifetime of seeking a medium through which she could talk to her father about the topic that dominated their home, she finally took recourse in poetry—a wise choice of genre because poetry, being spare, minimal, tight and unredundant, compels an engagement between writer and reader like no other art form. She wrote this poem and gave it to him:

> To my father
> Perhaps there are
> no limits to grief.
> Finding out
> forty-five years later
> that you lost a child
> whom you never knew
> whom you never knew had been born
> nor even conceived.
> Finding out,
> when all your tears
> were used up.
> When there was
> no more reason to weep,
> nor people to weep for.
> Finding out
> then,
> that a child of your making
> had been born in that place
> and died
> there
> a week after liberation.

He didn't respond.

Appendix:

Research Method

Τhis section details the step-by-step decision-making that steered
the collection and analysis of data.

The research trail

For the outcomes of research to have credibility and for the findings
to be meaningful to others, the research pathway needs to be transparent and available for scrutiny. That is the function of this appendix.

The key concepts here are validity and reliability. Research
validity is about being certain that you actually see what you think
you are seeing. Research reliability is about the applicability of your
findings to other contexts. For both to be achievable, there has to be
a clear audit trail of evidence.[1] An independent evaluator needs to see
the actual (not idealised) conditions and circumstances in which data
were collected and reduced, so as to be able to retrace your steps and,
as it were, recover your process. It is only when the precise context is
made explicit that a full and accurate reading can be made.[2] Glesne
and Peshkin assert that steps in the direction of 'other-verification'
are steps in the direction of transparency and verifiability.[3] The onus
is on the qualitative researcher to provide the means by which a
second researcher might want to make transfers across to a second
research context.[4] My view of this is that a researcher's efforts to
establish validity and reliability become one's gifts to the wider
research community, allowing others to build on what you have done
or draw meaning from your context to theirs.

The research trail is a set of reasoned decisions about what questions to explore and what to abandon, what to include and what leave
aside, what direction to take and not to take. The focus of my research

was on children of Holocaust survivors finding out about their parents' past. 'Finding out' is a key component because it is predicated on the notion that what the children learned is mediated by language. Essential questions were arranged almost concentrically, beginning with contextual circumstances and gradually honing into the 'finding out': What was it like being raised in a survivor home? How did your parents' wartime experience affect your life? What did you learn about their experiences as you were growing up? Most particularly, how did you find out what had happened to them?

Ultimately, the perspective offered as a qualitative interpretation of the experience is an integrated composite of the descendants' viewpoints.

Decisions about sampling

The sampling method for selection of respondents was criterion-based.[5] The explicit criterion was the understanding of 'descendant' and 'survivor' as defined in the early part of Chapter 2. Any descendant who identified with the definition and was willing to be interviewed and contribute to the project was eligible for interview. Often a respondent volunteered the names of other descendants who might be willing to be interviewed, creating the snowball effect of network sampling through participant referrals. As word of the research spread through the Sydney Jewish community, assisted by articles in the Jewish press and the *Sydney Morning Herald*, I was increasingly contacted by people who felt they fitted the description and wanted to participate.[6] Indeed, the number of available and willing respondents far exceeded my needs and resources.

It is usual practice in qualitative research for the data collection (in this case, interviewing) and data analysis to take place approximately at the same time, rather than in two distinct stages. In fact, the intertwining of the two steps is a key element in the 'grounding' process. It is the means by which we save 'all the soft nuances . . . the tones and shades of meaning'.[7] It allows early insights harvested from the data processing to inform and benefit later interviewing, so enabling the deepening insights of the researcher to feed back into the data collection process and enrich the emerging understanding. In any one week, then, I might be interviewing a descendant, summarising, transcribing the data, analysing the language, developing, adjusting and refining categories and codes, and also interviewing another descendant. It took about ten hours to process each respondent through these initial steps.

Interviewing and processing continued roughly in tandem until the point of 'saturation'. This perhaps is less a 'point' in time than a 'period' which happens when regularities and patterns in the data begin to 'firm up' and categories begin to 'stabilise'. Continuing data collection yields redundancy. When the quantity of new information slows down—from a flood to a current, then to a trickle and then to hardly any—we speak of 'category saturation'.[8] This is always a judgement call, and is contingent on a trade-off between resources and expectations. For me, saturation was reached when incoming data produced only tiny increments of new information in comparison to the effort expended to get them. As I watched the categories gradually begin to firm up, I sensed, with some relief, that the end was in sight.

The interview

Although data collection and reduction/analysis continued apace, they are here divided into separate sections for the sake of clarity. I begin with the interview.

The interview lasted between 60 and 90 minutes and was based on a structured interview protocol. As is customary in qualitative research, the final protocol emerged through successive refinements. After each interview, I evaluated the effectiveness of the protocol and never failed to make adjustments to it. By the time I had finished the research, and had no more need of the protocol, I thought it was just about as close to perfect as it could be!

Paradoxically, too, it was near the end of the interviewing when I realised what the core question was that I should have been asking the entire time. It emerged as a sudden realisation during an interview when I naively asked the question and had a very telling answer. My first reaction to this discovery was the desire to jettison all my data and start again, using this question as my 'perfect' elicitation instrument. Expediency made me desist. This was fortunate for I came to realise that discovering what the right question should have been was, in fact, the end-point of the research process, not the starting point. When I was despairing that it took me so long to find out what I should have been asking all along, I was reassured by the remark: 'But surely that's what research is . . . finding out what you need to ask. If you had known that at the start, you wouldn't have done the research'. Deceptively simple, but true—it is wisdom so palpable that I didn't see it without outside prompting. Nose too close up to the windowpane, again.

The interview format I used was both structured and open. By this I mean that although I had a protocol with set questions in a set order, I willingly digressed from the pre-determined format to follow my respondent's lead, down pathways that promised good harvest. I also supplemented direct questioning with verbal prompts (e.g., 'Tell me more about . . .'; 'Could you explain what you mean by . . .') in order to explore beyond the level of the superficial. Also, to establish my 'insider status' and allow a sense of a shared biographical world to draw on, I often disclosed information about my own home and childhood. Another motivation for this was my awareness that one-way disclosure too closely resembled 'therapy talk' and I wanted to avoid any suggestion of psychopathology.

The interviewing process was both facilitated and constrained by the fact that, as researcher and interviewer, I shared descendant status with the respondent. Being a descendant was advantageous in that the interview began with shared assumptions in matters such as background, upbringing and world view, providing a bond that broke down inhibitions and encouraged openness. However, at the same time the assumption of shared status was an impediment. Firstly, there were many cases where the assumption of shared views was simply not true. Secondly, the necessary characteristic of 'naivety' that qualitative researchers require is less easy to construct when the researcher has and is perceived to have 'insider' knowledge. Being 'naive' is an important element of the investigation. It requires the researcher to put aside assumptions, to flesh out respondents' explanations, to take on a learner role and to understand things as though you are coming to them for the first time. And very importantly, it requires respondents to see you in this way, as a willing *tabula rasa*. If they do, they are obliged to 'translate' terms that an insider would know. [9]

The topic area also served as a constraint during the interview. As a 'sensitive topic',[10] located in the private domain and emotionally charged, it does not lend itself to easy questioning, as probing may be perceived as intrusive. Most of the people I interviewed shed some tears during the interview, although the degree of distress varied widely. A few seemed devoid of emotion.

While psychological factors are unavoidable in any research of this kind, it is not an area in which I am qualified to comment. I am an applied linguist, not a psychologist, and my concern here is the communication event. However, that said, some explanation is required, at least to explain the matter of topic sensitivity. This is connected to the issue of the trans-generational transmission of trauma which others have investigated[11] and there are four points of connection.

Firstly, it is well documented that the kind and level of emotions that children of survivors have been reported as experiencing echo in a macabre way the emotions of their parents—anger, guilt, grief, shame—emotions that may well not have been resolved. One of my respondents said that even when he was young he was aware that children of survivors who had been in the camps were somehow qualitatively different from children of survivors who had not. In some cases, emotions may be compounded by bereavement issues bound up with the recent loss of a parent. These are issues where it is difficult to achieve closure. Through my interviews I discovered that the degree of insight into one's family and one's formation varied markedly.

Secondly, in some cases, the person I was interviewing had never before openly discussed the issues covered by the interview. Not surprisingly, such people usually had quite some difficulty: not knowing how to talk about a topic, looking about for the right words, feeling the lack of a scrip were unsettling.

Thirdly, even where there is a vocabulary to talk about them, such highly charged emotional events are not always readily retrievable, and may be recounted in an 'existential fog'.[12] As a result, I sometimes had to probe a topic from a number of angles, risking my interviewee's ire and non-co-operation.

Fourthly, because of all the foregoing elements, the stress associated with the interview had the potential of compromising composure and comfort.[13] It came as no surprise, therefore, that a number of people who were approached as potential interviewees declined, finding, if not stating, the topic 'uncomfortable'. Quite a few required lengthy explanation and assurance prior to giving their consent. Others said they 'knew nothing' on the topic and therefore had nothing to say. Even with such difficulties, however, I had more than the numbers I needed.

Informed consent was obtained at the time of the interview and the sessions were tape-recorded. Each interview began with biographical information about both the descendant and the survivor generation, including prewar data, wartime experiences and postwar settlement details. It then moved to how they came to find out about their parents' stories.

Each respondent was given a same-sex pseudonym and a code number, to preserve confidentiality and anonymity. The tape was transcribed shortly after the interview. During the data analysis phase, not all questions were accorded the same degree of attention, with questions related to communication taking priority. Focusing the analysis upon these helped to conserve resources as well as develop research priorities.[14]

Data reduction

This section deals with the way in which the raw data—recorded voices on audio cassettes—were converted into a manageable form.

The first stage

The first processing step was the creation of a tape script for each person interviewed.

Other than the very early ones, the tape scripts were not wholly verbatim, as this is an immensely time-consuming task, and largely unnecessary. Word-for-word scripting was reserved for chunks of talk where it was important to maintain the person's own words. Many such quotations have been included in this book. When not quoted verbatim, viewpoints were summarised. From the start then, the procedure had the nature of a selective transcription. Included too, on occasion, were commentaries of mine on contextual matters that I thought were relevant and likely to be lost if not recorded.

The second step was the summary profile. On the basis of the transcription, a one-page, third-person summary of the interview was made. The purpose of this was threefold. Firstly, being compact, it was very practical, being far more manageable than the transcripts. Secondly, it served the function of what Miles and Huberman call a 'contact summary sheet', designed to capture the researcher's immediate reflections following first contact with the information.[15] Thirdly, and very importantly, the summaries serve as a validity check—confirming that the understanding I reached through the interview was faithful to the respondent. Accordingly, a few days after the interview I would send the person a copy of the summary, with a request to evaluate its fidelity against their recollection of the interview. Space was made available for further comments to be added: information forgotten/overlooked during the interview, corrections to the summary, additional information considered relevant. When this was returned to me, I added their comments to my record of the interview. In this way the final draft of the summary was deemed to be a fairly robust record of events.

The third step was unitisation: carving the transcript into smaller components or units. The unit of analysis was a meaningful, topic-bounded, stand-alone chunk of text, irrespective of linguistic structure or size (clause, sentence, multi-sentence), containing one heuristic idea. These segments were awarded a descriptive code. The purpose of awarding codes is to tame or make manageable unwieldy word-data. As well as this, however, the coding is a step in the direction of formulating an explanatory account, or theory-building. While the initial step is flatly descriptive, subsequent re-codings carry increasingly higher-order inference and interpretation.

A start-list of codes was established as soon as coding began, allowing the codes to be well grounded in the data. The early codes were descriptive, quite rough and gross, with each aiming to identify a concept. Each code was given an operational definition so that it could be applied, repeatedly, without difficulty. The codes did not, of course, emerge in one sitting, but rather evolved through repeated revisits with the data. With time and use, they 'firmed up': some seemed to lose their usefulness, some merged with others, some solidified and saturated, some new ones developed. There then came a point at which I felt sufficient confidence in them. At the same time, of course, the interview protocol was being gently refined. The twin processes—the firming up of code categories and the refining of the data collection instrument—reinforced and complemented each other. All of the above—unitisation, descriptive coding, interview evolution—may be considered phases of the first stage of the investigation.

The second stage

After twelve or so interviews, totalling about 120 hours of data processing time, I started to feel the benefit of the massive exposure to my respondents' words. However, I realised too that for the codes to continue to be useful, they would have to do more than flatly describe substantive matters. I needed an organisational structure that would make sense of the existing codes and organise new incoming data. This realisation heralded the second stage of data reduction.

The next sweep for codes used inferential descriptors. If descriptive coding is a matter of identifying threads in the data, then inferential coding is a matter of bundling, or re-grouping the already identified threads into bundles that are meaningful given the research questions that guide the investigation. This interplay between the research focus and emergent threads is crucial. Second-level or pattern codes use inferential descriptors. They re-position information into larger 'bins' or categories which, being interpretive in nature, enable you to see what is salient and discard what is not. The beauty of second-level coding is that it is at this point that the data reduction process begins to offer explanations.

A new code list was developed. It reflected the second-level patterns, as well as the descriptive codes of the former start-list subsumed within them. The second stage is also represented graphically in the emergence of a tree map. The new codes were now applied to the pre-existing data (Respondents 1–12), with these transcripts being re-analysed (this time down the left-hand side of the transcript). This second sweep over the data, using codes that have already emerged from the data 'grounds' the study even more firmly. Through the re-sweep, refinements are continually made both to the list of codes and to the tree map.

The third stage

The third stage of the study involved fresh intake of new data (Respondents 13–26) and immediate analysis using the second-level coding. This process continued iteratively—collection and analysis and then more collection—with accompanying refinements being made to the coding system and the tree map, until the point of saturation was reached. This 'point' arrives rather as a dawning realisation. The progressive and continual adjustments that have thus far been made to the tree map begin to give way to a new 'integration' and gradually fewer new viable categories are generated. These dwindle nearly to zero and the codes and the tree map freeze into their final, permanent form.

The decision to discontinue data collection brings to a formal close the stage of data reduction, and necessitates the start of the write-up stage. Write-up is facilitated by the preparation, earlier in the study of a 'filing system' by which allocated codes were able to be stored and retrieved at will. Computer software is available to manage word-based data but, after an initial trial, I decided that being able to see and touch my data, to lay it out on the floor and physically move bits of it around, outweighed the efficiency software would offer.

Creating a trustworthy interpretation

This research seeks to interpret an aspect of the socially constructed world. To have value, such an interpretation must be trustworthy and to be deemed trustworthy, the research and the researcher must demonstrate that adequate care has been taken to pre-empt or avert or counter-act threats to the rigour of the study. This section will discuss ways in which I sought to shore up the rigour of this study.

The management of researcher bias

A major issue in the establishment of rigour is the notion of subjectivity or researcher bias or as Krueger terms it, 'selective perception'.[16] Because qualitative research makes such demands on subjectivity— understanding, inference, interpretation are all key ingredients of meaning-making—it is especially easy to attack its validity and reliability. An investigation may be dismissed because the research focus cannot be disentangled from particular sensibilities, thus compromising its validity. It may be dismissed as too idiosyncratic and context-embedded to be generalisable, hence compromising its reliability.

The difficulty here is that subjectivity can both enable and disable. On the enabling side, most qualitative researchers would contend that it is their very subjectivity that allows them to establish their research domain, and that makes them particularly alert and expert within this domain. Peshkin, for example, claims that everything that he learned as a researcher 'was rooted in those personal orientations . . . [called] subjectivity'.[17] Like many, he would assert that there is no such thing as value-free research.

Nevertheless, subjectivity can equally well disable, blurring one's vision, making one selectively sensitive. As a consequence, the researcher must monitor her own subjectivity, being continually alert to her own biases. This means becoming a devil's advocate or, as Miles and Huberman put it, being one's own harshest critic—a frame of mind that has you 'try to see what you are not seeing, to detect what you are making less of than could be made, so that you can temper as necessary that which your subjectivity is pressing you to focus on'.[18]

We need to distinguish between subjectivity and subjectivism 'which exalts personal feeling as the ultimate criterion of the good and the right'.[19]

In regard to subjectivity, a prime danger may derive from an over-attachment to one's topic or one's preconceptions, hunches or hypotheses.[20] Such an over-investment is incompatible with 'the open exploratory learner's attitude' that is the hallmark of good data collection and analysis.[21]

In a project such as this one, where the researcher belongs to the category of people interviewed, I am well aware of the fragility of my position and the potential for accusations of a disabling subjectivity. Clearly, I had to be on my guard from the outset against intrusions of biography. To help me accomplish this, I borrowed the procedure known in phenomenological research as 'bracketing'—suspending as far as is possible one's own beliefs, before entering the unique world of the interviewee. Bracketing allows the researcher to be 'other-sensitive'. In phenomenological research, this means 'using the matrices of that person's world-view in order to understand the meaning of what that person is saying, rather than what the researcher expects that person to say.[22] The procedure is not unrelated to the conscious creation of a map of oneself: a set of subjective 'I's.[23] Just as with the bracketing procedure, the acts of articulation and analysis in the subjective 'I's enable a degree of estrangement that allows researchers to monitor their own subjectivity.

Member checking

A series of measures was carried out through various phases of the research to ensure the internal validity of the project. One such measure was the use of 'member checks', also called 'participant verification'.[24] As described earlier, respondents were sent a summary of the transcript for verification or qualification. In addition, they were asked for supplementary non-verbal data. Using a bi-axis grid, they were asked to evaluate the discourse patterns in their parental home and mark a spot on the grid with an 'X'. This represented the point of intersection between a place on the horizontal continuum (representing the extremes of silence and talk) and a place on the vertical continuum (representing the extremes of direct and indirect discourse). The form was deliberately timed to arrive a few days after the interview so as to allow the respondent time to have reflected on the issues raised during the interview. It was an easy, non-verbal, X-marks-the–spot format and, subsequently, it enabled a comparison to be made between the verbal and non-verbal data. In all but two cases, I found there was a consonance between the data yielded by the two instruments. Regarding the two that were not consonant, both were followed up: one person had simply misunderstood the form; the other had had a confusion between whether she was mapping her mother or her father.

Member checking, in spirit and function, continued further into the project when an early draft on the findings was sent to part of the respondent population for further verification or qualification. This process of phenomenon recognition'[25] (by which you 'share the interpretive process with research respondents') served further to give me confidence in the validity of the study. Comments elicited from stakeholders were then knitted into a subsequent draft, not unlike the way in which respondents' comments on the draft profile summaries were earlier knitted back into the final profiles.

Another measure, related to member checking and employed to shore up validity, was the exploration and analysis of 'negative cases'.[26] The purpose here was to seek out and clarify the 'dissenting opinion'[27] and to knit these 'discrepant reports' into the write-up of the research. This allows the working hypothesis to be stretched and strengthened, and shores up the project's trustworthiness. Negative case exploration entailed giving a disproportionate amount of time to cases that lay outside the general thrust of the findings. This happened in the case of two male respondents, one from a Hungarian home and the other from a Czech home. In both these cases of respondents whose views tended to differ from my hunches and the emerging patterns among the majority of respondents, I conducted in-depth follow-up interviews until such time as I was happy with the quality of the data that derived from the interviews.

Triangulation

Triangulation is a well-respected research procedure that guards against threats to validity.[28] It obliges the researcher to approach the matter being researched from at least two, preferably three different perspectives. As a researcher you are at pains to discover and then to prove that the interpretation you have reached is as independent as you claim it to be, and is not, for example, a function of the data collection instrument or this particular population sample or your own particular orientations. Triangulated findings are an important means of establishing that the endpoint is not an artefact of the enterprise itself. Glesne and Peshkin, for example, contend that the more sources tapped for understanding, the more believable the findings.[29]

Finding 'another way in' was not easy. As the main study focused on the recollections of descendant respondents, it seemed logical to approach the survivor population to investigate whether there was some consonance of perception. I hoped too, that this would create a balance between the processes of interpretation (represented by descendants) and the processes of production (represented by survivors) in the speech act—the telling of Holocaust narrative— with which the study was centrally concerned.

I made several attempts with a pilot group of five survivors, to develop an instrument that would tap this resource. One of these, for example, surveyed them about the ease or difficulty encountered in telling their children about their Holocaust experience. Their answers showed a reluctance to return to that time in their lives or a failure to remember with any specificity. On occasion, there were answers that pointed to the kind of tension I wanted to explore, for example, 'I spoke to my daughter openly and honestly. However she tells me *now* that she was always a bit hesitant (and still is) to ask me anything beyond what I was saying. She never wanted to probe for fear of disturbing me'. However, this was the exception rather than the rule. Another instrument asked them to mark the spot on the bi-axes as it applied to their postwar households. This failed too as the survivors had difficulty interpreting the questions. After some efforts in this direction, I decided that the option of exploring survivors' perceptions in this way was untenable.

I tried a more oblique approach. Formality was reduced by replacing a written instrument with a short interview, in which a survey was completed by the survivor-interviewee with the investigator present to help out or explain issues. Obliqueness was achieved by changing the focus of the questions from 'How did you tell your children . . . ?' to 'How did your children respond to your stories?' By recasting the questions this way, I was hoping to sidestep issues of discomfort, guilt, and reluctance. This also, regrettably, led nowhere. Perhaps I was unable to establish the degree of trust that successful interviewing necessitates. Or perhaps the people involved had had half a lifetime in avoiding discomfort and were very expert at it.

A number of factors can be offered here in explanation. One is the advanced age of the survivors, and their health, failing memory and frailty. A second is their reluctance, at their stage of life, to examine more closely issues that are particularly painful or matters in which they might feel uncomfortable or remorseful.[30] Old age is a time of settling and putting one's house in order,[31] not of reshuffling the furniture, especially if pain and discomfort are the results. If, as I suspect, silence was the majority response, it may well be that in their fading years, in the expectation of taking silence to the grave, some regret and recrimination may be attached. Also, at an ethical level, I felt unjustified in stirring up people's pain.

In the end, in place of data collected from survivors, I decided to tap two other sources that I hoped would be more amenable. One was to probe for consonance with my findings in contemporary post-Holocaust literature, particularly that written by Holocaust descendants about the world they inherited and the homes they grew up in. In the last several years, there has been no shortage of such titles. Literary sources, such as literature and autobiography, have been validated as 'a fountain of experiences' to which a researcher may turn for insight.[32] Consequently, references to such reading are scattered through this book.

The other data source—people who have experienced a silence in the wake of trauma—was tapped to address issues of both validity and external reliability. I wanted to see whether my construct of post-trauma incommunicability would hold in other situations and contexts. In talking about my book with many people, I was urged to explore the application of its thesis to a context broader than the Holocaust. As a result, I decided to interview other trauma survivors to determine if similar patterns could be discerned in either generation. Thus, apart from the 27 Holocaust-related respondents, I also interviewed some ten other informants whose contact with trauma is in different ways conveyed by the experience of silence. Increasingly as I went about interviewing children of Holocaust survivors I found that their story of living with their parents' silent story resonated with other people, not involved in the Holocaust but with others of life's tragedies. In all I found that my interviews with such individuals tapped a wide variety of tragic circumstances whose aftermath was bathed in silence.

Notes

Chapter 1 A personal journey

1 This story was first published as an article, entitled 'On the Freedom to Talk about Dead Grandparents', *Australian Jewish News* 11 May 1990, and was reprinted as a short story in *Who Do You Think You Are? Second-generation Immigrant Women in Australia*, eds K. Herne, J. Travaglia and E. Weiss, Women's Redress Press, Sydney, 1992, pp. 160–3.

2 S. P. Oliner and P.M. Oliner, *The Altruistic Personality. Rescuers of Jews in Nazi Europe*, The Free Press, New York, 1988.

3 I am indebted to Jonathan Crichton for this expression.

4 T.S. Eliot, 'Little Gidding V', *Four Quartets*, Faber & Faber, London, 1966, p. 59.

5 Susan is not her real name. Pseudonyms are used throughout the book.

6 L. Brett, *Too Many Men*, Picador, Sydney, 1999.

Chapter 2 The story begins

1 Foxman was cited in *Australian Jewish News*, 14 February 1997, p. 8.

2 The term comes from E. Goffman, *Encounters. Two Studies in the Sociology of Interaction*, Bobbs-Merrill, Indianapolis, 1961, p. 44.

3 J.E. Young, *Writing and Rewriting the Holocaust: Narrative and the Consequences of Interpretation*, Indiana University Press, Bloomington and Indianoplis, 1988, p. vii.

4 M.J. Reddy, 'The conduit metaphor—a case of frame conflict in our language about language' in *Metaphor and Thought*, ed. A. Ortony, Cambridge University Press, Cambridge, 1979.

5 H.F. Wolcott, '"Problem-finding" in qualitative research', in *School and Society: Learning Content Through Culture*, eds H.T. Trueba, and C. Delgado-Gaitan, Praegar, New York, 1988, p. 30.

6 E. Eisner, 'On the difference between scientific and artistic approaches to qualitative research' *Educational Researcher*, vol. 10. no. 4, 1981.

7 J.B. Thompson, *Studies in the Theory of Ideology*, Cambridge, Polity Press, 1984, p. 133.

8 P. Novick, *The Holocaust in American Life*, Houghton Mifflin Co., Boston, 1999, p. 110.

9 M.E. Jucovy, 'Therapeutic work with survivors and their children: recurrent themes and problems' in *Healing their Wounds: Psychotherapy with Holocaust Survivors and their Families*, eds P. Marcus and A. Rosenberg, Praeger, New York, 1989, p. 51.

10 M. Hershman, *Safe in America*, HarperCollins, New York, 1995; A. Zable, *Jewels and Ashes*, Scribe Publications, Newham, Victoria, 1991.

11 The multi-functionality of silence is explored in D. Kurzon, *Discourse of Silence*, John Benjamins Publishing Company, Amsterdam, 1997.

Chapter 3 The silent aftermath of war

1 J. Freyberg, 'The emerging self in the survivor family', in P. Marcus and A. Rosenberg (eds), *Healing their Wounds: Psychotherapy with Holocaust Survivors and their Families*, Praeger, New York, 1989, p. 85.

2 P. Levi, *The Truce. A Survivor's Journey Home from Auschwitz*, Bodley Head, London, 1965.

3 *http://www.historyplace.com/worldwar2/timeline/knacht.httm*

4 U. Hegi, *Stones from the River*, Scribner, New York, 1994.

5 J. Kramer, 'The politics of memory' *The New Yorker*, 14 August 1995, pp. 48–65.

6 C. Lanzmann (dir.) *Shoah*, 1985.

7 M. Gilbert, *The Holocaust. The Jewish Tragedy*, Collins, London, 1986, p. 819.

8 D. Astrachan (dir.) *From Hell to Hell*, 1997.

9 M. Hershman, *Safe in America*, HarperCollins, New York, 1995.

10 P. Novick, *The Holocaust in American Life*, Houghton Mifflin Co., Boston, 1999.

11 S. Kramer (prod. & dir.), *Judgement at Nuremberg*, 1961.

12 P. Novick, op. cit., p. 85.

13 ibid., p. 86.

14 I. Buruma, *The Wages of Guilt. Memories of War in Germany and Japan*, Farrar Straus & Giroux, New York, 1994.

15 E. Wiesel, *From the Kingdom of Memory*, Summit Books, New York, p. 174.

16 P. Novick, op. cit.

17 L. Langer, *Admitting the Holocaust*, Oxford University Press, New York, 1995, p. 6.

18 I am indebted to Ursula Duba for this interpretation.

19 P. Novick, op. cit.

20 L. Langer, op. cit., p. 6.

21 U. Duba. 'Blind date', in 'Tales from a child of the enemy' (unpublished manuscript), New York, 1997, pp. 41-8; 'His blind date', in 'Inherited pain and defective genes. Descendants of the Shoah and the Third Reich', unpublished manuscript.

22 B. Schlink, *The Reader*, Phoenix, London, 1997.

23 U. Duba, 'Review of E. Schlant's *The Language of Silence: West German Literature and the Holocaust*', *http://users.rcn.com/duba/*, 13 August 2000.

24 C. James, 'Postcard from Munich' in *Flying Visits*, Picador, London, 1984, p. 169.

25 U. Duba, 'Review', op. cit.

26 I am indebted to Ursula Duba for this interpretation.

27 A. Hass, *The Aftermath. Living with the Holocaust*. Cambridge University Press, Cambridge, 1995, p. 134.

28 P. Novick, op. cit., p. 25.

29 M. Rosenbloom, 'Implications of the Holocaust for social work' *Social Casework: The Journal of Contemporary Social Work*, April, 1983, p. 205.

30 N. Fresco, cited in D. Laub, 'The empty circle: children of survivors and the limits of reconstruction' *Journal of the Psychoanalytic Association*, vol. 46, no. 2, 1998, p. 508.

31 H.I. Kaplan and B.J. Sadock, *Synopsis of Psychiatry: Behavioural Sciences/Clinical Psychiatry*, eighth edn, Williams & Wilkins, Baltimore, 1998, pp. 617–23.

32 J. Kestenberg, 'Psychoanalytic contributions to the problem of children of survivors from Nazi persecution' *Israel Annals of Psychiatry*, 311, 1972. p. 325; R. Krell, 'Alternative therapeutic approaches to Holocaust survivors' in P. Marcus, and A. Rosenberg (eds), op. cit. (n. 1).

33 D. Laub, cited in S. Felman and D. Laub, *Testimony. Crises of Witnessing in Literature, Psychoanalysis and History*, Routledge, New York and London, 1992, pp. 57 and xvii.

34 J. Freyberg, op. cit., (n. 1) p. 95.

35 R. Krell, op. cit., p. 218.

36 W. Ravel (dir.) *Primo Levi 1919–1987*, 1997.

37 N. Rosh White, 'Labelling Holocaust survivors: a reappraisal' *Journal of Intercultural Studies*, vol. 8, no. 2, 1987, p. 16.

38 G.M. Kren and L.H. Rappaport, cited in N. Rosh White, op. cit., p. 14.

39 E. Goffman, *Asylums: Essays on the Social Situation of Mental Patients and Other Inmates*, Doubleday/Anchor Books, New York, 1961.

40 R. Manne, *The Culture of Forgetting. Helen Demidenko and the Holocaust*, Text Publishing, Melbourne, 1996.

41 I. Clendinnen, *Reading the Holocaust*, Text Publishing, Melbourne, 1998.

42 N. Rosh White, op. cit., p. 18.

43 E. Apfelbaum. 'Uprooted communities, silenced cultures and the need for legacy', paper given at the Millennium World Congress in Critical Psychology, April–May 1999, University of Western Sydney, Nepean Campus, Sydney, Australia. 1999, p. 6.

44 J. Altounian, 'Putting aside words, putting to rest and putting aside the ancestors. How an analysand who was heir to the Armenian genocide of 1915 worked through mourning' *International Journal of Psychoanalysis*, vol. 80, pp. 439–48.

45 Cited in E. Apfelbaum, 'The impact of culture in the face of genocide. Struggling between a silenced home culture and a foreign host culture', paper given at the symposium on Culture in Psychology: A developing framework. Fifth European Congress of Psychology, Dublin, 1997, p. 6.

46 P. Novick, op. cit.

47 A. Hass, *In the Shadow of the Holocaust. The Second Generation*, Cornell University Press, New York, 1990, p. 72.

48 J. Misto, *The Shoehorn Sonata*, Currency Press, Sydney, 1996.

49 N. Rosh White, *From Darkness to Light*, Collins Dove, Melbourne, 1988; and L. Langer, *Holocaust Testimonies. The Ruins of Memory*, Yale University Press, New York, 1991.

50 S. Planalp, *Communicating Emotion. Social, Moral and Cultural Processes*, Cambridge University Press, Cambridge, 1999.

51 D. Kaye, *I Still Remember*, Fast Books, Sydney, 1996.

52 *Uncle Chatzkel* was written and directed by Ron Freeman, 1999, and produced by Film Australia and Robe Productions.

53 N. Rosh White cited in P. Read, *Returning to Nothing. The Meaning of Lost Places*, Cambridge University Press, Melbourne, 1996, p. 29.

54 D. Kaye, op. cit.; A. Riemer, *Inside, Outside, Inside Outside: Life Between Two Worlds*, Angus & Robertson, Sydney, 1992; L. Brett, *Too Many Men*, Picador, Sydney, 1999; and D. Astrachan, op. cit. (n. 8).

55 P. Read, op. cit.

56 W. Szymborska, cited in I. Clendinnen, op. cit., p. 207.

57 E. Apfelbaum, 'The impact of culture in the face of genocide', op. cit., p. 5.

58 For example, 'Tell your children of it and let your children tell their children, and their children another generation'. *Joel*, 1:3.

59 Y. Yerushalmi, 1982, cited in P. Novick, op. cit., p. 10.

60 E. Wiesel, cited in P. Read, op. cit., p. 47; L. Langer, op. cit. (n. 17); and A. Hass, op. cit., p. 163.

61 I am indebted to Fred Bedrich for permission to reprint his words.
62 I. Fonseca, *Bury Me Standing. The Gypsies and their Journey*, Vintage, London, 1996, p. 276.
63 D. Carroll, 'Foreword. The memory of devastation and the responsibility of thought: "And let's not talk about that"', in J.-F. Lyotard, *Heidegger and 'the Jews'*, University of Minnesota Press, Minneapolis. 1990, pp. vii–xxix.
64 W. Boyd, *Armadillo*, Penguin, London. 1998, p. 40.
65 B. Rommelspacher, 'About public speeches and private silence', *DieTageszeitung*, 19 December 1998, p. 1. Translated by U. Duba.
66 E. Wynhausen, cited in P. Read, op. cit., p. 47.
67 A. Zable, *Jewels and Ashes*, Scribe Publications, Newham Victoria, 1991.
68 S. Karas in P. Read, op. cit., p. 31.

Chapter 4 The context of incommunicability

1 L. Langer, *Holocaust Testimonies. The Ruins of Memory*, Yale University Press, New York, 1991, pp. 58 and 61.
2 D. Laub, in S. Felman and D. Laub, *Testimony. Crises of Witnessing in Literature, Psychoanalysis and History*, Routledge, New York and London, 1992, p. 69.
3 P. Levi, *The Drowned and the Saved*, (trans. R. Rosenthal), Michael Joseph, London, 1988.
4 S. Wiesenthal, cited in the Preface to P. Levi, op. cit., p. 1.
5 D. Laub, op. cit., p. 68.
6 H.R. Huttenbach, 'They didn't just die in Auschwitz' *Together*, vol. 10, no. 1, December 1995, pp. 9–10.
7 L. Brett, *Too Many Men*, Picador, Sydney, 2000, p. 530.
8 H.R. Huttenbach, op. cit., p. 9.
9 S. Friedlander, cited in J.E. Young, *Writing and Rewriting the Holocaust. Narrative and the Consequences of Interpretation*, Indiana University Press, Bloomington and Indianapolis, 1988, p. 16.
10 E. Wiesel, *From the Kingdom of Memory*, Summit Books, New York, 1990, p. 86.
11 T.S. Eliot, 'Burnt Norton Part V', *Four Quartets*, Faber & Faber, London, 1966, p. 19.
12 I. Clendinnen, *Reading the Holocaust*, Text Publishing, Melbourne, 1998. p. 38.
13 I am indebted to Jonathan Crichton for this observation.
14 These words were used by a reviewer of the *New York Times Book Review* (cited in J. Wheatley, 'Back from the dead', in the *Sydney Morning Herald* (*Good Weekend*, 26 February 2000, p. 32) about Inga Clendinnen's *Reading the Holocaust*.
15 U. Duba, 'The golden childhood', in U. Duba, *Tales from the Child of the Enemy*, Penguin, New York, 1997, pp. 93–9.
16 L. Brett, op. cit., p. 161.
17 A. Hass, *The Aftermath. Living with the Holocaust*. Cambridge University Press, Cambridge, 1995, p. 142.
18 E. Wiesel, op. cit., p. 245.
19 P. Novick, *The Holocaust in American Life*. Houghton Mifflin Co., Boston, 1999, p. 148.
20 T. Katriel, *Talking Straight: Dugri Speech in Israeli Sabra Culture*, Cambridge University Press, Cambridge, 1986.

21 T. Richmond, *Konin. A Quest*, Vintage, London, 1996, p. 376.

22 H. Yablonka, *Survivors of the Holocaust: Israel after the War*, New York University Press, New York, 1999.

23 L. Langer, op. cit., pp. 5–10.

24 Ursula Duba, personal communication with the author, November 2000.

25 Y. Danieli, 'Mourning in survivors and children of survivors: The role of group and community modalities', in D. Dietrich and P. Shabad (eds), The *Problem of Loss and Mourning. Psychoanalytic Perspectives*, International Universities Press, New York, 1986, p. 9.

26 M.S. Bergman and M.E. Jucovy, (eds), *Generations of the Holocaust*, Basic Books, New York, 1982, p. 59.

27 Y. Danieli, op. cit., p. 9.

28 G. Little, *The Public Emotions. From Mourning to Hope*, ABC Books, Sydney, 1999.

29 D. Hume, *An Inquiry Concerning Human Understanding*, ed. C.W. Hendel, Bobbs-Merrill, Indianapolis, 1955.

30 F. Nietzsche, *Twilight of the Idols and The Anti-Christ* (trans. R. J. Hollingdale), Harmondsworth, Penguin, 1978, p. 23.

31 I am grateful to Jonathan Crichton for this line of reasoning.

32 I am grateful to Jonathan Crichton for this insight.

33 A. Wajnryb, 'A letter to my children', unpublished manuscript, 1988, p. 166.

34 J.V. Jensen, 'Communicative functions of silence' *ETC: A Review of General Semantics*, vol. XXX, no. 3, 1973, pp. 249-57.

35 E. Goffman, *Forms of Talk*, Oxford, Basil Blackwell, 1981.

36 The term comes from E. Goffman, *Encounters. Two Studies in the Sociology of Interaction*, Bobbs-Merrill, Indianapolis, 1961, p. 55.

37 D. Laub, op. cit.

38 A. Wajnryb, op. cit.

39 Two books that treat the particular discourse of therapy are W. Labov and D. Fanshel, *Therapeutic Discourse: Psychotherapy as Conversation*, Academic Press, New York, 1977, and R. Lakoff, *Talking Power. The Politics of Language*, Basic Books, New York, 1990.

40 I am indebted to Jonathon Crichton for this line of reasoning.

41 J. Salamon, *The Net of Dreams. A Family's Search for a Rightful Place*, Random House, New York, 1996, p. 112.

42 E. Wiesel, cited in M.S. Bergmann and M.E. Jucovy (eds), op. cit., p. 6.

43 C. James, 'Postcard from Munich' in *Flying Visits*, Picador, London, 1984, p. 168.

44 G. Brown and G. Yule, *Discourse Analysis*, Cambridge University Press, Cambridge, 1983.

45 I am grateful to Jonathon Crichton for this line of reasoning.

46 V. Adelsward, 'The defendants' interpretation of encouragements in court: the construction of meaning in an institutionalized context' *Journal of Pragmatics*, 13, 5, 1989, pp. 741–9.

47 I am grateful to Jonathan Crichton for alerting me to this institutional parallel.

48 L. Langer, op. cit., p. 61.

49 B. Hills, 'Shock Tactics', *Sydney Morning Herald*, 13 June 1998, *Spectrum*, pp. 1 and 4.

50 I. Allende, *Of Love and Shadows*, Jonathan Cape, London, 1984, p. 32.

51 H. Epstein, *Where She Came From. A Daughter's Search for Her Mother's Memory*, Plume, London, 1997.
52 A. Hass, op. cit., p. 118.
53 A. Wajnryb, op. cit., p. 166
54 L. Langer, op. cit., p. 142.
55 D. Laub, 'Truth and testimony. The process and the struggle' *American Imago*, 48, 1991, pp. 75–91.
56 R. Melson, *Revolution and Genocide*, University of Chicago Press, Chicago, 1992.
57 E. Wiesel, in Y. Danieli, op. cit., p. 22.
58 T. Des Pres, cited in S. Felman and D. Laub, op. cit., p. xi.
59 H. Epstein, op. cit., p. 5.
60 Marietta Elliott has written about her experiences as a child survivor in 'Return ticket', *Idiom*, 23, 1994, pp. 62–5.
61 M. Lang, 'The long shadow' *Generation*, vol. 4, no. 1, 1994, p. 25.
62 D. Carroll, 'Foreword. The memory of devastation and the responsibility of thought: "And let's not talk about that"', in J.-F. Lyotard, *Heidegger and 'the Jews'*, University of Minnesota Press, Minneapolis, 1990, p. ix.
63 ibid., p. ix.
64 S. Felman and D. Laub, op. cit.
65 C. Delbo, cited in L. Langer, op. cit., p. 42.
66 R. Benigni (dir.), *Life is Beautiful*, 1999; S. Spielberg (dir.) *Schindler's List*, 1993. See also R. Manne, 'The Holocaust as a fairy tale' *Sydney Morning Herald*, 15 February 1999, p. 13; A. Bennie, 'Nothing beautiful about it' *Sydney Morning Herald*, 14 September 1999, p. 13.
67 I. Clendinnen, cited in A. Bennie, op. cit.
68 L. Brett, op. cit.
69 D. Berger, 2G-Legacy Mailing list, 22 March 1999, 13:52.
70 J. Salamon, op. cit., p. 113.
71 P. Roth, cited in P. Novick, op. cit., p. 32.
72 M.S. Bergmann and M.E. Jucovy (eds), op. cit., p. 59.
73 L. Peeters, 'The years that never were' *Australasian Psychiatry*, vol. 3, no. 3, June, 1995, p. 157.
74 B. Mahmoody, *For the Love of a Child*, Pan Macmillan, Sydney, 1992, p. 10.
75 D. Carroll, op. cit., p. x.
76 D. Laub, in S. Felman and D. Laub, op. cit.
77 U. Duba, 'Family portraits', in 'Inherited pain and defective genes. Descendants of the Shoah and the Third Reich', unpublished manuscript.
78 U. Duba, 'Missing—medical history', in 'Inherited pain and defective genes. Descendants of the Shoah and the Third Reich', unpublished manuscript.
79 T. Mostysser, 'The weight of the past. Reminiscences of a survivor's child', in L. Steinitz and D.M. Szonyi (eds), *Living After the Holocaust. Reflections by the postwar Generation in America*, Bloch Publishing Co., New York, 1975, p. 5.
80 ibid., pp. 4–5.
81 E. Hoffman, *Lost in Translation*, Minerva, London, 1991, pp. 252–3.
82 U. Dubarsky, *The First Book of Samuel*, Viking Australia, Sydney, 1995, p. 133.
83 H. Epstein, op. cit., p. 10.
84 M.S. Bergmann and M.E. Jucovy (eds), op. cit., p. 104.

Chapter 5 Born knowing: the descendants' experience

1 H. Epstein, *Where She Came From. A Daughter's Search for Her Mother's Memory*, Plume, London, 1997.
2 L. Brett, *Too Many Men*, Picador, Sydney, 1999.
3 H. Epstein, op. cit., p. 70.
4 M.S. Bergman and M.E. Jucovy (eds), *Generations of the Holocaust*, Basic Books, New York, 1982.
5 ibid.
6 H. Arendt, cited in E. Apfelbaum, 'The impact of culture in the face of genocide. Struggling between a silenced home culture and a foreign host culture', paper given at the symposium on Culture in Psychology: A developing framework. Fifth European Congress of Psychology, July, 1997, Dublin, p. 5.
7 K. Herne, J. Travaglia and E. Weiss (eds), *Who Do You Think You Are? Second-generation Immigrant Women in Australia*, Women's Redress Press, Sydney, 1992.
8 H. Epstein, op. cit.
9 E. Gandolfo, Abstract to 'Searching for a place to come from', paper delivered at Cultural Passports: Negotiating Home in Australia. Department of History, University of Sydney, 11 June, 1999.
10 L. Brett, op. cit.; A. Zable, *Jewels and Ashes*, Scribe Publications, Newham Victoria, 1991.
11 J. Altounian, cited in E. Apfelbaum, op. cit., p. 7.
12 E. Hoffman, *Lost in Translation*, Minerva, London, 1991.
13 L. Brett, op. cit., p. 390.
14 J.Dobies, 'One hour by bus' *Generation*, vol. 6, nos 1–2, 1997, p. 49.
15 M.S. Bergman and M.E. Jucovy, op. cit., p. 60.
16 L. Brett, op. cit., p. 487.
17 S. Varga, *Heddy and Me*, Penguin Australia, Sydney, 1994.
18 ibid., p. 223.
19 A. Erlich, *Short Eternity*, self-published, 1988, p. 19.
20 H. Epstein, *Children of the Holocaust. Conversations with Sons and Daughters of Survivors*, Putnam, New York, 1979, p. 11.
21 M. Hirsch, *Family Frames. Photography, Narrative and Memory*, Harvard University Press, Cambridge MA, 1997.
22 L. Brett, op. cit., p. 64.
23 A. Hass, *In the Shadow of the Holocaust. The Second Generation*, Cornell University Press, New York, 1990, p. 157.
24 N. Fresco, cited in S. Felman and D. Laub, *Testimony. Crises of Witnessing in Literature, Psychoanalysis and History*, Routledge, New York and London, 1992, p. 64.
25 H. Epstein, *Children of the Holocaust*, Putnam, New York, 1979.
26 A. Zable, op. cit., p. 164.
27 U. Duba, 'Still looking', in U. Duba, *Tales from a Child of the Enemy*, Penguin, New York, 1997, pp. 62–6.
28 P. Weir (dir.), *Gallipoli*, 1981.
29 Dr Deborah Saltman, a speaker on the panel of the colloquium, addressed herself to the pattern of survivors' children seemingly endlessly striving for achievement.
30 S.L. Gilman, *Smart Jews. The Construction of The Image of Jewish Superior Intelligence*, University of Nebraska Press, Lincoln, 1996.

31 D. Laub in S. Felman and D. Laub, op. cit., p. 73 (my emphasis).

32 H. Epstein, *Where She Came From*, Plume, London, 1997, p. 305.

33 E. Wiesel, cited in Y. Danieli, 'Mourning in survivors and children of survivors: The role of group and community modalities', in D. Dietrich and P. Shabad (eds), *The Problem of Loss and Mourning. Psychoanalytic Perspectives*, International Universities Press, New York, 1986, p. 9.

34 L. Brett, op. cit., p. 702.

35 M. Hirsch, op. cit., pp. 21–2 and xii.

36 L. Taxel, 'A sense of belonging. Sharing family history with children', in *Sydney's Child*, 1996, p. 4.

37 M. Hirsch, op. cit, p. 21.

38 D. Wardi, *Memorial Candles. Children of the Holocaust*, Routledge, New York, 1992.

39 H. Arendt, cited in E. Apfelbaum, op. cit., p. 5.

40 B. Bettleheim, cited in Y. Danieli, op. cit., p. 166.

41 A. Hass, op. cit., p. xv.

42 S. Rushdie, 'Giving up the dream of a tolerant Kosovo' *Sydney Morning Herald*, 12 August 1999, p. 19.

43 M. French, *The Bleeding Heart*, Andre Deutsch, London, 1980, p. 34.

44 S. Varga, op. cit., p. 232.

45 E. Apfelbaum, op. cit., p. 6.

46 E. Hoffman, op. cit., p. 8.

47 A. Wajnryb, 'A letter to my children', unpublished manuscript, 1988, p. 217.

48 One well-known journey is that recorded in M. Baker, *The Fiftieth Gate. A Journey through Memory*, Flamingo, Sydney, 1997. Deborah Ende researched these return journeys in her 'A healing journey: two generations of Holocaust survivors face the past', unpublished Masters thesis, Macquarie University, 1994.

49 M. Hirsch, op. cit., p. 242.

50 ibid., pp. 242–3.

51 J. Altounian, *Ouvrez-moi seulement les chemins d'Armenie. Un genocide aux deserts de l' inconscient*, Les Belles Lettres, Paris, 1990; J. Altounian, *La suivance. Traduire le trauma collectif*, Dunod, Paris, 2000.

52 M. Hirsch, op. cit., p. 268.

53 A. Erlich, op. cit., pp. 25 and 29.

54 J. Salamon, *The Net of Dreams. A Family's Search for a Rightful Place*, Random House, New York, 1996, p. 151 (my emphasis).

Chapter 6 Holocaust narrative

1 These are the words used by Mark Baker during a talk given on 16 April 1997 at the Sydney Jewish Museum on his recently published *The Fiftieth Gate. A Journey through Memory*, Flamingo, Sydney, 1997.

2 A. Zable, *Jewels and Ashes*, Scribe Publications, Newham Victoria, 1991, pp.164–5.

3 M.S. Bergman and M.E. Jucovy (eds), *Generations of the Holocaust*, Basic Books, New York, 1982, p. 20.

4 D. Maynard, 'On clinicians' co-implicating recipients' perspective in the delivery of diagnostic news', in P. Drew and J. Heritage (eds), *Talk at Work. Interaction in Institutional Settings*, Cambridge University Press, Cambridge, 1992, p. 336.

5 The importance of investigating discrepant evidence is discussed in D.A. Erlandson, E.L. Harris, B.L. Skipper, and S. D. Allen, *Doing Naturalistic Inquiry. A Guide to Methods*, Sage Publications, Newbury Park, 1993; and C. Glesne and A. Peshkin, *Becoming Qualitative Researchers. An Introduction*, Longman, New York, 1992.

6 D. Laub, 'Truth and testimony. The process and the struggle' *American Imago*, 48, 1991, p. 84.

7 A. Wajnryb, 'A letter to my children', unpublished manuscript, 1988; D. Kaye, *I Still Remember*, Fast Books, Sydney, 1996; G. Biggs, *Letter to my Sons*, Fast Books, Sydney, 1996; and H. Bochenek, *A Letter to Jane*, Fast Books, Sydney, 1994.

8 J.E. Young, *Writing and Rewriting the Holocaust. Narrative and the Consequences of Interpretation*, Indiana University Press, Bloomington and Indianapolis, 1988, p. 160.

9 ibid.

10 P. Hayes (ed.), *Lessons and Legacies: The Meaning of the Holocaust in a Changing World*, Northwestern University Press, Evanston, Illinois, 1991, p. 326.

11 A. Duranti, 'The audience as co-author: An introduction' *Text*, vol. 6, no. 3, pp. 239 and 244.

12 H. Epstein, *Where She Came From. A Daughter's Search for Her Mother's Memory*. Plume, London, 1997, p. 165.

13 ibid., p. 13.

14 N. Piatka, *Better Don't Talk. A Daughter Unlocks her Mother's Hidden Past*, performed in Sydney, February, 1998.

15 A. Hass, *The Aftermath. Living with the Holocaust*, Cambridge University Press, Cambridge, 1995, p. 138.

16 M. Hirsch, *Family Frames. Photography, Narrative and Memory*, Harvard University Press, Cambridge MA, 1997, p. 243.

17 All these references are cited in M. Hirsch, op. cit., p. 244.

18 A. Hass, 'Survivor guilt in Holocaust survivors and their children', in J. Lemberger (ed.), *A Global Perspective on Working with Holocaust Survivors and the Second Generation*, JDC—Brookdale Institute of Gerontology and Human Development, Jerusalem, 1995, p. 183.

19 I first read the metaphor of lamination in Erving Goffman, *Forms of Talk*, Basil Blackwell, Oxford, 1981, p. 154.

20 D. Grossman, *See Under: Love* (translated by Betsy Rosenberg), The Noonday Press, New York, 1989.

21 H. Gouri, cited in J. Baum, 'A literary analysis of traumatic neurosis in Israeli society: David Grossman's *See Under: Love' Other Voices, e-journal of Cultural Criticism*, vol. 2, no. 1, February 2000, p. 10.

22 D. Grossman, op. cit., p. 13.

23 The 'reversing un-' verb is explained in G. Pullam, 'Why you can't un-hear this talk' *Lingua Franca*, ABC Radio National, Saturday 15 January 2000.

24 W. Styron, *Sophie's Choice*, London, Cape, 1979.

25 M. Baker, *The Fiftieth Gate*, p. 177.

26 B. Schlink, *The Reader*, Phoenix, London, 1997.

27 A. Hass, op. cit., p. 138 (my emphasis).

28 M.S. Bergman and M.E. Jucovy (eds), op. cit., p. 6.

29 A. Hass, op. cit., p. 142.

30 S. Felman and D. Laub, *Testimony. Crises of Witnessing in Literature, Psychoanalysis and History*, Routledge, New York and London, 1992, pp. 70–1.

31 A. Hass, *In the Shadow of the Holocaust. The Second Generation*, Cornell University Press, New York, 1990, p. 157.

32 E. Goffman, op. cit., p. 146.

33 H. Epstein, op. cit., p. 277.

34 A. Erlich, *Short Eternity*, self-published, 1988, p. 21.

35 L. Brett *Too Many Men*, Picador, Sydney, 1999.

36 S. Hicks (dir.) *Shine*, 1996.

37 U. Duba, *Tales from a Child of the Enemy*, Penguin, New York, 1997, pp. 55–7.

38 B. Rubens, *I Dreyfus*, Abacus, London, 2000, p. 25.

39 A. Riemer, *Inside Outside. Life Between Two Worlds*, Angus & Robertson, Sydney, 1992.

40 For example, Rennie not only refers to traditional Polish anti-Semitism in understated terms ('harbouring negative attitudes', (p. 22)) but proceeds to claim that this is both an exaggeration and a simplification. He suggests that Polish hostility towards Jews was complemented by Jewish hostility to Poles, that it might be explained by the rampant nationalism of the time, and that serious incidents can be attributed to 'extremist elements', which he claims existed on both sides. He omits any mention of the fact that Poles were largely pleased to be rid of their three million Jews, and very often complicit in their murder. E. Rennie, *Poland. A Handbook in Intercultural Communication*, National Centre for English Language Teaching and Research, Macquarie University, Sydney, 1995.

Another version of this re-writing of history is seen in the Polish tendency to 'appropriate the Holocaust as their own experience', for example photographs of skeletal Jews at Auschwitz being captioned 'Poles at Oswiecim' (R. Hilberg, 1991, cited in C. Tatz, *Reflections on the Politics of Remembering and Forgetting*, Centre for Comparative Genocide, Macquarie University, 1994, p. 46.). For a detailed description of Polish anti-Semitism, see M. Gilbert, *The Holocaust, the Jewish Tragedy*, Collins, London, 1986.

41 E. Tonkin, *Narrating our Pasts. The Social Construction of Oral History*, Cambridge University Press, Cambridge, 1998, p. 130.

42 S. Hicks (dir.), *Shine*, 1996.

43 B. Rubens, op. cit., p. 19.

44 S. Varga, *Heddy and Me*, Penguin Australia, Sydney, 1994, p. 224.

45 N. Sokoloff, cited in J. Baum, op. cit., pp. 5 and 6.

46 H. Epstein, op. cit., p. 146.

47 S. Glass, *The Interpreter*, Century, London, 1999, p. 55.

48 H. Epstein, op. cit., p. 207.

49 A. Hass, *In the Shadow of the Holocaust*, pp. 39 and 41.

50 P. Novick, *The Holocaust in American Life*, Houghton Mifflin Co., Boston, 1999, pp. 138 and 244; and H. Arendt, *Eichmann in Jerusalem, A Report on the Banality of Evil*, Penguin, Harmondsworth, 1994.

51 C. Tatz, *Reflections on the Politics of Remembering and Forgetting*, pp. 47–8.

52 D. Grossman, op. cit., p. 84.

53 B. Rubens, op. cit., p. 276.

54 A. Erlich, op. cit., pp. 19–20.

55 E. Fogelman, *Breaking the Silence*, cited in J.E. Young, *Writing and Rewriting the Holocaust*, p. 162.

56 *Bringing Them Home. Report of the National Inquiry into the Separation of Aboriginal and Torres Strait Islander Children from their families*, 1997, Website: *www.austlii.edu.au/au/special/rsproject/rsjlibrary/breoc/stolen/*

57 A. Hass, *In the Shadow of the Holocaust*, p. 71.

58 A. Hass, *The Aftermath*, p. 137.

59 N. French, *The Memory Game*, Heinemann, London, 1997, p. 257.

60 M. Dobbs, *Wall Games*, HarperCollins, London, 1990, p. 299.

61 J. Salamon, *The Net of Dreams. A Family's Search for a Rightful Place*, Random House, New York, 1996, p. 217.

62 R. Krell, cited in N. Burchardt, 'The long shadow of the Holocaust', in *BJP Review of Books*, July, 1993, p. 6.

63 E. Hoffman, cited in E. Apfelbaum, 'The impact of culture in the face of genocide. Struggling between a silenced home culture and a foreign host culture', paper given at the symposium on Culture in Psychology: A developing framework. Fifth European Congress of Psychology, Dublin, 1997, p. 3.

64 J. Amery, *At the Mind's Limits*, Indiana University Press, Bloomington, 1966, p. 40.

65 H. Epstein, op. cit., pp. 275 and 165.

66 'One thing nobody mentions of the camps is the constant screaming . . . You were never spoken to, you were screamed at. There was no silence', in M. Lang (ed.), 'The long shadow' *Generation*, vol. 4, no. 1, 1994, p. 36.

67 J. Salamon, op. cit., p. 154.

68 D. Laub, op. cit., p. 79 (emphasis in original).

69 H. Epstein, op. cit., pp. 160 and 164.

70 S. Felman and D. Laub, *Testimony. Crises of Witnessing in Literature, Psychoanalysis and History*, Routledge, New York and London, 1992, p. 43.

71 S. Glass, op. cit., p. 55.

72 A. Hass, *The Aftermath*, p. 134.

73 D. Grossman, cited in J. Baum, op. cit., p. 9.

74 E. Goffman, op. cit., p. 3.

75 ibid., pp. 131–2.

76 A. Hass, *The Aftermath*, p. 141.

77 ibid., p. 136.

78 ibid.

79 A. Erlich, op. cit., p. 24.

Chapter 7 The unspoken text

1 U. Duba, 'As you wish, madam', in U. Duba, *Tales from a Child of the Enemy*, Penguin, New York, 1997, pp. 67–71.

2 A. Holland (dir.), *Europa Europa*, 1990.

3 S. Felman and D. Laub, *Testimony. Crises of Witnessing in Literature, Psychoanalysis and History*, Routledge, New York and London, 1992, p. 66.

4 H. Epstein, *Where She Came From. A Daughter's Search for Her Mother's Memory*, Plume, London, 1997, p. 68.

5   J. Salamon, *The Net of Dreams. A Family's Search for a Rightful Place*, Random House, New York, 1996, p. 179.

6   H. Epstein, op. cit., p. 75.

7   J. Krabbé (dir.), *Left Luggage*, 1998.

8   S. Glass, *The Interpreter*, Century, London, 1999, p. 56.

9   U. Duba, 'Carpet bombing', in *Tales from a Child of the Enemy*, pp. 4–5.

10 A. Erlich, *Short Eternity*, self-published, 1988, p. 23.

11 M. D'Orso, *Like Judgement Day. The Ruin and Redemption of a Town called Rosewood*, Grosset/Putnam, New York, 1996, p. 31.

12 A. Erlich, op. cit., p. 65.

13 H. Widdowson, 'Context, community, and authentic language', paper given at the 32nd Annual TESOL Convention, Seattle, March 1998.

14 S. Glass, op. cit., p. 115.

15 H. Epstein, op. cit., p. 308.

16 L. Brett, *Too Many Men*, Picador, Sydney, 1999, p. 341.

17 C. Clay (prod.), *Out of the Ashes*, 1995.

18 H.A. Barocas and C.B. Barocas, 'Wounds of the father: The next generation of Holocaust survivors' *International Review of Psycho-Analysis*, 6, 1979, pp. 331–40.

19 I am indebted to Jonathan Crichton for the 'visual field' metaphor.

Chapter 8 Other voices

1   A.R. Hochschild, *The Managed Heart. Commercialization of Human Feeling*, University of California Press, Los Angeles, 1983.

2   E. Goffman, *The Presentation of Self in Everyday Life*, Penguin, Harmondsworth, 1959.

3   T. Stephens, 'Vietnam project gives Catherine strength to mend war wounds' *Sydney Morning Herald*, 12 February 1999, p. 5; and C. Bowe, 'Discovering the silent screams from the Vietnam War', HSC Personal Interest Project, Society and Culture, 1998, Monte Sant' Angelo Mercy College, North Sydney.

4   A. Jaworski, *The Power of Silence. Social and Pragmatic Perspectives*, Sage Publications, London, 1993, p. 78.

5   I am indebted to Jonathan Crichton for these insights.

6   H. Sacks, *Lectures on Conversation* (ed. G. Jefferson), Basil Blackwell, Oxford, 1992, cited in D. Silverman, *Interpreting Qualitative Data: Methods for Analysing Talk, Text and Interaction*, Sage Publications, London, 1993.

7   Linda eschewed the use of a pseudonym for her story, sensing that fear of using her own name was a part of the silence that had traumatised her for so long.

8   See Report 22 of the Standing Committee on Social Issues following a parliamentary inquiry into adoption practices (1950–1998) at *www.parliament.nsw.gov.au*

9   *www.angelfire.com/or/originsnsw*

10 E. Goffman, *Forms of Talk*, Basil Blackwell, Oxford, 1981, pp. 144–5.

11 E. Apfelbaum, 'The impact of culture in the face of genocide. Struggling between a silenced home culture and a foreign host culture', paper given at the symposium on Culture in Psychology: A developing framework. Fifth European Congress of Psychology, Dublin, 1997, pp. 7–8.

12 *Bringing Them Home. Report of the National Inquiry into the Separation of Aboriginal*

and Torres Strait Islander Children from their Families, 1997, website:
www.austlii.edu.au/au/special/rsproject/rsjlibrary/hreoc/stolen/

13 D. Crystal, *Language Death*, Cambridge University Press, Cambridge, 2000.

14 L. Peeters, 'The years that never were' *Australasian Psychiatry*, vol. 3, no. 3, June, 1995.

15 ibid., p. 155.

16 A. Atkinson, 'Towards an understanding of evil: review of *Why Weren't We Told? A Personal Search for the Truth about Our History*' *Sydney Morning Herald*, 17 July 1999, *Spectrum*, p. 10.

17 H. Reynolds, *Why Weren't We Told? A Personal Search for the Truth about Our History*, Viking, Ringwood, Victoria, 1999.

18 ibid., p. 125.

19 ibid., p. 92.

Chapter 9 An emotional landscape

1 A. Zable, *Jewels and Ashes*, Scribe Publications, Newham Victoria, 1991, pp. 23–4.

2 It was in a conversation with Professor Konrad Kwiet that I was first alerted to the multiple meanings and symbolism of forests in Holocaust history and literature.

3 H. Epstein, *Where She Came From. A Daughter's Search for Her Mother's Memory*, Plume. London, 1997, pp. 150 and 17.

4 N. Fresco, 'Remembering the unknown', *International Review of Psycho-Analysis*, vol. 11, 1984, p. 421.

5 D. Laub, 'The empty circle: children of survivors and the limits of reconstruction' *Journal of the Psychoanalytic Association*, vol. 46, no. 2, 1998, p. 509.

6 D. Laub and N.C. Auerhahn, cited in D. Laub, op. cit., p. 509.

7 E.W. Eisner, *The Art of Educational Evaluation*, The Palmer Press, London, 1985, p. 193.

8 S. Sarangi and S. Selmbrouk, 'Non-co-operation in communication: a reassessment of Gricean pragmatics' *Journal of Pragmatics*, 17, 1992, p. 142.

9 R. Wajnryb 'The pragmatics of feedback', unpublished doctoral thesis, Macquarie University, 1994, p. 410.

10 A. Zable, op. cit., p. 102.

11 D. Laub, 'Truth and testimony. The process and the struggle' *American Imago*, 48, 1991, pp. 77–8.

Appendix: research method

1 R.A. Kreuger, *Focus Groups. A practical guide for applied research*, Sage, Thousand Oaks, CA, 1994.

2 A. Littlejohn and M. Melouk (eds) *Research Methods and Processes*, Department of Linguistics and Modern English Language, University of Lancaster, 1987.

3 C. Glesne and A. Peshkin, *Becoming Qualitative Researchers. An Introduction*, Longman, New York, 1992, p. 104.

4 D.A. Erlandson, E.L. Harris, B.L. Skipper and S.D. Allen, *Doing Naturalistic Inquiry. A Guide to Methods*, Sage Publications, London, 1993.

5 S.B. Merriam, *Case Study Research in Education. A Qualitative Approach*, Joss-Bass Publishers, San Francisco, 1991.

6 See S. Laub, 'Study of survivors' children under way' *The Australian Jewish News*, Sydney edition, 5 April 1996, p. 5; and H. Pitt, 'Quiet power of the unspoken word' *Sydney Morning Herald*, 18 April 1996, p. 9.

7   C. Glesne and A. Peshkin, op. cit., p. 149.
8   S.B. Merriam, op. cit., pp. 126 and 135.
9   J.P. Spradley, *The Ethnographic Interview*, Holt, Rinehart & Winston, Orlando, FLA, 1979.
10 R.M. Lee, *Doing Research on Sensitive Topics*, Sage Publications, London, 1993.
11 The transgenerational theme of much Holocaust research is explored in the following titles: M. Lang (ed.), 'The long shadow' *Generation*, vol. 4, no. 1, 1994; and H.A. Barocas and C.B. Barocas, 'Wounds of the father: the next generation of Holocaust survivors' *International Review of Psycho-Analysis*, 6, 1979. Bruno Bettelheim's words are cited in M. Lang (ed.), 1994, p. 35: 'What cannot be talked about can also not be put to rest: and if it is not, the wounds continue to fester from generation to generation'.
12 M. van Maanen, cited in R.M. Lee, op. cit., p. 103.
13 E. Goffman, *The Presentation of Self in Everyday Life*, Penguin, Harmondsworth, 1959.
14 R.A. Kreuger, op. cit.
15 M.B Miles and A.M. Huberman, *Qualitative Data Analysis*, Sage Publications Thousand Oaks, CA, 1984, pp. 50–1.
16 R.A. Kreuger, op. cit., p. 130.
17 C. Glesne and A. Peshkin, op. cit., p. 102.
18 M.B. Miles, and A.M. Huberman, op. cit., pp. 241–2.
19 C. Glesne and A. Peshkin, op. cit., p. 104.
20 A. Slimani, 'Designing and redesigning a qualitative study', in A. Littlejohn and M. Melouk (eds), *Research Methods and Processes*, Department of Linguistics and Modern English Language, University of Lancaster, 1987.
21 C. Glesne and A. Peshkin, op. cit., p. 15.
22 R.H. Hycner, 'Some guidelines for the phenomenological analysis of interview data', *Human Studies*, 8, 1985, p. 281.
23 C. Glesne and A. Peshkin, op. cit., pp. 104–5.
24 See E.G. Guba and Y.S. Lincoln, *Effective Evaluation*, Jossey-Bass Publishers, San Francisco, 1983, p. 186; D.A. Erlandson et al., op. cit., p. 31; and R.A. Kreuger, op. cit., p. 128.
25 Y.S. Lincoln and E.G. Guba, Naturalistic Inquiry, Sage Publications, Newbury Park, 1985.
26 C. Glesne and A. Peshkin, op. cit., p. 147.
27 D.A. Erlandson et al., op. cit., p. 121.
28 See, for example, S. Mathison, 'Why triangulate?' *Educational Researcher*, 17, March 1988, pp. 13–17; and M.B. Miles and A.M. Huberman, op. cit., pp. 234–5.
29 C. Glesne and A. Peshkin, op. cit.
30 See, for example, Y. Danieli, in M. Lang (ed.), 'The long shadow' *Generation*, vol. 4, no. 1, 1994, pp. 35–7.
31 E. H. Erickson, *Identity, Youth and Crisis*, Norton, New York, 1968.
32 M. Van Manen, *Researching Lived Experience*, University of New York Press, London and Canada, 1990, p. 70.

Index

Author's Note: When compiling the index for this book I started to index 'silence'. I quickly realised, however, that the notion of 'silence' permeates the whole book and that many of the entries in this index are subcategories of 'silence'. Accordingly, so as not to repeat myself, and to avoid confusion, I have not included a main entry for 'silence'. The same applies for 'Holocaust'. Other wide-ranging terms like 'language', 'war' and 'Jewishness' are similarly problematic (and unwieldy), but more able to be termed into indexed headings and subheadings.

Baum, J., 206
Belgium, 41, 45, 57, 64, 136
Bergen-Belsen *see* concentration camps
Berger, D., 114–15
Bergmann, M.S. and Jucovy, M.E., 127, 132
betrayal, 60, 115, 121, 155, 181, 184, 229
Bible, the, 78; Bible-reading, 307; Onan,
   story of, 160; Ruth, Book of, 160
biculturalism *see* bilingualism
Biderman, A., 84
Biggs, G., 173
bilingualism, 52–4
bizarre, 27, 48, 121, 134, 138, 151, 165,
   232–7
Bochenek, H., 174
boundaries: cultural, 68; and empathy,
   216–17; generational, 46, 68, 120, 121,
   123, 134, 139, 151, 179, 181, 151; and
   venue, 96
Bowe, C., 288
bread, 195, 266, 268
Breaking the Silence see film
Brett, L., 26–7, 76, 84, 89, 114, 124, 129,
   131, 132, 142, 149, 151, 197, 269
Bringing Them Home (report), 306–7
Brodsky, J., 92
Buenos Aires, 118
Buruma, I., 62
bystander, 61, 93, 183, 201

calico boxes, 14
Campbelltown, 9–10, 12
Canada, 130, 159
Carroll, D., 118
Catholic Church, the, 58–9, 90
cattle car *see* trains
census, 44, 46, 205
cherish, 51, 88–9, 134, 204, 205, 272
childhood: memories, of, 1–2, 5, 9, 24, 28,
   47–8, 52, 106, 128, 144, 146, 159, 167,
   177–8;
      discordance, 16, 162; incoherence,
      13–14, 123, 165
   see also nostalgia
chimney *see* concentration camps
choices, 188–9, 199, 281, 300, 316
Christian, 15–16, 28, 63–4, 117, 155;
   Brothers, 289–93; festivals:
      Christmas, 28, 128, 165;
      Easter, 28, 289;
   passing as, 41, 67, 205; Polish
      Christians, 181, 201, 204, 238;
   scripture class, 15–16, 49, 140
chronology, 33, 148, 179, 183, 218
Clendinnen, I., 72, 113
coherence: achieving, 161–9, 180, 191, 206,
   290; lack of, 6, 26, 28, 77, 80–1, 114, 131,
   156, 201;
      and the bizarre, 232–7; and
      dissonance, 212–13, 215

collaborator, 61, 69, 90, 183
communication: direct (explicit), 171–5;
      face-to-face, 171–3; recorded, 173, 175;
      written, 173–5;
   indirect, 171, 175–247 *passim*;
      bizarre, 232–7; choices, 188–9; cued
      messages, 237–9; and dissonance,
      212–26; fragments, 177–80; shame,
      226–32; shifts in participant roles,
      239–47; socialised messages, 191–212;
      vignettes, 180–7;
   unspoken, 171, 248–80 *passim*;
      excluded messages, 248–65; iconic
      messages, 265–76; omitted messages,
      276–80
communism, 62, 201 *see also* Soviet Union
composure, 30, 44, 96, 97, 119, 177, 186,
   262
concentration camps, 41, 44, 57–9, 62, 83,
   153, 100; camps:
      Auschwitz, 34, 45, 58, 64, 73, 77, 82,
      84, 106, 129, 132, 143, 149, 154, 156,
      180, 181, 197, 199, 207, 208, 222, 226,
      227, 246, 251, 252, 261, 268; Bergen-
      Belsen, 57, 154, 209, 223, 243;
      Birkenau, 27; near Boden Sea, 215;
      Dachau, 40, 63, 132; Drancy, 40, 63,
      132; in Estonia, xi; near Gdansk, 215;
      Majdanek, 185; Teresin, 132;
      Treblinka, xi, 24, 60, 115, 250;
   chimneys, 59, 266; crematoria, 59, 266;
   death marches, 196, 235, 252, 311; gas
   chambers, 24, 82, 164; hierarchy in, 40;
   photographs, 165; political prisoners, 40
conspiracy, 297–302; avoidance, 278; family,
   265; 'Jewish', the, 212; of silence, 56, 62
context: cues from, 37, 43–4, 151
   misinterpretations, 315–20;
   of the Holocaust, 134;
      politico-historical, 56–65;
      psycho-social, 66–75; linguistic, 84–6;
   inability to relate to, 114, 148, 153; lack
   of, 6, 161; study of language in, 20, 21,
   175–80; or venue, 95–100
crematoria *see* concentration camps
cues: to the past, 14, 44, 136, 138–9, 149,
   151, 162–3, 167, 179, 186, 193, 213,
   237–9; of the listener, 119, 190, 317; study
   of, 21
cyanide pills, 162
Czechoslovakia, 28, 29, 39, 41, 57, 76, 132,
   133, 163, 192, 201, 209, 234, 255

Dachau *see* concentration camps
Danieli, Y., 93
death march *see* concentration camps
Delbo, C., 111
Demidenko affair, the, 118
denial: of Aboriginal history, 309; of
   collaboration, 58–9; of escape, 58; by

definitions, 40–2; discrepant evidence, 173, 332; informed consent, 326; interview, 324–7; member checks, 331; non-Holocaust data, 50–4; participants, 38–42; patterns, 32; phenomenology, 331; premises, 33, 35; primary goal, 100; primary study, 38–40; qualitative, 36, 323; reliability of, 322; researcher bias, 330; researcher as insider, 325; sampling, 323; saturation, 324; sensitivity: intrusive questions, 37; of topic, 325–6; style, 310–11; summary profile, 327; Swedish, 102; tapescript, 327; tools of, 25; trail, 322–3; triangulation, 332–4; unitisation, 328; unit of analysis, 328; validity, 322; *see also* patterns

resistance, 63, 115, 172, 210, 226–7, 228; Partisans, 115, 187, 229; the Resistance, 111, 115, 229

revisionist *see* denial

Reynolds, H., 308–9

Richmond, T., vii, 91

Riemer, A., 76, 201

role: and behaviour, 94; distinct, 261–2; in Goffman's participation framework, 304; lack of, 96; of language, 55; of listener, 36, 68–9, 99–100, 102–4, 143, 175–6, 189–90, 239–47 *passim*; modelling, 45, 157, 230; multiple, 209; of narrative, 25; of non-Jews in the Holocaust, 61; of recasting, 71; of researcher, 3; reversal of, 169, 179, 262; in therapy, 98; *see also* participation framework

Romania, 39, 220

Rosenbloom, M., 67

Rosh White, N., 70, 72, 74

Roth, P., 117

Rubens, B., 200, 205, 216

Ruhr Valley, the, 57

Rushdie, S., 156

Russia *see* Soviet Union

Sacks, H., 295

Safe in America, 41, 61

Salamon, J., 99, 116, 167, 224, 230, 256

Schindler's List see film

Schlant, E., 65

Schlink, B., 65, 188

school, 5, 7, 10, 12, 15, 16, 27, 45, 49, 52–3, 57, 74, 138, 139, 146, 147

scripts, 96, 100, 131, 262, 267

searching, 40, 47, 145, 180

second generation, the *see* descendants

secrets, 43, 92, 131, 132, 137, 186–7, 217, 250, 270, 282–5, 305

separation: child's individuation, 271, 274–5; effect of silence, 78; effect of trauma, 104, 158, 203–4; forced, 45, 113, 179; removal of stolen children, 306; from witness and listener, 68; *see also* boundaries

severance: absence naturalised as normal, 276–80; discontinuity, 129–31, 153, 159, 180, 201, 208, 219, 244, 251, 257, 305–6, 311–13; growing up without a past, 6, 9, 205; lack of a language to talk of the past, 6, 9, 90; survivors' sealed-off past, 13

Shakespeare, 174

shame, 41, 67, 87–9, 116, 117, 132, 144, 148, 160, 164, 168, 207, 226–32 *passim*, 284

Shanghai, 40, 47, 49, 136, 146

Shine see film

Shoah: 'business', 79; as a term, 40; *see also* film

sibling, 10, 17, 82, 152, 153, 154, 181, 202, 204

Sicily, 129, 132

Singapore, Japanese occupation of, 74

slave labour *see* labour camps; concentration camps

sociology, 70

Solzhenitsyn, A., 80, 92

Sophie's Choice, 188; *see also* film

South Africa, 87

Soviet Union, the: as the enemy, 60; escape through, 49, 136, 146, 173–4; exposure of atrocities, 92; German retreat from, 143, 149; Hitler–Stalin pact, 203; liberating army of, 56, 172; and Stalin, 236; start of Cold War 62–3

speech, freedom of, 141, 215, 245

Spielberg Foundation, the, 175, 186, 209, 319

Stanner, W.E.H., 309

starvation, 13–14, 17, 43, 59, 61, 69, 125, 194–7, 203, 206, 214, 222, 235, 236

stigma *see* shame

stoicism, 78, 254, 296–7

stories *see* fragments; narrative; vignette

suicide, 51, 67, 104, 286–7, 297, 303

survivors: in the aftermath of war, 8, 55–6, 63–7; childhood of, 75; community of, 47, 126; definition of, 40–1; dysphoria in the home of, 32; going home, 60–1, 201; hierarchy, 41; losses, 39–40, 75–81 *passim*; pain threshold of, 271; public silence about, 73, 90–3; reconstruction, 75; relationship with their children, 88, 316–20; research questions about, 33; resilience of, 74, 126, 153, 198, 315; silence of, 107–16 *passim*; self-perception of, 41; sole, 24, 39, 69, 145, 149; survivor home, 33; 'survivor syndrome', 68, 69; surviving by accident, 77; *see also* luck

Switzerland, 58, 59, 90

synagogue, 57, 157, 188, 240, 274

taboo, 284; anniversaries, 139; descendants' involvement, 207, 244; display of emotion, 94, 174; music, 257; naturalised, 277; pain threshold, 271;